STUDY GUIDE
TO ACCOMPANY
McCONNELL

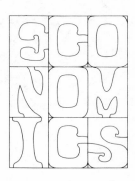

STUDY GUIDE
TO ACCOMPANY
McCONNELL

FIFTH EDITION

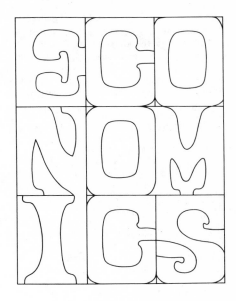

ROBERT C. BINGHAM
PROFESSOR OF ECONOMICS
KENT STATE UNIVERSITY

McGRAW-HILL BOOK COMPANY

New York   St. Louis   San Francisco   Düsseldorf   Johannesburg
Kuala Lumpur   London   Mexico   Montreal   New Delhi   Panama
Rio de Janeiro   Singapore   Sydney   Toronto

07-005290-5

1 2 3 4 5 6 7 8 9 0   BABA   7 9 8 7 6 5 4 3 2

This book was set in News Gothic by Monotype Composition
Company, Inc., and printed and bound by George Banta Company,
Inc. The designer was Betty Binns; the drawings were revised by
B. Handelman Associates, Inc. The editors were Jack R. Crutchfield,
Michael Elia, and Edwin Hanson. Ted Agrillo supervised production.

TO PQK

CONTENTS

HOW TO USE THE STUDY GUIDE IN ORDER TO
LEARN ECONOMICS   ix

AN INTRODUCTION TO AMERICAN CAPITALISM

1 THE NATURE AND METHOD OF ECONOMICS   1
2 AN INTRODUCTION TO THE ECONOMIZING PROBLEM   2
3 PURE CAPITALISM AND THE CIRCULAR FLOW   14
4 THE MECHANICS OF INDIVIDUAL PRICES:
   DEMAND AND SUPPLY   20
5 THE FIVE FUNDAMENTAL QUESTIONS AND THE PRICE SYSTEM   28
6 MIXED CAPITALISM AND THE ECONOMIC FUNCTIONS
   OF GOVERNMENT   34
7 THE FACTS OF AMERICAN CAPITALISM: HOUSEHOLDS   42
8 THE FACTS OF AMERICAN CAPITALISM: BUSINESSES   47
9 THE FACTS OF AMERICAN CAPITALISM: GOVERNMENT   54

NATIONAL INCOME, EMPLOYMENT, AND FISCAL POLICY

10 NATIONAL INCOME ACCOUNTING   59
11 THE BUSINESS CYCLE: UNEMPLOYMENT AND INFLATION   67
12 THE BACKGROUND AND ANALYTICAL TOOLS OF
    EMPLOYMENT THEORY   75
13 THE EQUILIBRIUM LEVELS OF OUTPUT, EMPLOYMENT,
    AND INCOME   83
14 THE ECONOMICS OF FISCAL POLICY   90
15 FISCAL POLICY AND THE PUBLIC DEBT   101

MONEY, MONETARY POLICY, AND ECONOMIC STABILITY

16 MONEY AND BANKING IN AMERICAN CAPITALISM   106
17 HOW BANKS CREATE MONEY   111
18 THE FEDERAL RESERVE BANKS AND MONETARY POLICY   118
19 ECONOMIC STABILITY: THEORY AND POLICY   126

AMERICAN ECONOMIC GROWTH: ACHIEVEMENTS, PROBLEMS, AND POLICIES

20 THE SIMPLE ANALYTICS OF ECONOMIC GROWTH 134

21 ECONOMIC GROWTH: THE AMERICAN EXPERIENCE 142

22 GROWTH IN AMERICAN CAPITALISM: COSTS, PROBLEMS, AND POLICIES 148

THE ECONOMICS OF THE FIRM AND RESOURCE ALLOCATION

23 THE MARKET STRUCTURES OF AMERICAN CAPITALISM 156

24 DEMAND, SUPPLY, AND ELASTICITY: SOME APPLICATIONS 162

25 FURTHER TOPICS IN THE THEORY OF CONSUMER DEMAND 173

26 THE COSTS OF PRODUCTION 179

27 PRICE AND OUTPUT DETERMINATION: PURE COMPETITION 187

28 PRICE AND OUTPUT DETERMINATION: PURE MONOPOLY 195

29 PRICE AND OUTPUT DETERMINATION: MONOPOLISTIC COMPETITION 202

30 PRICE AND OUTPUT DETERMINATION: OLIGOPOLY 208

31 PRODUCTION AND THE DEMAND FOR ECONOMIC RESOURCES 217

32 THE PRICING AND EMPLOYMENT OF RESOURCES: WAGE DETERMINATION 224

33 THE PRICING AND EMPLOYMENT OF RESOURCES: RENT, INTEREST, AND PROFITS 232

34 GENERAL EQUILIBRIUM: THE PRICE SYSTEM AND ITS OPERATION 238

CURRENT DOMESTIC ECONOMIC PROBLEMS

35 THE MONOPOLY PROBLEM: THE SOCIAL CONTROL OF INDUSTRY 246

36 RURAL ECONOMICS: THE FARM PROBLEM 252

37 URBAN ECONOMICS: THE PROBLEMS OF THE CITIES 260

38 THE ECONOMICS OF INEQUALITY AND POVERTY 267

39 LABOR UNIONS AND COLLECTIVE BARGAINING 274

40 THE ECONOMICS OF THE WAR INDUSTRY 280

41 THE SOCIAL IMBALANCE CONTROVERSY 286

INTERNATIONAL ECONOMICS AND THE WORLD ECONOMY

42 INTERNATIONAL TRADE AND THE ECONOMICS OF FREE TRADE 291

43 THE BALANCE OF PAYMENTS AND EXCHANGE RATES 298

44 INTERNATIONAL TRADE AND FINANCE: PROBLEMS AND POLICIES 306

45 THE UNDERDEVELOPED NATIONS: A SPECIAL PROBLEM IN ECONOMIC GROWTH 315

46 THE ECONOMIC CHALLENGE OF SOVIET RUSSIA 321

ANSWERS 329

This *Study Guide* was designed to help you read and understand Campbell R. McConnell's textbook, *Economics: Principles, Problems, and Policies,* Fifth Edition. If used properly, a guide can be a great aid to you in what is probably your first course in economics.

No one pretends that the study of economics is easy, but it can be made easier. Of course a study guide will not do your work for you, and its use is no substitute for reading the text. You must be willing to read the text, spend time on the subject, and work at learning if you wish to understand economics.

Many students do read their text and work hard on their economics course and still fail to learn the subject. This is because principles of economics is a new subject for them, and they have had no previous experience in learning economics. They want to learn but do not know just how to go about it. Here is where the *Study Guide* can come to their assistance. Let us first see what the *Study Guide* contains and then how to use it.

■ WHAT THE STUDY GUIDE IS

The *Study Guide* contains forty-six chapters —one for each chapter in the text—and an ANSWER SECTION. Each of the chapters has seven parts:
1. An *introduction* explains what is in the chapter of the text and how its subject matter is related to material in earlier and later chapters. It points out topics to which you should give special attention, and reemphasizes difficult or important principles and facts.
2. A *chapter outline* shows how the chapter is organized and summarizes briefly the essential points made in the chapter.
3. A list of the *important terms and concepts*

found in the chapter points out what you must be able to define in order to understand the material in the chapter.
4. *Fill-in questions* (short-answer and list questions) help you to learn and remember the crucial and important generalizations and facts in the chapter.
5. *Problems and projects* assist you in learning and understanding economic relationships and get you to think about certain economic problems.
6. *Objective questions* (true-false and multiple-choice) can be used to test yourself on the material in the chapter.
7. *Discussion questions* can be used to test yourself, to identify important questions in the chapter, and to prepare for examinations.

■ HOW TO STUDY AND LEARN WITH THE HELP OF THE STUDY GUIDE

For best results, quickly read the introduction, outline, and list of terms and concepts in the *Study Guide* before you read the chapter in the text. Then read the chapter in the text slowly, keeping one eye on the outline and the list of terms and concepts. Always read with pencil in hand and use your textbook as if you expected to sell it for wastepaper at the end of the year. The outline in the *Study Guide* contains only the major points in the chapter. Outline the chapter as you read it by identifying the major *and the minor* points and by placing appropriate numbers or letters (such as I or A or 1 or a) in the margins. It is also wise to underline the major and minor points in the chapter and to circle important terms and concepts. When you have completed the chapter, you will have the chapter outlined and your underlining will give you a set of notes on the chapter. It is not necessary to keep a separate notebook for textbook notes or outlines. Be careful to underline only the really important or summary statements.

After you have read the chapter in the text through once, turn again to the introduction, outline, and list of terms and concepts in the *Study Guide*. Reread the introduction and outline. Does everything there make sense? If not, return to the text and reread the topics that you do not remember well or that still confuse you. Look at the outline. Try to recall each of the minor topics or points that were contained in the text under each of the major points in the outline. When you come to the list of terms and concepts, go over them one by one. Define or explain each to yourself and then look it up in the text chapter. Check your own definition or explanation with that in the text. Make any correction or change in your own definition or explanation that is necessary. It is a good idea to put the page number or numbers on which the term or concept is discussed in the text after each term and concept on the list.

When you have done all this, you will have a pretty fair general idea of what is in the text chapter. Now take a look at the short-answer questions, the problems and projects, and the objective questions. Tackle each of these three sections one at a time, using the following procedure. (1) Answer as many questions as you can without looking in the text or in the answer section. (2) Check the text for whatever help you need. It is a good idea to do more than merely look for answers in the text; reread any section for which you were not able to answer questions. (3) Then consult the answer section for the correct answers and reread any section of the text for which you missed questions.

The questions in these three sections are not all of equal difficulty. Do not expect to get them all right the first time. Some are designed to pinpoint things of importance which you will probably miss the first time you read the text and to get you to read about them again. None of the questions is unimportant. Even those that have no definite answers will bring you to grips with many important economic questions and increase your understanding of economic principles and problems.

In answering the discussion questions—for which no answers are given—it is not neces-

sary to write out answers. All you need to do is mentally outline your answer. For the more difficult discussion questions you may want to write out a brief outline of the answer or a full answer. Do not avoid the difficult questions just because they are more work. Answering these questions is often the most valuable work a student can do toward acquiring an understanding of economic relationships and principles.

■ SOME FINAL WORDS

Perhaps the method of using *Study Guide* outlined above seems like a lot of work. It is. Study and learning necessarily entail work on your part. This is a fact you should willingly accept.

After you have used the *Study Guide* to study three or four chapters, you will find that some sections are of more value to you than others. Let your own experience determine how you will use it. But do not discontinue use of the *Study Guide* after three or four chapters merely because you are not sure whether it is helping you. Stick with it.

In addition to the material in the *Study Guide*, there are questions at the end of each chapter in the text. Some of these questions are similiar to questions in the *Study Guide*, but none is identical. It will be worthwhile for you to examine all the questions at the end of each chapter and to work out or outline answers for them. The student who has trouble with the problems in the *Study Guide* will find the end-of-chapter problems useful in determining whether he has actually mastered his difficulties. All students will find many of the end-of-chapter questions more thought-provoking than the discussion questions in the *Study Guide*.

For students who either have trouble with or wish to learn more rapidly the sections of the text containing explanations of economic theory (or principles), let me recommend my *Economic Concepts: A Programmed Approach*. A programmed book is a learning device which speeds and increases comprehension. Its use will greatly expand the student's understanding of economics.

Robert C. Bingham

THE NATURE
AND METHOD
OF ECONOMICS

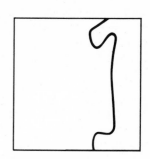

Chapter 1 introduces the reader to the study of economics. Its aim is to explain the subject matter of economics and the methods economists employ in the study of this subject matter.

While this chapter attempts to indicate the value to be derived from the study of economics and the importance of economic questions and problems to every individual, the heart of the chapter is the discussion of economic principles. Economic principles are generalizations grounded on facts; but, because the subject matter of economics is human behavior and because the economist cannot employ laboratory experiments to test his generalizations, these principles are always imprecise and subject to numerous exceptions. Economics is a science but it is not an exact science.

If the study of economics is to be of any worth to a student, it is necessary to understand from the very beginning that economic principles are simplifications—approximations—of a very complex real world and that both the formulation and application of these principles present many opportunities for the making of serious mistakes. Economic principles are not the answers to economic questions but are tools—intellectual tools—for analyzing economic problems and finding policies to solve these problems. Selection of the economic policies to follow depends not only upon economic principles but also upon the

value judgments of society—that is, upon the goals of the economy.

Pages 13 to 18 of the textbook outline a few of the almost innumerable errors of commission and omission of which the beginner in economics ought to beware. The study of economics is difficult enough without compounding the difficulty with emotional, logical, and semantical errors.

■ CHAPTER OUTLINE

1. Citizens in a democracy must understand elementary economics in order to understand the present-day problems of their society and to make intelligent decisions when they vote. Economics is an academic rather than a vocational subject, but a knowledge of it is valuable to businessmen, consumers, and workers.

2. Economists gather relevant facts to obtain economic principles that may be used to formulate policies which will solve economic problems.

a. Descriptive economics is the gathering of relevant facts about the production, exchange, and consumption of goods and services.

b. Economic theory is the analysis of the facts and the derivation of economic principles. These principles are generalizations and abstractions (or approximations) of reality.

1

c. Policy economics is the combination of economic principles and economic values (or goals) to control economic events.

3. Straight thinking in the study and use of economic principles requires strict application of the rules of logic—rules in which personal emotions are irrelevant, if not detrimental. There are at least nine pitfalls encountered in studying and applying economic principles.

■ IMPORTANT TERMS

Descriptive economics	Complementary goals
Economic principle (law)	Emotionally loaded terminology
Economic theory (analysis)	Dual terminology
	Fallacy of composition
Applied (policy) economics	Macroeconomics
Economy policy	"Other things equal" assumption
Generalization	Microeconomics
Abstraction	*Post hoc, ergo propter hoc* fallacy
Economic model	Intentions vs. realizations
Directly related	
Inversely related	Expectations (anticipations)
Social point of view	
Mutually exclusive goals	

■ FILL-IN QUESTIONS

1. The study of economics is the study of the _____,

_____,

and _____ of goods and services.

2. Economic laws are _____ concerning man's economic behavior and as such necessarily involve _____ from reality.

3. Economic laws are imprecise and subject to exceptions because _____

_____

4. Economic principles enable the economist to predict the result of a certain economic act or of certain economic behavior; this ability to predict is valuable because it makes it possible to _____

5. Six widely accepted economic goals in the United States are _____,

_____, _____,

_____, _____,

and _____

6. The three steps involved in the formulation of economic policy are:

a. _____

b. _____

c. _____

7. What three dangers are inherent in the construction and application of economic models?

a. _____

b. _____

c. _____

8. The correct economic policy to employ today to achieve a given end may be inappropriate for the achievement of the same end tomorrow because _____

_____

9. Economists often use "dual terminology." This means that they _____

10. Macroeconomics is concerned with the

_____

output of the economy and the _____ level of prices, while microeconomics is concerned with output in a(n) _____

_____

and the price of a(n) _____

_____

■ PROBLEMS AND PROJECTS

1. "In 1969 the demand for wheat in Chicago increased and caused the price of wheat at Chicago to rise." This is a *specific* instance of a more *general* economic principle. Of which economic *generalization* is this a particular example? _____

_____

_____

2. Following is a list of factors—economic and noneconomic—which may or may not be related to the number of automobiles produced in the United States in a year and the average price at which the automobiles are sold. In the space to the right of each factor indicate whether you think the factor is relevant (R) or irrelevant (I) and whether in your opinion the factor is economic (E) or noneconomic (N).

a. The cost of living in Detroit   _____

b. The price of Volkswagens   _____

c. The political party of the President of the United States   _____

d. The average price of stocks on the New York Stock Exchange   _____

e. The rate at which corporation profits are taxed   _____

f. The extent to which automation has been introduced into the production of automobiles   _____

g. The price of gasoline in the United States   _____

h. The size of the budget deficit of the United States government   _____

i. The percentage of the United States population living in rural areas   _____

j. Bus fares in Hoboken, New Jersey   _____

k. The rate at which the more than 83 million automobiles in the United States are polluting the air   _____

l. The star of a television program sponsored by the Ford Motor Company   _____

m. The chief of the Antitrust Division of the U.S. Department of Justice   _____

n. The price of wheat in Kansas City, Missouri   _____

3. Below are several current economic questions or problems. Indicate in a few words what you believe the answer to the question is or what should be done to solve the problem. You are not really expected to have, at this point in your study of economics, well-thought-out and/or correct answers, but you probably have some opinions or ideas on these questions and problems.

a. How to prevent inflation.   _____

_____

b. How to prevent unemployment.   _____

_____

c. Whether to impose quotas on goods imported into the United States.   _____

_____

d. How to reduce poverty in the United States. _____

e. How to help underdeveloped and backward nations to raise their standards of living.

_____

f. Whether the public (national) debt is too large.   _____

4. Examine your answers to question 3, using the following criteria.

a. Is your solution or answer based on what others have told you the solution or answer should be? _____

b. Is your solution or answer practical? Is it politically feasible? _____

c. Are you employing a theory to arrive at a solution or answer? _____

d. Do you need more facts to answer the question? If so, what kind of facts? _____

_____

e. Are you guilty of being an "economic quack," or biased? Have you based your answer on some preconceived notions which might be completely wrong? _____

5. Below are four statements. Each of them is an example of one of the pitfalls frequently encountered in the study of economics. Indicate in the space following each statement the type of pitfall involved.

a. "Thrift (or saving) promotes the welfare of the economy." _____

b. "An unemployed worker can find a job

if he looks diligently and conscientiously for employment; therefore, all unemployed workers can find employment if they are diligent and conscientious in looking for a job." _____

_____

c. *Jones:* "Underdeveloped nations are unable to increase their standards of living because they are unable to accumulate capital." *Smith:* "This is not correct. They are unable to increase their standards of living because they are consuming all they produce." _____

d. "The stock market crash of 1929 was followed by and resulted in 10 years of depression." _____

6. Below are two exercises in making graphs. On the graphs plot the economic relationships contained in each exercise. Be sure to label each axis of the graph and to indicate the unit of measurement and scale used on each axis.

a.

National income, billions of dollars	Consumption expenditures, billions of dollars
$100	$100
150	145
200	185
250	220
300	250
350	275
400	300

Graph national income on the horizontal axis and consumption expenditures on the vertical

axis; connect the seven points and label the curve "Consumption Schedule."

b.

Rate of interest, %	Investment expenditures, billions of dollars
8	$15
7	17
6	20
5	24
4	29
3	35
2	42

Graph investment expenditures on the horizontal axis and the rate of interest on the vertical axis; connect the seven points and label the curve "Investment Schedule."

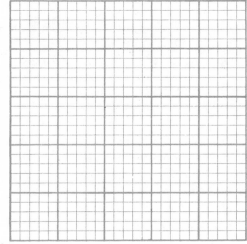

0

c. The relationship between:
(1) National income and consumption expenditures is a(n) _____ one.
(2) The rate of interest and investment expenditures is a(n) _____ one.

■ SELF-TEST

Circle the T if the statement is true, the F if it is false.

1. Economics is academic and of little value because it does not teach the student how to earn a living.   T **F**

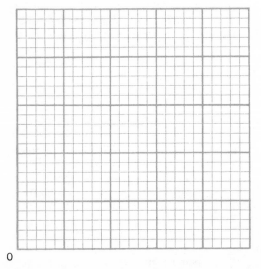

0

2. Economic principles are derived from the facts of economic behavior. Ⓣ F

3. Economics deals with the activities by which man earns a living and improves his standard of living. Ⓣ F

4. The ability to predict the economic consequences of various acts is important because it enables both businessmen and government officials to formulate policies that will tend to bring about the results they desire. Ⓣ F

5. The first step in the formulation of an economic policy, the statement of the goal or desired result, may be an occasion for disagreement because different people may have different and conflicting goals. Ⓣ F

6. Once a single goal or end has been determined as the sole objective of economic policy, there is seldom any question of which policy to adopt to achieve that goal. T Ⓕ

7. If you speak of "capital" to the average person, he understands you to be referring to money. The economist, therefore, is obligated to use the term "capital" to mean money. T Ⓕ

8. "Business expects to be able to sell 10,000 pairs of shoes this year and so produces 10,000 pairs. They actually sell 12,000 pairs." This illustrates the difference between macroeconomics and microeconomics. T Ⓕ

9. It is relatively easy to distinguish propositions involving economic quackery from those based on scientific economic principles by a careful examination of economic statistics and by testing the propositions in the harsh light of economic reality. T Ⓕ

10. The Law of Demand is an example of an economic policy. T Ⓕ

Underscore the letter that corresponds to the best answer.

1. Economics is a practical field of study in several ways. Which one of the following is *not* an element of its practicality? (a) every person affects and is affected by the operation of the economy; (b) every person has to earn a living in some manner, and economics develops skills and trains the student in the art of making a living; (c) every person in a democracy is confronted with its political problems, many of which are economic in nature; (d) every person who understands the overall operation of the economy is in a better position to solve his personal economic problems.

2. One economic principle states that the lower the price of a commodity, the greater will be the quantity of the commodity which consumers will wish to purchase. On the basis of this principle *alone,* it can be concluded that (a) if the price of mink coats falls, more mink coats will be purchased by consumers; (b) if the price of mink coats falls, Mrs. James will purchase two instead of one; (c) if the price of mink coats falls and there are no important changes in the other factors affecting their demand, the public will probably purchase a greater quantity of mink coats than it did at the higher price; (d) if more mink coats are purchased this month than last month, it is because the price of mink coats has fallen.

3. Knowing that as the price of a commodity rises the quantity of the commodity sold decreases and that the imposition of a tax on a commodity increases its price, the economist concludes that if the government taxes cigarettes, fewer cigarettes will be sold. This is an example of: (a) prediction; (b) control; (c) policy; (d) the fallacy of composition.

4. An economic model is *not:* (a) an ideal type of economy or an economic policy for which we ought to work; (b) a tool which the economist employs to enable him to predict; (c) one or a collection of economic principles; (d) an explanation of how the economy or a part of the economy functions in its essential details.

5. Which of the following is *not* a danger to be encountered in the construction or application of economic models? (a) it may contain irrelevant facts and omit more relevant data; (b) it may come to be accepted as "what ought to be" rather than as "what is"; (c) it may be overly simplified and so be a very poor approximation of the reality it explains; (d) it may result in a conclusion that is unacceptable to the citizens or the government of a nation.

6. Which of the following economic goals is subject to reasonably accurate measurement? (a) economic security; (b) full employment; (c) economic freedom; (d) an equitable distribution of income.

7. To say that two economic goals are mutually exclusive means that: (a) it is not possible to achieve both goals; (b) these goals are not accepted as goals in the U.S.S.R. (c) the achievement of one of the goals results in the achievement of the other; (d) it is possible to quantify both goals.

8. During World War II the United States employed price controls to prevent inflation; this was referred to as "a fascist and arbitrary restriction of economic freedom" by some and as "a necessary and democratic means of preventing ruinous inflation" by others. Both labels are examples of: (a) economic quackery; (b) the fallacy of composition; (c) the misuse of commonsense definitions; (d) emotionally loaded terminology.

9. The government increases its expenditures for road-construction equipment and the average price of this equipment falls. To reason that the lower price was due to the increase in government expenditures may be an example of: (a) the *post hoc, ergo propter hoc* fallacy; (b) the fallacy of composition; (c) a generalization that is true during a depression but untrue during prosperity; (d) using dual terminology.

10. If an individual determines to save a larger percentage of his income, he will no doubt be able to save more money. To reason, therefore, that if all individuals determine to save a larger percentage of their incomes they will all be able to save more money is an example of: (a) the *post hoc, ergo propter hoc* fallacy; (b) the fallacy of composition; (c) a generalization that is true during a depression but untrue during prosperity; (d) using dual terminology.

■ DISCUSSION QUESTIONS

1. What is the relationship between facts and theory? Can a theory be *proved?* Can a theory be *disproved?*

2. What is a "laboratory experiment under controlled conditions"? Does the science of economies have any kind of laboratory? Why do economists employ the "other things equal" assumption?

3. What is meant by an "economic model"? Can you think of any models employed in the other courses you are taking (or have taken)? (Omit from your consideration courses in the Art Department.)

4. "Good economic policy depends upon the development of good economic theories." Is this true? Are good economic theories all that is necessary to bring about improved economic conditions?

5. Of the six economic goals of American capitalism listed in the text, which one would you *rank* first, second, third, etc.? Would you add any other goals to this list?

6. If economic goals 2 and 3 were mutually exclusive, which goal would you prefer? Why? If goals 1 and 4 were mutually exclusive, which would you prefer? Why?

7. Explain briefly the difference between macroeconomics and microeconomics.

8. Define and explain the relationships between descriptive economics, economic theory, and applied economics.

9. Why are economic principles and models necessarily abstract and generalized?

10. What are the principal reasons for studying economics?

11. What procedure should be followed in formulating sound economic policies?

12. In what ways are the construction and application of economic models dangerous?

AN INTRODUCTION
TO THE ECONOMIZING
PROBLEM

The aim of Chapter 2 is to explain the central problem of economics and the Five Fundamental Questions into which this central problem can be divided.

The central problem of economics is that resources—the ultimate means of satisfying material wants—are scarce *relative* to the insatiable wants of society. Economics as a science is concerned with the study of the various aspects of the behavior of society in its effort to allocate the scarce resources—land, labor, capital, and entrepreneurial ability—in order to satisfy as best it can its unlimited desire for consumption. This basic problem becomes, in reality, five problems: what to produce, how to produce it, for whom to produce it, the achievement of full employment of resources, and the maintenance of economic flexibility.

The production possibilities table and curve are used in this chapter to illustrate the meaning of the scarcity of resources and of increasing costs. It is only an illustrative device, but it should help the student to understand the nature of several economic concepts and problems.

Every economy is faced with the problem of scarce resources and has to find answers to the Five Fundamental Questions. But no economy arrives at solutions to its fundamental economic problems in the same way that another economy does. Between the extremes of pure laissez faire capitalism and communism lie various economic systems; all systems are simply different devices—different methods of organization—for finding answers or systems which are employed to find economic answers; Chapters 3 to 7 explain in greater detail how the American economy is built and operates.

Throughout Chapter 2 of the textbook there are numerous economic definitions and classifications. It would be well for the student to learn these definitions and classifications *now*. They will be used later on and it will be necessary for the student to know and understand them if he is to understand what follows.

■ CHAPTER OUTLINE

1. The bases upon which the study of economics rests are two facts.
   a. Society's material resources are unlimited.
   b. The economic resources which are the ultimate means of satisfying these wants are scarce in relation to the wants.

2. Economics, then, is the study of how society's scarce resources are used (administered) to obtain the greatest satisfaction of its material wants.
   a. To be efficient in the use of its resources an economy must achieve both full employment and full production.
   b. The production possibilities table and curve indicate the alternative combinations of goods and services an economy is capable of

producing when it has achieved full employment and full production.

   c. Which of these alternative combinations
society chooses—which product-mix it selects
—depends upon the preferences of that society; and preferences are subjective and nonscientific.

   d. Because resources are not completely
adaptable to alternative uses, the production
of any product is subject to the law of increasing costs.

3. Failure to achieve full employment and
full production reduces the output of goods
the economy produces, but improvements in
technology and increased amounts of resources augment the output the economy is
capable of producing. The combination of
goods and services an economy chooses to
produce now helps to determine its production possibilities in the future.

4. Faced with unlimited wants and scarce resources, every economy must determine in
some manner what goods to produce, how
much of them to produce, how to produce
them, how to divide the total output among
the members of society, and how to ensure
full employment of its resources and a flexible
economic system.

5. Different economic systems—capitalism,
socialism, and communism—are based on
different philosophies and institutions and
employ different methods to obtain answers
to these Five Fundamental Questions.

■ IMPORTANT TERMS

The economizing problem	Economics
Unlimited wants	Full employment
Scarce resources	Full production
Land, capital, labor, and entrepreneurial ability	Unemployment
	Disguised unemployment
Real capital	Consumer goods
Money (financial) capital	Capital goods
Rental income, interest income, wages, and profit	Economic efficiency
	Production possibilities table
Factors of production	Production possibilities curve

Law of increasing costs	Liberal or democratic socialism
Five Fundamental Economic Questions	Communism or authoritarian socialism
Economic flexibility	
Laissez faire capitalism	Opportunity cost
	Economic growth

■ FILL-IN QUESTIONS

1. The two fundamental facts which provide
the foundations of economics are:

   a. _____

   b. _____

2. Complete the following classification of resources:

   a. _____

   (1) _____

   (2) _____

   b. _____

   (1) _____

   (2) _____

3. The incomes of individuals are received
from supplying resources. Four types of in-

comes are _____ ,

_____ ,

_____ ,

and _____

4. Economics can be defined as _____

_____

_____

5. When a production possibilities table or
curve is constructed, three assumptions are
made. These assumptions are:

   a. _____

   b. _____

   c. _____

6. Both consumer goods and capital goods
satisfy material wants. However, consumer

goods satisfy human wants _____

while capital goods satisfy human wants _____

_____

7. Below is a production possibilities curve for tractors and suits of clothing.

Tractors

0   Suits of clothing

a. If the economy moves from point *A* to point *B* it will produce (more, fewer) _____

_____ tractors and (more, fewer)

_____ suits of clothing.
b. If the economy is producing at point *X*, some of the resources of the economy are

either _____ or _____
c. If the economy moves from point *X* to

point *B* (more, fewer) _____

tractors and (more, fewer) _____
suits will be produced.
d. If the economy is to produce at point *Y*,

it must either _____

or _____

8. The more an economy consumes of its

current production, the (more, less) _____
it will be capable of producing in future years, other things being equal.

9. The cost of producing a commodity tends to increase as more of the commodity is

produced because _____

_____

10. Four functions which the entrepreneur performs are:

a. _____

b. _____

c. _____

d. _____

11. List the Five Fundamental Questions which every economy must attempt to answer.

a. _____

b. _____

c. _____

d. _____

e. _____

12. The quantity of other goods and services an economy must go without in order to pro-

duce low-cost housing is the _____
of producing low-cost housing.

13. Unemployment can take two forms: _____

_____

unemployment and _____
unemployment.

14. Economic efficiency requires that there

be both _____

of resources and _____

15. The extent to which resources are used in an economy depends upon the degree to

which the economy is _____
to use its resources and the extent to which it

is _____
to use its resources.

16. An economy needs flexibility because

_____,

_____,

and _____
are constantly changing.

17. All the combinations of products shown in the production possibilities table (or on the curve) can be achieved only if there are both full employment and full production in the economy; the best combination of products

depends upon the _____

of that society and is a _____ matter.

18. Different societies have different output _____ and employ different economic _____ and _____ to achieve them. The two extreme systems of economic organization in the modern, industrially advanced nations are _____ and _____ .

■ PROBLEMS AND PROJECTS

1. Below is a list of resources. Indicate in the space to the right of each whether the resource is land, capital (C), labor, entrepreneurial ability (EA), or some combinations of these.

a. Fishing grounds in the North Atlantic _____

b. A cash register in a retail store _____

c. Uranium deposits in South Africa _____

d. An irrigation ditch in Nebraska _____

e. The work performed by the late Henry Ford _____

f. The oxygen breathed by human beings _____

g. The U.S. Steel plant in Gary, Indiana _____

h. The goods on the shelf of a retail store _____

i. The work done by a laborer on an assembly line _____

j. The tasks accomplished in perfecting color television for commercial sales _____

2. A production possibilities table for two commodities, wheat and automobiles, follows. The table is constructed employing the usual three assumptions. Wheat is measured in units of 100,000 bushels and automobiles in units of 100,000.

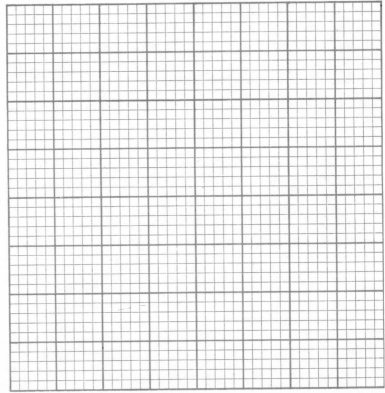

0

Combination	Wheat	Automobiles
A	0	7
B	7	6
C	13	5
D	18	4
E	22	3
F	25	2
G	27	1
H	28	0

a. Follow the general rules for making graphs (Chapter 1), plot the data in the table on the graph (page 10) to obtain a production possibilities curve. Place wheat on the vertical axis and automobiles on the horizontal axis.

b. Fill in the table below showing the *opportunity cost per unit* of producing the 1st through the 7th automobile.

Automobiles	Cost of production
1st	_____
2d	_____
3d	_____
4th	_____
5th	_____
6th	_____
7th	_____

c. Fill in the table below showing the *opportunity cost per unit* of producing the 7th through the 28th unit of wheat.

Wheat	Cost of production
7th	_____
13th	_____
18th	_____
22d	_____
25th	_____
27th	_____
28th	_____

3. Below is a production possibilties curve. Draw on this graph:

a. A production possibilties curve which indicates greater efficiency in the production of good *A*.

b. A production possibilities curve which indicates greater efficiency in the production of good *B*.

c. A production possibilities curve which indicates an increase in the resources available to the economy.

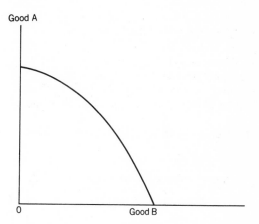

4. Below is a list of economic goods. Indicate in the space to the right of each whether the good is a consumer good (CON), a capital good (CAP), or whether the answer depends (DEP) upon who is using it and for what purpose.

a. An automobile _____

b. A tractor _____

c. A taxicab _____

d. A house _____

e. A factory building _____

f. An office building _____

g. An ironing board _____

h. An icebox _____

i. A telephone _____

j. A quart of Scotch whisky _____

k. A cash register _____

l. A screwdriver _____

■ SELF-TEST

Circle the T if the statement is true, the F if it is false.

1. The wants with which economics is concerned include only those wants which can be satisfied by goods and services.　Ⓣ　F

2. Resources are scarce because society's material wants are unlimited.　Ⓣ　F

3. Money, as a resource, is classified as "capital."　T　Ⓕ

4. It is not possible for an economy capable of producing just two goods to increase its production of both.　T　Ⓕ

5. The cost of producing a good tends to increase as more of it is produced, because resources less suitable to its production must be employed.　Ⓣ　F

6. At full employment and full production, the more capital goods an economy produces today, the smaller the amount of consumer goods it will be able to produce today.　Ⓣ　F

7. If an economy increases the percentage of the current output it consumes, its production possibilities curve will move to the left.　T　Ⓕ

8. The more capital goods an economy produces today, the greater will be the total output of all goods it can produce in the future, other things being equal.　Ⓣ　F

9. The opportunity cost of producing woolen mittens is the other goods and services the economy is unable to produce because it has decided to produce mittens.　Ⓣ　F

10. It is economically desirable to have unemployed resources at the outbreak of a war because resources need not be shifted from consumer-good production in order to produce military goods.　T　Ⓕ

Underscore the letter that corresponds to the best answer.

1. An "innovator" is defined as an entrepreneur who: (a) makes basic policy decisions in a business firm; (b) combines factors of production to produce a good or service; (c) invents a new product or process for producing a product; (d) introduces new products on the market or employs a new method to produce a product.

2. A farmer who produces his crops by inefficient methods is: (a) an unemployed worker; (b) an underemployed worker; (c) a fully employed worker; (d) an apparently unemployed worker.

3. At point A on the production possibilities curve in the illustration below: (a) more wheat than tractors is being produced; (b) more tractors than wheat are being produced; (c) the economy is employing all its resources; (d) the economy is not employing all its resources.

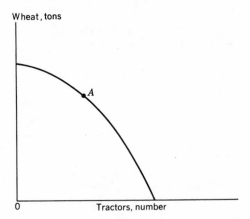

Wheat, tons

0　　　　　　　Tractors, number

4. If the production possibilities curve on the graph below moves from position A to position B, then: (a) the economy has increased the efficiency with which it produces wheat; (b) the economy has increased the efficiency with which it produces tractors; (c) the economy has put to work previously idle resources; (d) the economy has gone from a full-employment situation to a less-than-full-employment situation.

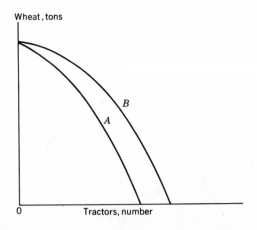

Wheat, tons

0　　　　　　　Tractors, number

5. If there is an increase in the resources available within the economy: (a) more goods and services will be produced in the economy; (b) the economy will be capable of producing more goods and services; (c) the standard of living in the economy will rise; (d) the technological efficiency of the economy will improve.

6. Which one of the following is *not* one of the Five Fundamental Economic Questions which every economy must answer? (a) determining what is to be produced; (b) deciding the level of resource use; (c) distributing output; (d) enforcing the law of increasing costs.

7. During the Middle Ages the feudal society found answers to the Fundamental Economic Questions through a system of: (a) custom and tradition; (b) laissez faire capitalism; (c) democratic socialism; (d) communism.

8. If the economic system of a nation is liberal or democratic socialism, there is: (a) public ownership and control of the bulk of industry and agriculture; (b) virtually no government planning or control; (c) a mixture of public and private ownership and decision making; (d) reliance on the price system only as a means of implementing central planning.

9. The combination of products in a society's production possibilities table which is its optimum product-mix depends upon that society's: (a) resources; (b) technology; (c) level of employment; (d) values or priorities.

10. An economy is efficient when it has achieved: (a) full employment; (b) full production; (c) either full employment or full production; (d) both full employment and full production.

■ DISCUSSION QUESTIONS

1. Explain what is meant by the "economizing problem." Why are resources scarce?

2. In what sense are wants satiable and in what sense are they insatiable?

3. What are the four economic resources? How is each of these resources defined? What is the income earned by each of them called?

4. Every individual has his own personal economic problem—just as every economy has its economic problem. How would you state this individual economic problem?

5. When is a society economically efficient? What is meant by "full production" and how does it differ from "full employment"?

6. Why cannot an economist determine which of the combinations in the production possibilities table is "best"? What determines the optimum product-mix? How and why do the product-mixes of the U.S. and the U.S.S.R. differ?

7. Explain the difference between a "good" and a "service."

8. Why is the production possibilities curve "concave" to the origin? What would such a curve show if it were convex to the origin or a straight line connecting the two axes?

9. What three assumptions are made in drawing a production possibilities curve or schedule? How do technological advance and an increased supply of resources in the economy affect the curve or schedule?

10. What is the important relationship between the *composition* of the economy's current output and the *location* of future production possibilities curves?

11. Many people do not spend all their income on goods and services but rather *save* some of it. Does this indicate to you that their desires for goods and services have been fully satisfied, or does it indicate that money saved satisfies some other human desire?

12. What is opportunity cost? What is the law of increasing costs? Why do costs increase?

13. What are the Five Fundamental Economic Questions and how are they related to the economizing problem?

14. Laissez faire capitalism, democratic socialism, and communism differ in their underlying assumptions, institutions, and methods for solving their fundamental economic problems. Contrast these economic systems.

15. Explain the difference between "full employment" and "full production."

PURE CAPITALISM
AND THE
CIRCULAR FLOW

Chapter 3 has three principal aims: to outline the six ideological and institutional characteristics of pure capitalism, to explain three practices found in all modern economics, and to sketch in extremely simple terms the fundamental operation of a capitalistic economy. A more detailed explanation of the institutions, practices, and behavior of the American economy—which is not *purely* capitalistic—is found in the chapters that follow. If the aims of this chapter are accomplished, the student can begin to understand the system and methods employed by our economy to find answers to the Five Fundamental Economic Questions discussed in Chapter 2.

The resources of the American economy are owned by its citizens, who are free to use them as they wish in their own self-interest; prices and markets serve to express the self-interests of resource owners, consumers, and business firms; and competition serves to regulate self-interest—to prevent the self-interest of any person or any group from working to the disadvantage of the economy as a whole and to make self-interest work for the benefit of the entire economy.

Based on comparative advantage and specialization, trade is made more convenient by the use of money as a medium of exchange. Trade increases the production possible in an economy with a given quantity of resources. Trade also increases the interdependence of the members of the economy. The principle of comparative advantage is the basis for all trade between individuals, firms, regions, and nations; and the student ought to be sure to understand what is meant by comparative advantage, how specialization is determined on the basis of comparative advantage, and why trade and specialization tend to increase the total production of the economy.

The circular-flow-of-income model (or diagram) is a device which illustrates for a capitalistic economy the relation between households and businesses, the flow of money and economic goods and services between households and businesses, their dual role as buyers and sellers, and the two basic types of markets essential to the capitalistic process.

Understand these essentials of the economic skeleton first; then a little flesh—a little more reality, a little more detail—can be added to the bones. Understanding the skeleton makes it much easier to understand the whole body and its functioning.

■ CHAPTER OUTLINE

1. The American economy is not pure capitalism; but it is a close approximation of pure capitalism. Pure capitalism has six important peculiarities that distinguish it from other economic systems.

2. In common with all other advanced economies of the world, the American economy has three major characteristics.

a. It employs complicated and advanced methods of production and vast amounts of capital equipment to produce goods and services.

b. It is a highly specialized economy; specialization is based on the principle of comparative advantage and increases the productive efficiency of the economy.

c. It also uses money extensively to facilitate trade and specialization.

3. The circular flow model is a device used to clarify the relationships between households and business firms in a purely capitalistic system, the part that each of them plays in the economy, and their respective roles in the resource and product markets.

■ IMPORTANT TERMS

Private property	**Terms of trade**
Self-interest	**Money**
Competition	**Medium of exchange**
Freedom of choice	**Barter**
Freedom of enterprise	**Coincidence of wants**
Roundabout production	**Circular flow of income**
Specialization	**Household**
Division of labor	**Resource market**
Comparative cost	**Product market**
Comparative advantage	

■ FILL-IN QUESTIONS

1. The institution of _____ entails the ownership of the means of production by private individuals and institutions.

2. Two basic freedoms encountered in a capitalistic economy are the freedoms of _____

_____

and _____

3. Self-interest means that each economic

unit _____

_____;
this self-interest might work to the disadvantage of the economy as a whole if it were not

regulated and constrained by _____

4. According to the economist, competition is present if two conditions prevail; these two conditions are:

a. _____

b. _____

5. If the number of buyers and sellers in a market is large, no single buyer or seller is

able to _____

6. In a capitalistic economy no one individual determines the answers to the fundamental questions of what and how to produce and how the product will be distributed. These decisions are made by many individuals and

are made effective through a _____

_____

system in a _____
type of economy.

7. In a capitalistic economy new products and more efficient methods of production are

introduced by _____

_____

motivated by the desire for _____

_____

8. The three practices or institutions common to all modern economies are _____

_____,

_____,

and _____

9. If an economy engages in extensive specialization the individuals living in the econ-

omy are extremely _____;

and _____
among the individuals is necessary if they are to enjoy the benefits of specialization.

10. In modern economies money functions

chiefly as a _____

11. Barter between two individuals will take

place only is there is a _____

12. In the circular flow model, households

are buyers and businesses sellers in the _____

_____

market; and businesses are buyers and house-

holds sellers in the _____
market.

13. For an item to be "money," it must be

_____

14. The income of any household depends

upon two things: _____

and _____ ;
the income of any business also depends upon

two things: _____

and _____

_____

■ PROBLEMS AND PROJECTS

1. The countries of Lilliput and Brobdingnag
have the production possibilities tables for
apples and bananas shown below.

LILLIPUT PRODUCTION POSSIBILITIES TABLE (lbs.)

Product	Production alternatives					
	A	B	C	D	E	F
Apples	40	32	24	16	8	0
Bananas	0	4	8	12	16	20

BROBDINGNAG PRODUCTION POSSIBILITIES TABLE (lbs.)

Product	Production alternatives					
	A	B	C	D	E	F
Apples	75	60	45	30	15	0
Bananas	0	5	10	15	20	25

Note that the costs of producing apples and
bananas are constant in both countries.
  a. In Lilliput the cost of producing:

  (1) 8 apples is _____ bananas

  (2) 1 apple is _____ bananas
  b. In Brobdingnag the cost of producing:

  (1) 15 apples is _____ bananas

  (2) 1 apple is _____ bananas
  c. In Lilliput the cost of producing:

  (1) 4 bananas is _____ apples

  (2) 1 banana is _____ apples
  d. In Brobdingnag the cost of producing:

  (1) 5 bananas is _____ apples

  (2) 1 banana is _____ apples
  e. The cost of producing 1 apple is lower

in the country of _____
and the cost of producing 1 banana is lower

in the country of _____
  f. Lilliput has a comparative advantage in

the production of _____
and Brobdingnag has a comparative advantage

in the production of _____
  g. The information in this problem is not
sufficient to determine the exact terms of
trade; but the terms of trade will be *greater*

than _____ apples for 1 banana and *less* than

_____ apples for 1 banana. We can also say

that the terms of trade will be between _____

bananas for 1 apple and _____ bananas for
1 apple.
  h. If neither nation could specialize, each
would produce production alternative C. The
combined production of apples in the two

countries would be _____ apples and the com-

bined production of bananas would be _____
bananas.
  (1) If each nation specializes in producing
the fruit for which it has a comparative advantage, their combined production will be

_____ apples and _____ bananas.
  (2) Their gain from specialization will be

_____ apples and _____ bananas.

2. Here is another problem to help you understand the principle of comparative advantage and the benefits of specialization. A
tailor named Hart has the production possibilities table for trousers and jackets given
below. He chooses production alternative D.

HART'S PRODUCTION POSSIBILITIES TABLE

Product	Production alternatives					
	A	B	C	D	E	F
Trousers	75	60	45	30	15	0
Jackets	0	10	20	30	40	50

Another tailor, Schaffner, has the production possibilities table below and produces production alternative E.

SCHAFFNER'S PRODUCTION POSSIBILITIES TABLE

Product	Production alternatives						
	A	B	C	D	E	F	G
Trousers	60	50	40	30	20	10	0
Jackets	0	5	10	15	20	25	30

a. To Hart

(1) the cost of one pair of trousers is _____ jackets

(2) the cost of one jacket is _____ pairs of trousers
b. To Schaffner

(1) the cost of one pair of trousers is _____ jackets

(2) the cost of one jacket is _____ pairs of trousers
c. If Hart and Schaffner were to form a partnership to make suits

(1) _____ should specialize in the making of trousers because he can make a pair of trousers at the cost of _____ of a jacket while it costs his partner _____ of a jacket to make a pair of trousers.

(2) _____ should specialize in the making of jackets because he can make a jacket at the cost of _____ pairs of trousers while it costs his partner _____ pairs of trousers to make a jacket.
d. Without specialization and between them Hart and Schaffner were able to make 50 pairs of trousers and 50 jackets. If each specializes completely in the item in the production of which he has a comparative advantage, their combined production will be _____ pairs

of trousers and _____ jackets. Thus the gain from specialization is _____.

e. When Hart and Schaffner come to divide the income of the partnership between them, the manufacture of a pair of trousers should be treated as the equivalent of from _____ to _____ jackets (and a jacket should be treated as the equivalent of from _____ to _____ pairs of trousers).

3. In the circular flow diagram below, the upper pair of flows (*a* and *b*) represent the product market and the lower pair (*c* and *d*) the resource market.

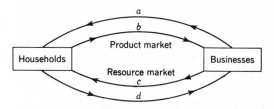

Supply labels or explanations for each of the four flows:

a. _____

b. _____

c. _____

d. _____

■ SELF-TEST

Circle the T if the statement is true, the F if it is false.

1. The American economy can correctly be called "pure capitalism." T **(F)**

2. There are definite legal limits to the right of private property. **(T)** F

3. The consumer is sovereign in a capitalistic economy because it is he who ultimately determines what the economy will produce. **(T)** F

4. Businessmen and resource owners always act only to further their own self-interest. T **(F)**

5. If a person, firm, or region does not have a comparative advantage in the production of a particular commodity, it should not specialize in the production of that commodity. Ⓣ F

6. Money is a device for facilitating the exchange of goods. Ⓣ F

7. "Coincidence of wants" means that two persons desire to acquire the same good or service. T Ⓕ

8. Cigarettes may serve as money if buyers and sellers are generally willing to accept them as money. Ⓣ F

9. In the circular flow of income, the household functions on the demand side of the resource and product markets. Ⓣ F

10. The price system is not employed in communistic and socialistic economies. T Ⓕ

Underscore the letter that corresponds to the best answer.

1. Two regions, Slobovia and Utopia, have the production possibilities tables below.

SLOBOVIA PRODUCTION POSSIBILITIES TABLE

Product	Production alternatives					
	A	B	C	D	E	F
Cams	1,500	1,200	900	600	300	0
Widgets	0	100	200	300	400	500

UTOPIA PRODUCTION POSSIBILITIES TABLE

Product	Production alternatives				
	A	B	C	D	E
Cams	4,000	3,000	2,000	1,000	0
Widgets	0	200	400	600	800

In Slobovia the comparative cost: (a) of 1 cam is 3 widgets; (b) of 1 widget is ⅓ cam; (c) of 1 cam is ⅓ widget; (d) of 3 widgets is 1 cam.

2. Using the production possibilities tables in the question above, which of the following statements is *not* true? (a) Slobovia should specialize in the production of widgets; (b) Slobovia has a comparative advantage in the production of widgets; (c) Utopia should specialize in the production of widgets; (d) Utopia

has a comparative advantage in the production of cams.

3. Employing the same information contained in question 1, the terms of trade will be: (a) greater than 7 cams for 1 widget; (b) between 7 cams for 1 widget and 5 cams for 1 widget; (c) between 5 cams for 1 widget and 3 cams for 1 widget; (d) less than 3 cams for 1 widget.

4. Still using the schedules in question 1, assume that if Slobovia did not specialize it would produce alternative C and that if Utopia did not specialize it would select alternative B. The gains from specialization are: (a) 100 cams and 100 widgets; (b) 200 cams and 200 widgets; (c) 400 cams and 500 widgets; (d) 500 cams and 400 widgets.

5. Which of the following is *not* a necessary consequence of specialization? (a) people will use money; (b) people will engage in trade; (c) people will be dependent upon each other; (d) people will produce more of some things than they would produce in the absence of specialization.

6. In an economy in which there are full employment, constant amounts of resources, and unchanging technology: (a) to increase the production of capital goods requires an increase in the production of consumer goods; (b) to decrease the production of capital goods necessitates a decrease in the production of consumer goods; (c) to increase the production of capital goods is impossible; (d) to increase the production of capital goods a decrease in the production of consumer goods is needed.

7. Which of the following is *not* a characteristic of competition as the economist sees it? (a) the widespread diffusion of economic power; (b) a large number of buyers in product markets; (c) at least several sellers of all products; (d) the relatively easy entry to and exit of producers from industries.

■ DISCUSSION QUESTIONS

1. Explain the several elements—institutions and assumptions—embodied in capitalism.

2. What do each of the following seek if they pursue their own self-interest? Consumers, resource owners, and businessmen.

3. Explain what economists mean by competition. Why is it important in an economy whose members are motivated by self-interest?

4. What are the advantages of "indirect" or "roundabout" production?

5. How does an economy benefit from specialization and the division of labor?

6. What disadvantages are there to specialization and the division of labor?

7. Why do specialization and an advanced technology go hand in hand?

8. Explain what is meant by comparative cost and comparative advantage. What determines the terms of trade? What is the gain that results from specialization in the products in the production of which there is a comparative advantage?

9. What are the principal disadvantages of barter?

10. What is money? What important function does it perform? Explain how money performs this function and how it overcomes the disadvantages associated with barter. Why are people willing to accept paper money in exchange for the goods and services which they have to sell?

11. In the circular-flow-of-income model: (a) What two markets are involved? (b) What role do households play in each of these markets? (c) What role do businesses play in each of these markets? (d) What two income flows are pictured in money terms? In real terms? (e) What two expenditure flows are pictured in money terms? In real terms?

12. What are the five shortcomings of the circular-flow-of-income model?

THE MECHANICS
OF INDIVIDUAL
PRICES:
DEMAND AND SUPPLY

Chapter 4 is an introduction to the most fundamental tool of economic analysis: demand and supply. If you are to progress successfully into the later chapters it is essential that you understand what is meant by demand and supply and how to use this powerful tool.

Demand and supply are simply "boxes" or categories into which all the forces and factors that affect the price and the quantity of a good bought and sold in a competitive market can conveniently be placed. It is necessary to see that demand and supply do determine price and quantity exchanged and to see *why* and *how* they do this.

Many students never do understand demand and supply because they never learn to define demand and supply *exactly* and because they never learn (1) what is meant by an increase or decrease in demand or supply, (2) the important distinctions between demand and quantity demanded and between supply and quantity supplied, (3) the equally important distinctions between an increase (or decrease) in demand and an increase (or decrease) in quantity demanded and between an increase (or decrease) in supply and an increase (or decrease) in quantity supplied.

Having learned these, however, it is no great trick to comprehend the so-called "law of supply and demand." The equilibrium price—that is, the price which will tend to prevail in the market as long as demand and supply do not change—is simply the price at which quantity demanded and quantity supplied are equal. The quantity bought and sold in the

market (the equilibrium quantity) is the quantity demanded and supplied at the equilibrium price. If you can determine the equilibrium price and quantity under one set of demand and supply conditions, you can determine them under any other set and so will be able to analyze for yourself the effect of changes in demand and supply upon equilibrium price and quantity.

In analyzing equilibrium price and quantity, two important assumptions are made. One is that the higher the price of a good, the smaller will be the quantity demanded of the good (and vice versa); this assumption is called the law of demand. The second is that the higher the price of a good, the larger will be the quantity supplied of that good (and vice versa); this second assumption is the law of supply.

The chapter includes a brief examination of the factors that influence demand and supply and of the ways in which changes in these influences will affect and cause changes in demand and supply. A graphic method is employed in this analysis in order to facilitate an understanding of demand and supply, equilibrium price and quantity, changes in demand and supply, and the resulting changes in equilibrium price and quantity. In addition to understanding the definitions of demand and supply *exactly*, it is necessary to understand the two counterparts of demand and supply: the demand *curve* and the supply *curve*. These are simple graphic (or geometric) representations of the same data contained in the schedules of demand and supply—and demand and supply can only be expressed in terms of schedules or these graphic counterparts.

■ CHAPTER OUTLINE

1. Demand is a schedule of prices and the quantities which buyers will purchase at each of these prices during some period of time.

a. As price rises buyers will purchase smaller quantities, and as price falls they will purchase larger quantities; this is the law of demand.

b. The demand curve is a graphic representation of demand and the law of demand.

c. Market (or total) demand for a good is a summation of the demands of all individuals in the market for that good.

d. The demand for a good depends upon the tastes, income, and expectations of buyers; the number of buyers in the market; and the prices of related goods.

e. A change (either an increase or a decrease) in demand is caused by a change in any of the factors (in *d*) which determine demand, and means that the demand schedule and demand curve have changed.

(1) If an increase in the income of a consumer increases his demand for a good, the good is a normal one; if it decreases his demand, the good is an inferior one.

(2) If an increase (decrease) in the price of one good causes the demand for another good to increase (decrease), the two goods are substitute goods; if it causes the demand for the other good to decrease (increase), the two goods are complementary; and if it causes no change, the two goods are independent goods.

f. A change in demand and a change in the quantity demanded are *not* the same thing.

2. Supply is a schedule of prices and the quantities which sellers will sell at each of these prices during a given period of time.

a. The law of supply indicates that as the price of the good rises larger quantities will be offered for sale, and that as the price of the good falls smaller quantities will be offered for sale.

b. The supply curve is a graphic representation of supply and the law of supply; the market supply of a good is the sum of the supplies of all sellers of the good.

c. The supply of a good depends upon the prices of the resources used to produce it, the prices of other goods which might be produced, the techniques which are used to produce it, price expectations, and the number of sellers of the product.

d. Supply will change when any of the determinants of supply changes; a change in supply is a change in the entire supply schedule or curve.

e. A change in supply must be distinguished from a change in quantity supplied.

3. The market or equilibrium price of a commodity is that price at which quantity demanded and quantity supplied are equal; and the quantity exchanged in the market (the equilibrium quantity) is equal to either the quantity demanded or the quantity supplied.

a. The rationing function of prices is the elimination of either a shortage or surplus of the commodity.

b. Change in demand, supply, or both affects both the equilibrium price and quantity in definite ways.

c. In resource markets suppliers are households and demanders are business firms, and in product markets suppliers are business firms and demanders are households; supply and demand are useful in the analysis of prices and quantities exchanged in both these markets.

■ IMPORTANT TERMS

Demand schedule	**Law of supply**
Law of demand	**Supply curve**
Demand curve	**Increase (or decrease) in supply**
Individual demand	
Total or market demand	**Quantity supplied**
	Equilibrium price
Increase (or decrease) in demand	**Equilibrium quantity**
	Rationing function of prices
Normal (superior) good	
	Price-increasing effect
Inferior good	
Substitute (competing) good	**Price-decreasing effect**
	Quantity-increasing effect
Complementary good	
Independent good	
Quantity demanded	**Quantity decreasing effect**
Supply schedule	

■ FILL-IN QUESTIONS

1. In resource markets prices are determined by the demand decisions of _____ and the supply decisions of _____; in product markets they are determined by

_____

and _____

2. When demand is graphed, price is placed on the _____

axis and quantity on the _____ axis.

3. The relationship between price and quantity in the demand schedule is a(n) _____

_____

relationship; in the supply schedule the relationship is a(n) _____ one.

4. When a consumer demand schedule or curve is drawn up, it is assumed that five factors that determine demand are fixed and constant. These five determinants of consumer demand are:

a. _____

b. _____

c. _____

d. _____

e. _____

5. A decrease in demand means that consumers will buy (larger, smaller) _____ quantities at every price or will pay (more, less) _____ for the same quantities.

6. If a consumer's demand for a product decreases when his income increases, the product is a(n) _____ good; if his demand for it increases when his income increases, the product is a(n) _____

_____

good.

7. If a consumer's demand for a product decreases when the price of another product increases, the two products are _____ goods; if a consumer's demand for a product increases when the price of another product increases, the two products are _____

_____

goods.

8. A change in income or in the price of another product will result in a change in the (demand for, quantity demanded of) _____

_____

the given product, while a change in the price of the given product will result in _____

_____

9. The fundamental factors which determine the supply of any commodity in the product market are:

a. _____

b. . _____

c. _____

d. _____

e. _____

10. An improvement in the technology of producing a product is apt to _____

_____ the supply of that product; a(n) (increase, decrease) _____ in the prices of resources used to produce the product will have the same effect.

11. If quantity demanded exceeds quantity supplied, price is (greater, less) _____ than the equilibrium price.

12. In the spaces below each of the following, indicate the effect [increase (+), decrease (—), no change (0), or indeterminate (?)] upon equilibrium price and equilibrium quantity of each of these changes in demand and/or supply.

a. Increase in demand, supply constant

_____   _____

b. Increase in supply, demand constant

_____ _____

c. Decrease in demand, supply constant

_____ _____

d. Decrease in supply, demand constant

_____ _____

e. Increase in demand, increase in supply

_____ _____

f. Increase in demand, decrease in supply

_____ _____

g. Decrease in demand, decrease in supply

_____ _____

h. Decrease in demand, increase in supply

_____ _____

13. If supply and demand establish a price for a good such that there is no shortage or surplus of the good, then price is successfully

performing its _____
function.

14. The equilibrium price of a commodity is the price at which _____

_____

■ PROBLEMS AND PROJECTS

1. Using the demand schedule below, plot the demand curve on the graph. Label the axes and indicate for each axis the units being used to measure price and quantity.

Price	Quantity demanded, 1,000 bushels of soybeans
$1.20	10
1.00	15
.80	20
.60	25
.40	30
.20	35

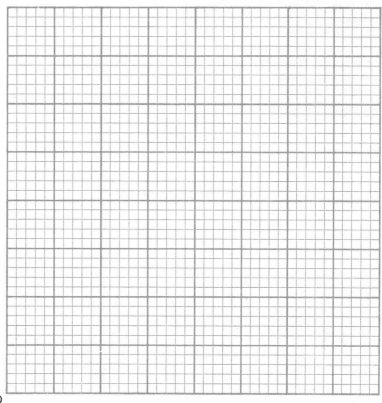

0

Demand for A (per week)			Demand for B (per week)		
(1) Price	(2) Quantity demanded	(3) Quantity demanded	(4) Price	(5) Quantity demanded	(6) Quantity demanded
$.90	10	0	$5.00	4	7
.85	20	10	4.50	5	8
.80	30	20	4.00	6	9
.75	40	30	3.50	7	10
.70	50	40	3.00	8	11
.65	60	50	2.50	9	12
.60	70	60	2.00	10	13

2. The demand schedules of three individuals (Roberts, Charles, and Lynn) for loaves of bread are shown below. Assuming there are only three buyers of bread, draw up the total or market demand schedule for bread.

Price	Quantity demanded, loaves of bread			Total
	Roberts	Charles	Lynn	
$.30	1	4	0	_____
.16	3	5	1	_____
.12	6	6	5	_____
.08	10	7	10	_____
.04	15	8	16	_____

3. Below is a demand schedule for bushels of apples. In columns 3 and 4 supply any new figures for quantity which represent in column 3 an increase in demand, in column 4 a decrease in demand.

(1) Price	(2) Quantity demanded	(3) Demand increases	(4) Demand decreases
$2.00	400	_____	_____
1.90	500	_____	_____
1.80	600	_____	_____
1.70	700	_____	_____
1.60	800	_____	_____
1.50	900	_____	_____

4. Assume that O'Rourke has, when his income is $100 a week, the demand schedule for good A shown in columns 1 and 2 of the table above and the demand schedule for good B shown in columns 4 and 5. Assume that the prices of A and B are $.80 and $5, respectively.

a. How much A will O'Rourke buy? _____

How much B? _____

b. Suppose that, as a consequence of a $10 increase in O'Rourke's weekly income, the quantities demanded of A become those shown in column 3 and the quantities demanded of B become those shown in column 6.

(1) How much A will he now buy? _____

How much B? _____

(2) What type of good is A? _____

(3) What type of good is B? _____

5. The market demand for good X is shown in columns 1 and 2 of the next table. Assume the price of X to be $2 and constant.

(1) Price	(2) Quantity demanded	(3) Quantity demanded	(4) Quantity demanded
$2.40	1,600	1,500	1,700
2.30	1,650	1,550	1,750
2.20	1,750	1,650	1,850
2.10	1,900	1,800	2,000
2.00	2,100	2,000	2,200
1.90	2,350	2,250	2,450
1.80	2,650	2,550	2,750

a. If as the price of good Y rises from $1.25 to $1.35 the quantities demanded of good X become those shown in column 3, it can be concluded that X and Y are _____ goods.

b. If as the price of good Y rises from $1.25 to $1.35 the quantities demanded of good X become those shown in column 4, it can be concluded that X and Y are _____ goods.

6. Plot the supply schedule which follows on the same graph on which you plotted demand in problem 1.

Price	Quantity supplied, 1,000 bushels of soybeans
$1.20	40
1.00	35
.80	30
.60	25
.40	20
.20	15

a. The equilibrium price of soybeans will be

$_____

b. _____ thousand bushels of soybeans will be exchanged at this price.

c. Indicate clearly on the graph the equilibrium price and quantity by drawing lines from the intersection of the supply and demand curves to the price and quantity axes.

7. In a local market for hamburger on a given date, each of 300 sellers of hamburger has the following supply schedule. In column 3 construct the market supply schedule for hamburger.

(1) Price	(2) Quantity supplied— one seller, lb.	(3) Quantity supplied— all sellers, lb.
$.65	150	_____
.60	110	_____
.55	75	_____
.50	45	_____
.45	20	_____
.40	0	_____

8. Below is the market demand schedule for hamburger on the same date and in the same market as that given in problem 7. The equilibrium price of hamburger will be between

$ _____

and $ _____ ;

the equilibrium quantity will be between ____

_____

and _____ pounds.

Price	Quantity demanded, lb.
$.65	28,000
.60	31,000
.55	36,000
.50	42,000
.45	49,000
.40	57,000

9. Each of the following events would tend to affect (that is, increase or decrease) either the demand for or the supply of television sets, and thus affect the price of television sets. In the first blank indicate the effect upon demand or supply and in the second the effect (increase or decrease) upon price.

a. It becomes known that a local department store is going to have a sale on television sets within the next three months. _____ ;

b. The workers who produce the sets go on strike for over two months. _____ ;

c. The workers in the industry receive a 90-cent-an-hour wage increase. _____ ;

d. The average price of movie tickets increases. _____ ; _____

e. The firms producing the sets undertake to produce a large volume of missile components for the Defense Department. _____ ;

f. Several large areas in the country, previously without television stations, become regions in which programs can be received. ___

_____; _____

g. Because of the use of mass-production techniques, the amount of labor necessary to produce a set decreases. _____;

_____

h. The price of high-fidelity phonograph

sets decreases. _____; _____

i. The average consumer believes that a shortage of sets is developing in the econ-

omy. _____; _____

j. The general level of personal income tax

rates increases. _____; _____

10. Below is the supply schedule for a certain product. In column 3 place *any* new *price* figures which indicate an increase in supply; in column 4 put new *price* figures which indicate a decrease in supply.

(1) Price	(2) Quantity supplied	(3) Supply increase	(4) Supply decrease
$10	950	$_____	$_____
8	900	_____	_____
6	850	_____	_____
4	800	_____	_____
2	750	_____	_____

■ SELF-TEST

Circle the T if the statement is true, the F if it is false.

1. Demand is the amount of a commodity or service which a buyer will purchase at a particular price.   T ⃝F

2. The law of demand states that as price increases, the quantity of the product demanded increases.   T ⃝F

3. In graphing supply and demand schedules, supply is put on the horizontal axis and demand on the vertical axis.   T ⃝F

4. If price falls, there will be an increase in demand.   T ⃝F

5. If the demand curve moves from D_1 to D_2 in the graph below, demand has increased.   ⃝T F

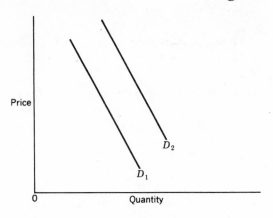

6. A fall in the price of a good will cause the demand for goods which are substitutes for it to increase.   T ⃝F

7. If two goods are complementary, an increase in the price of one will cause the demand for the other to increase.   T ⃝F

8. If the market price of a commodity is for a time below its equilibrium price, the market price will tend to rise because demand will decrease and supply will increase. T ⃝F

Underscore the letter that corresponds to the best answer.

1. Which of the following can cause a decrease in consumer demand for product X? (a) a decrease in consumer income; (b) an increase in the prices of goods which are good substitutes for product X; (c) an increase in the price which consumers expect will prevail for product X in the future; (d) a decrease in the supply of product X.

2. If two goods are substitutes for each other, an increase in the price of one will necessarily: (a) decrease the demand for the other; (b) increase the demand for the other; (c) decrease the quantity demanded of the other; (d) increase the quantity demanded of the other.

3. The income of a consumer decreases and he increases his demand for a particular good. It can be concluded that the good is: (a) normal; (b) inferior; (c) a substitute; (d) a complement.

4. If the supply curve moves from S_1 to S_2 on the graph below, there has been: (a) an increase in supply; (b) a decrease in supply; (c) an increase in quantity supplied; (d) a decrease in quantity supplied.

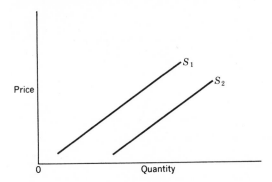

5. An increase in demand and a decrease in supply will: (a) increase price and increase the quantity exchanged; (b) decrease price and decrease the quantity exchanged; (c) increase price and the effect upon quantity exchanged will be indeterminate; (d) decrease price and the effect upon quantity exchanged will be indeterminate.

6. An increase in supply and an increase in demand will: (a) increase price and increase the quantity exchanged; (b) decrease price and increase the quantity exchanged; (c) affect price in an indeterminate way and decrease the quantity exchanged; (d) affect price in an indeterminate way and increase the quantity exchanged.

7. Which of the following could not cause an increase in the supply of cotton? (a) an increase in the price of cotton; (b) improvements in the art of producing cotton; (c) a decrease in the price of the machinery and tools employed in cotton production; (d) a decrease in the price of corn.

8. The law of supply states that as price increases: (a) supply increases; (b) supply decreases; (c) quantity supplied increases; (d) quantity supplied decreases.

■ DISCUSSION QUESTIONS

1. Explain the difference between an increase in demand and an increase in quantity demanded, and between a decrease in supply and a decrease in quantity supplied.

2. Neither demand nor supply remain constant for long because the factors which determine demand and supply do not long remain constant. What are these factors? How do changes in them affect demand and supply?

3. How are normal, inferior, substitute, complementary, and independent goods defined, and how can these concepts be used to predict the way in which a change in income or in the prices of other goods will affect the demand for a given good?

4. Given the demand for and the supply of a commodity, what price will be the equilibrium price of this commodity? Explain why this price will tend to prevail in the market and why higher (lower) prices, if they do exist temporarily, will tend to fall (rise).

5. Would you define a decrease in supply as a decrease in the amounts that would be supplied at various prices or as an increase in the prices necessary to ensure various amounts of the good being offered for sale? Explain your preference.

6. Analyze the following quotation and explain the fallacies contained in it. "An increase in demand will cause price to rise; with a rise in price, supply will increase and the increase in supply will push price down. Therefore, an increase in demand results in little change in price because supply will increase also."

7. What is meant by the "rationing function of prices"?

8. What is the difference between individual and market demand; and what is the relationship between these two types of demand? Does this distinction and relationships also apply to individual and market supply?

9. "The law of demand depends upon the ability of consumers to substitute, and the law of supply depends upon the ability of producers to substitute." Explain for both laws the kind of substitution that takes place.

10. If you were a consumer buying a product in a competitive market and hoping for the price of the product to fall, for what events on the demand side and on the supply side would you hope?

THE FIVE
FUNDAMENTAL QUESTIONS
AND THE
PRICE SYSTEM

In Chapters 2, 3, and 4 we examined the institutions and characteristics of pure capitalism and saw how supply and demand determine both equilibrium price and equilibrium quantity in resource and product markets. Chapter 5 draws these elements together into an explanation of the ways in which the market system finds answers for the first four of the Five Fundamental Economic Questions. This explanation is only an approximation—a simplified version or a model—of the methods actually employed by American capitalism. Yet this simple model, like all good models, contains enough realism to be truthful and is general enough to be understandable.

The model is intentionally and specifically unrealistic because the economic role of government is ignored and because actual competition in American capitalism is probably much less effective than is assumed in Chapter 5. These shortcomings, however, do not invalidate the major points made in the chapter about the functioning of the price-market system; and the shortcomings are corrected in later chapters to make the model more realistic.

The section entitled "Operation of the Price System" (beginning on page 75 of the textbook) is both the most important part of this chapter and the part the student will find most difficult. If the student will try to understand how the American system of prices and markets finds answers for each of the four basic questions by examining them *individually* and in the order in which they are presented, he will understand more easily how the price system as a whole operates. Actually the price system finds answers for all these questions simultaneously, but for purposes of explanation and comprehension it is much simpler to consider them as if they were separate questions.

In addition to explaining how the price system operates, Chapter 5 also takes up the question of *how well* it operates. Here the student will find the going much easier. It should be particularly noted, however, that the price-market system is a widely accepted method of allocating scarce resources because it is economically quite efficient in the allocation of resources. But even so, it, like every other economic system devised by man, is not perfectly efficient. The specific criticisms leveled against the price-market system are well worth noting because, as will be seen in Chapter 6, many of government's functions in the economy are directed toward the correction of the system's faults which have been pointed out by its critics; in fact, one of the reasons for ignoring the role of government in Chapter 5 is to emphasize the shortcomings of pure capitalism in the absence of government.

A few final words of advice to the student. He should be sure he understands the *importance* and *role* of each of the following in the operation of the price-market system: (1) the rationing and directing functions of prices,

(2) substitutability between different products and between different resources, (3) the profit motive of business firms, (4) the entry and exodus of firms from industries, (5) competition, and (6) consumer sovereignty.

■ CHAPTER OUTLINE

1. The price system consists of product and resource markets in which prices and quantities exchanged are determined. In the product markets households demand the products supplied by business firms, while in the resource markets businesses demand the resources supplied by households.

2. Household and business firms in their functions as both demander and suppliers are faced with the necessity of making choices: what, how much and how to produce, what resources to employ, how to spend incomes, and to whom to supply resources. Choices are necessary because resources are scarce. Choices are possible only to the extent that there is substitutability between resources and between products.

3. The system of prices and markets and the choices of households and business firms furnish the economy with answers to the first four Fundamental Economic Questions.
   a. The demands of consumers for products and the desire of business firms to maximize their profits determine what and how much of each product is produced and its price.
   b. The desire of business firms to maximize profits by keeping their costs of production as low as possible guide them to employ the most efficient techniques of production and determines their demand for and prices of the various resources; competition forces them to use the most efficient technique and ensures the most efficient will be able to stay in business.
   c. With resource prices determined, the money income of each household is determined; and with product prices determined, the quantity of goods and services which these money incomes will buy is determined.
   d. The price-market system communicates changes in consumer tastes, the availability of resources, and techniques of production to business firms.
   (1) The desire for maximum profits and competition will then result in a new set of

answers to the first three Fundamental Economic Questions.
   (2) Competition and the desire to increase profits promote both better techniques of production and capital accumulation.
   e. Competition in the economy compels firms seeking to promote their own interests to promote (as though led by an "invisible hand") the best interest of society as a whole: an allocation of resources appropriate to consumer wants, production by the most efficient means, and the lowest possible prices.

4. The price system has been both praised and damned because it has both merits and faults. But it does work; it is one way of finding answers for the Fundamental Economic Questions. The analysis of the price system contained in this chapter is only a rough approximation of how the American economy actually operates, because competition is often weak and because the economic role of government has been ignored.

■ IMPORTANT TERMS

Substitutability	Economic efficiency
Economic choice	Consumer sovereignty
Normal profit	Directing (guiding) function of prices
Economic cost	
Economic profit	Invisible hand
Prosperous industry	Least-cost technique
Unprosperous industry	Self-limiting adjustment

■ FILL-IN QUESTIONS

1. The competitive price system is a mechanism for both _____ the decisions of producers and households and

_____ these decisions.

2. Given its money income, each household tries to spend its income on that combination of products which _____

_____

3. The economy—producers and households

—must make economic choices because _____
_____;
choices are only possible because different products and different resources are, to some degree, _____
for each other.

4. A normal profit is an economic cost because _____
_____

5. If firms in an industry are earning economic profits, firms will _____
the industry, the price of the industry's product will _____, and the industry will employ a _____ quantity of resources and produce a _____ quantity of output; the industry's economic profits will _____
_____
to _____

6. In determining the distribution of total output in the economy, the price system is involved in two ways, which are:

a. _____

b. _____

7. In deciding whether an economy is flexible, the two questions which must be answered are:

a. _____

b. _____

8. The *opportunity* for technological advance exists in the capitalistic system because there are no _____
to restrict it.

9. The entrepreneur uses money which he obtains either from _____
or from _____
to acquire capital goods.

10. If the price system is competitive, there is an identity of _____ interests and the _____ interest: firms seem

to be guided by an _____
to allocate the economy's resources efficiently.

11. The chief economic advantage of the price system, it is said, is that _____
_____;
its chief noneconomic advantage is that _____
_____

12. Four criticisms often made of the price system are:

a. _____

b. _____

c. _____

d. _____

13. Competition, it is argued, tends to break down because _____
_____
and _____
_____

■ PROBLEMS AND PROJECTS

1. Assume that a firm can produce either product A, product B, or product C with the resources it is currently employing. These resources cost the firm a total of $50 per week. Assume, for the purposes of the problem, that the firm's employment of resources cannot be changed. The market prices of and the quantities of A, B, and C these resources will produce per week are given below.

Product	Market price	Output	Economic profit
A	$7.00	8	$_____
B	4.50	10	_____
C	.25	240	_____

a. Which product will the firm produce? ___
_____

b. If the price of A rose to $8, the firm would _____

c. If the firm were producing A and selling it at a price of $8, what would tend to happen to the number of firms producing A?

---

2. Suppose that a firm can produce 100 units of product X by combining labor, land, capital, and entrepreneurial ability in four different ways. If it can hire labor at $2 per unit, land at $3 per unit, capital at $5 per unit, and entrepreneurship at $10 per unit; and if the amounts of the resources required by the four methods of producing 100 units of product X are as indicated in the table, answer the questions below.

Resource	Method			
	1	2	3	4
Labor	8	13	10	6
Land	4	3	3	2
Capital	4	2	4	7
Entrepreneurship	1	1	1	1

a. Which method is the least expensive way of producing X? _____

b. If X sells for 50 cents per unit, what is the economic profit of the firm? $_____ What is its profit if X sells for 60 cents per unit? $_____

c. If the price of labor should rise from $2 to $3 per unit and if at the same time the price of X should rise from 50 cents to 70 cents per unit,

(1) The firm's use of:

Labor would change from _____ to _____

Land would change from _____ to _____

Capital would change from _____ to _____
Entrepreneurship would not change.

(2) The firm's economic profit would change from $_____ to _____

3. Assume that the market prices of products A, B, and C are $1, $2, and $3, respectively, and that the market prices of labor, land, capital, and entrepreneurial ability are $2, $4, $6, and $10, respectively. There are four

methods of producing A, B, and C *in lots of 100 units;* the quantities of resources needed to produce the products in lots of 100 are shown in the tables below.

Resource	Method			
	1	2	3	4
	Product A			
Labor	25	20	15	10
Land	5	6	6	7
Capital	6	6	7	8
Entrepreneurship	1	1	1	1
	Product B			
Labor	40	35	30	25
Land	9	13	13	14
Capital	10	11	12	12
Entrepreneurship	1	1	1	1
	Product C			
Labor	90	85	80	75
Land	12	13	15	20
Capital	12	14	16	20
Entrepreneurship	1	1	1	1

If these are the only opportunities open to the firm:

a. What product should it produce? _____
b. The firm will wish to hire

(1) _____ units of labor

(2) _____ units of land

(3) _____ units of capital

(4) _____ units of entrepreneurial ability.

c. How much economic profit will the firm receive? $_____

d. If the price of product C rose from $3 to $4 per unit:

(1) What product would the firm produce? _____

(2) What would happen to the firm's employment of:

Labor _____

Land _____

Capital _____

Entrepreneurship _____

(3) What would happen to the economic profit of the firm? _____

■ SELF-TEST

Circle the T if the statement is true, the F if it is false.

1. Prices are indicators of the relative scarcity of resources and products.　　(T) F

2. Industries in which economic profits are earned by the firms in the industry will attract the entry of new firms into the industry.　(T) F

3. If firms have sufficient time to enter and leave industries, the economic profits of industry will disappear.　　(T) F

4. Resources will tend to be used in those industries capable of earning normal or economic profits.　　(T) F

5. If the market price of resource A increases, firms will tend to employ smaller quantities of resource A.　　(T) F

6. Changes in the tastes of consumers are reflected in changes in consumer demand for products.　　(T) F

7. The incentive which the price system provides to induce technological improvement is the opportunity for economic profits.　(T) F

8. Contraction in the size of an industry is always the consequence of improved methods of production in that industry.　　T (F)

9. In a capitalistic economy it is from the entrepreneur that the demand for capital goods arises.　　(T) F

10. An increase in the size of the firms in an industry generally leads to a smaller number of firms in the industry.　　(T) F

Underscore the letter that corresponds to the best answer.

1. The wants of consumers are expressed on: (a) the demand side of the resource market; (b) the demand side of the product market; (c) the supply side of the resource market; (d) the supply side of the product market.

2. Which of the following best defines economic costs? (a) total payments made to workers, landowners, suppliers of capital, and entrepreneurs; (b) only total payments made to workers, landowners, suppliers of capital,

and entrepreneurs which must be paid to obtain the services of their resources; (c) total payments made to workers, landowners, suppliers of capital, and entrepreneurs *less* normal profits; (d) total payments made to workers, landowners, suppliers of capital, and entrepreneurs *plus* normal profits.

3. If normal profits are not being earned by the firms in an industry, the consequences will be that: (a) lower-priced resources will be drawn into the industry; (b) firms will leave the industry, causing the price of the industry's product to fall; (c) the price of the industry's product will rise and fewer resources will be employed by the industry; (d) the price of the industry's product will fall and thereby cause the demand for the product to increase.

4. Which of the following would *not* necessarily result, sooner or later, from a decrease in consumer demand for a product? (a) a decrease in the profits of the industry producing the product; (b) a decrease in the output of the industry; (c) a decrease in the supply of the product; (d) an increase in the prices of resources employed by the firms in the industry.

5. If firm A does not employ the most "efficient" or least costly method of production, which of the following will *not* be a consequence? (a) firm A will fail to earn the greatest profit possible; (b) other firms in the industry will be able to sell the product at lower prices; (c) new firms will enter the industry and sell the product at a lower price than that at which firm A now sells it; (d) firm A will be spending less on resources and hiring fewer resources than it otherwise would.

6. Which of the following is *not* a factor in determining the *share* of the total output of the economy received by any household: (a) the prices at which the household sells its resources; (b) the quantities of resources which the household sells; (c) the tastes of the household; (d) the prices which the household must pay to buy products.

7. If an increase in the demand for a product and the resulting rise in the price of the product causes the supply of the product, the size of the industry producing the product, and the amounts of resources devoted to its production to expand, price is successfully performing its: (a) guiding function; (b) rationing function; (c) medium-of-exchange function; (d) standard-of-value function.

8. In a capitalistic economy characterized by competition, if one firm introduces a new and better method of production, other firms will be forced to adopt the improved technique: (a) to avoid less-than-normal profits; (b) to obtain economic profits; (c) to prevent the price of the product from falling; (d) to prevent the price of the product from rising.

9. Which of the following would be an indication that competition does not exist in an industry? (a) less-than-normal profits in the industry; (b) inability of the firms in the industry to expand; (c) inability of firms to enter the industry; (d) wages lower than the average wage in the economy paid to workers in the industry.

10. Economic criticism of the price system is widespread and has pointed out many of the failures of the system. However, the chief economic virtue of the system remains that of: (a) allowing extensive personal freedom; (b) efficiently allocating resources; (c) providing an equitable distribution of income; (d) eliminating the need for decision making.

■ DISCUSSION QUESTIONS

1. To what extent are firms "free" to produce what they wish by methods which they choose? Do resource owners have freedom to use their resources as they wish?

2. Explain the difference between a price system which is adaptable to change and a price system which is conducive to change.

3. What is meant when it is said that competition is the mechanism which "controls" the price-market system? How does competi-

tion do this? What do critics of the price system argue tends to happen to this controlling mechanism as time passes, and why do they so argue?

4. "An invisible hand operates to identify private and public interests." What are private interests and what is the public interest? What is it that leads the economy to operate as if it were directed by an invisible hand?

5. What reasons are advanced to explain why modern technology results in firms which are large both in absolute size and in relation to the size of their markets?

6. What arguments do critics of the price system advance to refute the contention that the price system allocates resources efficiently?

7. To what extent is this chapter unrealistic?

8. In what way does the desire of entrepreneurs to obtain economic profits and to avoid losses make consumer sovereignty effective?

9. Why is the ability of firms to enter industries which are prosperous important to the effective functioning of competition?

10. What are the two important functions of prices? Explain the difference between these two functions.

11. If the basic economic decisions are not made in a capitalistic economy by a central authority, how are they made?

12. Explain in detail how an increase in the consumer demand for a product will result in more of the product being produced and in more resources being allocated to its production.

13. Explain why the substitutability of resources for each other and the substitutability of products for each other is important if an economy is to allocate its resources efficiently and best satisfy human wants.

MIXED CAPITALISM AND THE ECONOMIC FUNCTIONS OF GOVERNMENT

Chapter 6 introduces the student to the five basic functions performed by Federal, state, and local governments in America's mixed capitalistic economy. This is an examination of the actual role of government in an economy which is neither a purely planned nor a purely market-type economy. The discussion points out the degree and the ways in which government causes the American economy to differ from a purely market-type economy. The chapter does not attempt to list all the *specific* ways in which government affects the behavior of the economy. Instead it provides a *general* classification of the tasks performed by government.

Following an explanation of each of the five functions of government in the American economy, the chapter attempts to evaluate the economic role of government in the United States. Here it is pointed out that people generally agree that government should perform these functions. But they disagree on how far government should go in performing them and over whether specific government actions and programs are needed for government to perform these functions. Governments today frequently employ benefit-cost analysis to determine whether they should or should not undertake some specific action—a particular act, project, or program. This kind of analysis forces government to estimate both the costs and the benefits of the project or program; to expand its activities only where the benefits exceed the costs; and to reduce or eliminate

programs and projects when the costs exceed the benefits.

The author concludes this chapter by making several important observations about the role of government in the American economy. First, we cannot expect perfection from government when there is so much imperfection in the rest of our society. Second, we cannot avoid the important issue of whether governmental activity increases or decreases our personal freedoms. And finally, the large role played by government is attributable to definite causes but has not yet reduced significantly the importance of private enterprise in the American economy.

■ CHAPTER OUTLINE

1. The American economy is neither a pure market economy nor a purely governmentally directed or planned economy. It is an example of mixed capitalism and is predominantly a market economy with some government direction and planning.

2. Government in the American economy performs five economic functions. The first two of these functions are designed to enable the price system to operate more effectively; and the other three functions are designed to eliminate the major shortcomings of a purely market-type economy.

3. The first of these functions is to provide the legal and social framework that makes the effective operation of the price system possible.

4. The second function is the maintenance of competition and the regulation of monopoly.

5. Government performs its third function when it redistributes income to reduce the extent of income inequality.

6. Government reallocates resources and performs its fourth function in order to:
   a. Take account of spillover costs and benefits.
   b. Provide society with social goods and services.

7. Its fifth function is stabilization of the price level and the maintenance of full employment.

8. In evaluating government's role in the economy:
   a. It is generally agreed that it is desirable for government to perform these functions.
   b. There is a good deal of controversy concerning how far it should go in performing them.

9. It should be observed that:
   a. Government does not have a monopoly on inefficiency in the economy.
   b. The nature and amount of government activity and the extent of individual freedom may be related to each other.

10. It is not possible to measure accurately the size of government's role, but government purchases (and taxes) have increased over the past fifty years in both absolute and relative terms because of expenditures for war and national defense and because of the public's desire for more and better social goods and services.

■ IMPORTANT TERMS

Market economy	**Social (collective) goods**
Planned economy	
Monopoly	**Individual (private) goods**
Mixed capitalism	
Spillover	**Exclusion principle**
Spillover costs	**Benefit-cost analysis**
Spillover benefits	**Fallacy of limited decisions**

■ FILL-IN QUESTIONS

1. All actual economies are "mixed" because they combine elements of a _____ economy and a _____ economy.

2. List the five economic functions of government:

   a. _____

   b. _____

   c. _____

   d. _____

   e. _____

3. Monopoly can be defined as _____

_____

4. To control monopoly in the United States government has:

   a. created commission to _____ the prices and the services of the _____ monopolies;

   b. taken over at the local level the _____

_____
electric and water companies;

   c. enacted _____
laws to maintain competition.

5. The price system, because it is an impersonal mechanism, results in _____ in the distribution of income. To redistribute income from the upper to lower income groups the Federal government has:

   a. enacted _____ programs;

   b. engaged in _____ intervention;

   c. used the _____
tax to raise much of its revenues.

6. In a competitive market for a product:
   a. the benefits to consumers from using the product is expressed by the _____ curve for the product;
   b. the cost of producing the product is expressed by the _____ curve;

c. in equilibrium the extra or marginal ____

_____ of the last unit of the product consumed is equal to the extra or marginal

_____ of producing that last unit.

7. Competitive markets bring about an optimum allocation of resources only if there are

no _____

or _____
in the consumption and production of the good or service.

8. There is a spillover whenever some of the costs of producing a product or some of the

benefits from consuming it accrue to _____

_____

9. Whenever in a competitive market there are:
a. spillover costs the result is an (over-,

under-) _____allocation of resources to the product because units of the product

whose _____ exceed their ____

_____ are produced;

b. spillover benefits the result is an _____

_____allocation of resources to the product because units of the product whose

_____ exceed their _____

_____ are not produced.

10. What two things can government do to:
a. Make the market reflect spillover costs?

(1) _____

(2) _____
b. Make the market reflect spillover benefits?

(1) _____

(2) _____

11. Private goods are _____ and

yield satisfaction largely to _____

while social goods are _____

with large _____ benefits.

12. When the production of a commodity benefits *only* those who pay the price that is necessary to induce its production, that commodity is subject to the _____ principle. This principle, in general, applies to

_____ goods but not to _____ goods.

13. To reallocate resources from the production of private to the production of social goods government reduces the demand for

private goods by _____ consumers and

firms and then _____social goods.

14. To stabilize the economy government:

a. _____ aggregate demand by ____

_____ its expeditures for social

goods and services and _____
taxes when there is less than full employment;

b. _____aggregate demand by ____

_____ its expenditures for social

goods and services and _____
taxes when there are inflationary pressures.

15. Throughout most of its history government in the United States has performed in some degree each of the five functions except

that of _____

16. In applying benefit-cost analysis, government should employ more resources in the public sector if the benefits from the addi-

tional _____
exceed the costs that result from having

fewer _____

17. When government employs benefit-cost analysis it often finds that:

a. it is difficult to _____
the benefits and the costs of a program;
b. the program not only reallocates re-

sources but also affects the _____

of the economy and the _____
of income.

18. Despite the recognition of governmental inefficiency, it should be noted that there is

also inefficiency in the _____

_____ of the economy.

19. To reason that increased governmental activity necessarily reduces private economic activity is an example of the fallacy of _____

---

20. During the past fifty or so years, government spending in the United States has increased, both absolutely and relatively, because of _____
and _____
Today government expenditures equal about

_____th of the economy's total output of goods and services.

■ PROBLEMS AND PROJECTS

1. Below is a list of various government activities. Indicate in the space to the right of each into which of the five classes of government functions the activity falls. If the activity falls under more than one of the five functions, indicate this.

  a. Maintaining an army _____
  b. Providing for a system of unemployment compensation _____
  c. Establishment of the Federal Reserve Banks _____
  d. Insuring employees of business firms against industrial accidents _____
  e. Establishment of an Antitrust Division in the Department of Justice _____
  f. Making it a crime to sell stocks and bonds under false pretenses _____
  g. Providing low-cost lunches to school children _____
  h. Taxation of whiskey and other spirits _____

---

  i. Regulation of organized stock, bond, and commodity markets _____
  j. Setting tax *rates* higher for large incomes than for smaller ones _____

2. On the graph above are the demand and supply curves for a product bought and sold in a competitive market. Assume that there are no spillover benefits or costs.

  a. Were this market to produce an output of Q_1 there would be an underallocation of resources to the production of this product because at output Q_1 the benefit from the last unit consumed equals _____ and exceeds the _____ cost of producing that last unit.
  b. Were this market to produce Q_2 there would be an overallocation of resources because at Q_2 the _____ cost of producing the last unit exceeds the _____ benefit obtained from consuming that last unit.
  c. At the equilibrium output of Q_e there is an _____ allocation of resources to the production of this product because the cost and the benefit obtained from the last unit of the product produced both equal _____

---

3. On two graphs on page 38 are product demand and supply curves that do *not* reflect the spillover costs of producing the product or the spillover benefits obtained from its consumption.
  a. On the first graph draw in another curve that reflects the inclusion of spillover *costs*.
  (1) The inclusion of spillover costs in the total cost of producing the product (increases, decreases) _____ the output of the product and _____ its price.

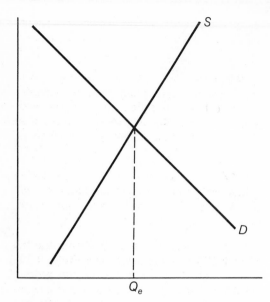

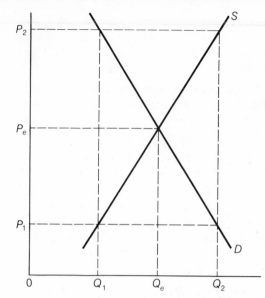

(2) Were the output Q_e produced there would be an overallocation of resources to this product because at Q_e the extra cost is

_____ than the extra benefit to the economy.

b. On the second graph draw in another curve that reflects the inclusion of spillover *benefits*.

(1) The inclusion of the spillover benefits in the total benefits obtained from consuming

the product (increases, decreases) _____

the output of the product and _____ its price.

(2) Were the output Q_e produced there would be an underallocation of resources to this product because at Q_e the extra cost is

_____ than the extra benefit to the economy.

4. Imagine that a state government is considering the construction of a new highway to link its two largest cities. Its estimate of the total costs and the total benefits of building 2, 4, 6, and 8 lane highways between the two cities are shown in the table below. (All figures are in millions of dollars.)

a. Compute the marginal cost and the marginal benefit of the 2, 4, 6, and 8 lane highways.

b. Will it benefit the state to allocate resources to construct a highway? _____

c. If the state builds a highway:

(1) It should be a _____ lane highway.

(2) The total cost will be $_____

(3) The total benefit will be $_____

(4) The *net* benefit to the state will be $___

Project	Total cost	Marginal cost	Total benefit	Marginal benefit
No highway	$ 0		$ 0	
2 lane highway	500	$_____	650	$_____
4 lane highway	680	_____	750	_____
6 lane highway	760	_____	800	_____
8 lane highway	860	_____	825	_____

■ SELF-TEST

Circle the T if the statement is true, the F if it is false.

1. The American economy cannot be called "capitalistic" because its operation involves some "planning."   **T   F**

2. When the Federal government provides for a monetary system, it is functioning to provide the economy with social goods and services.   **T   F**

3. An economy in which strong and effective competition is maintained will find no need for programs designed to redistribute income.   **T   F**

4. Competitive product markets ensure an optimal allocation of an economy's resources.   **T   F**

5. In a competitive product market and in the absence of spillover costs, the supply curve or schedule reflects the marginal cost of producing the product.   **T   F**

6. If demand and supply reflected all the benefits and costs of a product, the equilibrium output of a competitive market would be identical with its optimum output.   **T   F**

The graph below should be used to answer true-false question 7 and multiple-choice questions 3 and 4.

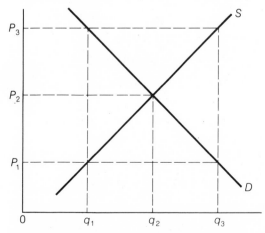

7. Assuming there are no spillover costs or benefits, the production of q_1 units of this product would result in an overallocation of resources to the production of the product.   **T   F**

8. The inclusion of the spillover benefits would increase the demand for a product.   **T   F**

9. When there are spillover costs involved in the production of a product, more resources are allocated to the production of that product and more of the product is produced than there would be if there were no spillover costs.   **T   F**

10. Reduced taxation of firms producing goods which provide spillover benefits will usually result in a better allocation of reserves.   **T   F**

11. If the economic role of government in the United States is evaluated objectively, it becomes clear that the scope of the government's activities is too large and that government's efficiency in performing its role has been inadequate.   **T   F**

12. In a democracy, government tends generally to perform those tasks which the majority of society demands of it.   **T   F**

13. Reduced government spending is the same as economy in government.   **T   F**

14. Both liberals and conservatives agree that the expansion of government's role in the economy has reduced personal freedom in the United States.   **T   F**

15. In practice it is usually quite simple to estimate the costs and the benefits of a project financed by government.   **T   F**

Underscore the letter that corresponds to the best answer.

1. Which of the following is *not* one of the methods utilized by government to control monopoly? (a) the imposition of special taxes on monopolists; (b) government ownership of monopolies; (c) government regulation of monopolies; (d) antitrust laws.

2. One of the following is *not* employed by government to redistribute income. Which one? (a) the negative income tax; (b) direct market intervention; (c) income taxes which take a larger part of the incomes of the rich than the poor; (d) public assistance programs.

Use the graph preceding true-false question 7 to answer the following two questions.

3. If there are neither spillover costs nor spillover benefits, the output which results in the optimum allocation of resources to the production of this product is (a) q_1; (b) q_2; (c) q_3; (d) none of these outputs.

4. If there are no spillover costs or benefits, the marginal benefit (or satisfaction) from producing q_3 units of this product is (a) p_1; (b) p_2; (c) p_3; (d) none of these.

5. When the production and consumption of a product entails *both* spillover costs and benefits, a competitive product market results in (a) an underallocation of resources to the product; (b) an overallocation of resources to the product; (c) an optimum allocation of resources to the product; (d) an allocation of resources that may or may not be optimum.

6. Which of the following is the best example of a good or service providing the economy with spillover benefits? (a) an automobile; (b) a drill press; (c) a high school education; (d) an operation for appendicitis.

7. In the American economy the reallocation of resources needed to provide for the production of social goods is accomplished mainly by means of: (a) government subsidies to the producers of social goods; (b) government purchases of social goods from producers; (c) direct control of producers of both private and social goods; (d) direct control of producers of social goods only.

8. In assessing the desirability of government performing the five basic economic functions in the United States, there seems to be rather general agreement that: (a) the functions ought to be increased in number and government's role in the economy expanded; (b) the functions ought to be decreased in number and government's role in the economy reduced to a minimum; (c) the functions are those which the government ought to perform, but there is no general agreement as to the extent to which government should go in performing them; (d) with the exception of stabilizing the economy, these are legitimate tasks for government to perform as long as government, in performing them, does not interfere with the operation of the economy.

9. Which of the following is characteristic of social goods? (a) they have large spillover benefits; (b) they are divisable; (c) they are subject to the exclusion principle; (d) they can be produced only if large spillover costs are incurred.

10. Which of the following functions of government most affects the area of macroeconomics? (a) maintaining competition; (b) redistributing income; (c) reallocating resources; (d) stabilizing the economy.

11. Assume that a government is considering a new antipolution program and has a choice of four different projects. The total cost and the total benefits of each of the four projects is given below.

Project	Total cost	Total benefit
#1	$2 million	$5 million
#2	$5 million	$7 million
#3	$10 million	$10 million
#4	$20 million	$15 million

Which projects should it adopt? (a) #1; (b) #1 and #2; (c) #1, #2, and #3; (d) all of the projects.

12. Governments in the United States now purchase what fraction of the economy's total output of goods and services? (a) $\frac{1}{10}$; (b) $\frac{1}{5}$; (c) $\frac{1}{4}$; (d) $\frac{1}{3}$.

■ DISCUSSION QUESTIONS

1. Why is it proper to refer to the United States economy as "mixed capitalism"?

2. What are the five economic functions of government in America's mixed capitalistic economy? Explain what the performance of each of these functions requires government to do.

3. Would you like to live in an economy in which government undertook only the first two functions listed in the text? What would be the advantages and disadvantages of living in such an economy?

4. Why does the market system provide some people with lower incomes than it provides others?

5. Explain why, when there are neither spillover costs nor spillover benefits, competitive product markets bring about an optimum allocation of resources to the production of the goods and services bought and sold in these markets. Why do spillover costs and benefits bring about a less than optimum allocation of resources?

6. What is meant by a spillover, a spillover cost, and a spillover benefit? What specific spillover costs and benefits seem to you to be significant in the American economy? How would the inclusion of spillover costs and the inclusion of spillover benefits affect the allocation of the economy's resources?

7. What methods do governments employ to (a) redistribute income; (b) reallocate resources to take account of spillover costs; (c) reallocate resources to take account of spillover benefits?

8. What is meant by the "exclusion principle"? How is this principle related to the distinction made between private and social goods?

9. What basic method does government employ in the United States to reallocate resources away from the production of private goods and toward the production of social goods?

10. Is there agreement on whether government should perform its five economic functions? Why is there criticism of government activity?

11. Explain what benefit-cost analysis is and how it is used. What is the major problem encountered when benefit-cost analysis is utilized by government?

12. Is government, in your opinion, more or less efficient than the private sector of the economy? Explain the difference between "economy in government" and "reduced government spending."

13. Do you think government limits or expands personal freedom by performing its economic functions?

14. Even though approximately one-fifth of the total output of the American economy is produced by or for government, is this an accurate measure of the degree to which private enterprise has been eliminated from the American economic scene?

15. What factors explain why government today spends more than it did fifty years ago?

THE FACTS OF AMERICAN CAPITALISM: HOUSEHOLDS

Chapters 7, 8, and 9 are concerned with the sources and the spending of the incomes of American households, businesses, and governments. These three chapters aim to acquaint the student with a few economic facts relevant to an understanding of modern capitalism in the United States. Chapter 7 describes the ways in which households get their incomes and the uses to which they put these incomes.

In these chapters the student will find a number of statistics—tables, averages, percentages—and he ought to make no attempt to memorize exact figures. Rather he should try to remember trends and approximate values and whether these values are less than or greater than other comparable values. Another word or two of advice: The student should be sure he understands what is meant by *absolute size* and *relative size*. The latter is always measured as a *percentage* of some total, while the former is measured in *units* such as dollars, pounds, persons, etc.

The first part of the chapter deals with the distribution of income in the United States; the distribution of income means simply the way in which the total income which people receive is divided up (distributed) among them. Two different ways of viewing the distribution of income are stressed: the way in which it is distributed among people according to the function which they perform in the economy (these functions are supplying labor, land, capital, and entrepreneurship) and the

way in which it is distributed among the various households in the economy. The latter way, the personal distribution of income, is of special importance because it influences the level of total income production, and employment and the types and quantities of the various goods and services produced in the economy. Attention should be concentrated on the *general* facts of income distribution (not the exact figures), the conclusions which are drawn from these general facts, and the definitions of the new terms employed.

The second part of the chapter discusses the three uses to which American households put the income they receive. Several new terms and concepts are introduced, and figures are employed in this discussion. Again, attention should be paid to the generalizations, the new terms, and such significant distinctions as those between durable and nondurable goods and between saving and savings. In addition to increasing one's knowledge of American capitalism, the effort expended on this chapter will pay large dividends beginning with Chapter 10.

■ CHAPTER OUTLINE

1. Households play a dual role in the economy: They supply the economy with resources, and they purchase the greatest share of the goods and services produced by the economy.

2. Households obtain their incomes in exchange for the resources they furnish the economy. The way in which the total income of all households is divided among (or shared by) them is called the distribution of income.

a. A functional distribution of income indicates the way in which total income is divided into wages, rent, interest, and profits.

b. A personal distribution of income indicates the way in which total income is divided among households in various income classes and is of particular importance because it influences total consumption spending in the economy and the types of goods and services demanded by consumers.

3. Households use their incomes to purchase consumer goods, to pay taxes, and to accumulate savings.

a. Personal taxes constitute a deduction from a household's total income; what remains after taxes can be either saved or spent.

b. Saving is what a household does not spend of its after-tax income, while "savings" is the sum of all its past saving.

c. Households spend for durable goods, nondurable goods, and services.

d. Consumer protection and the improvement of consumer knowledge results in a better allocation of society's resources.

■ IMPORTANT TERMS

Functional distribution of income

Personal distribution of income

Absolute size of income

Relative share of income

Personal consumption expenditures

Durable good

Nondurable good

Personal taxes

Personal saving

Personal savings

■ FILL-IN QUESTIONS

1. Households play a dual role in a capitalistic system in that they _____ and _____

2. The relative share of national income going for wages and salaries is about _____ _____ percent.

3. The personal distribution of income is of particular importance because it affects the

_____

and the _____

of national income, output, and employment.

4. In a price-market system the money income of a family or person depends roughly

upon its _____

5. The total income of households is disposed

of in three ways: _____ ,

_____ ,

and _____

6. Households use about _____ percent of their total income to pay personal taxes, the

greater part of which goes to the _____

government to pay their personal _____ taxes.

7. Based on their durability, consumer spending is classified as spending for _____

_____ ,

_____ ,

and _____

8. Savings are a _____

and saving is a _____

9. Households save primarily in order to obtain

_____

and for purposes of _____

10. Both personal consumption expenditures

and personal saving _____ as after-tax increases.

■ PROBLEMS AND PROJECTS

1. On page 44 is the *absolute* distribution of income in the United States for the year 1969. In the space at the right, place the figures which indicate the *relative* shares of income. (Because of rounding, the sum of the shares may not equal the total.)

	Billions of dollars	Relative share
Wages and salaries	$564.2	_____
Proprietors' income	66.8	_____
Corporate profits	85.8	_____
Interest	30.7	_____
Rents	22.0	_____
National income	$769.5	100.0

2. In the table below are figures which indicate the amount spent on personal consumption at various levels of after-tax income.

a. Compute personal saving at each level of income.

b. On the adjoining graph, with income on the horizontal axis, plot both personal consumption expenditures and personal saving. Connect all the points which indicate personal consumption expenditures and all those which indicate personal saving; label these two curves. Label the vertical axis "Personal consumption expenditures and Personal saving."

c. Now compute the percentage of income spent on consumption and the percentage saved at each of the eight levels of income.

d. As income increases, the amount

(1) Spent for consumption _____

(2) Saved _____

e. As income increases, the percentage of income

(1) Spent for consumption _____

(2) Saved _____

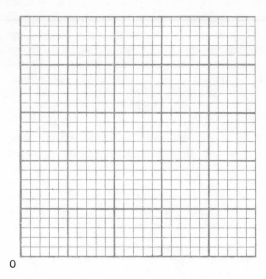

0

■ SELF-TEST

Circle the T if the statement is true, the F if it is false.

1. During a period of depression the *absolute* amount of rent and interest being received in the American economy tends to increase.

T F

2. The personal distribution of income describes the manner in which society's total income is divided among wages, rent, interest, and profit. **T F**

3. Corporate profits over the years have tended to be an unstable percentage of national income. **T F**

After-tax income	Personal consumption expenditures	Personal saving	Percent of income spent	Percent of income saved
$100	$120	$_____	_____	_____
150	160	_____	_____	_____
200	200	_____	_____	_____
250	240	_____	_____	_____
300	280	_____	_____	_____
350	320	_____	_____	_____
400	360	_____	_____	_____
450	400	_____	_____	_____

4. A distribution of income which is based on the productivity of resources usually results in considerable *in*equality in the size of incomes.   **T   F**

5. In both relative and absolute terms, personal taxes have exceeded personal saving in recent years.   **T   F**

6. A "durable good" is defined as a good which has an expected life of one year or more.   **T   F**

7. As personal consumption expenditures decline, the percentage of these expenditures going for durable goods tends to increase.

T   F

8. Savings is defined as a stock and as the accumulation of financial assets held by households.   **T   F**

9. The upper 10 percent of families, ranked on the basis of size of income, account for most of the personal saving done in the United States.   **T   F**

10. *Dissaving* means that personal consumption expenditures exceed after-tax income.

T   F

Underscore the letter that corresponds to the best answer.

1. There are in the United States approximately how many households (families)? (*a*) 40 million; (*b*) 50 million; (*c*) 60 million; (*d*) 70 million.

2. As national income increases, wages and salaries tend to: (*a*) increase both absolutely and relatively; (*b*) increase absolutely and decrease relatively; (*c*) decrease absolutely and increase relatively; (*d*) increase absolutely and remain unchanged relatively.

3. When national income declines (as in a recession or depression), *in absolute terms:* (*a*) wages remain constant and the other distributive shares of national income decrease; (*b*) wages decrease and the other distributive shares increase; (*c*) wages increase and other distributive shares decrease; (*d*) wages and the other distributive shares decrease.

4. Which of the following is *not* a factor affecting the amount of money income received by the individual household? (*a*) the quantity of resources the household has available to supply to business firms; (*b*) the amount of saving done by the household; (*c*) the prices paid for the various resources in the market; (*d*) the actual level of employment of the household's resources.

5. Expenditures for *nondurable* goods in recent years have amounted to approximately what percentage of personal consumption expenditures? (*a*) 30%; (*b*) 45%; (*c*) 60%; (*d*) 75%.

6. Which of the following is a true statement? (*a*) The durable goods and service parts of personal consumption expenditures vary more over time than do the expenditures for nondurables; (*b*) expenditures for nondurables vary more than do the expenditures for durable goods and services; (*c*) expenditures for nondurables vary more than the expenditures for services and less than the expenditures for durables; (*d*) expenditures for nondurables vary more than the expenditures for durables and less than the expenditures for services.

7. In recent years personal taxes have been approximately what percentage of total income? (*a*) 15%; (*b*) 18%; (*c*) 24%; (*d*) 30%.

8. Since the end of World War II, personal taxes in the United States have: (*a*) increased absolutely and relatively; (*b*) increased absolutely and decreased relatively; (*c*) decreased absolutely and increased relatively; (*d*) decreased absolutely and relatively.

■ DISCUSSION QUESTIONS

1. Explain the difference between a functional and a personal distribution of income.

2. How do the relative functional shares of national income change as the level of national income changes? How do the absolute shares vary as national income varies?

3. The present personal distribution of income affects both the level of resource use and the allocation of resources in the economy. What is the connection between the distribution of income and the employment and allocation of resources?

4. What determines how large a money income an individual household will have? In what way is a household's income related to its productivity? Why does a personal distribution of income based on productivity lead to personal income inequality?

5. Which, in your opinion, would result in a greater total saving out of a national income of a given size: a more or less nearly equal distribution of income?

6. Explain how a resource's or a group's share of national income can increase absolutely and decrease relatively or decrease absolutely and increase relatively.

7. The purchase of what type of consumer goods is largely postponable? Why is this?

8. What is the difference between a stock and a flow? Is saving a stock or a flow? Why? Are savings a stock or a flow? Why?

9. How is it possible for a family's personal consumption expenditures to exceed its after-tax income?

10. What is meant by "consumer protection"? Why might consumer protection and increased consumer knowledge lead to a better allocation of resources? Are there any problems that might arise as a result of the imposition by government of quality standards for products?

THE FACTS
OF AMERICAN
CAPITALISM:
BUSINESSES

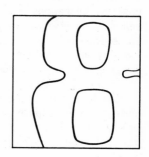

Chapter 8 is the second of the three chapters dealing with the relevant facts of American capitalism and is specifically concerned with the business firms of the United States. There are thousands of pages which might be written on business in the United States, but this chapter is in no sense a summary of all these pages. Rather, it is an introduction to a few of the more important characteristics of business and a broad picture of the role of the producer in the American economy.

It is apparent early in the chapter that what most characterizes American business is the differences existing among firms insofar as their size, legal form, and life span are concerned, as well as in the products they produce. The student should note the distinction between a proprietorship, a partnership, and a corporation and the advantages and disadvantages (especially their abilities to raise money capital and the liabilities of their owners) of each.

Other things of particular importance are the problem of the separation—often called the "divorce"—of the ownership and control of the modern corporation; the conclusions brought out by an examination of the distribution of the roughly eleven and one-half million firms among the major sectors of the economy; and the relative importance, numerically and financially, of the three forms of business organization.

The chapter contains an introduction to what many economists consider a serious economic

and political problem in the United States today: the large size, both absolutely and relatively, of a relatively few manufacturing firms. There is an examination of the degree to which "big business" prevails in the economy and an explanation of why and how firms get to be giants. The answer to the question of whether these giants are good or bad for the economy as a whole turns out to be a question of whether the advantages of increased productive efficiency outweigh the disadvantages associated with the lessening of competition which follows the emergence of a few large firms.

In addition to looking at the privately owned profit-seeking business firms, the author examines briefly two new forms of business institution in the American economy. There are those firms which are privately owned but are not motivated by a desire for profit. And there are those privately owned firms which for all practical purposes have become branches of government because they are regulated by government or depend upon government to buy their products.

The device employed in the last section of the chapter to explain the receipts and expenditures of business is the income (or profit and loss) statement. This statement simply shows from whom a firm or a group of firms received their income during some period of time—usually a year—and what they did with it after they got it. The device is used here for two purposes: (1) to show the relative and absolute importance of the various types of business allocations and business receipts, and (2) to serve as an introduction to the procedures which will be used in Chapter 10 when the measurement of national income is examined. Special attention should be paid to the item in the income statement that is most difficult for students to understand: *depreciation.* Unlike the other items on the allocations side of the income statement, depreciation represents *not* a cash payment to those who have supplied the firm with resources, but an accounting notation that a part of the firm's income was obtained at the "expense" of the wearing out of some of the firm's equipment and that this expense has to be covered by income before a profit can be shown. If a firm buys equipment which lasts a year or a number of years, the firm's income must in both cases exceed all its expenses, including the cost of the equipment, before the firm can show a profit. Depreciation is merely a bookkeeping device for allocating the cost of equipment which is used more than one year to those years in which it is used, rather than to the year in which it is purchased.

■ CHAPTER OUTLINE

1. The business population of the American economy consists of many imperfectly defined and overlapping industries; business firms which operate one or more plants and produce one or more products are the components of these industries. Firms vary greatly in size and in the length of time they remain in business.

2. The three principal legal forms of organization of firms are the proprietorship, the partnership, and the corporation; each form has special characteristics, advantages, and disadvantages. The form of organization which any business firm should adopt depends primarily upon the amount of money capital it will require to carry on its business. Although the proprietorship is numerically dominant in the United States, the corporation accounts for the major portion of the economy's output.

3. A relatively large percentage of the total output of and employment in the American economy is generated by the relatively small percentage of firms in the manufacturing sector of the economy.

4. Big business is characteristic of the American economy; the economy and many of its industries are dominated by giant firms which produce a relatively large proportion of the total output.

a. While no simple measure exists to calculate the extent of industrial concentration, statistics do reveal that concentration exists in many industries.

b. Business firms have grown large in order to increase their productive efficiency, their power and prestige, their chances of survival, and their profits by the elimination of competition. This growth has resulted both from the internal expansion of firms and from the combination of firms.

c. Whether big firms should be feared depends upon the answer to this question: Do the advantages associated with large-scale production outweigh the disadvantages associated with a decline in competition?

5. There are in the American economy today a number of institutions which are neither privately owned business firms seeking profits nor governments.

a. The nonprofit sector of the economy consists of those private organizations whose goal is not profit but who employ resources to produce goods and services.

b. There are also firms which are privately owned and seeking profits but which have become quasi-public institutions.

6. Business's dual role in the economy consists of producing and selling goods and services which satisfy human wants *and* employing the economy's resources and thereby creating income for the suppliers of resources.

a. The income statement of an individual firm shows the receipts of a firm (from sales) and the allocation (or use) of these receipts during some period of time.

b. The consolidated income statement for all business firms in the economy shows the receipts of these firms from sales to the three major classes of customers and the allocation of these receipts to suppliers of resources, government, and owners during a given time period.

■ IMPORTANT TERMS

Plant

Firm

Industry

Horizontal com-
bination

Vertical combination

Conglomerate
combination

Sole proprietorship

Partnership

Corporation

Unlimited liability

Limited liability

Separation ("divorce")
of ownership and
control

Internal growth

Combination

Income (profit and
loss) statement

Depreciation

Nonprofit sector

■ FILL-IN QUESTIONS

1. There are about _____
business firms in the United States.

2. The liabilities of a sole proprietor and of

partners are _____
while the liabilities of stockholders in a cor-

poration are _____

3. Indicate in the spaces to the right of each
of the following whether these business characteristics are associated with the proprietorship (PRO), partnership (PART), corporation
(CORP), two of these, or all three of these
legal forms.
  a. Much red tape and legal expense in be-

ginning the firm _____

  b. Unlimited liability _____

  c. No specialized management _____
  d. Has a life independent of its owner(s)

_____

  e. Decided tax advantage if its profits are

large _____
  f. Greatest ability to acquire funds for the

expansion of the firm _____
  g. Permits some but not a great degree of

specialized management _____
  h. Possibility of an unresolved disagreement

among owners over courses of action _____

  i. Makes it possible for a businessman to

avoid responsibility for illegal actions _____

4. What are the four basic reasons why business firms desire to grow big?

  a. _____

  b. _____

  c. _____

  d. _____

5. Small firms become large firms either as

consequence of _____,

or _____,
or both. Most large firms have depended to a

large degree upon _____

6. List below six kinds of organizations which
are found in the nonprofit sector of the economy.

  a. _____

  b. _____

  c. _____

  d. _____

  e. _____

  f. _____

7. Nonprofit organizations are like private
business firms and governments because they

_____

and _____
But they are unlike private business firms be-

cause _____

_____

8. The dual role of business in the economy

is _____

and _____

9. An income (or profit and loss) statement

shows _____

and _____

10. Depreciation is an estimate of _____

_____

11. On the receipts side of a consolidated income statement for the business sector of the
economy, "sales of output" are subdivided, in

the order of their relative importance, into

sales to _____,

_____,

and _____

12. A consolidated income statement for the business sector of the economy shows only those sales to other businesses where _____

_____ ;
to include *all* sales would *not* result in an accurate measure of _____

_____

because _____

■ PROBLEMS AND PROJECTS

1. Indicate to the best of your ability what you would call the industries in which the following firms operate:
  a. Sears, Roebuck and Company
  b. The General Electric Company
  c. A used-car dealer in your town
  d. Gimbels department stores
  e. Your local gas or electric company
  f. A new-car dealer
  g. The Mars Candy Company
  h. The Aluminum Company of America
  i. The Anaconda Copper Company
  j. The William Wrigley Chewing Gum Company

2. Without looking at Table 8–2 in the text, indicate as best you can how each of the following industries ranks (1, 2, 3, 4, or 5) among the five industries insofar as number of firms, national income produced, and number of employees are concerned. Then check your answers with Table 8–2.
  a. Wholesale and retail trade

  _____ _____ _____

  b. Services _____ _____ _____

  c. Agriculture, forestry, and fishing

  _____ _____ _____

  d. Construction _____ _____ _____

  e. Manufacturing _____ _____ _____

3. Below are items taken from the income statement of a single corporation.

	Thousands of dollars
Indirect business taxes	$ 1
Interest	2
Payroll taxes	4
Rent	5
Depreciation	6
Dividends	7
Undistributed profits	8
Corporate profits taxes	16
Materials	37
Wages and salaries	42
Sales of output	128

Arrange these items in the form used in Table 8–4 of the text on the blank income statement provided at the top of page 51. Compute any totals not provided above.

4. Arrange the data in the table below in a consolidated income statement for the business sector of the economy on the blank statement provided on page 51. Follow the form used in Table 8–5 in the text. Compute by addition or subtraction any figures not included in the data.

	Billions of dollars
Payroll taxes	$ 5
Interest	6
Rents	11
Dividends	11
Corporate profits after taxes	19
Corporate income taxes	24
Indirect business taxes	35
Depreciation	37
Sales to government	47
Proprietors' income	52
Sales to other businesses	58
Wages and salaries	186
Sales to consumers	270

Allocations		Receipts	
(1)	$_____	(8)	$_____
(2)	_____		
(3)	_____		
(4)	_____		
(5)	_____		
(6)	_____		
(a)	$_____		
(b)	_____		
(c)	_____		
(7)	_____		
(a)	_____		
(b)	_____		
Total allocations	$_____	Total receipts	$_____

Allocations		Receipts	
(1)	$_____	(8)	$_____
(2)	_____	(a)	$_____
(3)	_____	(b)	_____
(4)	_____	(c)	_____
(5)	_____		
(a)	$_____		
(b)	_____		
(c)	_____		
(6)	_____		
(a)	_____		
(b)	_____		
Total allocations	$_____	Total receipts	$_____

■ SELF-TEST

Circle the T if the statement is true, the F if it is false.

1. A plant is defined as a group of firms under a single management.   **T   F**

2. An industry is a group of firms that produce the same or nearly the same products.   **T   F**

3. The corporate form of organization is the least used by firms in the United States.   **T   F**

4. Corporations account for over one-half the total output of the privately owned business firms in the United States. **T F**

5. The corporation in the United States today always has a tax advantage over other legal forms of business organization. **T F**

6. Whether a business firm should incorporate or not depends chiefly upon the amount of money capital it must have to finance the enterprise. **T F**

7. Most giant firms in the United States have grown and become big by internal growth rather than through combination with other firms. **T F**

8. Not all economists and observers agree that modern technology requires firms as large as some of those in the United States today. **T F**

9. On the receipts side of the business sector's consolidated income statement, the largest single item is sales to government. **T F**

10. It is not proper to include the capital equipment owned by a firm in its income statement. **T F**

11. Organizations in the nonprofit sector of the economy compete with the private sector for economic resources, but the goods and services they produce do not compete with those produced in the private sector. **T F**

Underscore the letter that corresponds to the best answer.

1. If we include self-employed farmers and professional people, there are approximately how many million business firms in the United States? (a) 5; (b) 8; (c) 11½; (d) 15.

2. A group of three plants which is owned and operated by a single firm and which consists of a farm growing wheat, a flour milling plant, and a plant which bakes and sells bakery products is an example of: (a) a horizontal combination; (b) a vertical combination; (c) a conglomerate combination; (d) a corporation.

3. Limited liability is associated with: (a) only proprietorships; (b) only partnerships; (c) both proprietorships and partnerships; (d) only corporations.

4. Which of the following forms of business organization can most effectively raise money capital? (a) corporation; (b) partnership; (c) proprietorship; (d) vertical combination.

5. Which of the following industries has the largest number of firms? (a) agriculture, forestry, and fishing; (b) manufacturing; (c) wholesale and retail trade; (d) mining.

6. Which of the following industries produces the largest percentage of the national income? (a) agriculture, forestry, and fishing; (b) manufacturing; (c) wholesale and retail trade; (d) government.

7. The 100 largest manufacturing firms in the United States today own approximately what percentage of the net capital assets of all manufacturing firms? (a) 30%; (b) 50%; (c) 60%; (d) more than 60%.

8. Approximately what percentage of the total sales of business firms consists of sales to consumers? (a) 40%; (b) 50%; (c) 60%; (d) 70%.

9. If a farmer produces $60 worth of wheat and sells it to a miller, who uses it to produce $80 worth of flour and in turn sells it to a baker, who produces bread which he sells for $150, the value of the production which has taken place is: (a) $60; (b) $80; (c) $150; (d) $290.

10. For the business sector of the economy as a whole, the largest allocation is for: (a) wages and salaries; (b) taxes; (c) depreciation; (d) profits.

11. Which of the following would *not* be in the nonprofit sector of the economy? (a) a savings and loan association; (b) the Federal government; (c) a private university; (d) the Ford Foundation.

■ DISCUSSION QUESTIONS

1. What does it mean when it is said that the business population in the United States is both "diverse" and "fluid"?

2. What is the difference between a plant and a firm? Between a firm and an industry?

Which of these three concepts is the most difficult to apply in practice? Why? Distinguish between a horizontal, a vertical, and a conglomerate combination.

3. What are the principal advantages and disadvantages of each of the three legal forms of business organization? Which of the disadvantages of the proprietorship and partnership account for the employment of the corporate form among the big businesses of the American economy?

4. Explain what "separation of ownership and control" of the modern corporation means. What problems does this separation create for stockholders and the economy?

5. What figures can you cite to show that the typical firm engaged in agriculture is relatively small and that the average firm engaged in manufacturing is relatively large? Are firms engaged in wholesaling and retailing; mining; and finance, insurance, and real estate relatively large or relatively small?

6. Is manufacturing in the United States an industry dominated by big business? What evidence do you use to reach this conclusion?

7. What are the two opposing views often advanced in answer to the question, "Is big business bad for the economy"?

8. Explain what is meant by the nonprofit sector of the economy. How are organizations in the nonprofit sector like and unlike organizations in the private and public sectors? For what reasons have some observers been critical of the nonprofit sector? Why do others defend the nonprofit sector?

9. What is meant by "private-public amalgamation"? What are the two forms of such amalgamation?

10. What are the seven main items which appear on the allocation side of an *individual* firm's income statement? One of these items has two subitems and another has three. What are these subitems?

11. There are seven main items on the allocation side of a *consolidated* income statement for the business sector of the economy, but they are not the same seven that appear in an individual firm's income statement. What item has been added and what item has been eliminated? Why is this done?

12. Explain carefully what is meant by depreciation.

THE FACTS OF AMERICAN CAPITALISM: GOVERNMENT

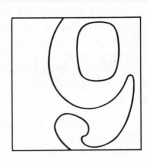

The facts of government finance in the United States presented in Chapter 9 center on two questions: Where do governments get their incomes? On what do they spend these incomes?

The organization of the chapter is relatively simple. First, the trends which taxes collected and expenditures made by all levels of government—Federal, state, and local—have taken during the past thirty years are examined briefly. Second, a closer look is given to the major items upon which governments spend their incomes, the principal taxes they levy to obtain their incomes, and the relative importance of these taxes. Third, the chapter looks at the Heller Plan for reducing the mismatch between the fiscal needs and resources of the Federal government on the one hand, and the needs and resources of state and local government on the other hand. Fourth, the chapter examines the principles applied in levying taxes, the way tax rates vary as personal incomes change, who really pays the taxes levied against various groups in the economy, and how much of their incomes Americans pay to government in the form of taxes.

What should the student get out of this chapter? There are at least six important sets of facts: (1) the trend which taxes and government expenditures have taken in recent years and why; (2) the relative importance of the principal taxes and the relative importance of the various expenditure items in the budgets of the three levels of government;

(3) the nature of the fiscal imbalance between the Federal government and state and local governments, how the Heller Plan proposes to remedy this imbalance, and the advantages and disadvantages of the Heller Plan; (4) the meaning and philosophy of the benefits-received and ability-to-pay principles; (5) the meaning of progressive, regressive, and proportional taxation, the shifting and incidence of taxes, and the incidence of the major types of taxes; and (6) the degree of progressiveness that exists in the taxing systems of Federal, state, and local government; and the percentages of income turned over to government by all households and by families with different incomes.

The student is cautioned again to avoid memorizing statistics. He should look instead for the trends and generalizations which these statistics illuminate. He should spend his time, also, on the terms used, the classifications employed, and the conclusions which are drawn and which embody these terms and classifications.

■ CHAPTER OUTLINE

1. Government's dual role in the economy consists of collecting revenue by taxation and expending this revenue for goods and services.

2. In both absolute and relative terms, government tax collections and spending have increased during the past thirty years.

a. The increased tax collections and spending are the result of hot and cold wars, population increases, urbanization and the greater demand for social goods, pollution of the environment, and inflation.

b. Government spending consists of expenditures for goods and services and transfer payments.

3. The principal taxes employed and the principal purposes for which these taxes are spent are different at the three governmental levels.

a. The Federal government relies heavily upon personal and corporate income taxes and payroll taxes, and spends a very large percentage of its income for national defense.

b. State and local governments employ chiefly sales, excise, and property taxes to finance their expenditures, most important of which are for education and highways.

4. Because of an imbalance between the ability of state and local governments to expand their tax collections and the growing need for these governments to deal with serious social and economic problems, the Heller Plan proposes that from 2 to 3 percent of the personal income taxes collected by the Federal government be distributed to the states.

5. Although the overall level of taxes is important to the economy, the question of who pays the tax bill is equally important.

a. Two philosophies, the benefits-received principle and the ability-to-pay principle, are widely employed to determine how the tax bill should be apportioned among the economy's citizens.

b. Taxes can be classified as progressive, regressive, or proportional according to the way in which the *tax rate* changes as income increases.

c. A tax levied upon one person or group of persons may be shifted partially or completely to another person or group; to the extent that a tax can be shifted or passed on through lower prices paid or higher prices received, its incidence is passed on. The incidence of the four major types of taxes is only probable and is not known for certain.

d. Federal taxes tend to be progressive in nature, and state and local taxes regressive; the tax system as a whole in the income range which includes most American families is roughly proportional.

■ IMPORTANT TERMS

Government transfer payment	Payroll tax
	Property tax
Personal income tax	Heller Plan
Marginal tax rate	
Average tax rate	Benefits-received principle
Corporation income tax	Ability-to-pay principle
Double taxation	Progressive tax
Capital gain	Regressive tax
Depletion allowance	Proportional tax
Sales tax	Tax incidence
Excise tax	Tax shifting

■ FILL-IN QUESTIONS

1. It is through the _____ and the _____ of government that the functions of government are most directly felt by the economy.

2. Transactions in the private sector of the economy are _____ while those in the public sector, by and large, are _____

3. Government transfer payments are _____ _____

4. The most important source of revenue for the Federal government is the _____ tax; next in importance are the _____ taxes. The major portion of Federal expenditures is for _____

5. Corporation income is said to be "taxed double" because _____ _____

6. State and local governments rely primarily upon _____ and _____ taxes for their incomes, which they spend mostly on _____ , _____ , and _____

7. The purpose of the _____ is to increase the revenues of state and local governments and enable them to expand their efforts to solve the serious social and economic problems facing them. This proposal would have the Federal government distribute from _____ to _____ percent of the revenue it collects from the _____ tax to the states.

8. The two philosophies of apportioning the tax burden which are most evident in the American economy are the _____ principle and the _____ principle.

9. As the income *decreases*, a proportional tax involves a _____ tax rate, a regressive tax, an _____ tax rate, and a progressive tax, a _____ _____ tax rate.

10. Indicate in the space to the right of each of the following taxes whether that tax (as applied in the United States) tends to be regressive (R) or progressive (P).

a. Personal income tax   _____

b. Sales tax   _____

c. Excise tax   _____

d. Property tax   _____

e. Corporation income tax   _____

f. Inheritance tax   _____

11. The tax systems of state and local governments in the United States tend to be _____ _____, that of the Federal government _____ and that of all levels of government combined tends to be _____

■ PROBLEMS AND PROJECTS

1. Below are several levels of taxable income and hypothetical marginal tax rates applicable to each $1,000 increase in income. Compute for each income level the tax and the average tax rate.

Taxable income	Marginal tax rate, %	Tax	Average tax rate, %
$1,500	20	$300	20
2,500	22	_____	_____
3,500	25	_____	_____
4,500	29	_____	_____
5,500	34	_____	_____
6,500	40	_____	_____
7,500	47	_____	_____

2. In the table below are seven levels of taxable income and the amount paid at each of the seven levels under three tax laws: A, B, and C. Compute for each of the three taxes the *average* rate of taxation of each of the seven income levels and indicate whether the tax is regressive, proportional, progressive, or some combination thereof.

Income	Tax A Tax paid	Av. tax rate %	Tax B Tax paid	Av. tax rate %	Tax C Tax paid	Av. tax rate %
$ 500	$ 15.00	_____%	$ 5.00	_____%	$ 50.00	_____%
1,500	45.00	_____	30.00	_____	135.00	_____
3,000	90.00	_____	90.00	_____	240.00	_____
5,000	150.00	_____	150.00	_____	350.00	_____
7,500	225.00	_____	187.50	_____	450.00	_____
10,000	300.00	_____	200.00	_____	500.00	_____
15,000	450.00	_____	300.00	_____	600.00	_____
Type of tax:	_____		_____		_____	

3. Assume a government levies a 4 percent sales tax on all consumption expenditures. Consumption expenditures at six income levels are shown in the table below.

Income	Consumption expenditures	Sales tax paid	Average tax rate, %
$ 5,000	$5,000	$ _____	_____
6,000	5,800	_____	_____
7,000	6,600	_____	_____
8,000	7,400	_____	_____
9,000	8,200	_____	_____
10,000	9,000	_____	_____

a. Compute the sales tax paid at each income.

b. Compute the average tax rate at each income.

c. Using income as the tax base, the sales tax is a _____ tax.

■ SELF-TEST

Circle the T if the statement is true, the F if it is false.

1. Taxes collected by, and expenditures of, all levels of government in the United States exceed $250 billion per year.　**T　F**

2. The chief source of revenue for the Federal government is the corporation income tax.　**T　F**

3. The level of Federal expenditures in 1971 was about $150 million.　**T　F**

4. The chief difficulty in applying the benefits-received principle of taxation is to determine who receives the benefits of many of the goods and services which government supplies.　**T　F**

5. The Heller Plan is a proposal to have the Federal government give to the states a portion of the revenue it receives from the personal income tax.　**T　F**

6. A sales tax generally turns out to be a proportional tax.　**T　F**

7. Total taxes collected by the Federal government are approximately equal to the amount of taxes collected by all state and local governments.　**T　F**

8. The state and Federal taxes on gasoline are good examples of taxes levied on the benefits-received principle.　**T　F**

Underscore the letter that corresponds to the best answer.

1. Today all government expenditures equal approximately what percentage of the American economy's total output? (a) 8%; (b) 15%; ⓒ 23%; (d) 28%.

2. Which of the following would *not* be a government transfer expenditure? ⓐ contributions of employers to support the social security program; (b) social security payments to the aged; (c) unemployment compensation benefits; (d) payments to the widows of war veterans.

3. Which of the following pairs represents the chief source of income and the most important type of expenditure of *state* governments? ⓐ personal income tax and expenditures for education; (b) personal income tax and expenditures for highways; (c) sales and excise taxes and expenditures for public welfare; ⓓ sales and excise taxes and expenditures for highways.

4. Which of the following pairs represents the chief source of income and the most important type of expenditure of *local* governments? (a) property tax and expenditures for highways; ⓑ property tax and expenditures for education; (c) sales and excise taxes and expenditures for public welfare; (d) sales and excise taxes and expenditures for police, fire, and general government.

5. Which of the following is *not* true of the ability-to-pay principle as applied in the United States? (a) it is more widely applied than the benefits-received principle; (b) income is generally taken as the measure of the ability to pay; ⓒ it is more widely applied by state and local than by Federal government; (d) as the tax base increases, taxes paid increase both absolutely and relatively.

6. Which of the following tends to be a progressive tax in the United States? ⓐ inheritance tax; (b) property tax; (c) sales tax; (d) excise tax.

7. Past, present, and future wars account for approximately what percentage of all Federal expenditures? (a) 50%; ⓑ 55%; (c) 60%; (d) 65%.

8. Which of the following taxes can be least easily shifted? ⓐ personal income tax; (b) corporation income tax; (c) sales tax; (d) excise tax.

■ DISCUSSION QUESTIONS

1. What is meant by the "dual role" of government in the economy? How do transactions in the public sector differ from those in the private sector of the economy?

2. What have been the causes which have contributed to the absolute and relative increases in government spending over the last thirty years?

3. Government expenditures fall into two broad classes: expenditures for goods and services, and transfer payments. Explain the difference between these and give examples of expenditures which fall into each of the two classes.

4. Explain the difference between exhaustive and nonexhaustive government spending.

5. Explain precisely the difference between the marginal tax rate and the average tax rate.

6. What is a tax "loophole"? What are the three principal loopholes in the Federal tax system? How do these loopholes affect the distribution of income?

7. What different kinds of taxes do the various governments in the United States employ to raise revenues?

8. Explain in detail the differences that exist between Federal, state, and local governments in the taxes upon which they primarily rely for their revenues and the major purposes for which they use these revenues.

9. What is the Heller Plan? Why does it seem easier to have the Federal government raise additional revenues, and why does it seem necessary to have state and local governments spend this additional revenue? What are the advantages and disadvantages of this plan?

10. What are the two basic philosophies for apportioning the tax burden in the United States? Explain each. What are the difficulties encountered in putting these philosophies into practice?

11. Explain the differences among progressive, regressive, and proportional taxes. Which taxes fall into each of these three categories? What can be said about the progressivity or regressivity of Federal, state, and local taxes and the overall tax system?

12. Which of the following taxes tends to be shifted? (a) personal income tax; (b) corporate income tax; (c) sales and excise taxes; (d) property tax. From whom is the tax shifted and upon whom is the tax incidence?

NATIONAL INCOME ACCOUNTING

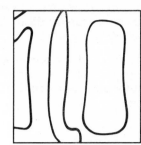

National income (or social) accounting is the subject matter of Chapter 10. This type of accounting aims to measure or estimate five things: (1) the gross national product, the total output of all final goods and services in the economy during a year; (2) the net national product, the annual output of all final goods and services over and above (in excess of or "net of") the stock of goods with which the economy began the year; (3) the national income, the total income or output earned by owners of land and capital and suppliers of labor and entrepreneurial ability during a year; (4) personal income, the total income or output actually received—whether earned or unearned—by these suppliers of resources (or the total income earned and received plus unearned income) before the payment of personal taxes; and (5) disposable income, the total income or output available to resource suppliers after the payment of personal taxes.

This is national income (or social) accounting because it involves estimating output or income for the nation or society as a whole, rather than for an individual business firm or family. Note that the terms "output" and "income" are interchangeable because the nation's output and income are identical: The value of the nation's output equals the total expenditures for this output, and these expenditures become the receipts or the income of those in the nation who have produced this output. Consequently, there are two equally acceptable methods, both discussed in the chapter, for obtaining each of the five income-output measures listed above. These two methods are the output (or expenditures) method (or approach) and the income (or allocations) method (or approval).

Accounting is essentially a process of adding up. This chapter explains in detail and lists the items which must be added and/or subtracted to obtain by both methods each of the five income-output measures. It is up to the student to learn precisely *what* to add and subtract, i.e., how to compute GNP, NNP, NI, PI, and DI by both methods. This is a fairly difficult chapter, and the only way to learn the material is simply to sit down and learn it—memorize it if necessary! A careful reading of the chapter, however, will enable the student to avoid the necessity of memorizing. He should first try to understand what each of the five income-output measures attemps to measure and the two alternative approaches to these measurements. Then the item added and/or subtracted will be simpler.

In addition to explaining the two methods of computing the five income-output measures and each of the items used in the computation process, the chapter discusses the purpose of social accounting; the means by which income-output measures for different years may be adjusted to take account of changes in the price level so that comparisons between years are possible; and the shortcomings and dangers inherent in national income accounting. Chapter 10 is essential background for Parts Two and Three, which explain the history of and the factors determining the level of total output and income in the economy. The chapter is important in itself because it presents one of the several means of measuring or estimating the well-being of the economy and the individuals comprising the economy in a given year and over the years.

■ CHAPTER OUTLINE

1. National income (or social) accounting consists of concepts which enable those who use them to measure the economy's output, to compare it with past outputs, to explain its size and the reasons for changes in its size, and to formulate policies designed to increase it.

2. The gross national product (GNP) is the market value of the output of all final goods and services produced in the economy during a year.
   a. GNP is measured in dollar terms rather than in terms of physical units of output.
   b. Because the value of the dollar (and the price level) changes over time, it is necessary to adjust dollar GNP figures when comparing GNPs in different years.
   c. To adjust dollar GNP figures for changes in the price level, divide the dollar GNP in any year by the price index for that year.
   d. To avoid double counting, GNP includes only *final* goods and services—goods and services that will not be processed further during the *current* year.
   e. Nonproductive transactions are not included in GNP; purely financial transactions and secondhand sales are, therefore, excluded.
   f. GNP is not an ideal measure of national economic well-being for several reasons.
   g. Measurement of GNP can be accomplished by two methods—the expenditures and the income methods—but the same result is obtained by either method.

3. Computation of GNP by the expenditures method requires the accountant to add the four types of spending which occur in the economy for final goods and services: the personal consumption expenditures of households; government spending for goods and services; business spending for capital goods; and the *net* spending of foreign citizens, firms, and governments for American goods and services.

4. Computation of GNP by the income method requires the accountant to total the nine uses to which the income derived from the production and sale of final goods and services are put: depreciation, indirect business taxes, compensation of employees, rents, interest, proprietors' income, corporate income taxes, dividends, and undistributed corporate profits.

5. In addition to GNP, four other national income measures are useful and important in evaluating the output and health of the economy: the Net National Product, National Income, Personal Income, and Disposable Income. Each has a distinct and different meaning and can be computed by either the expenditures or the income method. All five are related to each other in a definite way, and each can be computed by making certain additions to or deductions from the other measures.

■ IMPORTANT TERMS

National income (social) accounting

Gross national product

Real gross national product

Inflating

Deflating

Price index

Base year

Given year

Final goods

Intermediate goods

Double counting

Value added

Nonproductive transaction

Nonmarket transaction

Output (expenditures) approach

Income (allocations) approach

Personal consumption expenditures

Government purchases of goods and services

Gross private domestic investment

Noninvestment transaction

Net private domestic investment

Expanding (growing) economy

Stationary (static) economy

Declining (contracting) economy

Net exports

Nonincome charges

Capital consumption allowances

Indirect business taxes

Compensation to employees

Wage and salary supplements

Net national product

National income

Personal income

Disposable income

Personal saving

■ FILL-IN QUESTIONS

1. Social accounting is invaluable because it provides a means of keeping track of the ____

_____

and the information necessary to devise and put into effect _____

_____

2. Gross national product is a monetary measure of all final goods and services produced during a year; to measure the value of these goods and services, the goods and services are valued at their _____

3. In order to compare the gross national product in two different years, it is necessary to adjust money GNP because _____

_____

4. In measuring GNP only final goods and services are included; if intermediate goods and services were included, the accountant would be _____

5. A firm buys materials for $200 and produces from them a product which sells for $315. The $115 is the _____ by the firm.

6. The total value added to a product at all stages of production equals _____

_____

7. Public transfer payments, private transfer payments, and security transactions are all examples of the _____ type of nonproductive transactions.

8. Depreciation and indirect business taxes, by the income or allocations approach, are referred to as _____ charges or allocations.

9. Gross private domestic investment basically includes _____,

_____,

and _____

Net private domestic investment is less than

gross private domestic investment by an amount equal to _____

10. If gross private domestic investment is greater than capital consumption, the economy is _____; if it is less than capital consumption, the economy is _____; and if it equals capital consumption, the economy is _____

11. The compensation of employees in the system of social accounting consist of actual wages and salaries and wage and salary ____ which are the payments employers make to

_____

and to _____

12. Corporate profits are disposed of in three ways: _____,

_____,

and _____

13. Gross national product overstates the economy's production in a given year because it fails to _____

14. Net national product equals gross national product minus _____

15. National income equals net national product minus _____; this deduction is made because national income is income _____ and the subtracted item is not considered to be a factor of production which contributes to the production of output.

16. _Transfer payments_ include the following five items:

a. _____

b. _____

c. _____

d. _____

e. _____

17. Personal income equals national income

plus _____

and minus _____ ,

_____ ,

and _____ .

It also equals the sum of _____ ,

_____ ,

_____ ,

and _____

18. Disposable income equals personal income minus _____ ;

disposable income also equals _____

plus _____

plus _____

19. Personal saving equals disposable income minus _____

and· _____

20. Net private domestic investment plus

_____

equals gross private domestic investment.

■ PROBLEMS AND PROJECTS

1. Price indices, deflating and inflating:
a. Below are hypothetical figures for five different years showing the prices of a typical commodity for each of the five years.

Year	Price	Price index (1927 equals 100)	Price index (1935 equals 100)
1927	$ 9	_____	_____
1929	11	_____	_____
1931	6	_____	_____
1933	7	_____	_____
1935	8	_____	_____

(1) Using 1927 as the base year, compute the index of prices in each of the five years.
(2) Using 1935 as the base year, compute the index of prices in each of the five years.

b. Below are hypothetical figures for money or unadjusted gross national product in each of the five years.

Year	Money or unadjusted GNP, billions of dollars	Adjusted GNP in 1927 dollars	Adjusted GNP in 1935 dollars
1927	$ 90	$_____	$_____
1929	120	_____	_____
1931	60	_____	_____
1933	65	_____	_____
1935	70	_____	_____

(1) Compute the real (or adjusted) gross national product measured in 1927 dollars.
(2) Compute the real (or adjusted) gross national product measured in 1935 dollars.

2. You are given the following national income accounting data.

	Billions of dollars
Personal taxes	$ 37
Social security contributions	10
Indirect business taxes	19
Corporate income taxes	38
Transfer payments	17
Gross national product	468
Undistributed corporate profits	34
Gross private domestic investment	74
Personal consumption expenditures	310
Net private domestic investment	51
Interest paid by consumers	8

Compute each of the following:

a. Net national product: $_____

b. National income: $_____

c. Personal income: $_____

d. Disposable income: $_____

e. Personal saving: $_____

3. Following are hypothetical social accounting figures for the United States.

	Billions of dollars
Exports	$ 12
Interest paid by consumers	5
Dividends	13
Depreciation (capital consumption allowances)	22
Government expenditures for goods and services	71
Rents	9
Indirect business taxes	11
Compensation to employees	238
Gross private domestic investment	56
Personal saving	29
Corporate income taxes	15
Transfer payments	26
Interest	6
Proprietors' income	21
Personal consumption expenditures	217
Imports	7
Social security contributions	7
Undistributed corporate profits	14
Personal taxes	55

Complete the table below in which the five income-output measures are computed by both methods. Identify each of the several amounts which you add (and/or subtract) to compute each of the five measures.

4. Below is a list of items which may or may not be included in the five income-output measures. Indicate in the space to the right of each which of the income-output measures includes this item; it is possible for the item to be included in none, one, two, three, four, or all of the measures. If the item is included in none of the measures, indicate why it is not included.

a. Interest on the national debt _____

b. The sale of a used air conditioner _____
c. The production of shoes which are not sold by the manufacturer _____
d. The income of a bootlegger in a "dry" state _____

Income (allocations) method	Output (expenditures) method
Gross National Product	
(1) $	(1) $
(2)	(2)
(3)	(3)
(4)	(4)
(5)	Gross national product $_____
(6)	
(7)	
(8)	
(9)	
Gross national product $_____	
Net National Product	
(1) $	(1) $
(2)	(2)
(3)	(3)
(4)	(4)
(5)	Net national product $_____
(6)	
(7)	
(8)	
Net national product $_____	

Income (allocations) method		Output (expenditures) method	
		National Income	
(1)	$	(1)	$
(2)		(2) Less:	
(3)		National income	$_____
(4)			
(5)			
(6)			
(7)			
National income	$_____		
		Personal Income	
(1)	$	(1)	$
(2) Plus:		(2)	
(3) Less:		(2)	
(4) Less:		(4)	
(5) Less:		Personal income	$_____
Personal income	$_____		
		Disposable Income	
(1)	$	(1)	$
(2) Less:		(2)	
Disposable income	$_____	(3)	
		Disposable income	$_____

e. The purchase of a share of common stock on the New York Stock Exchange _____

f. The interest paid on the bonds of the General Motors Corporation _____

g. The labor performed by a housewife _____

h. The labor performed by a paid baby-sitter _____

i. The monthly check received by an idler from his rich aunt _____

j. The purchase of a new tractor by a farmer _____

k. The labor performed by an assembly-line worker in repapering his own kitchen _____

l. The services of a lawyer _____

m. The purchase of shoes from their manufacturer by a shoe retailer _____

n. The monthly check received by the government by a student studying on the GI Bill of Rights _____

o. The rent a homeowner would receive if he did not live in his own home _____

■ SELF-TEST

Circle the T if the statement is true, the F if it is false.

1. Gross national product measures at their market value the total output of all goods and services produced in the economy during a year.   **T   F**

2. Comparison of gross national product with the gross national product of an earlier year when the price level has risen between the two years necessitates the "inflation" of the GNP figure in the later year. **T   F**

3. To adjust money gross national product for a given year so that a comparison between GNP in that year and in the base year can be made, it is necessary to divide money GNP in the given year by the price index—expressed as a decimal—for that year. **T   F**

4. The total value added to a product and the value of the final product are equal. **T   F**

5. The two approaches to the measurement of the gross national product yield identical results because one approach measures the total amount spent on the products produced by business firms during a year while the second approach measures the total income of business firms during the year. **T   F**

6. In computing gross national product, net national product, and national income by the expenditures (or output) approach, transfer payments are excluded because they do not represent payments for currently produced goods and services. **T   F**

7. If gross private domestic investment is greater than depreciation during a given year, the economy has declined or contracted during that year. **T   F**

The data in the table below should be used to answer true-false questions 8 through 10 and multiple-choice questions 8 through 10.

	Billions of dollars
Net private domestic investment	$ 32
Personal taxes	39
Transfer payments	19
Indirect business taxes	8
Corporation income taxes	11
Personal consumption expenditures	217
Depreciation	7
Interest paid by consumers	4
United States exports	15
Government purchase of goods and services	51
Undistributed corporate profits	10
Social security contributions	4
United States imports	17

8. Gross private domestic investment is equal to $25 billion. **T   F**

9. National income equals the net national product minus $8 billion. **T   F**

10. Disposable income is equal to $245 billion. **T   F**

Underscore the letter that corresponds to the best answer.

1. Which of the following is *not* an important use to which social accounting is put? (a) provides a basis for the formulation and application of policies designed to improve the economy's performance; (b) permits measurement of the economic efficiency of the economy; (c) makes possible an estimate of the output of final goods and services in the economy; (d) enables the economist to chart the growth or decline of the economy over a period of time.

2. If both money gross national product and the level of prices are rising, it is evident that: (a) real GNP is constant; (b) real GNP is rising but not as rapidly as prices; (c) real GNP is declining; (d) no conclusion can be drawn concerning the real GNP of the economy on the basis of this information.

3. To include the value of the parts used in producing the automobiles turned out during a year in gross national product for that year would be an example of: (a) including a nonmarket transaction; (b) including a nonproductive transaction; (c) including a noninvestment transaction; (d) double counting.

4. The sale in 1969 of an automobile produced in 1968 would not be included in the gross national product for 1969; doing so would involve: (a) including a nonmarket transaction; (b) including a nonproductive transaction; (c) including a noninvestment transaction; (d) double counting.

5. The service a baby-sitter performs when she stays at home with her baby brother while her parents are out and for which she receives no payment is not included in the gross national product because: (a) this is a nonmarket transaction; (b) this is a nonproductive transaction; (c) this is a noninvestment transaction; (d) double counting would be involved.

6. Which of the following does *not* represent investment? (*a*) an increase in the quantity of shoes on the shelves of a shoe store; (*b*) the construction of a house which will be occupied by its owner; (*c*) the purchase of newly issued shares of stock in the General Motors Corporation; (*d*) the construction of a factory building using money borrowed from a bank.

7. A refrigerator is produced by its manufacturer in 1968, sold during 1968 to a retailer, and sold by the retailer to a final consumer in 1969. The refrigerator is: (*a*) counted as consumption in 1968; (*b*) counted as investment in 1969; (*c*) counted as investment in 1968 and consumption and disinvestment in 1969; (*d*) not included in the gross national product of 1968.

Questions 8 through 10 use the national income accounting data given in the table in the true-false section.

8. The net national product is equal to: (*a*) $298 billion; (*b*) $302 billion; (*c*) $317 billion; (*d*) $321 billion.

9. National income exceeds personal income by: (*a*) $6 billion; (*b*) $15 billion; (*c*) $21 billion; (*d*) $44 billion.

10. Personal saving is equal to: (*a*) −$24 billion; (*b*) −$7 billion; (*c*) $7 billion; (*d*) $24 billion.

■ DISCUSSION QUESTIONS

1. Of what use is national income accounting to the economist and to the policy makers in the economy?

2. Why are GNP, NNP, etc., monetary measures, and why is it necessary that they be monetary measures?

3. Why do economists find it necessary to inflate and deflate GNP when comparing GNP in different years? How do they do this?

4. Why is GNP not an ideal measure of the economic welfare of society? Are there any better measures? For what purposes are NNP, NI, PI, and DI used?

5. Why does GNP exclude nonproductive transactions? What are the two principal types of nonproductive transactions? List some examples of each.

6. Why are there two ways, both of which yield the same answers, of computing GNP, NNP, etc?

7. What is meant by a nonincome charge or allocation? What are the two principal nonincome charges included in GNP? Why are they excluded from NI?

8. Why are transfer payments excluded from GNP, NNP, and NI?

9. Is residential construction counted as investment or consumption? Why?

10. How do you define a static, an expanding, and a contracting economy? What is the relationship between gross private domestic investment and depreciation in these three economies?

11. Why are indirect business taxes "indirect"?

12. Under what conditions can personal saving be negative? How is this possible?

THE BUSINESS CYCLE: UNEMPLOYMENT AND INFLATION

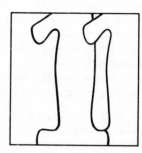

This chapter begins the explanation of what determines the level of gross national product, net national product, national income, etc., actually achieved in any year. In the preceding chapter the student learned how to compute these income-output measures and what each of them means. In the chapters that follow he should learn what causes income and output to be what they are, what causes them to fluctuate, and how they can be controlled for the welfare of the economy as a whole.

Chapter 11 is concerned with the ups and downs which occur in employment, output, income, and price level over the years. These ups and downs are usually referred to as the business cycle. The chapter is in part historical and descriptive. It examines recent American economic history to see how prices, employment, income, and output have changed; the relationships between changes in these variables; and the immediate causes of these changes. One purpose of the chapter is to give the student a few historical facts which will be used in the next two chapters as a basis for generalizations about the determinants of income and output. The chapter is not purely descriptive and historical, however. Sections of it deal with the reasons the economic variables behave the way they do and why certain relationships exist between them.

Particular attention should be paid to the following: (1) the basic cause of changes in employment, output, income, and the price level; (2) the relationship between the level of employment in the economy and the effect of increased spending upon prices and employment; (3) what full employment and unemployment mean; (4) the relationship between the level of employment in the economy and the effect of increased spending upon the output of durable and nondurable goods and upon the incomes received by different groups in the economy; (5) the effect of price inflation upon the real incomes of various groups in the economy; (6) who is hurt by and who benefits from inflation and deflation; (7) the specific causes of the periods of prosperity, depression, and inflation experienced by the American economy during the last fifty years or so; and (8) what seem to be the prospects for economic stability in the future.

The facts, relationships, and explanations in Chapter 11 are too important to be overlooked, and they must be mastered if the student is to understand the chapters that follow.

■ CHAPTER OUTLINE

1. The macroeconomic trilogy is evident in the history of the American economy: economic growth interrupted by price stability and by employment and output instability.

2. The levels of employment, output, and prices actually achieved by the economy depend upon the level of total spending in the economy.

a. The relationships between total spending, employment, output, and the price level are generally positive (direct).

b. These relationships are not rigid; the way in which a change in the level of spending affects employment, output, and prices depends upon the levels of employment and output already achieved.

3. Full employment means that there are jobs available for all those who wish to work; it does not mean that all who wish to work are employed, because there is always some frictional unemployment in the economy.

a. The economic cost of unemployment is wasted resources and unproduced output.

b. Unemployment also leads to serious social problems.

4. Inflation and deflation mean increases and decreases, respectively, in the level of prices in the economy. These increases and decreases operate to the advantage of some groups in the economy and to the disadvantage of other groups. Creeping inflation involves small annual increases in the level of prices and it, too, can both benefit and hurt different groups in the economy.

5. The business cycle means alternating periods of prosperity and depression. These recurrent ups and downs in employment, output, and prices are irregular in their occurrence and intensity.

a. Not all changes in employment and output which occur in the economy are cyclical; some are due to seasonal and secular influences.

b. The business cycle affects almost the entire economy, but it does not affect all parts in the same way and to the same degree. In particular, the production of durable and nondurable goods and the incomes of various groups do not fluctuate to the same degree during the cycle.

6. Since 1920 the American economy has witnessed great changes in the levels of employment, output, and prices; these changes can best be understood by reviewing the ways in which total spending changed during this period and the reasons for these changes in total spending.

7. Most economists agree that the economy will be more stable in the future than in the

past because of the growth of economic knowledge, better public policies to combat recession and inflation, changes in its institutions and structure, and the expansion in the public sector of the economy.

■ IMPORTANT TERMS

Macroeconomic trilogy	**Premature inflation**
Full unemployment	**Pure inflation**
Frictional unemployment	**Hyper-(galloping) inflation**
Business cycle	**Demand-pull inflation**
Seasonal variation	**GNP gap**
Secular trend	**Creeping unemployment**
Inflation	
Deflation	**Money income**
Creeping inflation	**Real income**

■ FILL-IN QUESTIONS

1. The basic determinant of the level of employment is the volume or level of _____

_____ in the economy.

2. Complete the following chain (using such words as more, less, larger, smaller, increase, decrease, etc.): An increase in total spending in the economy will make it profitable for

business to produce a _____ output; to do this it must employ _____ resources and this _____ the incomes received in the economy and *may*

_____ the price level.

3. Increases in total spending when the economy is at *less* than full employment may result in a rise in the price level; this is termed _____ inflation. Increases in spending when the economy is at full employment result only in a rise in the price level; and this is called _____ inflation.

4. Full employment in the American economy is achieved when approximately _____ percent of the labor force is employed; even at full employment there is always some ____

_____ unemployment.

5. The GNP gap is equal to _____

GNP *minus* _____ GNP.

6. Inflation means a _____

and deflation a _____

_____

7. A person's *real* income depends upon his

_____

and _____

_____

8. List under the appropriate headings in the table below as many of those groups as you can who are affected by inflation and deflation.

9. Creeping inflation means an increase in the level of prices of from about _____

to _____

percent per year.

10. If the business cycle is divided into four phases, these phases are often called _____

_____,

_____,

_____,

and _____;

if it is divided into two phases, it is common

to call these phases _____

and _____

or _____

and _____

11. In addition to the changes brought about by the operation of the business cycle, changes in output and employment may be

due to _____

and _____

12. Production and employment in the ____

_____ goods industries are affected to a greater degree by depression and expansion than they are in the _____ goods industries; prices vary to a greater extent in the (low-, high-) _____ concentration industries.

13. During the period from 1922 to 1929 in the United States, GNP tended to _____

_____,

unemployment was _____,

and prices were _____.

The basic cause of these conditions was a

_____ level of

investment spending on _____

and _____

14. Three important factors contributing to the prosperity of the 1920s were:

a. _____

b. _____

c. _____

Inflation		Deflation	
Hurt	Benefit	Hurt	Benefit
_____	_____	_____	_____
_____	_____	_____	_____
_____	_____	_____	_____
_____	_____	_____	_____
_____	_____	_____	_____

15. In the 1930s investment spending was low largely because of _____

_____

and _____

_____

16. By and large, the prosperity of the World War II years was due to increased government spending; during this period consumer spending _____

and private investment spending _____

_____

17. Following World War II consumer spending in the United States greatly increased because consumers had both _____

and _____

and because the level of prices was _____

_____

18. In addition to a high level of consumer spending, prosperity in the United States between 1946 and 1949 was due to:

a. _____

b. _____

c. _____

d. _____

19. The decade of the 1950s was, in general, a period of prosperity and rising *real* GNP. But there were brief recessions in _____

and _____; and inflation was accompanied by a slowing down of the _____

_____ rate and a _____
level of unemployment.

20. The American economy in 1961 began a period of unprecedented economic expansion. The principal reasons for this expansion were:

a. _____

b. _____

c. _____

d. _____

e. _____

21. During the period of economic expansion that began in early 1961, the *rate* of growth _____ and *un*employment

_____.

Until 1965 the price level was _____;

but after 1965 the economy experienced ___

_____

22. The anti-inflationary policies undertaken by the Federal government in 1969 did not curb the inflation but did decrease _____

and _____. The stubbornness of this inflation is probably the result of inflationary _____

■ PROBLEMS AND PROJECTS

1. In the table on page 71 are statistics* dealing with population, the labor force, employment, etc., in the United States during the years 1968, 1969, and 1970. Make the computations necessary to complete the statistics. (Numbers of persons are in thousands.)
  a. How was it possible to have *both* employment and unemployment increase between 1968 and 1969? _____

_____

  b. In relative terms, if unemployment increases employment will decrease. Why? ___

_____

  c. Would you say that 1968 and 1969 were years of full employment? Why? What about 1970? _____

  d. Why is the task of maintaining full employment over the years more than just a problem of finding jobs for those who happen to be involuntarily idle in any given year? ___

_____

* Board of Governors of the Federal Reserve System, *Federal Reserve Bulletin*, vol. 57, no. 3, March, 1971, p. A64.

	1968	1969	1970
Total noninstitutional population over 15 years of age	135,562	137,841	140,182
Population not in the civilian labor force	53,291	53,602	54,280
Armed Forces	3,534	3,506	3,187
Civilian labor force	_____	_____	_____
Percent of noninstitutional population over 15 years of age in the civilian labor force	_____	_____	_____
Total employment	75,920	77,902	78,627
Total unemployment	_____	_____	_____
Percent of civilian labor force employed	_____	_____	_____
Percent of civilian labor force unemployed	_____	_____	_____

2. In the space below, indicate for each of the following situations the effects of an increase in total spending on *incomes, output, employment,* and the *price level,* respectively, using the following symbols: A, no effect or slight increase; B, increase; and C, sharp increase.

a. Depression and widespread unemployment

_____ _____ _____ _____

b. Prosperity, but moderate unemployment

_____ _____ _____ _____

c. Prosperity and full employment

_____ _____ _____ _____

3. The table below gives the average prices charged and the outputs of two different industries during a boom year and a depression year. Indicate in the appropriate spaces the percentages by which prices and output declined between the boom year and the depression year in each of the two industries.

a. In which industry was the relative price decline the greatest? _____

b. In which industry was the relative output decline the greatest? _____

c. Of the two, which industry would you say produced "hard" goods (capital goods and consumer durable goods)? _____

d. Which industry of the two would you suspect was concentrated? _____

4. Indicate in the space to the right of each of the following the effect—beneficial (B), detrimental (D), or indeterminate (I)—of inflation and deflation on these persons:

a. A retired schoolteacher living on her savings _____ _____

b. A retired schoolteacher living on the dividends she receives on the shares of stock she owns _____ _____

c. A farmer who has mortgaged his farm at the local bank for $20,000, which must be paid off in ten years _____ _____

d. A pensioner _____ _____

e. A widow whose income consists entirely

Industry	Prices			Output		
	Boom	Depression	% Decline	Boom	Depression	% Decline
A	$ .65	$ .43	_____	90,000	70,000	_____
B	7.50	7.00	_____	120,000	75,000	_____

of interest received on the corporate bonds
she owns   _____ _____

  f. A schoolteacher   _____ _____
  g. A union member who works in a steel
plant   _____ _____
  h. A state government employee

                          _____ _____

5. Suppose that in 1984 the economy is at full employment and has a GNP of $1,200 billion. GNP is capable of growing at a rate of 5 percent per year.

  a. Compute the economy's *potential* GNP in 1985 and 1986 and enter them in the table below. (*Hint:* Potential GNP in any year is equal to 105 percent of the potential GNP in the previous year.)

Year	Potential GNP	Actual GNP	GNP gap
1984	$1,200	$1,200	$ 0
1985	_____	1,236	_____
1986	_____	1,286	_____

  b. *Actual* GNP in 1985 and 1986 is shown in the table. Complete the table by computing the GNP gap in these two years.

■ SELF-TEST

Circle the T if the statement is true, the F if it is false.

1. In practical terms, full employment means that approximately 96 to 97 percent of the total work force is employed.   **T F**

2. With a moderate amount of unemployment in the economy, an increase in total spending will generally increase both the price level and the output of the economy.   **T F**

3. If the economy is operating at full employment a decrease in total spending can be expected to reduce both the price level and employment in the economy.   **T F**

4. During prosperity, labor's share of the national income tends to increase.   **T F**

5. Not all changes which occur in output and

employment in the economy are due to the business cycle.   **T F**

6. Industries which are highly concentrated show small relative decreases in output and large relative decreases in prices during a downswing of the business cycle.   **T F**

7. Inflation tends to work to the advantage of those persons whose income is derived from corporate profits and to the disadvantage of those whose income is derived from interest on corporate bonds.   **T F**

8. Economists agree that creeping inflation benefits the economy as a whole.   **T F**

9. The 1920s, in general, were years of rising GNP and prices and little unemployment.   **T F**

10. The World War II years were a period characterized by a high level of private investment spending.   **T F**

11. During World War II the increased taxes paid by consumers and the increased saving done by consumers were significant factors contributing to inflation.   **T F**

12. The economy's GNP gap is measured by deducting its actual GNP from its potential GNP.   **T F**

Underscore the letter that corresponds to the best answer.

1. Which of the following is *not* part of the macroeconomic trilogy? (a) price stability; (b) economic growth; (c) full employment; (d) full production.

2. If the resources of the economy are fully employed, an increase in total spending will cause: (a) output and employment to increase; (b) output and prices to increase; (c) incomes and prices to increase; (d) employment and incomes to increase.

3. If the economy is experiencing a depression with substantial unemployment, an increase in total spending will cause: (a) a decrease in the *real* income of the economy; (b) little or no increase in the level of prices; (c) an increase in the *real* income and a decrease in the *money* income of the economy; (d) proportionate increases in the price level, output, and income in the economy.

4. Total employment in December of this year was greater than total employment in December of 1928. This is no doubt due to the effect of: (a) seasonal variations; (b) secular trend; (c) the business cycle; (d) the diverse impact of the business cycle.

5. If employment in the agricultural sector of the American economy during last August and September was 112 percent of what it normally is in those months, this is probably a consequence of: (a) seasonal variations; (b) secular trend; (c) the business cycle; (d) both seasonal variations and the business cycle.

6. Production and employment in which of the following industries would be least affected by a depression? (a) nondurable consumer goods; (b) durable consumer goods; (c) capital goods; (d) iron and steel.

7. Which of the following would *not* benefit from deflation? (a) those living on fixed incomes; (b) those who find prices falling faster than their incomes; (c) those who have money savings; (d) those who became debtors during a period when prices were higher.

8. In late 1929 and the early 1930s a severe depression occurred in the United States. Which of the following was *not* a factor which contributed to the depression? (a) a decline in residential construction; (b) an expansion in the nation's money supply; (c) excess industrial capacity; (d) a large volume of personal indebtedness.

9. Which of the following was characteristic of economic conditions in the United States during the 1920s? (a) a backlog of demand for capital; (b) excess industrial capacity; (c) diminishing consumer debt; (d) rising prices and wage rates.

10. Which of the following was characteristic of the American economy between 1946 and 1949? (a) decreased government spending and a rising price level; (b) decreased consumer spending and decreased private investment spending; (c) increased consumer spending and decreased net exports; (d) declining employment and a rising price level.

11. Which of the following was *not* characteristic of the decade of the 1950s? (a) inflation; (b) two recessions; (c) an increase in the rate of economic growth; (d) significant economic growth.

12. Which of the following has *not* been characteristic of the American economy since 1961? (a) a decline in the level of consumer prices; (b) a decline in the percentage of the labor force that is unemployed; (c) an increased rate of economic growth; (d) increased spending by Federal, state, and local governments.

■ DISCUSSION QUESTIONS

1. What is meant by the macroeconomic trilogy?

2. Explain why and how total spending determines output, employment, and income in the economy.

3. Explain what will tend to happen to employment, output, income, and the price level if total spending increases and the resources of the economy are: (a) widely unemployed, (b) moderately unemployed, (c) fully employed. If total spending *decreased* would the effects on employment, output, income, and the price level be just the opposite? Why?

4. When is there full employment in the American economy? How is the concept of frictional (or normal) unemployment related to the concept of full employment?

5. Why will the price level tend to increase as a consequence of an increase in total spending in the economy *before* all the resources of the economy are fully employed?

6. What are the phases of the business cycle called? How often do business cycles occur?

7. The business cycle is only one of three general causes of changes in output, income, and employment in the economy. What are the other influences which affect these variables?

8. Compare the manner in which the business cycle affects output, prices, and incomes in the industries producing capital and durable goods with industries producing nondurable goods and services. What causes these differences?

9. What are inflation and deflation? What groups benefit from and what groups are hurt by inflation and deflation? Why?

10. Why do some economists believe that creeping inflation is beneficial to the economy?

11. What are the two principal arguments against creeping inflation? How can creeping inflation turn into hyperinflation and eventually result in depression and unemployment?

12. In what sense did the prosperity of the 1920s "cause" the depression of the 1930s?

13. The level of total spending in the economy is the basic determinant of the levels of income, output, employment, and prices. What were the fundamental factors affecting total spending during: (a) the 1920s; (b) the 1930s; (c) the 1940s; (d) the 1950s; (e) the 1960s?

14. It was forecast that with the end of World War II a decrease in government spending would cause the economy to have a major depression. Why did the depression fail to appear?

15. What reasons do economists offer to support their belief that the American economy will be more stable and less prone to depressions in the future than it has been in the past?

THE BACKGROUND
AND ANALYTICAL
TOOLS OF
EMPLOYMENT THEORY

Chapters 12 and 13 are really one chapter which has been divided into two parts and are probably the most important and crucial chapters in the first half of the text. They both concern the critical question of what determines the actual levels of employment and output the economy achieves in a given year.

Most of the material contained in the two chapters deals with the Keynesian theory or modern explanation of how employment and output are determined. This modern explanation is not the only possible explanation, however. It is with an alternative explanation called the classical theory of employment that the first part of Chapter 12 deals. The classical theory is described there for several reasons: to impress upon the student the fact that an alternative theory does exist; to examine the assumptions upon which the theory rests; to point out the weaknesses—both in fact and in logic—of the explanation; to provide an understanding of the reasons lying behind the "cures" for depression often advanced both in the past and at the present time; and, finally and most important, to enable the student to understand and evaluate the modern theory.

The outstanding thing about the classical theory is its conclusion that the economy will *automatically* function to produce the maximum output the economy is capable of producing and to provide employment for all those who are willing and able to work. Compare this with the conclusion drawn by the exponents of the modern theory that the economy functions in no such way, that both depression and inflation can prevail with no automatic tendency to be corrected, and that full employment and maximum output, when achieved, are accidental. Compare also the political philosophies of the proponents of the two theories. Those accepting the classical theory have advocated as little government interference with the economy as possible in the belief that such interference would only prevent the achievement of full employment and maximum output; adherents of the modern theory have proposed that government action is necessary to eliminate the periods of depression and periods of inflation that can occur.

In studying this part of Chapter 12 the student should focus his attention on the following: (1) the three specific assumptions listed on page 202 of the text which are used throughout Chapters 12 and 13 to simplify the explanation, (2) Say's Law, (3) how the classical economists were able to conclude that whatever part of their incomes people choose to save will nevertheless be spent, (4) the part played by flexible prices and flexible wages in ensuring that all workers will be employed and that the economy will produce its maximum output, and (5) why the classical theory is not a good explanation of how the economy actually operates.

The basic proposition contained in the modern theory is that the level of total spending (aggregate demand) in the economy determines the size of the economy's output (NNP) and the total amount of employment. The latter part of the chapter analyzes the economic factors which determine the two principal components of aggregate demand—consumption demand and investment demand. The student should pay particular attention to the relationships called the consumption schedule, the saving schedule, and their characteristics; and to the four propensity concepts as well as to the "nonincome" determinants of consumption and saving. Investment demand depends basically upon the expected profitability of investment; six factors which influence profit expectations are analyzed. Here the student will do well to know how changes in these factors will affect investment.

In the next chapter the tools and ideas developed and explained in Chapter 12 are put together to form a complete and coherent picture of how aggregate demand determines the level of NNP.

■ CHAPTER OUTLINE

1. The classical theory of employment reached the conclusion that the economy would automatically tend to employ its resources fully and produce a full-employment level of output; this conclusion was based on Say's Law and the assumption that prices and wages were flexible.

a. Say's Law stated that the production of goods produced an equal amount of income to buy these goods; changes in the rate of interest would ensure that all income not spent (that is, income saved) by consumers would be loaned to investors, who would spend these borrowed funds on capital goods.

b. If there were an excess supply of goods or an excess supply of labor (unemployment), prices and/or wages would fall until the excesses were eliminated and full employment and maximum output again prevailed in the economy.

c. Believing that capitalism would automatically ensure a full-employment level of output, the classical economists saw no need for government interference with the operation of the economy.

2. J. M. Keynes, in his *General Theory of Employment, Interest, and Money*, denied that flexible interest rates, prices, and wages would automatically promote full employment; he set forth the modern theory that there was nothing automatic about full employment and that both depression and inflation might prevail without any tendency existing for them to be self-correcting.

3. Aggregate output and employment are directly related to the level of total spending in the economy; to understand what determines the level of total spending at any time it is necessary to explain the factors that determine the levels of consumption and investment spending, the two principal components of total spending.

4. Consumption is the largest component of total spending; saving is income not spent for consumer goods.

a. Disposable income is the most important determinant of both consumption and saving; the relationships between income and consumption and between income and saving are both direct (positive) ones.

b. The consumption schedule shows the amounts that households will spend for consumer goods at various levels of income, and the saving schedule shows the amounts they will save.

c. The average propensities to consume and to save and the marginal propensities to consume and to save can be computed from the consumption and saving schedules.

d. In addition to income, there are several other important determinants of consumption and saving; changes in these nonincome determinants will cause the consumption and saving schedules to change. A change in the amount consumed (or saved) is not the same thing as a change in the consumption (or saving) schedule.

5. The most important determinant of the level of investment in the economy is the net profit which business expects to realize from the purchase of additional capital goods. At least six factors influence the net profit expectations of business, and because these factors are subject to sudden and rapid change the investment schedule is highly unstable.

■ IMPORTANT TERMS

Classical theory of employment	Marginal propensity to consume
Say's Law	Marginal propensity to save
Rate of interest	Change in amount consumed
Money market	
Saving	Change in amount saved
Investment	
Price-wage flexibility	Change in the consumption schedule
Consumption schedule	Change in the saving schedule
Saving schedule	
Average propensity to consume	Nonincome determinants of consumptions and saving
Average propensity to save	

■ FILL-IN QUESTIONS

1. Three "simplifying assumptions" used throughout most of the chapter are that the economy is a _____,
that all saving is _____ saving, and that the government _____ _____ _____.
A consequence of these assumptions is that
_____ = _____ = _____ = _____

2. According to Say's Law, the production of goods and services creates an equal _____
_____

3. Changes in _____,
according to the classical economists, ensure that what is not spent on consumer goods is spent on capital goods.

4. In the classical theory, if saving is greater than investment the rate of interest will _____
_____
and if investment is greater than saving it will
_____;
the rate of interest will have a tendency to __

where saving and investment are equal.

5. Full employment, in the classical theory, was assured by _____
and _____
_____

6. According to the classical way of thinking, if the interest rate did not equate saving and investment, and if total output exceeded the level of spending, prices in the output
markets would tend to _____
because of competition among business firms; this would make production unprofitable and
temporarily cause _____
in resource markets; but competition among resource suppliers would tend to drive resource prices _____
and _____
employment. This process would continue until _____

7. Keynes, in attacking the classical theory of employment, contended that price-wage flexibility would not guarantee full employment, first, because _____
_____
and, second, because wage reductions would
simply lead to _____,
_____,
and _____

8. Reasoning that if a price and wage rate reduction would increase the output and employment of an individual firm, then a general reduction in prices and wages will increase output and employment in the economy as a
whole involves the fallacy called _____
_____

9. According to the modern theory of employment, saving and investment are done by
_____
and for _____

10. Keynes argued that _____
is the most important determinant of the level
of saving in the economy and that saving will

_____

as this determinant increases in size.

11. The largest single component of total

spending is _____
spending.

12. As disposable income falls, the average

propensity to consume will _____

and the average propensity to save will _____

_____

13. The most important determinants of consumption spending, other than the level of disposable income, are:

a. _____

b. _____

c. _____

d. _____

e. _____

f. _____

14. A change in the consumption (or saving)

schedule means that _____

_____

while a change in the amount consumed (or

saved) means that _____

_____

15. Fundamentally, it is _____

_____

which determines the level of investment, investment being defined as spending for addi-

tional _____

16. Six factors which affect profit expectations and investment demand are:

a. _____

b. _____

c. _____

d. _____

e. _____

f. _____

17. The consumption schedule and the saving schedule tend to be (stable or unstable)

_____

while investment demand tends to be _____

_____

18. The demand for new capital goods tends

to be unstable because of the _____

of capital goods, the _____ of

innovation, and the _____ of actual
and expected profits.

■ PROBLEMS AND PROJECTS

1. Suppose that the amounts savers plan to save at various rates of interest and the amounts investors plan to invest at various rates of interest are as given in the table below.

Amount savers plan to save	Rate of interest, %	Amounts investors plan to invest
$60	8	$40
55	7	45
50	6	50
45	5	55
40	4	60
35	3	65
30	2	70
25	1	75
20	0	80

a. What rate of interest will prevail in the

economy? _____%

How much will be saved? $_____

How much will be invested? $_____
 b. If the saving schedule should:
 (1) increase, the rate of interest would ____

_____,

saving would _____,

and investment would _____

(2) decrease, the rate of interest would _____

_____ ,

saving would _____ ,

and investment would _____

c. If the investment schedule should:

(1) increase, the rate of interest would _____

_____ ,

saving would _____ ,

and investment would _____

(2) decrease, the rate of interest would _____

_____ ,

saving would _____ ,

and investment would _____

d. According to modern economists:

(1) A(n) _____

in _____

would cause the saving schedule to increase.

(2) A(n) _____

in _____

would cause the saving schedule to decrease.

e. If the saving and investment schedules were as given in the table below, answer the following questions.

(1) What rate of interest would ensure the

equality of saving and investment? _____

_____

(2) Why is it not possible for this rate of

Amount savers plan to save	Rate of interest, %	Amounts investors plan to invest
$20	9	$ 1
19	8	2
18	7	3
17	6	4
16	5	5
15	4	6
14	3	7
13	2	8
12	1	9
11	0	10

interest to prevail? _____

_____

(3) Under what economic conditions might such saving and investment schedules exist?

_____

(4) Either a(n) _____

in the saving schedule or a(n) _____
in the investment schedule would eliminate these unusual saving and investment conditions.

2. On page 80 is a consumption schedule. Assume taxes and transfer payments are zero.

a. Compute saving, the average propensity to consume, and the average propensity to save for each of the eight levels of NNP.

b. Compute the marginal propensity to consume and the marginal propensity to save for each of the seven changes in NNP.

c. Graph the consumption schedule, the saving schedule, and the 45° line.

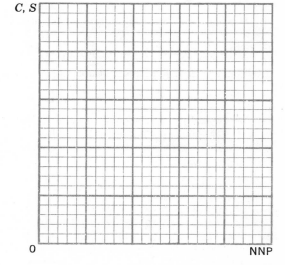

C, S

0   NNP

3. Indicate in the space to the right of each of the following events whether the event will tend to increase (+) or decrease (−) the saving schedule.

a. Development of consumer expectations

that prices will be higher in the future _____

b. Gradual shrinkage in the stock of durable

goods owned by consumers   _____

c. Increase in the volume of consumer in-

debtedness   _____

NNP	C	S	APC, %	APS, %	MPC, %	MPS, %
$350	$351	-1	100.3	___		
360	360	0	100	___	90	10
370	369	1	___	___	90	90
380	377	3	___	___	80	20
390	385	5	___	___	80	20
400	392	8	___	___	70	30
410	399	11	___	___	70	30
420	405	15	___	___	60	40

d. Growing belief that disposable income will be lower in the future _____

e. Rumors that a current shortage of consumer goods will soon disappear _____

f. Rise in the actual level of disposable income _____

g. A build-up in the dollar size of liquid assets owned by consumers _____

h. Development of a belief by consumers that the Federal government can and will prevent depressions in the future _____

4. Indicate in the space to the right of each of the following events whether the event would tend to increase (+) or decrease (−) the level of investment demand.

a. Rising stock market prices _____

b. Decrease in interest rates _____

c. Development of expectations by businessmen that business taxes will be higher in the future _____

d. Step-up in the rates at which new products and new production processes are being introduced _____

e. Business belief that wage rates may be lower in the future _____

f. A mild recession _____

g. A belief that business is "too good" and the economy is due for a period of "slow" consumer demand _____

h. Rising costs in the construction industry

i. A rapid increase in the size of the economy's population _____

j. A period of a high level of investment spending which has resulted in productive capacity in excess of the current demand for goods and services _____

■ SELF-TEST

Circle the T if the statement is true, the F if it is false.

1. Say's Law states that demand for goods and services creates an equal supply of goods and services. **T F**

2. In the classical theory, if saving exceeds investment the rate of interest will rise until saving and investment are equal. **T F**

3. According to the classical economists involuntary unemployment is impossible. **T F**

4. The level of saving in the economy depends primarily upon the level of disposable income, while investment spending is determined by the net profit which business expects to receive on new investments. **T F**

5. The consumption schedule which is employed as an analytical tool is also a historical record of the relationship of consumption to disposable income. **T F**

6. Statistics show and economists agree that the marginal propensity to consume falls and the marginal propensity to save rises as disposable income rises. **T F**

7. Both the consumption schedule and the saving schedule tend to be relatively stable over time. **T F**

8. If business adds to its stock of capital goods by financing investment out of undistributed profits, the rate of interest is not a consideration in determining the level of investment spending. **T F**

Underscore the letter that corresponds to the best answer.

1. If government neither taxes nor spends, and all saving done in the economy is personal saving: (a) gross national product equals net national product; (b) gross national product equals national income; (c) net national product equals disposable income; (d) disposable income equals personal consumption expenditures.

2. Which of the following could *not* be called a classical economist? (a) John Maynard Keynes; (b) J. B. Say; (c) A. C. Pigou; (d) John Stuart Mill.

3. If the rate of interest did not equate saving and investment and total output was greater than total spending, the classical economists argued, competition would tend to force: (a) product and resource prices down; (b) product prices up and resource prices down; (c) product prices up and resource prices up; (d) product prices down and resource prices up.

4. Which of the following is *not* involved in Keynes's criticism of the classical theory of employment? (a) a reduction in wage rates will lead only to a reduction in total spending, not to an increase in employment; (b) investment spending is not influenced by the rate of interest; (c) prices and wages are simply not flexible downward in modern capitalistic economies; (d) saving in modern economies depends largely upon the level of disposable income and is little influenced by the rate of interest.

5. If consumption spending increases from $358 to $367 billion when disposable income increases from $412 to $427 billion, it can be concluded that the marginal propensity to consume is: (a) 0.4; (b) 0.6; (c) 0.8; (d) 0.9.

6. If when disposable income is $375 billion

the average propensity to consume is 0.8, it can be concluded that: (a) the marginal propensity to consume is also 0.8; (b) consumption is $325 billion; (c) saving is $75 billion; (d) the marginal propensity to save is 0.2.

7. Which of the following would *not* cause the consumption schedule to increase (that is, cause the consumption curve to rise)? (a) a decrease in consumers' stocks of durable goods; (b) an increase in consumers' ownership of liquid assets; (c) a decrease in the amount of consumers' indebtedness; (d) an increase in the income received by consumers.

8. A decrease in the level of investment spending would be a consequence of: (a) a decline in the rate of interest; (b) a decline in the level of wages paid; (c) a decline in business taxes; (d) a decline in stock market prices.

■ DISCUSSION QUESTIONS

1. According to the classical economists, what level of employment would tend to prevail in the economy? On what two basic assumptions did their analysis of the level of employment rest?

2. What is Say's Law? How were the classical economists able to reason that whatever is saved is spent?

3. In the classical analysis Say's Law made it certain that whatever was produced would be sold. How did flexible prices, flexible wages, and competition drive the economy to full employment and maximum output?

4. On what grounds did J. M. Keynes argue that flexible interest rates would not ensure the operation of Say's Law? What were his reasons for asserting that flexible prices and wages would not ensure full employment?

5. "Savers and investors are largely different groups and are motivated by different factors." Explain in detail who these groups are and what motivates them. Does the rate of interest play any role in determining saving and investment?

6. Explain briefly how the average propensity to consume and the average propensity to save vary as disposable income varies. Why do APC and APS behave this way? What happens to consumption and saving as disposable income varies?

7. Why do the sum of the APC and the APS and the sum of the MPC and the MPS always equal exactly one?

8. Explain briefly and explicitly *how* changes in the six nonincome determinants will affect the consumption schedule and the saving schedule and *why* such changes will affect consumption and saving in the way you have indicated.

9. Explain briefly and explicitly *how* changes in the six determinants of profit expectations will affect investment demand and *why*.

10. Why does the level of investment demand tend to be highly unstable?

THE EQUILIBRIUM LEVELS OF OUTPUT, EMPLOYMENT, AND INCOME

Chapter 13 explains in simple terms what determines the equilibrium level of NNP—the actual size of the NNP which will tend to be produced in the economy. The student *must* understand this chapter if he is to acquire an understanding of what causes NNP to rise and fall; of what causes unemployment, depression, inflation, and prosperity; and of what can be done to prevent recession and inflation and to foster price stability, full employment, and economic growth.

The equilibrium level of NNP is determined by the level of total spending or *aggregate demand* in the economy. In Chapter 12, the two principal components of aggregate demand, consumption demand and investment demand, were analyzed. In this chapter the equilibrium level of NNP is explained with both tables and graphs, first by using the aggregate demand–aggregate supply approach and then by employing the saving-investment approach. These two approaches are complementary and are simply two different ways of analyzing the same process and of reaching the same conclusions. For each approach it is important for the student to know, given the consumption (or saving) schedule and the level of investment demand, *what* NNP will tend to be produced and *why* this will be the NNP which will be produced.

It is also important that the student understand the significant distinctions between intended (planned) saving and actual (realized) saving; and between intended (planned) investment and actual (realized) investment. Actual saving is always equal to actual investment because both are defined in exactly the same way: the output of the economy minus its consumption. Intended saving and intended investment are not, however, equal by definition; they are equal only when NNP is at its equilibrium level. When NNP is *not* at its equilibrium level, intended saving and intended investment are *not* equal; but actual saving and investment will, as always, be equal because actual investment includes unintended (or unplanned) investment. Remember: Equilibrium NNP is achieved when *intended* saving and investment—*not actual* saving and investment—are equal.

The consumption (and the saving) schedule and investment demand—especially the latter —are subject to change, and when they change NNP will also change. The relationship between a change in investment (or a change in the consumption schedule) and a change in NNP is called the multiplier. Three things to note here are: *how* the multiplier is defined, *why* there is a multiplier effect, and upon *what* the size of the multiplier depends. Because of the multiplier, the paradoxical consequence of an attempt by the economy to save more is either no increase or a decrease in the level of saving in the economy. The explanation of this paradox will be evident to the student when he understands equilibrium NNP and the multiplier effect.

The final portion of the chapter emphasizes

that equilibrium NNP is not necessarily the NNP at which full employment is achieved without the creation of inflationary pressures. Equilibrium NNP may be greater or less than full-employment NNP: if it is greater there is an inflationary gap, and if it is less there exists a deflationary gap. The next chapter deals with the fiscal policies that can be employed by government to eliminate these gaps. Chapter 13 has purposely ignored government and assumed an economy in which government neither taxes nor spends. But Chapter 14 does not ignore the role of government in the economy and discusses fiscal policies and their effects upon equilibrium NNP.

■ CHAPTER OUTLINE

1. Two alternative approaches are used to explain what level of NNP will tend to prevail in the economy (that is, will be the equilibrium NNP). Both approaches yield the same answer. Using the aggregate demand—aggregate supply approach, equilibrium NNP will be that NNP at which aggregate quantity demanded (planned consumption + planned investment) equals aggregate quantity supplied (NNP or planned consumption + planned saving).

2. Using the saving-investment approach, equilibrium NNP will be that NNP at which planned saving and planned investment are equal.

3. The saving and investment schedules indicate what consumers and investors *plan* to do; if planned saving and planned investment are not equal, NNP will change until they become equal. *Realized* saving and investment are always equal.

4. Changes in the investment schedule or in the consumption and saving schedules will cause the equilibrium level of NNP to change.
    a. If investment changes, NNP will change in the same direction by an amount greater than the change in investment; this is called the multiplier effect; the size of the simple multiplier depends upon the size of the marginal propensity to save.
    b. The paradox of thrift is that an increase in the saving schedule results in no increase, and may result in a decrease, in saving; the

decrease in the saving schedule causes a multiple contraction in NNP and at the lower NNP the same amount or even less saving takes place.

5. The equilibrium level of NNP may turn out to be an equilibrium at less than full employment, at full employment with stable prices, or at full employment with inflation.
    a. If the equilibrium NNP is *less* than the NNP consistent with full employment and stable prices, there exists a deflation gap; the size of the deflationary gap equals the amount by which aggregate demand must increase to increase *real* equilibrium NNP to full-employment NNP without creating inflation.
    b. If equilibrium NNP is *greater* than the NNP consistent with full employment and stable prices, there is an inflationary gap. The size of the inflationary gap equals the amount by which aggregate demand must decrease to decrease *money* NNP without creating unemployment.

■ IMPORTANT TERMS

Aggregate demand	Actual (realized) saving
Aggregate supply	
Aggregate quantity demanded	Actual (realized) investment
Aggregate quantity supplied	Equilibrium level of NNP
Aggregate demand—aggregate supply approach	Multiplier effect
	Multiplier
Saving-investment approach	Complex multiplier
	Simple multiplier
Planned (intended) saving	Paradox of thrift
	Supermultiplier
Planned (intended) investment	Deflationary gap
	Inflationary gap

■ FILL-IN QUESTIONS

1. Two complementary approaches which are employed to explain the equilibrium level of

output, employment, and income are the _____

_____

approach and the _____
approach.

2. In the modern theory of employment, income, employment, and output depend directly upon the level of _____ in the economy.

3. Assuming a governmentless economy, the equilibrium level of NNP is that NNP at which

NNP equals _____

plus _____ ;

and the NNP at which _____

equals _____

4. If:

a. Aggregate quantity demanded is greater than aggregate quantity supplied, planned

saving is _____

planned investment, and NNP will tend to __

_____

b. Aggregate quantity demanded is less than aggregate quantity supplied, planned saving is

_____

planned investment, and NNP will tend to __

_____

c. Aggregate quantity demanded is equal to aggregate quantity supplied, planned saving is

_____

planned investment, and NNP will tend to __

_____

5. At every level of NNP _____

saving and _____ investment are equal. But if planned investment is greater than planned saving by $10, NNP will tend to

_____

by an amount _____ $10; and if planned saving is greater than planned investment by $5, NNP will tend to

_____

by _____

6. When full employment has been achieved, if aggregate quantity demanded is greater than aggregate quantity supplied, planned in-

vestment will be _____

planned saving, prices will tend to _____ ,

output to _____ ,

income to _____ ,

employment to _____ ,

and _____
will be the result.

7. The value of the simple multiplier equals

_____

or _____ .
The fact that NNP will increase by more than an increase in investment demand is due to

two facts: _____

and _____

8. If the economy decides to save more (consume less) at every level of NNP, the equilib-

rium NNP will _____
and the equilibrium level of saving in the

economy will either _____

or _____ ;
this consequence of an increased desire to

save is called the _____

9. A deflationary gap exists when equilibrium

NNP is (greater, less) _____
than the full-employment NNP; to bring NNP to the full-employment level, aggregate de-

mand must _____ by an amount equal to the difference between equilibrium

and full-employment NNP divided by _____

_____

10. When equilibrium money NNP is greater than the full-employment NNP at which prices

are stable, there is a(n) _____

_____ gap; to eliminate this gap

_____ must decrease by

_____

divided by the multiplier.

■ PROBLEMS AND PROJECTS

NNP	C	S	I	C + I
$300	$290	$ 10	$ 22	$ 312
310	298	12	22	320
320	306	14	22	328
330	314	16	22	336
340	322	18	22	344
350	330	20	22	352
360	338	22	22	360
370	346	24	22	368
380	354	26	22	376
390	362	28	22	384
400	370	30	22	392

1. The table at the right shows consumption demand at various levels of NNP. Assume taxes and government spending are zero and that investment demand is $22.

   a. Complete the saving, investment, and consumption-plus-investment columns.

   b. The equilibrium level of NNP will be

$ _____ 360 _____

   c. The marginal propensity to consume is

_____ .80 _____,

and the marginal propensity to save is __ .20 __

   d. The value of the simple multiplier is __ 5 __
   e. If investment demand should increase by

$3, NNP would increase by $__ 15 __
   f. If investment demand should decrease by

$4, NNP would decrease by $__ 20 __

   g.
   (1) On the graph below, plot C, C + I, and aggregate supply, and indicate the equilibrium NNP.

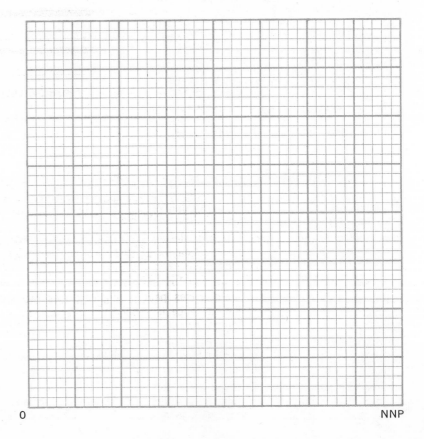

0   NNP

(2) On the graph below, plot S and I and indicate the equilibrium NNP.

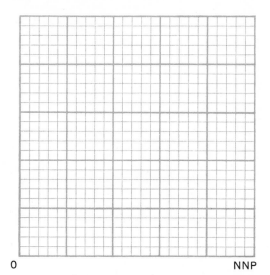

0   NNP

2. Assume the marginal propensity to consume is 0.8 and the change in investment demand is $10. Complete the table below, modeled after Table 13–2 in the textbook.

3. In the next column are a saving schedule and two investment schedules—one (I_a) indicating that investment spending is constant and the other (I_i) indicating that the investment demand schedule is upsloping.

a. Using either investment schedule, the equilibrium NNP is $_____ and saving is $_____

b. The marginal propensity to save is _____ and the simple multiplier is _____

NNP	S	I_a	I_i
$300	$ 5	$15	$10
310	7	15	11
320	9	15	12
330	11	15	13
340	13	15	14
350	15	15	15
360	17	15	16
370	19	15	17
380	21	15	18
390	23	15	19
400	25	15	20

c. A $2 rise in the I_a schedule will cause NNP to rise by $_____, while a $2 rise in the level of the I_i schedule will cause NNP to rise by $_____

d. The value of the supermultiplier in the second case is, therefore, _____

e. Use the two investment schedules given in the table and assume a $2 increase in the saving schedule in the table—that is, planned saving at every NNP increases by $2.

(1) If the investment schedule is I_a, equilibrium NNP will _____ to $_____ and at this NNP saving will be $_____

(2) If the investment schedule is I_i, equilibrium NNP will _____ to $_____ and at this NNP saving will be $_____

(3) The effect of the increase in the saving schedule is to _____ equilibrium NNP and either to _____ or to _____ saving; this is called the _____

	Change in income	Change in consumption	Change in saving
Increase in investment of $10	+ 10	_____	_____
Second round	_____	_____	_____
Third round	_____	_____	_____
Fourth round	_____	_____	_____
Fifth round	_____	_____	_____
All other rounds	_____	_____	_____
Totals	_____	_____	_____

(4) The amount by which NNP changes depends upon the size of the change in the saving schedule and the size of _____

4. In the table below are consumption and saving schedules. Assume that the level of NNP at which full employment without inflation is achieved is $590.

NNP	C	S
$550	$520	$30
560	526	34
570	532	38
580	538	42
590	544	46
600	550	50
610	556	54
620	562	58
630	568	62

a. The value of the multiplier is _____
b. If investment demand is $58, equilibrium

NNP is $_____ and exceeds the full-employment noninflationary NNP by

$_____. There is a(n) _____

gap of $_____
c. If investment demand is $38, equilibrium

NNP is $_____ and is less than

full-employment NNP by $_____.

There is a(n) _____

gap of $_____

■ SELF-TEST

Circle the T if the statement is true, the F if it is false.

1. Both the saving schedule and the investment schedule are schedules of plans rather than schedules of saving and investment actually realized.   T   F

2. The larger the marginal propensity to consume, the larger the size of the multiplier.   T   F

3. Actual saving at any level of NNP equals planned investment plus unintended investment (or minus unintended disinvestment).   T   F

4. The existence of a deflationary gap in the economy is characterized by the full employment of labor.   T   F

The following two questions are based on the data supplied for multiple-choice questions 1 and 2.

5. If saving at each level of NNP decreased by $5 and if investment demand remained constant at $24, equilibrium NNP would decrease by $16⅔ and saving in the economy would decrease by $5.   T   F

6. If consumption spending at each level of NNP increased by $10, the equilibrium level of NNP would tend to rise by $30.   T   F

7. If NNP were to decline by $40, consumers would probably reduce their consumption expenditures by an amount less than $40.   T   F

8. Realized saving and realized investment are always equal.   T   F

Underscore the letter that corresponds to the best answer.

Questions 1 and 2 below, as well as true-false questions 5 and 6, are based on the following consumption schedule.

NNP	C
$200	$200
240	228
280	256
320	284
360	312
400	340
440	368
480	396

1. If investment demand is $60, the equilibrium level of NNP will be: (a) $320; (b) $360; (c) $400; (d) $440.

2. If investment demand were to increase by $5, NNP would increase by: (a) $5; (b) $7½; (c) $15; (d) $16⅔.

3. If the value of the marginal propensity to consume is 0.6 and NNP falls by $25, this was caused by a decrease in aggregate demand of: (a) $10; (b) $15; (c) $16⅔; (d) $20.

4. The paradox of thrift means that: (a) an increase in saving lowers the level of NNP; (b) an increase in the average propensity to save lowers or leaves unchanged the level of savings; (c) an increase in the marginal propensity to save lowers the value of the multiplier; (d) an increase in NNP increases investment demand.

5. If the marginal propensity to consume is 0.6⅔ and if both investment demand and the saving schedule increase by $25, NNP will: (a) increase by $75; (b) not change; (c) decrease by $75; (d) increase by $25.

6. If NNP is $275 billion, consumption $250 billion, and investment $20 billion, NNP: (a) will tend to remain constant; (b) will tend to increase; (c) will tend to decrease; (d) equals aggregate demand.

7. If planned saving is greater than planned investment: (a) businesses will be motivated to increase their investments; (b) aggregate quantity demanded will be greater than aggregate quantity supplied; (c) NNP will be greater than planned investment plus planned consumption; (d) realized saving will tend to increase.

8. To eliminate an inflationary gap of $50 in an economy in which the marginal propensity to save is 0.1 it will be necessary to: (a) decrease aggregate demand by $50; (b) decrease aggregate demand by $5; (c) increase aggregate demand by $50; (d) increase aggregate demand by $5.

■ DISCUSSION QUESTIONS

1. Explain why the equilibrium level of NNP is that level of NNP at which NNP equals aggregate demand and at which saving equals investment. What will cause NNP to rise if it is below this level and what will cause it to fall if it is above this level?

2. What is meant by "the distinction between saving and investment plans or intentions and the actual amounts which households manage to save and businesses to invest"? Are the saving schedule and the investment schedule planned or realized saving and investment? What adjustment causes planned and realized saving and investment to become equal?

3. What is the multiplier effect? Why does there tend to be a multiplier effect (that is, on what basic economic facts does the multiplier effect depend)? What determines how large the simple multiplier effect will be?

4. What is meant by the paradox of thrift? When would an increase in the saving schedule cause saving (at equilibrium) to decrease?

5. What relationship is there between the equilibrium level of NNP and the level of NNP at which full employment without inflation is achieved?

6. Explain what is meant by a deflationary gap and an inflationary gap. What economic conditions are present in the economy when each of these gaps exists? How is the size of each of these gaps measured?

THE ECONOMICS OF FISCAL POLICY

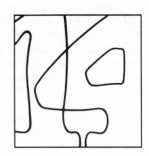

Chapter 14 is really a continuation of the two preceding chapters and is concerned with the chief practical application of the principles discussed in those chapters. It is worth recalling that principles of economics are generalizations about the way the economy works— *how* and *why* the economic system functions —and that these principles are studied in order that policies may be devised to solve real problems. Over the past one-hundred years or so, the most difficult problems which have confronted the economy have been those associated with the business cycle. Knowing the problems and what determines the level of output, income, and employment in the economy, the economist is in a position to offer advice on how the economy can be "controlled" to bring about full employment, maximum output, and stable prices—to suggest policies designed to eliminate deflationary and inflationary gaps.

Government spending and taxation have a strong influence on output, employment, and prices. Federal policies with respect to expenditures (both for goods and services and for transfer payments) and taxation, designed to affect total production and employment and the price level, are fiscal policies. These variables, of course, are not affected solely by fiscal measures. The central banks of the United States (the Federal Reserve Banks) are also in a position to affect the economy's operation by applying monetary measures (monetary policy), but the selection and application of monetary policies is a topic which

must await analysis of the effect of banks on the operation of the economy (Chapters 16, 17, 18).

In the opening section of Chapter 14 the author points out that Congress in the Employment Act of 1946 committed the Federal government to using fiscal (and monetary) policy to achieve a trio of economic goals— economic growth, stable prices, and full employment. This act also established the Council of Economic Advisors to advise the President and the Joint Economic Committee to advise Congress on matters pertaining to national economic policy.

The second major section of the chapter introduces government taxing and spending into our analysis of equilibrium NNP. It is important to note that government spending for goods and services adds to aggregate demand and that taxation reduces the disposable income of consumers, thereby reducing both the amount of consumption and the amount of saving that will take place at any level of NNP. Both "approaches" are again employed, and the student is again warned that he must know *what* NNP will tend to be produced and *why*. Special attention should be directed to the exact effect taxes have upon the consumption and saving schedules and the multiplier effects of changes in government spending and taxes.

An important point needs to be made here. Fiscal policy affects aggregate demand either directly or indirectly. Changes in government spending for goods and services alter aggregate demand directly by the same amount and in the same direction as the changes in government spending and have a multiplier effect on NNP. Changes in taxes alter aggregate demand indirectly, change the consumption schedule by an amount equal to the change in taxes times the marginal propensity to consume (which is less than 1.0), and change it in the opposite direction. This change in the consumption schedule then has a multiplier effect on NNP.

In addition to this, what should the student learn from Chapter 14? He should be aware (1) that there are two broad categories of fiscal policy, nondiscretionary and discretionary, the meaning of each, and the differences between them; (2) that fiscal policy can be either expansionary or contractionary, what is meant by each, and when each is used; (3) that the kind (progressive, proportional, or regressive) of tax system the economy uses determines how much built-in stability there will be; (4) that fiscal policy determines both the slope and location of the "budget line" and thereby affects the "rate of utilization" and the size of the Federal government's surplus or deficit; (5) that the fiscal policy and budget line needed to bring about full employment change as potential GNP grows; (6) that if the government "runs" a deficit or a surplus, there are several ways of financing the deficit or disposing of the surplus, and that the way the deficit or surplus is handled can affect the economy's operation almost as much as the size of the deficit or surplus and the level of expenditures and taxes at which the deficit or surplus is incurred; and (7) that there are quite a few specific problems connected with the actual application of fiscal policy and what some of the most important of these problems are.

■ CHAPTER OUTLINE

1. Fiscal policy is the manipulation by the Federal government of its expenditures and tax receipts in order to affect total spending in the economy (and thereby to affect growth, employment, and prices). The Employment Act of 1946 set the goals of American fiscal policy and provided for a Council of Economic Advisors to the President.

2. Discretionary fiscal policy involves congressional changes in tax rates and expenditure programs in order to eliminate deflationary and inflationary gaps.

a. Government expenditures for goods and services add to aggregate demand and increase equilibrium NNP; an increase in these expenditures has a multiplier effect upon equilibrium NNP.

b. Taxes decrease planned consumption and aggregate demand by the amount of the tax times the MPC; an increase in taxes thus decreases equilibrium NNP by a multiplier which is equal to MPC/MPS.

c. If the government both taxes and spends, equilibrium NNP will be the NNP at which

(1) Aggregate quantity demanded (planned consumption + planned investment + government spending for goods and services) equals aggregate quantity supplied (NNP or planned consumption + planned saving + net taxes).

(2) Planned investment + government spending for goods and services equals planned saving + net taxes.

d. Equal increases (decreases) in taxes and in government expenditures increase (decrease) equilibrium NNP by the amount of the change in taxes (or in expenditures).

e. The elimination of the inflationary (deflationary) gap is accomplished by contractionary (expansionary) fiscal policy and by increasing (decreasing) taxes, decreasing (increasing) expenditures, and incurring budget surpluses (deficits).

3. Nondiscretionary fiscal policy is a "built-in" stabilizer of the economy.

a. Tax collections in the American economy increase (decrease) without congressional action when the NNP rises (falls).

b. Such transfer payments as unemployment compensation and such subsidies as those paid to farmers decrease (increase) when the NNP rises (falls).

c. These automatic changes in tax collections and government disbursements, by lessening the size of the marginal propensity to consume and the multiplier, reduce fluctuations in the NNP.

4. A progressive tax system gives the economy more stability than a proportional tax system; and a regressive tax system has no built-in stability.

5. Discretionary and nondiscretionary fiscal

policy and the differences between them are better understood with the help of budget lines.

a. The 1964 reduction in personal and corporate income tax rates moved the budget line downward and thereby increased the utilization rate, tax collections, and the rate of economic growth.

b. But when the economy is growing, the size of its potential real GNP at full employment is continually increasing. Given the tax rates and expenditure programs of the Federal government, the budget surplus it would incur at full employment is also constantly increasing and has a progressively contractionary effect upon the economy.

6. Discretionary fiscal policy is needed if growth, employment, and prices are to be affected by fiscal policy because nondiscretionary fiscal policy is not strong enough by itself to ensure full employment, economic growth, and stable prices.

a. In addition to the size of the deficit or surplus, the manner in which the government finances its deficit or disposes of its surplus affects the level of total spending in the economy.

b. And the types of taxes and the types of expenditures upon which the government relies to operate its fiscal policy help to determine the effectiveness of that fiscal policy in promoting economic stability.

7. Certain other specific complications arise in enacting and applying fiscal policy, and the degree of success achieved in solving these problems determines whether fiscal policy will actually be employed and whether it will be appropriate and effective.

■ IMPORTANT TERMS

Fiscal policy

Employment Act of 1946

Council of Economic Advisors

Joint Economic Committee

Nondiscretionary fiscal policy

Discretionary fiscal policy

Built-in stability

Balanced-budget multiplier

Expansionary fiscal policy

Contractionary fiscal policy

Budget line

Utilization rate

Full-employment surplus

Fiscal drag

■ FILL-IN QUESTIONS

1. The use of monetary and fiscal policy to reduce inflationary and deflationary gaps became national economic policy in the _____

_____ Act of _____.

This act also established the _____

to the President and the _____ in Congress.

2. In an economy in which government both taxes and spends, the equilibrium level of NNP is that NNP at which NNP is equal to

_____

plus _____

plus _____ ;

or where _____

plus _____

equals _____

plus _____

3. Taxes tend to reduce consumption demand at each level of NNP by an amount equal to the taxes multiplied by the _____

_____ ;

saving will decrease by an amount equal to

the taxes multiplied by the _____

_____

4. Equal reductions in taxes and government

spending will _____

NNP by an amount equal to _____

5. In order to increase NNP during a period

of depression, taxes should be _____

and government expenditures _____ ;
to decrease NNP during a period of inflation,

taxes should be _____

and government expenditures _____
6. If fiscal policy is to have a countercyclical

effect, a budget _____
should be incurred during a depression and a

budget _____ during inflation.

7. If the MPS were 0.2, a $1 billion increase in government expenditures for goods and services would increase NNP by $_____ billion; but a $1 billion tax reduction would increase NNP by only $_____ billion.

8. If a nondiscretionary fiscal policy is employed, tax *rates and structures* and expenditure *programs* are not changed by Congress but _____ and _____ do change to offset the business cycle.

9. If an economy is to have built-in stability, tax receipts should _____ as NNP rises and _____ as NNP falls; government expenditures should

_____ as NNP rises and _____ as NNP falls.

10. The two principal means available to the Federal government for financing budget deficits are _____ and _____; the (former, latter) _____ is least contractionary because _____

_____

11. There are two reasons for the belief that public works expenditures have a stronger expansionary effect than transfer payments; they are:

a. _____

b. _____

12. Most, though not all, economists would agree that a $5 billion increase in a (progressive, regressive) _____ would be the *least* deflationary.

13. What are the three principal reasons why there is a problem of timing in the use of discretionary fiscal policy?

a. _____

b. _____

c. _____

14. A (progressive, regressive, proportional) _____ tax system does the most to promote built-in stability, while a _____ _____ does nothing to bring about built-in stability.

15. The reduction in 1964 of personal and corporate income tax rates moved the budget line _____-ward and _____ both the full-employment surplus and the amount of fiscal drag.

■ PROBLEMS AND PROJECTS

1. On page 94 is a consumption function.
   a. Assume the government levies $10 in taxes at all levels of NNP and the marginal propensity to consume remains constant. Compute the new consumption column (C'), the saving column (S'), and the saving plus taxes column (S' + T) at each of the 13 levels of NNP.
   b. Suppose that investment demand is $15 and government spending for goods and services is $20. Complete the investment-plus-government-spending column (I + G) and the consumption-plus-investment-plus-government-spending column (C' + I + G).
   c. On the graphs on the next two pages plot:
   (1) C', I + G and C' + I + G, and aggregate supply. Show the equilibrium NNP.
   (2) S' + T and I + G. Show the equilibrium NNP.
   d. The equilibrium level of NNP will be $_____
   e. If taxes remained at $10 and government expenditures rose by $10, NNP would rise by $_____
   f. If government expenditures remained at $20 and taxes increased by $10, NNP would fall by $_____
(To answer the question above it is not necessary to recompute C, S, S + T, and C + I + G. Use the multipliers.)
   g. The effect of a $10 increase in taxes *and* a $10 increase in government spending is to _____ NNP by an amount equal to $_____

NNP	C	C'	S'	S' + T	I + G	C' + I + G
$350	$325	——	——	——	——	——
360	334	——	——	——	——	——
370	343	——	——	——	——	——
380	352	——	——	——	——	——
390	361	——	——	——	——	——
400	370	——	——	——	——	——
410	379	——	——	——	——	——
420	388	——	——	——	——	——
430	397	——	——	——	——	——
440	406	——	——	——	——	——
450	415	——	——	——	——	——
460	424	——	——	——	——	——
470	433	——	——	——	——	——

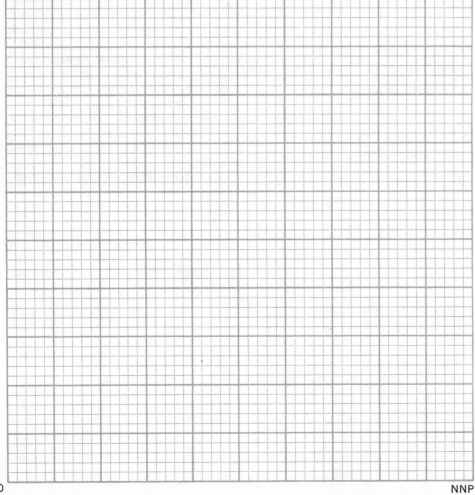

0

NNP

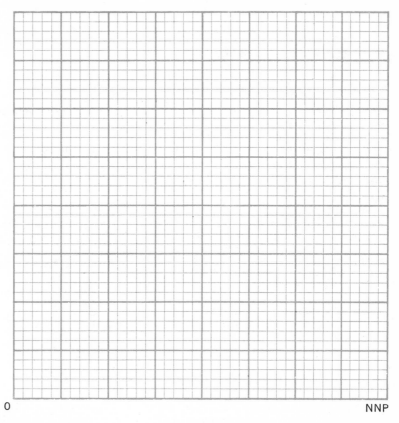

0   NNP

2. Assume that the government's budget is initially balanced and that the marginal propensity to save is 0.2.

a. If the government increases its expenditures for goods and services by $20 and its taxes by $10, NNP will increase by $_____

b. If the government increases its expenditures for goods and services by $30 and its taxes by $20, NNP will increase by $_____

c. Although the size of the budget deficit is $10 in both (a) and (b) above, the expansionary effect of this deficit was greater in the (first, second) _____ case.

d. If the government decreases its expenditures for goods and services by $10 and its taxes by $5, NNP will decrease by $_____

e. If the government decreases its expenditures for goods and services by $25 and its taxes by $20, NNP will decrease by $_____

f. Although the size of the budget surplus is $5 in both (d) and (e) above, the deflationary effect of this surplus was greater in the (first, second) _____ case.

3. Indicate in the space to the right of each of the following the effect—increase (+), decrease (−), or no effect (0)—on money NNP, output, and employment.

a. The economy is at less than full employment and:

(1) Government reduces its expenditures for goods and services ____ ____ ____

(2) Government reduces net taxes

____ ____ ____

(3) Investment increases

____ ____ ____

(4) Households plan to save more

____ ____ ____

(5) Households plan to consume more

____ ____ ____

b. The economy is operating at full employment and:

(1) Government increases its expenditures for goods and services ____ ____ ____

(2) Government increases transfer payments

____ ____ ____

(3) Investment increases

_____ _____ _____

(4) Households plan to save more

_____ _____ _____

(5) Households plan to consume less

_____ _____ _____

4. Below is a schedule which shows the budget-line schedule. It is drawn up on the assumption that the Federal government has a given fiscal program.

Federal budget surplus (+) or deficit (−) as a % of GNP	Utilization rate (%)
−1	93
0	94
1	95
2	96
3	97
4	98
5	99
6	100

a. Plot this schedule on the graph below.

b. The fact that the budget line slopes upward from left to right indicates that there is

_____

in the economy.

c. This budget line would shift upward if the Federal government:

(1) _____ its expenditures for goods and services

(2) _____ its transfer payments program

(3) _____ tax rates.

d. The slope of this budget line would become steeper if the Federal government made

the tax system (more, less) _____ progressive.

e. The full-employment surplus is equal to

_____ percent of the GNP. If GNP at a utilization rate of 100 percent were $600 billion, the full-employment surplus would be

equal to $_____ billion. And if this

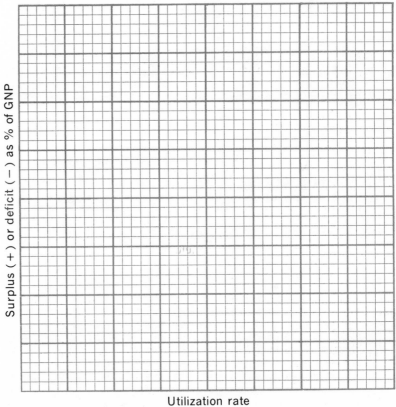

Utilization rate

100 percent utilization rate GNP were to increase by 10 percent, the full-employment surplus would increase by $_____ billion.

5. In the table below are four different NNPs and the amount that would be spent for consumption (C_0) and the amount saved (S_0) at each NNP if there were no taxes in the economy.

a. The MPC in the economy is _____ and the value of the multiplier is _____

b. Three different tax systems might be used in this economy: system No. 1, system No. 2, and system No. 3. The amounts of consumption, saving, and taxes paid under each tax system are shown in the remainder of the table. Under each system the tax rate (taxes collected divided by the NNP) is 10 percent and the amount of taxes collected is $50 when the NNP is $500.

(1) Which of the tax systems is proportional? _____

(2) Which is regressive? _____

(3) Which is progressive? _____

c. In system No. 1—the regressive system—when NNP increases by $50,

(1) consumption increases by $_____, saving by $_____, and taxes by $_____

(2) the MPC is _____ and the multiplier is equal to _____

d. In the second, or proportional, tax system, when NNP increases by $50,

(1) consumption increases by $_____, saving by $_____, and taxes by $_____

(2) the MPC is _____ and the multiplier is equal to _____

(Hint: To compute the value of the multiplier,

divide 1 by 1 minus the MPC. Do not divide 1 by the MPS. This won't work when taxes collected change as NNP changes!)

e. Tax system No. 3 is progressive. In this tax system, when NNP increases by $50

(1) from $500 to $550,

(a) consumption increases by $_____, saving by $_____, and taxes by $_____

(b) the MPC is _____ and the multiplier is _____

(2) from $550 to $600,

(a) consumption increases by $_____, saving by $_____, and taxes by $_____

(b) the MPC is _____ and the multiplier is _____

(3) from $450 to $500,

(a) consumption increases by $_____, saving by $_____, and taxes by $_____

(b) the MPC is _____ and the multiplier is _____

f. The conclusions to be drawn from this problem are:

(1) The adoption of a regressive tax system (does, does not) _____ change the value of the MPC and the multiplier.

(2) The adoption of a proportional tax system (increases, decreases, does not affect) _____ _____ the MPC and the multiplier.

(3) The adoption of a progressive tax system _____ the MPC and the multiplier.

(4) With a progressive tax system the MPC and the multiplier _____ as NNP rises and _____ as NNP falls.

NNP	No taxes		System No. 1			System No. 2			System No. 3		
	C_0	S_0	C_1	S_1	T_1	C_2	S_2	T_2	C_3	S_3	T_3
$450	410	40	370	30	50	374	31	45	381.2	32.8	36
500	450	50	410	40	50	410	40	50	410.0	40.0	50
550	490	60	450	50	50	446	49	55	437.2	46.8	66
600	530	70	490	60	50	482	58	60	462.8	53.2	84

■ SELF-TEST

Circle the T if the statement is true, the F if it is false.

1. The Employment Act of 1946 commits the Federal government to using monetary and fiscal policy to achieve economic stability.   T   F

2. Automatic or built-in stabilizers are not sufficiently strong to prevent recession or inflation, but they can reduce the severity of recession or inflation.   T   F

3. Even a balanced budget can be a weapon in fighting depression and inflation.   T   F

4. If taxes only are reduced by $10 and the marginal propensity to save is 0.4, equilibrium NNP will rise by $25.   T   F

5. If the MPS were 0.3 and taxes were levied by the government so that consumers paid $20 in taxes at each level of NNP, consumption expenditures at each level of NNP would be $14 less.   T   F

6. It is generally believed that public works expenditures have a greater expansionary effect than transfer payments and that regressive taxes are more contractionary than progressive taxes.   T   F

7. The fiscal policies of state and local governments have tended to assist and reinforce the efforts of the Federal government to mitigate depression and inflation.   T   F

8. A governmental deficit is contractionary.   T   F

9. A regressive tax system is more conducive to built-in stability than a progressive one.   T   F

10. An increase in personal income tax rates would move the budget line upward.   T   F

11. Fiscal drag refers to the facts that as potential GNP grows, the dollar size of the full-employment surplus also grows, and that this growing full-employment surplus makes it progressively more difficult to reach a 100 percent utilization rate.   T   F

12. The fiscal program that results in a 1 percent full-employment surplus is more expansionary than the program that brings about a 2 percent full-employment surplus.   T   F

Underscore the letter that corresponds to the best answer.

The first four questions are based on the consumption schedule below.

1. If taxes were zero, government expenditures for goods and services $10, and investment $6, equilibrium NNP would be: (*a*) $310; (*b*) $320; (*c*) $330; (*d*) $340.

NNP	C
$300	$290
310	298
320	306
330	314
340	322
350	330
360	338

2. If taxes were $5, government expenditures for goods and services $10, and investment $6, equilibrium NNP would be: (*a*) $300; (*b*) $310; (*c*) $320; (*d*) $330.

3. Assume investment is $42, taxes $40, and government spending for goods and services zero. If the full-employment level of NNP is $340, the gap can be eliminated by reducing taxes by: (*a*) $8; (*b*) $10; (*c*) $13; (*d*) $40.

4. Assume that investment is zero, that taxes are zero, and that government spending for goods and services is $20. If the full-employment-without-inflation level of NNP is $330, the gap can be eliminated by decreasing government expenditures by: (*a*) $4; (*b*) $5; (*c*) $10; (*d*) $20.

5. Which of the following policies would do the *most* to reduce inflation? (*a*) increase taxes by $5 billion; (*b*) reduce government expenditures for goods and services by $5 billion; (*c*) increase taxes and government expenditures by $5 billion; (*d*) reduce both taxes and government expenditures by $5 billion.

6. If the economy is to have built-in stability, when NNP falls: (*a*) tax receipts and government transfer payments should fall; (*b*) tax receipts and government transfer payments should rise; (*c*) tax receipts should fall and government transfer payments should rise;

(d) tax receipts should rise and government transfer payments should fall.

7. If the government wishes to increase the level of NNP, it might: (a) reduce taxes; (b) reduce its expenditures for goods and services; (c) reduce transfer payments; (d) reduce the size of the budget deficit.

8. If the marginal propensity to consume is 0.6⅔ and both taxes and government expenditures for goods and services increase by $25, NNP will: (a) fall by $25; (b) rise by $25; (c) fall by $75; (d) rise by $75.

9. Which of the following by itself is the most expansionary (least contractionary)? (a) redemption of government bonds held by the public; (b) borrowing from the public to finance a budget deficit; (c) a build-up in the size of the government's checking account in the central banks; (d) creating new money to finance a budget deficit.

10. Which of the following would be the most contractionary? (a) increased personal income taxes, the receipts being used to retire part of the national debt; (b) increased sales and excise taxes, the receipts being used to retire part of the national debt; (c) increased personal income taxes, the receipts being used to increase the cash balance of the government; (d) increased sales and excise taxes, the receipts being used to increase the cash balance of the government.

11. Which of the following would cause an upward shift in the budget line? (a) an increase in the utilization rate; (b) an increase in the full-employment surplus; (c) an increase in government expenditures for goods and services; (d) an increase in tax rates.

12. Suppose the fiscal program of the Federal government is constant. Which of the following would not be the result of an increase in the utilization rate? (a) an increase in the employment rate; (b) an increase in the full-employment surplus; (c) an increase in tax collections; (d) an increase in real GNP.

■ DISCUSSION QUESTIONS

1. What is meant by fiscal policy? What methods can government use to increase

NNP? What policies can it follow to reduce NNP?

2. In the Employment Act of 1946, (a) what responsibility was given to the Federal government; (b) what tasks were assigned to the Council of Economic Advisors and the Joint Economic Committee; and (c) what specific kinds of policy were to be used to achieve the goals established by the act?

3. What is the difference between discretionary and nondiscretionary fiscal policy?

4. What is the exact effect which taxes will have on the consumption schedule? On the saving schedule?

5. If both taxes and government spending increase by equal amounts, NNP will increase by that amount. Why?

6. How does a nondiscretionary type of fiscal policy work to offset rises and falls in the level of NNP?

7. What are the alternative means of financing deficits and disposing of surpluses available to the Federal government? What is the difference between these methods insofar as their expansionary and contractionary effect is concerned?

8. What are the chief advantages and disadvantages of public works programs as a means of controlling deflation?

9. In what sense has state and local fiscal policy been procyclical rather than countercyclical? What accounts for this fiscal perversity?

10. What kind of tax system works best to promote built-in stability? Why? Which tax system does the least to promote built-in stability? Why?

11. Explain (a) what the budget line is; (b) what determines its slope; (c) what causes upward and downward shifts in the budget line; and (d) what the full-employment surplus is.

12. Explain why, with government taxing and spending, the equilibrium NNP is that NNP at which NNP equals aggregate demand (consumption plus investment plus government spending for goods and services); and saving plus taxes equals investment plus government spending. What will cause NNP to move to its equilibrium level?

13. What is fiscal drag? What measures can be taken to reduce or eliminate fiscal drag? What will be the effect of these measures on the utilization rate and the Federal budget surplus or deficit?

14. Suppose there are strong inflationary pressures and a 100 percent utilization rate in the economy. To reduce these inflationary pressures, in what direction should the budget line move? What changes in the fiscal program of the Federal government would move the budget line in this direction?

FISCAL POLICY AND THE PUBLIC DEBT

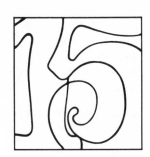

Whenever the Federal government applies fiscal policy and incurs either a budget defict or a budget surplus, the size of the public (i.e., the national) debt is affected. Budget deficits lead to an increase in the public debt, while surpluses cause the debt to decrease. Whether the government will incur deficits and surpluses to stabilize the economy and whether the public debt will increase, decrease, or remain constant depends upon which one of three basic budget philosophies the government follows. Chapter 15 has three major sections and is chiefly concerned with two related topics: the budget philosophy and the public debt.

The first section of Chapter 15 deals with the three budget philosophies. The student should learn from this section what each of the philosophies is and how they differ. He should also discover the effects of applying each philosophy upon national output, employment, and the price level; and upon the size of the public debt.

In the second section of the chapter the public debt is considered. Here the student should become aware of how large the debt and interest on the debt are, both absolutely and relatively; how public debt differs from private debt; and how and why the debt has grown. He should understand that the existence of the public debt both causes several economic problems and has its economic advantages—but that the problems are *not*

those of bankrupting the government or of shifting the cost of a war (or of other government programs) to future generations.

The third, very short, section of Chapter 15 makes it clear that an increasing public debt is the result of government borrowing private saving. Private saving by business firms and by households is constantly increasing as the NNP grows. To maintain full employment and growth, all this saving must be borrowed and spent. To the extent that businesses and households fail to borrow all that is saved at full employment, government must take up the slack by borrowing and increasing the public debt if we are to continue to have full employment and economic growth.

Overall, it should become apparent that the size of the national debt is not of great importance. Changes in its size are important because they are the result of either deficits or surpluses; and a deficit or a surplus reflects the application of fiscal policy to affect the performance of the economy.

■ CHAPTER OUTLINE

1. Three budgetary philosophies may be followed by a government; the adoption of any of these philosophies will affect the employment, the output, and the price level of the economy.

a. Proponents of an annually balanced budget would have government expenditures and tax revenues equal in every year; but such a budget is pro- rather than countercyclical.

b. Those who advocate a cyclically balanced budget propose matching surpluses (in years of prosperity) with deficits (in depression years) to stabilize the economy; but there is no assurance that the surpluses will equal the deficits over the years.

c. Advocates of functional finance contend that deficits, surpluses, and the size of the debt are of minor importance; that the goal of full employment without inflation should be achieved regardless of the effects of the necessary fiscal policies upon the budget and the size of the national debt.

2. Any government surplus or deficit automatically affects the size of the public debt.

a. The large public debt is primarily the result of Federal borrowing during World War II and is almost entirely internally held. To assess the quantitative importance of the public debt, it should be noted that the relative size of the debt and the interest payments on it have not grown so rapidly as have the absolute size of the debt and the interest payments.

b. Because of basic differences between public and private debt, it is not proper to attribute to public debt the same disadvantages and problems associated with private debt.

c. The public debt incurred during World War II cannot be passed on to future generations because it is an internally held debt. The economy has continued to grow and prosper even though the debt has grown.

d. There are at least five economic problems which a large public debt creates (although they are not the ones usually attributed to it).

e. But, on the other hand, in at least three respects a large public debt is desirable.

3. If we are to have continual full employment and growth in an already growing economy, all the private saving done at full employment must be borrowed and spent—by business firms, consumers, or governments. All this private saving not borrowed and spent privately will have to be borrowed and spent publicly; and this increases the public debt.

■ IMPORTANT TERMS

Annually balanced budget	**Externally held public debt**
Cyclically balanced budget	**Retiring the public debt**
Functional finance	**Refunding the public debt**
Internally held public debt	

■ FILL-IN QUESTIONS

1. Three prevailing philosophies of fiscal policy are:

a. _____

b. _____

c. _____

2. An annually balanced budget is procyclical rather than countercyclical because _____

_____

3. A cyclically balanced budget suggests that to ensure full employment without inflation, the government incur deficits during periods

of _____

and surpluses during periods of _____

_____

with the deficits and surpluses equaling each other over the business cycle. The budget over the cycle may not balance, however, because

_____

_____

4. Functional finance has as its main goal

the achievement of _____ ;

and would regard budget _____

and increases in the _____
as of secondary importance.

5. Today the public debt is about _____ percent, and interest charges on the debt are

approximately _____ percent of GNP in the United States.

6. What are the three chief *differences* between public debt and private debt?

a. _____

b. _____

c. _____

7. The public debt of the United States is almost entirely _____ held.

8. The cost of World War II was not passed on to future generations because the generation that fought the war had to go without _____ ; and the generations being taxed to pay interest on the debt also _____

9. The existence of a large public debt may dampen _____ incentives in the economy, increase _____ _____ , and make it difficult to use _____ to control inflation.

10. The existence of a large public debt is desirable to the extent that it provides _____ _____ , cushions the impact of _____ , and provides a means of applying _____ _____ policies.

11. As the full-employment NNP of the economy increases, the amount of saving done at full employment _____ . To maintain full employment, all this saving must be _____ and _____

12. If the saving done at full employment is not all borrowed and spent by business and consumers, _____ must borrow and spend the saving. If it:
  a. does *not* borrow and spend it, NNP and the rate of economic growth will _____
  b. does borrow and spend it, the public debt will _____

■ PROBLEMS AND PROJECTS

1. In the table below are figures showing the GNP, the size of the public debt, and interest on the debt during six years in a hypothetical economy.

Year	GNP	Debt	Interest on debt	Debt as % of GNP	Interest as % of GNP
1	$450	$100	$60	____	____
2	500	400	20	____	____
3	600	600	24	____	____
4	650	780	32	____	____
5	750	900	45	____	____
6	800	950	76	____	____

  a. Compute
  (1) the size of the debt as a percentage of GNP in each year.
  (2) the size of the interest payments as a percentage of GNP in each year.
  b. The size of the debt relative to GNP
  (1) rose between years _____ and _____
  (2) was constant between years _____ and
  (3) fell between years _____ and _____
  c. The size of the interest payments relative to GNP
  (1) rose between years _____ and _____
  (2) was constant between years _____ and
  (3) fell between years _____ and _____

■ SELF-TEST

Circle the T if the statement is true, the F if it is false.

1. Proponents of functional finance argue that a balanced budget, whether it is balanced annually or over the business cycle, is of minor importance when compared with the objective of full employment without inflation.
                                                    T   F

2. There is no assurance that a nation can both use fiscal policy to promote full employment and balance its budget cyclically.

T   F

3. The public debt is about $390 billion.

T   F

4. The primary reason for the large increase in the public debt since 1930 is the deficit spending during the years of the Great Depression.

T   F

5. A nation can experience prosperity and growth in its real output even though its national debt is increasing rapidly.

T   F

6. The chief disadvantage of the public debt of the United States is that as the debt becomes payable, the government may be unable to tax or to borrow sufficient money to redeem its securities.

T   F

7. The amount of saving done at full employment in a growing economy increases both absolutely and relatively.

T   F

8. To maintain full employment in a growing economy it is necessary for the total of public and private debt to increase.

T   F

Underscore the letter that corresponds to the best answer.

1. Which of the following would involve reducing government expenditures and increasing tax rates during a depression? (a) an annually balanced budget policy; (b) functional finance; (c) cyclically balanced budget policy; (d) a policy employing built-in stability.

2. As a percentage of the gross national product, the public debt and interest on the debt are, respectively, about: (a) 50% and 1%; (b) 40% and 1.9%; (c) 105% and 3%; (d) 125% and 6%.

3. Which of the following is characteristic of an internally held public debt? (a) it must be retired; (b) payment of interest on the debt decreases the nation's standard of living; (c) retirement of the debt would decrease the nation's productive capacity; (d) it is held within a single economic unit.

4. Incurring internal debts to finance a war does not pass the cost of the war on to future generations because: (a) the opportunity cost of the war is borne by the generation that

fought it; (b) the government need not pay interest on internally held debts; (c) there is never a need for government to refund the debt; (d) wartime inflation reduces the relative size of the debt.

5. Which of the following is a consequence of the public debt of the United States? (a) it increases incentives to work and invest; (b) it provides some built-in stability during a recession; (c) it reduces income inequality; (d) it leads to greater saving at the various levels of disposable income.

6. Which of the following would be a consequence of the total retirement of the public debt? (a) a reduction in the nation's productive capacity; (b) a reduction in the nation's standard of living; (c) a redistribution of the nation's wealth among its citizens; (d) an increase in aggregate demand in the economy.

7. Suppose the average propensity to save is constant and equal to 0.2 of NNP. If the full-employment NNP increases from $600 billion to $660 billion, saving at full employment will increase by: (a) $3 billion; (b) $6 billion; (c) $9 billion; (d) $12 billion.

8. Suppose the multiplier is 3. Were the amount of saving done at full employment to increase by $20 and were private borrowing to increase by $5, to maintain full employment, public borrowing and the public debt would have to increase by: (a) $5; (b) $15; (c) $45; (d) $60.

■ DISCUSSION QUESTIONS

1. Explain why an annually balanced budget is not "neutral" and how it can intensify, rather than reduce the tendencies for NNP to rise and fall.

2. How does a cyclically balanced budget philosophy differ from the philosophy of functional finance?

3. Why do advocates of functional finance argue that budget deficits and a mounting public debt are of secondary importance?

4. How big is the national debt of the United States absolutely and relatively? How large are the interest charges on the debt absolutely and relatively? What has happened to the size of the debt and interest charges since 1930? Why?

5. In what ways does public debt differ from private debt when the public debt is held internally?

6. Why does government borrowing to finance a war pass the cost of the war, plus interest, on to future generations if the debt is externally held? If the debt is internally held, the cost is not passed on. Why? Express your answers to the above in both real and monetary terms. Are there any exceptions to the generalizations above?

7. What are the principal advantages and disadvantages of a public debt internally held? Which of its disadvantages seems most important to you at this point in your study of economics?

8. In what ways does the existence of a large public debt contribute to inflation? Why does an increase in the size of the debt abet inflation? Which tends to be more inflationary, the existence of the debt or increases in its size?

9. What tends to happen to the absolute and the relative amounts of saving done at full employment as the full-employment NNP grows?

10. Why, in a growing economy, must borrowing and debt increase in order to maintain full employment and economic growth? What will happen to NNP if private borrowing and private debt do not increase? What must government do to maintain full employment if private borrowers do not increase their borrowings and debt enough to maintain full employment? What will this do to the public debt?

MONEY AND BANKING IN AMERICAN CAPITALISM

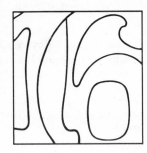

By and large, Chapter 16 is descriptive and factual. It contains no explanation of how the banking system affects the operation of the economy. The purpose of this chapter is, however, to prepare the student for such an explanation. Of special importance are many terms and definitions which will probably be new to the student. These must be learned if the following two chapters and their analysis of how the banking system affects the performance of the economy are to be clearly understood. Chapter 16 also contains a factual description of the institutions which comprise the American banking system—the Board of Governors of the Federal Reserve System, the Federal Reserve Banks, and the commercial banks—and the functions of these institutions.

The student will do well to pay particular attention to the following points: (1) what money is and the functions it performs, what types of money exist in the American economy and their relative importance, and what constitutes the money supply; (2) what gives value to or "backs" American money; and (3) the three principal institutions of the American banking system, their functions, and their relationships.

Several points are worth repeating here because so much depends upon their being fully understood. First, money is whatever performs the three functions of money, and in the

United States money consists of the debts (promises to pay) of the Federal government or of banks. In the United States, this money is "backed" by no more than the goods and services for which its owners can exchange it—not by gold, because Americans cannot exchange their money for gold.

Second, the central bank in the United States is the twelve Federal Reserve Banks and the Board of Governors of the Federal Reserve System, which oversees their operation. These banks, while privately owned by the commercial banks, are operated more or less as an agency of the Federal government —not for profit, but primarily to regulate the nation's money supply in the best interests of the economy as a whole and secondarily to perform other services for the banks, the government, and the economy. They are able to perform their primary function because they are bankers' banks where commercial banks can deposit and borrow money. They do not deal directly with the public.

Third, commercial banks, like many other financial institutions, accept deposits and make loans, but they also—and this distinguishes them from other financial institutions —are literally able to create money by lending demand deposits. Because they are able to do this, they have a strong influence on the size of the money supply and the value of money. The Federal Reserve Banks exist primarily to regulate the money supply and its value by influencing and controlling the amount of money commercial banks create.

Finally, banks—both Federal Reserve and commercial—are dealers in debt. Their assets consist almost entirely of the debts of others —the Federal government, other banks, or private borrowers—in the form of currency, bonds, and other types of promises to pay; their liabilities are debts to others in the form of currency and deposits (which "the others" consider assets).

■ CHAPTER OUTLINE

1. Money is whatever performs the three basic functions of money: a medium of exchange, a standard of value, and a store of value.

2. In the American economy the supply of money consists (in order of relative importance) of demand deposits, paper money, and coins—not owned by banks or the government.

a. Currency (paper money plus coins) is money created by the government, and demand deposits are money which has been created by private commercial banks.

b. Such paper assets as government bonds and savings accounts are near-monies because they can easily and quickly be converted into money; the amount of near-money is important because it affects consumer saving and spending and because changes in the money supply would occur if near-money were converted.

3. In the United States:

a. Money is the promise of either some bank or the Federal government to pay (it is a bank or government debt), but these debts cannot be redeemed for anything tangible.

b. Money has value only because people have faith in their ability to exchange it for desirable goods and services.

c. The value of money is inversely related to the price level.

d. Money is "backed" by the confidence which the public has that the value of money will remain stable; and the Federal government can use monetary and fiscal policy to keep the value of money relatively stable.

4. The centralized American banking system consists of thousands of privately owned and operated commercial banks and the twelve Federal Reserve Banks, which are owned by the commercial banks and whose operation is directed by the Board of Governors of the Federal Reserve System.

a. The banking system is centralized because the absence of centralization in the past led to an inflexible supply of money, a multitude of different kinds of money, and a mismanagement of the money supply which caused recurrent financial panics and speculation.

b. The Federal Reserve System is composed of:

(1) The Board of Governors, which exercises control over the supply of money and the banking system

(2) The Federal Reserve Banks, which are central, quasi-public, bankers' banks

(3) Over 13,000 commercial banks—either state or national banks—which perform the two essential functions of holding deposits and making loans

c. The Board of Governors and the Federal Reserve Banks perform six functions aimed at providing certain essential services, supervision of the private commercial banks, and the regulation of the supply of money.

■ IMPORTANT TERMS

Medium of exchange
Standard of value
Store of value
Token money
Intrinsic value
Face value
Paper money
Federal Reserve Note
Treasury currency
Currency
Bank money
Demand deposit
Near-money
Time deposit
Money supply
Fiat money
Legal tender
Board of Governors

Federal Open Market Committee
Federal Advisory Committee
Federal Reserve Bank
Central bank
Quasi-public bank
Bankers' bank
Commercial bank
State bank
National bank
Member bank
Member bank deposits (or reserves)
Collection of checks
Quantitative credit controls
Qualitative (selective) credit controls

■ FILL-IN QUESTIONS

1. Three functions of money are:

a. _____

b. _____

c. _____

2. The supply of money in the United States consists of _____ ,

_____ ,

and _____

not owned by _____

or _____

3. Money in the United States consists of the debt of _____

or the debt of _____

4. Insofar as their dollar size is concerned, the two most important near-monies in the United States are _____

and _____

5. Money in the United States has value because _____

_____ ;

the value of money varies _____

with changes in the _____

6. Money = _____ + _____

7. The Board of Governors of the Federal Reserve System has as its chief responsibility

_____ ;

two groups which assist it in formulating policies to achieve this end are the _____

and the _____

8. What are the three basic quantitative controls employed by the Federal Reserve Banks?

a. _____

b. _____

c. _____

9. The three principal characteristics of the Federal Reserve Banks are:

a. _____

b. _____

c. _____

10. If a bank is a banker's bank it means that _____

and _____

11. The six major functions of the Federal Reserve Banks are:

a. _____

b. _____

c. _____

d. _____

e. _____

f. _____

12. Commercial banks are banks which _____

_____

and _____

and in doing so _____

13. Commercial banks differ from other financial institutions (savings banks, savings and loan associations, etc.) because they _____

_____

and _____

and the other institutions do not.

14. When it is said that the Federal Reserve Banks act as a fiscal agent for the Federal government, it is meant that the Federal Reserve Banks _____ ,

_____ ,

and _____

15. The most important of the functions which the Federal Reserve Banks perform is that of _____

■ PROBLEMS AND PROJECTS

1. From the data in the table below, it can be concluded that on the date to which the figures pertain:

	Billions of dollars
Total Federal Reserve Notes outstanding	$ 53.7
Total savings accounts of the public	230.2
Total treasury coin outstanding	6.5
Commercial bank reserves at the Federal Reserve Banks	29.9
Demand deposits of the Federal government at the Federal Reserve Banks	6.0
Currency owned by commercial banks	10.4
Currency owned by the Federal Reserve Banks	0.2
Total treasury paper money outstanding	0.6
Demand deposits of the public in commercial banks	171.9
Government bonds owned by the public	166.7
Currency owned by the Federal government	0.1

a. The money supply is $_____ billion.

b. The amount of near-money is $_____ billion.

2. If you were to deposit $500 in currency in your checking account in a commercial bank, the *size* of the supply of money, as a consequence of your deposit, would have ____

_____;
and the *composition* of the money supply would have _____

3. If the price level:
a. Fell by 20 percent, the value of money would _____ by _____ percent.
b. Rose by 10 percent, the value of money would _____ by _____ percent.

■ SELF-TEST

Circle the T if the statement is true, the F if it is false.

1. If a coin is "token money," its face value is less than its intrinsic value.   T F

2. The larger the volume of near-monies owned by consumers, the larger will be their average propensity to save.   T F

3. If money is to have a fairly stable value, its supply must be limited relative to the demand for it.   T F

4. The Board of Governors of the Federal Reserve System is appointed by the President of the United States and confirmed by the Senate.   T F

5. The Federal Reserve Banks are owned and operated by the United States government.   T F

6. All national banks are members of the Federal Reserve System.   T F

7. The most important function of the Federal Reserve Banks is the control of the size of the economy's money supply.   T F

8. Federal Reserve Banks are bankers' banks because they make loans to and accept deposits from commercial banks.   T F

Underscore the letter that corresponds to the best answer.

1. Which of the following constitutes the largest element in the nation's money supply? (a) treasury currency; (b) Federal Reserve Notes; (c) time deposits; (d) demand deposits.

2. Demand deposits are money because they are (a) legal tender; (b) fiat money; (c) a medium of exchange; (d) token money.

3. Which of the following best describes the "backing" of money in the United States? (a) the gold bullion stored at Fort Knox, Kentucky; (b) the belief of holders of money that it can be exchanged for desirable goods and services; (c) the willingness of banks and the government to surrender something of value in exchange for money; (d) the faith and confidence of the public in the ability of government to pay its debts.

4. If a person deposits $75 in currency in his checking account at a commercial bank, the supply of money has (a) decreased by $75; (b) increased by $75; (c) not changed in any way; (d) not changed in amount, but its composition has changed.

5. Which of the following is *not* a quantitative credit control? (a) regulation of consumer credit for purchasing homes; (b) open-market operations; (c) setting of the reserve requirement; (d) setting of the discount rate.

6. Which of the following functions distinguishes a commercial bank from other financial institutions? (a) accepts deposits; (b) creates and destroys money; (c) makes loans; (d) deals in debts.

7. Less than one-half of all commercial banks are members of the Federal Reserve System; these member banks have about what percentage of all deposits in commercial banks? (a) 20%; (b) 40%; (c) 60%; (d) 80%.

8. If the price level increases 20 percent, the value of money decreases: (a) 14½%; (b) 16⅔%; (c) 20%; (d) 25%.

■ DISCUSSION QUESTIONS

1. How would you define money? What constitutes the supply of money in the United States? Which of these is the largest element in the money supply?

2. Why are savings accounts (time deposits) and United States government bonds near-monies? Of what importance is the existence of near-monies?

3. For what reasons are demand deposits included in the money supply?

4. What "backs" the money used in the United States? What determines the value of money? Explain the relationship between the value of money and the price level.

5. Why is it necessary to have central banks in the United States?

6. Outline the structure of the Federal Reserve System and the chief functions of each of the segments of the system.

7. As briefly as possible outline the characteristics of the Federal Reserve Banks and explain the meaning of these characteristics.

8. How are commercial banks *like* other financial institutions? How do commercial banks *differ* from other financial institutions?

9. What are the chief functions which the Federal Reserve Banks perform? Explain briefly the meaning of each of these functions. Which function is the most important?

10. What is a commercial bank? What functions does it perform in the United States?

HOW BANKS CREATE MONEY

Chapter 16 outlined the institutional structure of banking in the United States today, the functions which banks and money perform, and the composition of the money supply in the United States. Chapter 17 explains how banks literally create money—checking account money—and the factors which determine and limit the money-creating ability of commercial banks.

The device (and a most convenient and simple device it is) employed to explain commercial banking operations and money creation is the balance sheet. All banking transactions affect this balance sheet, and the first step to understanding how money is created is to understand how various simple and typical transactions affect the commercial bank balance sheet.

In reading this chapter the student must analyze for himself the effect upon the balance sheet of each and every banking transaction discussed. The important items in the balance sheet are demand deposits and reserves, because demand deposits *are* money, and the ability of a bank to create new demand deposits is conditioned by the amount of reserves the bank owns. Expansion of the money supply depends upon the possession by commercial banks of excess reserves, which do not appear explicitly in the balance sheet but which do appear there implicitly because excess reserves are the difference between the actual reserves and the required reserves of commercial banks.

Three cases—the single commercial bank, the monopoly bank, and the banking system —are presented in order to help the student build an understanding of banking and money creation slowly and methodically. It is important here to understand that the money-creating potential of a single commercial bank differs in an important way from the money-creating potential of a monopoly bank and the entire banking system; it is equally important to understand how the money-creating ability of many single commercial banks is *multiplied* and results in the money-creating ability of the banking system as a whole.

Certain assumptions are used throughout most of the chapter to analyze money-creating ability; in certain instances these assumptions may not be completely realistic and may need to be modified. The chapter concludes with a discussion of how the earlier analysis must be modified—but not changed in its essentials— to take account of these slightly unrealistic assumptions.

■ CHAPTER OUTLINE

1. The balance sheet of the commercial bank is a statement of the assets, liabilities, and net worth of the bank at a specific point in time.

2. By examining the ways in which the balance sheet of the commercial bank is affected by various transactions, it is possible to understand how a single commercial bank in a multibank system can create money.

a. Certain reserve concepts are vital to this understanding.

(1) The *legal reserve deposit* (required reserve) which a commercial (member) bank must maintain at its Federal Reserve Bank (or as vault cash—which can be ignored) equals the reserve ratio multiplied by the deposit liabilities of the commercial bank.

(2) *Excess reserves* equal the *actual* deposit (reserve) of a commercial bank at the Federal Reserve Bank (plus the vault cash—which can be ignored) less its required reserve.

b. The deposit of cash in a commercial bank does not affect the total money supply; it only changes its composition, substituting demand deposits (bank money) for currency in circulation.

c. The writing of a check upon one bank and its deposit in a second bank results in a loss of reserves and deposits for the first and gain in reserves and deposits for the second bank.

d. A single commercial bank can only safely make loans (or buy securities) in an amount equal to its excess reserves because it fears the loss of reserves and deposits to other banks. When lending (or buying securities), a bank increases its own deposit liabilities and, therefore, the supply of money by the amount of the loan.

3. A monopoly bank can safely make loans (or buy securities) and thus increase its deposit liabilities and the supply of money by an amount equal to its excess reserves multiplied by the reciprocal of the reserve ratio. The monopoly bank can lend more than can a single commercial bank because it does not fear the loss of reserves to other banks.

4. The lending ability of a banking system composed of many individual banks is the same as the lending ability of a monopoly bank.

a. The system can lend (or buy securities), thereby creating money and deposits, in an amount equal to the excess reserves of the system multiplied by the deposit multiplier (the reciprocal of the reserve ratio).

b. The banking system as a whole can do this even though no single commercial bank lends an amount greater than its excess re-

serves because the banking system, like the monopoly bank, does not lose reserves.

c. The potential lending ability of the banking system may not be fully achieved because of "leakages."

■ IMPORTANT TERMS

Balance sheet

Vault cash (till money)

Legal (required) reserve

Reserve ratio

Fractional reserve

Actual reserve

Excess reserve

The lending potential of an individual commercial bank

Monopoly bank

The lending potential of a monopoly bank

Commercial banking system

The lending potential of the banking system

Profit vs. liquidity

Deposit multiplier

Leakage

Willingness vs. ability to lend

■ FILL-IN QUESTIONS

1. The balance sheet of a commercial bank is a statement of the bank's _____ and _____ at some specific point in time.

2. The coins and paper money which a bank has in its possession are called _____ _____ or _____

3. Another name for a checking account is a _____; a savings account is also called a _____ _____

4. The legal reserve deposit of a commercial bank (ignoring vault cash) must be kept in the _____ and must equal (at least) its _____ multiplied by the _____

5. The excess reserves of a commercial bank

equal its _____

less its _____

6. If commercial banks are allowed to accept (or create) deposits in excess of their reserves, the banking system is operating under a system of _____ reserves.

7. When a person deposits cash in a commercial bank and receives a demand deposit in return, the size of the money supply has (increased, decreased, not changed) _____

_____

8. When a check is drawn upon bank X, deposited in bank Y, and cleared, the reserves of bank X are (increased, decreased, not changed) _____ and the reserves of bank Y are _____; deposits in bank X are _____ and deposits in bank Y are _____

9. A single commercial bank in a multibank system can safely make loans equal in amount to the _____ of that commercial bank.

10. When a commercial bank makes a new loan of $10,000, it (increases, decreases) ____

_____

the supply of money by $_____

11. When a commercial bank sells a $2,000 government bond to a private business firm the supply of money (increases, decreases)

_____

by $_____

12. A banker ordinarily pursues two conflicting goals; they are _____ and _____

13. A monopoly bank can safely make loans and create money in an amount equal to its excess reserves multiplied by the _____

_____

14. The greater the reserve ratio is, the (larger, smaller) _____ is the deposit multiplier.

15. If the required reserve ratio is 16⅔ percent, the banking system is $6 million short of reserves and the banking system is unable to increase its reserves, the banking system must _____ the money supply by $_____

■ PROBLEMS AND PROJECTS

1. Below is a simplified balance sheet for a commercial bank. Assume that the given figures show the balance sheet of the bank *prior* to each of the following transactions. Draw up the balance sheet as it would appear after each of the transactions is completed, and place the balance sheet figures in the appropriate column.

	(1)	(2)	(3)	(4)
Assets:				
Cash	$100	$__	$__	$__	$__
Reserves	200	__	__	__	__
Loans	500	__	__	__	__
Securities	200	__	__	__	__
Liabilities:				
Demand deposits	900	__	__	__	__
Capital stock	100	__	__	__	__

a. A check for $50 is drawn by one of the depositors of the bank, given to a person who deposits it in another bank, and cleared (column 1).

b. A depositor withdraws $50 in cash from the bank, and the bank restores its vault cash by obtaining additional cash from its Federal Reserve Bank (column 2).

c. A check for $60 drawn on another bank is deposited in this bank and cleared (column 3).

d. The bank sells $100 in government bonds to the Federal Reserve Bank in its district (column 4).

2. In column 1 below are several reserve ratios. Compute the deposit multiplier for each of the reserve ratios and enter the figures in column 2. In column 3 show the maximum amount by which a single commercial bank in a multibank system can increase its loans for each dollar's worth of excess reserves it possesses. In column 4 indicate the maximum amount by which the banking system can increase its loans for each dollar's worth of excess reserves in the system.

(1)	(2)	(3)	(4)
12½%	____	$____	$____
16⅔%	____	____	____
20%	____	____	____
25%	____	____	____
30%	____	____	____
33⅓%	____	____	____

3. Below are five balance sheets for a commercial bank (columns 1a–5a). The required reserve ratio is 20 percent.

a. Compute the required reserves (A) and—ignoring vault cash—the excess reserves* (B) of the bank.

b. If this bank is one bank in a multibank system, compute the amount of new loans it can extend (C).

c. If this bank is a monopoly bank, compute the amount of new loans it can extend (D).

d. Draw up for the individual bank in a multibank system the five balance sheets as they appear after the bank has made the new loans that it is capable of making safely (columns 1b–5b).

e. Draw up for the monopoly bank the balance sheet as it would appear after the bank has made the new loans that it is capable of making safely (columns 1c–5c).

* If the bank is short of reserves and must reduce its loans or obtain additional reserves, show this by placing a minus sign in front of the amounts by which it is short of reserves.

	(1a)	(2a)	(3a)	(4a)	(5a)
Assets:					
Cash	$ 10	$ 20	$ 20	$ 20	$ 15
Reserves	40	40	25	40	45
Loans	100	100	100	100	150
Securities	50	60	30	70	60
Liabilities:					
Demand deposits	175	200	150	180	220
Capital stock	25	20	25	50	50
A. Required reserve	$__	$__	$__	$__	$__
B. Excess reserve	__	__	__	__	__
C. New loans—single bank	__	__	__	__	__
D. New loans—monopoly bank	__	__	__	__	__

	(1b)	(1c)	(2b)	(2c)	(3b)	(3c)	(4b)	(4c)	(5b)	(5c)
Assets:										
Cash	$__	$__	$__	$__	$__	$__	$__	$__	$__	$__
Reserves	__	__	__	__	__	__	__	__	__	__
Securities	__	__	__	__	__	__	__	__	__	__
	__	__	__	__	__	__	__	__	__	__
Liabilities:										
Demand deposits	__	__	__	__	__	__	__	__	__	__
Capital stock	__	__	__	__	__	__	__	__	__	__

4. Below is a simplified consolidated balance sheet for all commercial banks in the economy. The reserve ratio is 20 percent. Assume that this is the balance sheet as it appears *prior* to the following transactions.

a. The public deposits $5 in cash in the banks and the banks send the $5 to the Federal Reserve, where it is added to their reserves. Fill in column 1. If the banking system extends the new loans it is capable of extending, show in column 2 the balance sheet as it would then appear.

		(1)	(2)	(3)	(4)	(5)	(6)
Assets:							
Cash	$ 50	$___	$___	$___	$___	$___	$___
Reserves	100	___	___	___	___	___	___
Loans	200	___	___	___	___	___	___
Securities	200	___	___	___	___	___	___
Liabilities:							
Demand deposits	500	___	___	___	___	___	___
Capital stock	50	___	___	___	___	___	___
Loans from Federal Reserve	0	___	___	___	___	___	___
Excess reserves		___	___	___	___	___	___
Maximum possible expansion of the money supply		___	___	___	___	___	___

b. The banking system sells $8 worth of securities to the Federal Reserve. Complete column 3. Assuming the system extends the maximum amount of credit of which it is capable, fill in column 4.

c. The Federal Reserve lends $10 to the commercial banks; complete column 5. Complete column 6 showing the condition of the banks after the maximum amount of new loans which the banks are capable of making is granted.

■ SELF-TEST

Circle the T if the statement is true, the F if it is false.

1. The balance sheet of a commercial bank shows the transactions in which the bank has engaged during a given period of time.   **T   F**

2. Tom Roberts deposits $300 in cash in a commercial bank and receives a demand deposit in return; an hour later the Lincoln Coal and Iron Company borrows $300 from the same bank. The money supply has increased $300 as a result of the two transactions.   **T   F**

3. A single commercial bank in a multibank system of banking can safely loan an amount equal to its excess reserves multiplied by the required reserve ratio.   **T   F**

4. A commercial bank which is a member of the Federal Reserve System may maintain its legal reserve either as a deposit in its Federal Reserve Bank or as government bonds in its own vault.   **T   F**

5. The legal reserve which a commercial bank maintains must equal at least its own deposit liabilities multiplied by the required reserve ratio.   **T   F**

6. The actual reserves of a commercial bank equal excess reserves plus required reserves.   **T   F**

7. A commercial bank's assets plus it net worth equal the bank's liabilities.   **T   F**

8. The reserve of a commercial bank in the Federal Reserve Bank is an asset of the Federal Reserve Bank.   **T   F**

9. A check for $1,000 drawn on bank X by a depositor and deposited in bank Y will increase the excess reserves of bank Y by $1,000.   **T   F**

10. To say that a commercial bank seeks *profits* and *liquidity* is an example of dual terminology—using two different words to mean the same thing.　　　　　　T　F

11. When a borrower repays a loan of $500, either in cash or by check, the supply of money is reduced by $500.　　　　T　F

12. The granting of a $5,000 loan and the purchase of a $5,000 government bond from a private citizen by a commercial bank have the same immediate effect on the money supply.　　　　　　　　　　　T　F

13. If a monopoly bank has $10 million in excess reserves and if the reserve ratio is 25 percent, it can safely increase its loans by $40 million.　　　　　　　　　T　F

14. While a single commercial bank in a multibank system can only safely increase its loans by an amount equal to its excess reserves, the entire banking system can increase its loans by an amount equal to its excess reserves multiplied by the reciprocal of the reserve ratio.　　　　　　T　F

15. If borrowers from a commercial bank wish to have cash rather than demand deposits, the money-creating potential of the banking system will be increased.　　T　F

Underscore the letter that corresponds to the best answer.

1. A bank has excess reserves of $3,000 and deposit liabilties of $30,000; the required reserve ratio is 20 percent. The actual reserves of the bank are: (a) $3,000; (b) $6,000; (c) $9,000; (d) $10,000.

2. A bank has excess reserves of $5,000 and deposit liabilities of $50,000 when the required reserve ratio is 20 percent. If the reserve ratio is raised to 25 percent, the bank's excess reserves will be: (a) $1,000; (b) $1,500; (c) $2,000; (d) $2,500.

3. A depositor places $750 in cash in a bank, and the reserve ratio is 33⅓ percent; the bank sends the $750 to the Federal Reserve Bank. As a result, the *reserves* and the *excess reserves* of the bank have been increased, respectively, by: (a) $750 and $250; (b) $750 and $500; (c) $750 and $750; (d) $500 and $500.

4. A bank has deposit liabilities of $100,000, reserves of $37,000, and a required reserve ratio of 25 percent. The amount by which a *single commercial bank* and the amount by which a *monopoly bank* could safely increase their loans are, respectively: (a) $12,000 and $48,000; (b) $17,000 and $68,000; (c) $12,000 and $60,000; (d) $17,000 and $85,000.

5. A bank has no excess reserves to start with, but then a depositor places $600 in cash in the bank, and the bank adds the $600 to its reserves by sending it to the Federal Reserve Bank. The bank then loans $300 to a borrower. As a consequence of these transactions the size of the money supply has: (a) not been affected; (b) increased by $300; (c) increased by $600; (d) increased by $900.

6. A bank has excess reserves of $500 and a required reserve ratio of 20 percent; it grants a loan of $1,000 to a borrower. If the borrower writes a check for $1,000 which is deposited in another bank, the first bank will be short of reserves, after the check has been cleared, in the amount of: (a) $200; (b) $500; (c) $700; (d) $1,000.

7. A monopoly bank has excess reserves of $700 and decides it can make new loans of $2,100 and be just meeting its reserve requirements. The required reserve ratio is: (a) 20%; (b) 25%; (c) 30%; (d) 33⅓%.

8. A bank sells a $1,000 government security to a private business firm. The business firm pays for the bond in cash, which the bank adds to its vault cash. The money supply has: (a) not been affected; (b) decreased by $1,000; (c) increased by $1,000; (d) increased by $1,000 multiplied by the reciprocal of the required reserve ratio.

9. The commercial banking system, because of a recent change in the reserve ratio required, finds that it is $50 million short of reserves. Before the change in the reserve ratio, it was loaned up but not short of reserves. It has deposit liabilities of $500 million and reserves of $100 million. The change in the reserve ratio which took place was: (a) from 20 to 30%; (b) from 25 to 30%; (c) from 20 to 33⅓%; (d) 25 to 33⅓%.

10. Only one bank in the commercial banking system has excess reserves, and its excess reserve is $100,000. This bank makes a new loan equal to the maximum amount it can safely loan. The borrower receives half the loan in the form of a demand deposit and half in cash, which the bank obtains from its Federal Reserve Bank. The required reserve ratio for all banks is 20 percent, and the cash is *not* redeposited in a bank. The maximum amount that the money supply can be expanded by the banking system as a result of the entire transaction is: (a) $250,000; (b) $300,000; (c) $500,000; (d) $600,000.

■ DISCUSSION QUESTIONS

1. Commercial banks seek both profits and safety. Explain how the balance sheet of the commercial banks reflects the desires of bankers for income and for liquidity.

2. Do the reserves held by commercial banks satisfactorily protect the deposits of the bank's depositors? Are the reserves of commercial banks needed, and are they sufficient to ensure the safety of deposits? Explain your answers.

3. Explain why the granting of a loan by a commercial bank increases the supply of money. Why does the repayment of a loan decrease the supply of money?

4. A store owner writes a check on his account in a New York City bank and gives it to one of his suppliers, who deposits it in his bank in Albany, New York. How does the Albany bank obtain payment from the New York City bank? If the two banks were in New York City and San Francisco, how would one bank pay the other? How are the excess reserves of the two banks affected?

5. Why is a single commercial bank in a multibank system only able to loan safely an amount equal to its excess reserves, while a monopoly bank can safely loan an amount equal to its excess reserve multiplied by the reciprocal of the reserve ratio required?

6. In a multibank system of banking, no one commercial bank ever lends an amount greater than its excess reserve, but the banking system as a whole is able to extend loans and expand the money supply by an amount equal to the system's excess reserves multiplied by the reciprocal of the reserve ratio. Explain why this is possible and how the multiple expansion of credit and money takes place.

7. On the basis of a given amount of excess reserves and a given reserve ratio, a certain expansion of the money supply may be possible. What are the reasons why the potential expansion of the money supply may not be fully achieved?

THE FEDERAL
RESERVE BANKS
AND MONETARY POLICY

Chapter 18 is the third chapter dealing with money and banking; and it is concerned with how the Board of Governors of the Federal Reserve System and the Federal Reserve Banks affect output, income, employment, and the price level in the economy. Central-bank policies designed to affect these variables are called monetary policies, the goal of which in the present economy is full employment without inflation.

The student should have little difficulty with this chapter if he has understood the material in Chapter 17. In Chapter 18 attention should be concentrated on the following: (1) the cause-effect chain between monetary policy; commercial bank reserves and excess reserves; the supply of money; the cost and availability of credit; and investment spending, aggregate demand, output, employment, and the price level; (2) the principal items on the balance sheet of the Federal Reserve Banks; (3) the three principal quantitative controls available to the Federal Reserve Banks, and how employment of these controls can affect the reserves, excess reserves, the actual money supply, and the money-creating potential of the banking system; (4) the other (qualitative) controls which the Federal Reserve banks use or have used to influence in the economy; (5) the actions the Federal Reserve would take if it were pursuing a tight money policy to curb inflation, and the actions it would take if it were pursuing an easy money policy to prevent or eliminate depression; and (6) the relative effectiveness of the

various types of monetary controls and of monetary policy in general in curbing inflation and depression.

In order to acquire a thorough knowledge of the manner in which each of the Federal Reserve transactions affects reserves, excess reserves, the actual money supply, and the potential money supply, the student must study very carefully each of the sets of balance sheets which are used to explain these transactions. On these balance sheets the items to watch are again reserves and demand deposits! Be sure that you know why each of the balance-sheet changes is made and are able, on your own, to make the appropriate balance-sheet entries to trace through the effects of any transaction.

To increase the student's understanding of how changes in the money supply affect the output of an economy and its price level, Chapter 18 offers the student a second way of looking at the economic forces that determine output and prices. This is the monetary approach. It employs the equation of exchange to reach conclusions that do not differ from those obtained from the saving-investment (or aggregate demand–aggregate supply) approach. But it emphasizes the effects of a change in the money supply rather than the effects of changed saving and investment plans upon NNP and prices. Changes in saving and investment plans affect either V (the income velocity of money), M (the money supply) or both V and M in the equation of exchange and thereby affect either output (Q), the price level (*P*), or both. *V* and *M* are the connecting link between the two approaches. The student should learn how and why changes in saving and investment plans affect *V* and *M*. In addition, the student must understand the equation of exchange and each of its four terms and how a change in any one of the four terms affects the other terms in the equation.

■ CHAPTER OUTLINE

1. The objective of monetary policy is full employment in the economy without inflation; the Federal Reserve Banks attempt to accomplish this objective by exercising control over the size of commercial bank reserves, thereby influencing the size of the money supply, the rate of interest, investment, and the level of total spending.

2. By examining the consolidated balance sheet and the principal assets and liabilities of the Federal Reserve Banks, an understanding of the ways in which the Federal Reserve can control and influence the reserves of commercial banks and the money supply can be obtained.

3. The Federal Reserve Banks employ three general or quantitative controls to affect the total amount of bank credit and the size of the money supply.

a. The Federal Reserve can change the reserve ratio.

b. It can buy and sell government bonds in the open market.

c. And it can also change the discount rate.

d. Changes in the discount rate and the purchase and sale of government bonds affect the amount of Reserve Bank credit and the amount of commercial bank reserves.

e. A tight (easy) money policy involves increasing (decreasing) the reserve ratio, selling (buying) bonds in the open market, and increasing (decreasing) the discount rate.

4. The Federal Reserve also employs selective or qualitative controls to affect the volume of credit available for and the amount of spending on certain types of goods and securities.

a. These controls consist of setting the margin requirements for the purchase of stocks,

the terms of credit available to purchasers of homes and durable consumer goods, and the maximum interest rate commercial banks may pay on time deposits.

b. In addition, moral suasion is used to influence commercial bank lending.

5. Open-market operations are probably the most effective device for controlling credit and the money supply.

6. A second approach to the relationships between the money supply, national output, and the price level employs the equation of exchange.

a. The equation of exchange is a useful truism: Total spending for the national output (*MV*) equals the total amount of money received from the sale of the national output (*PQ*). If *V* is constant, increases in *M* increase total spending and either *P*, *Q*, or both; and vice versa.

b. Most economists believe *V* is not constant and that it increases when consumer and business expectations improve or the rate of interest increases; and vice versa.

c. The value of the multiplier in any time period depends directly on the magnitude of *V*.

d. The saving-investment and equation-of-exchange approaches yield the same conclusions and reinforce each other; but each approach emphasizes the economic forces underemphasized by the other.

7. Whether monetary policy is effective in promoting full employment without inflation is a debatable question, but monetary policy has both shortcomings and advantages in fighting recession and inflation.

■ IMPORTANT TERMS

Monetary policy	Margin requirement
Easy money policy	Regulation *Q*
Tight money policy	Equation of exchange
Gold certificates	Income (circuit) velocity of money
Quantitative control	
Qualitative control	Resting time of money
Reserve Bank credit	Monetary approach
Open-market operations	Financial intermediaries
Discount rate	Cost-push inflation
Moral suasion	

■ FILL-IN QUESTIONS

1. The general objective of monetary policy in the United States is _____;
the _____
is generally responsible for the monetary policies which are put into effect by _____
_____

2. To eliminate inflation the monetary authority should seek to _____
the reserves of commercial banks, which would _____
the supply of money, causing the rate of interest to _____
and investment spending to _____

3. The two largest assets of the Federal Reserve Banks are _____
and _____. Their two largest liabilities are _____ and
_____

4. Government securities are bought and sold in the open market by the Federal Reserve Banks in order to _____
and to _____

5. Reserve Bank credit is the sum of _____
_____
and _____

6. The three quantitative (or general) controls employed by the monetary authority are

changing _____,

charging _____,

and _____

7. Changes in the reserve ratio affect the ability of commercial banks to create money in two ways: they affect the _____
_____
and the _____

8. To increase the supply of money, the Federal Reserve Banks should _____
the reserve ratio, _____
the discount rate, and/or _____
government securities in the open market; **to** decrease the supply of money, it should _____
_____
the reserve ratio, _____
the discount rate, and/or _____
securities in the open market.

9. If the Federal Reserve Banks were to sell $10 million in government bonds to the public and the reserve ratio were 25 percent, the supply of money would immediately be reduced $_____,
the reserves of commercial banks would be reduced $_____,
and the excess reserves of the banks would be reduced $_____;
if these bonds were sold to the commercial banks, the supply of money would immediately be reduced _____,
the reserves of the banks would be reduced $_____,
and the excess reserves of the banks would be reduced $_____

10. Indicate in the space to the right of each of the following transactions whether it will increase (+) or decrease commercial bank excess reserves (−).
a. Federal Reserve sells bonds in the open market _____
b. Commercial banks borrow from the Federal Reserve _____
c. Federal Reserve reduces the reserve ratio _____

11. The qualitative or selective controls are changes in:
a. _____
b. _____
c. _____

12. In the equation of exchange, $MV = PQ$. Indicate below what each of the four letters in the equation represents.

M: _____

V: _____

P: _____

Q: _____

13. Indicate in the spaces provided the effects—increase (+), decrease (−), or no change (0)—upon P and Q of the following:

a. The economy is at full employment, M increases, and V remains constant.

_____ _____

b. The economy is in a recession, V increases, and M remains constant. _____ _____

c. The economy is close to but not at full employment, and both M and V increase.

_____ _____

d. The economy is in a recession, M increases, and V remains constant. _____ _____

e. The economy is at full employment, and both M and V increase. _____ _____

14. If each firm *and* household wishes to hold an amount equal to $\frac{1}{12}$ of its annual income:

a. The "resting time" of a dollar in each firm and household would be _____

b. V would be _____

15. V would tend to *decrease* if:

a. The interest rate _____

b. The business outlook changed from _____

to _____

c. The economy felt that there would be _____ rather than _____ in the future.

16. Suppose the marginal propensity to consume is 0.9. If V is 4, a $10 billion increase in investment will increase the NNP by $_____ during the *first* year following the investment.

17. Monetary policy will *not* be effective in pulling a nation out of a depression if commercial banks _____ or if the public _____

18. One of the advantages of monetary policy is that it tends to have more _____ than fiscal policy.

■ PROBLEMS AND PROJECTS

1. Below are various items which belong in the balance statement of the Federal Reserve Banks. Place them in their proper place in the blank balance sheet, listing them either on the asset or on the liability side and in the order of their dollar importance.

Member bank reserves	Treasury deposits
Securities	Cash
Loans to member banks	Gold certificates
Federal Reserve Notes	

Assets	Liabilities
_____	_____
_____	_____
_____	_____
_____	_____

2. Assume that the consolidated balance sheet below is for all commercial banks. Assume also that the required reserve ratio is 25 percent, that cash is *not* a part of the commercial banks' legal reserve, and that the demand schedule below shows the amounts of commercial bank loans from the Federal Reserve that will be outstanding at various rates of interest.

Assets		Liabilities	
Cash	$ 50	Demand deposits	$400
Reserves	100	Loans from Federal	
Loans	150	Reserve	25
Securities	200	Net worth	75
	$500		$500

Discount rate, %	Amounts commercial banks will borrow from Federal Reserve
3.0	$ 0.0
2.5	12.5
2.0	25.0
1.5	37.5
1.0	50.0
0.5	62.5

a. To increase the supply of money by $100, the Federal Reserve Banks could *either:*

(1) _____

the reserve ratio to _____
percent

(2) _____

securities worth $_____
in the open market

(3) _____

the discount rate to _____
percent

b. To reduce the supply of money by $50,
the Federal Reserve Banks could *either:*

(1) _____

the reserve ratio to _____
percent

(2) _____

securities worth $_____

in the open market

(3) _____

the discount rate to _____
percent

3. Below are the initial consolidated balance sheets of the Federal Reserve and of commercial banks. Assume that the reserve ratio for commercial banks is 25 percent, that cash is *not* a part of a bank's legal reserve, and that the balance-sheet figures in column 1 prevail at the start of each of the following problems. Place the new balance-sheet figures in the appropriate columns and complete A, B, C, and D. *Do not cumulate your answers!*

a. The Federal Reserve Banks sell $3 in securities to the public, which pays by check (column 2).

b. The Federal Reserve Banks buy $4 in securities from the commercial banks (column 3).

	(1)	(2)	(3)	(4)	(5)	(6)
Federal Reserve Banks						
Assets:						
Gold certificates	$ 25	$___	$___	$___	$___	$___
Securities	30	___	___	___	___	___
Loans to commercial banks	10	___	___	___	___	___
Liabilities:						
Reserves of commercial banks	50	___	___	___	___	___
Treasury deposits	5	___	___	___	___	___
Federal Reserve Notes	10	___	___	___	___	___
Commercial Banks						
Assets:						
Reserves	$ 50	$___	$___	$___	$___	$___
Securities	70	___	___	___	___	___
Loans	90	___	___	___	___	___
Liabilities:						
Demand deposits	200	___	___	___	___	___
Loans from Federal Reserve	10	___	___	___	___	___
A. Required reserves		___	___	___	___	___
B. Excess reserves		___	___	___	___	___
C. Initial change in the money supply		___	___	___	___	___
D. Total potential change in the money supply		___	___	___	___	___

THE FEDERAL RESERVE BANKS AND MONETARY POLICY 123

c. The Federal Reserve Banks lower the required reserve ratio for commercial banks to 20 percent (column 4).

d. The U.S. Treasury buys $5 worth of goods from American manufacturers and pays the manufacturers by checks drawn on its accounts at the Federal Reserve Banks (column 5).

e. Because the Federal Reserve Banks have raised the discount rate, commercial banks repay $6 which they owe to the Federal Reserve (column 6).

4. In the table below are the values of three of the four terms in the equation of exchange during six different years.

Year	M	V	P	Q
1	$300	3	$2	____
2	400	3	____	600
3	400	____	2²⁄₇	700
4	____	5	3	750
5	600	5	____	750
6	600	6	4⁸⁄₁₀	____

a. Complete the table by computing the value of the term not given in each year.

b. Between years:

(1) 1 and 2, a 33⅓ percent increase in M caused _____ to increase by _____%.

(2) 2 and 3, a 33⅓ percent increase in V caused _____ to increase by _____% and _____ to increase by _____%.

(3) 3 and 4, a 12½ percent increase in M and a 25 percent increase in V caused P to increase by _____% and Q to increase by _____%.

(4) 4 and 5, a 33⅓ percent increase in M caused _____ to increase by _____%.

(5) 5 and 6, a 20 percent increase in V caused _____ to increase by _____%.

■ SELF-TEST

Circle the T if the statement is true, the F if it is false.

1. Consumer spending is more sensitive to changes in the rate of interest than is investment demand.   T   F

2. If the monetary authority wished to follow a tight money policy, it would seek to reduce the reserves of commercial banks.   T   F

3. The securities owned by the Federal Reserve Banks are almost entirely U.S. government bonds.   T   F

4. A change in the reserve ratio will affect the multiple by which the banking system can create money, but it will not affect the actual or excess reserves of member banks.   T   F

5. If the Federal Reserve Banks buy $15 in government securities from the public in the open market, the effect will be to increase the excess reserves of commercial banks by $15.   T   F

6. If the reserve ratio is lowered, some required reserves are turned into excess reserves.   T   F

7. Statistical evidence indicates that the income velocity of money is almost constant.   T   F

8. A decline in interest rates tends to increase the velocity of money.   T   F

9. The policies of the Federal Reserve Banks during a period of inflation are reinforced by the desire of the United States Treasury to keep interest rates low.   T   F

10. It is generally agreed that fiscal policy is more effective than monetary policy in controlling the business cycle because fiscal policy is more flexible.   T   F

Underscore the letter that corresponds to the best answer.

1. The agency directly responsible for monetary policy in the United States is: (a) the twelve Federal Reserve Banks; (b) the Board of Governors of the Federal Reserve System; (c) the Congress of the United States; (d) the U.S. Treasury.

2. The largest single asset in the Federal Reserve Banks' consolidated balance sheet is: (a) securities; (b) gold certificates; (c) cash; (d) the reserves of member banks.

3. The largest single liability of the Federal Reserve Banks is: (a) the reserves of member banks; (b) the deposits of the U.S. Treasury; (c) Federal Reserve Notes; (d) loans to member banks.

4. If the banking system had actual reserves of $140 and excess reserves of $20, to eliminate the excess reserves the Federal Reserve Banks would have to: (a) raise the reserve ratio from 18 to 20 percent; (b) raise the reserve ratio from 20 to 23⅓ percent; (c) raise the reserve ratio from 23⅓ to 25 percent; (d) raise the reserve ratio from 25 to 27½ percent.

5. Assuming that the Federal Reserve Banks sell $20 million in government securities to member banks and the reserve ratio is 20 percent, then the effect will be: (a) to reduce the actual supply of money by $20 million; (b) to reduce the actual supply of money by $4 million; (c) to reduce the potential money supply by $20 million; (d) to reduce the potential money supply by $100 million.

6. Which of the following acts would *not* have the same general effect upon the economy as the other three? (a) the Federal Reserve Banks sell bonds in the open market; (b) the Federal Reserve increases the discount rate; (c) the Federal Reserve lowers the down payments required for the purchase of consumer durables; (d) the Federal Reserve raises the reserve ratio.

7. If V in the equation of exchange is constant, an increase in M will necessarily increase: (a) P; (b) Q; (c) both P and Q; (d) P times Q.

8. Changes in the saving plans of consumers and the investment plans of business firms have an initial and direct effect upon: (a) M; (b) V; (c) either M or V but not both; (d) either M or V or both M and V.

9. If the "resting time" of a dollar in each firm and household in the economy is 3 months, (a) firms and households wish to hold an amount of money equal to ⅓ of their annual incomes; (b) firms and households wish to hold an account of money equal to ½ of their annual incomes; (c) the velocity of money is 3; (d) the velocity of money is 2.

10. If the income velocity of money is 4 and the marginal propensity to consume is 0.8, a $10 increase in planned investment will *during the first year* increase NNP by: (a) $18; (b) $24.40; (c) $29.52; (d) $50.

■ DISCUSSION QUESTIONS

1. Explain how the Board of Governors and the Federal Reserve Banks can influence investment, output, employment, and the price level. In your explanation, employ the following concepts: reserves, excess reserves, the supply of money, the availability of bank credit, and the rate of interest.

2. Why are changes in the rate of interest more likely to affect investment spending than consumption and saving?

3. What are the principal assets and liabilities of the Federal Reserve Banks? Which of these items seems most crucial in its effect on the levels of income, output, employment, and prices in the economy?

4. What is Reserve Bank credit? Why is it so called? How is it related to commercial bank reserves and the supply of money?

5. Explain how the quantitative controls of the Federal Reserve Banks would be used to contract the supply of money. How would they be used to expand the supply of money?

6. What is the difference between the effects of the Federal Reserve's buying (selling) government securities in the open market from (to) commercial banks and from (to) the public?

7. How do the selective or qualitative controls differ from general or quantitative controls? What are the principal selective controls? Explain how the Federal Reserve would use these controls in following a tight and an easy money policy.

8. Explain how the Federal Reserve employs Regulation Q to prevent the impact of a tight money policy from falling heavily upon the residential construction industry.

9. Which of the control devices available to the Federal Reserve is most effective? Why is it more effective than other quantitative controls?

10. Explain the terms in the equation of exchange and why the equation is truism.

11. Explain how a change in M or in V in the equation of exchange will affect P and Q during a recession, during a period of prosperity without full employment, and during a period of full employment. What causes V to change?

12. Why is monetary policy more effective in controlling inflation than in reducing unemployment?

13. Why did the Federal Reserve and the Treasury disagree in the post–World War II period of inflation over the policy the Federal Reserve should follow with respect to its open-market operations?

14. If the Federal Reserve is following a tight money policy and trying to reduce the reserves of commercial banks, but the commercial banks are acquiring new reserves by selling government securities to the Federal Reserve Banks, is there anything the Federal Reserve can do to prevent this?

15. Looking back at your answer to question 1, explain why monetary policy may be ineffectual in controlling inflation and preventing depression.

ECONOMIC STABILITY: THEORY AND POLICY

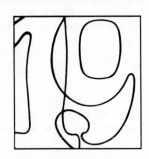

Chapter 19 is in part a summary of the previous nine chapters. The first two major sections of the chapter recall for the student the main outline of the theory of employment and the principal public policies that may be used to promote full employment without creating inflation. They help the student to see that the various principles discussed in the previous chapters are *not* separate theories but are, in fact, connected parts of the one theory of employment; and that the public policies discussed in earlier chapters are *not* really separate policies but are alternative means of achieving the goal of economic stabilization.

This one theory of employment and the alternative means of achieving this one goal are summarized for the student in Figure 19–1. This is probably the single most important figure in the textbook. But the student should be aware that it *is* a summary and that a summary necessarily sacrifices detail and completeness in exchange for generality and briefness. A few of the "Complications and Problems" which are hidden by Figure 19–1 and which are an essential part of a full understanding of the theory of employment and of stabilization policy are reviewed for the student in the third section of the chapter.

The fourth section of Chapter 19 examines two sharply opposing views. Keynesians stress the impact of the Federal budget on national output and the price level; and they believe that the way to achieve full employment without inflation is fiscal policy. Monetarists stress the impact of the money supply on output and price levels; and they contend that monetary policy is the best way to achieve these goals. The theories employed by the Keynesians and the Monetarists are really one theory. The student should try to see that what divides them is not the theory but the question of what method, fiscal or monetary policy, is the best means of promoting economic stability.

Just as Professor McConnell sent the manuscript for Chapter 19 to the printer in August 1971 President Nixon announced a "New Economic Policy." The freeze on wages, prices, and rents (as well as certain other parts of the program) announced by the President were to be temporary. By the time the student reads the last section of the chapter a more permanent means of limiting inflation will in all likelihood have replaced this freeze. This last section may record only an incident in history. But it seems likely that the New Economic Policy will be a turning point in the history of economic policy in the United States. For this reason Professor McConnell hastened to revise Chapter 19 to include in it a record of this turning point.

In order to increase the student's comprehension of this single theory in its entirety and the alternative fiscal and monetary policies which are available to promote economic stability and in order to clarify the controversy between Keynesians and Monetarists, the "Problems and Projects" section of the *Study Guide* contains a series of three numérical problems. The problems begin with familiar concepts and principles and from these familiar ideas develop several entirely new concepts and tools. These new concepts enable the student to understand better the theory of employment and public policy as a whole—rather than in parts—and to see the connections between the parts. In working these new and more difficult problems the student cannot rely on the textbook for help. Instead he must depend on what he has already learned and on carefully following the instructions given him in the problems. The only words of caution that need be given are: (1) start at the beginning of the series of problems; and (2) check your answer with those in the Answers section (at the back of the *Study Guide*) at every step of the way.

■ CHAPTER OUTLINE

1. The income, employment, output, and prices of an economy are positively related to the level of aggregate demand, which has three principal components.

 a. Consumption spending depends upon the income of the economy and the several factors which affect the location of the consumption schedule.

 b. Investment spending is the more unstable component because it depends upon profit expectations which are themselves highly variable.

 c. Government spending depends partly on what level of spending is necessary to achieve full employment and price stability.

2. To achieve economic stability, government employs both fiscal and monetary policy.

 a. Fiscal policy utilizes both automatic and discretionary changes in government spending and in taxes.

 b. Monetary policy utilizes both quantitative and selective controls to affect the money supply and interest rates.

3. The use of the theory of employment to achieve economic stability is complicated by several considerations.

 a. The connections between cause and effect are more complex and interdependent than the theory may suggest.

 b. The quantitative relationships between the components of the theory can only be esti-

mated; and stabilization policies will, therefore, never be completely successful.

 c. Economic stabilization is but one goal of the American economy, and at times it may be made subordinate to other more pressing goals.

4. Economists disagree over whether fiscal or monetary policy is the more effective means of stabilizing the economy.

 a. Keynesians believe fiscal policy is more effective.

 b. The Monetarists believe monetary policy is more effective and argue that:

 (1) because the demand for money is a fixed percentage of national income (and the velocity of money is, therefore, constant) the level of national income can be controlled by varying the money supply

 (2) the economic history of the United States shows that the changes in the money supply caused the observed changes in national income

 (3) fiscal policy is ineffective unless accompanied by changes in the money supply and it is, therefore, money-supply change that changes the level of economic activity

 (4) discretionary changes in the money supply bring about instability and a fixed rate of growth in the money supply is necessary for stability

 c. The Keynesians deny the contentions of the Monetarists by offering a number of counterarguments.

5. The New Economic Policy announced by President Nixon in August 1971 aimed to reduce unemployment, slow inflation, and increase net exports.

 a. To increase consumption and investment spending and thereby expand employment, an investment tax credit, a reduction in the excise tax on automobiles, and an earlier increase in personal income tax exemptions were proposed.

 b. To prevent inflation the President imposed a ninety-day freeze on wages and salaries, prices, and rents; and established a Cost of Living Council to recommend measures to prevent inflation after the freeze ends.

 c. To increase net exports he imposed a surcharge on imports subject to tariffs and eliminated the fixed relation between the dollar and foreign money.

 d. While well received by most economists,

at least three criticisms were levied against this policy.

e. The end of the freeze may bring about a more permanent incomes policy.

■ IMPORTANT TERMS

Keynesian position	**New Economic Policy**
Monetarist position	**Cost of Living Council**
Monetary rule	

■ FILL-IN QUESTIONS

1. The levels of output, employment, income, and prices depend upon the level of _____ _____ which in turn depends (in a closed economy) upon the amounts of _____, _____, and _____

2. The theory of employment explains each of the three primary components of aggregate demand as follows:

a. Consumption depends upon the level of _____ and the position of the _____

b. Net investment depends upon the _____ _____ of business firms.

c. Government expenditures for goods and services depend upon _____ _____

3. Government seeks to stabilize the economy by employing _____ and _____ policies.

4. Fiscal policy entails changing:

a. _____ spending to affect _____ directly.

b. _____ revenues in order to affect the _____ and _____ components of aggregate demand.

5. Monetary policy entails changing the supply of _____ to bring about a change in

the _____ and thereby affect _____ spending in the economy.

6. Applying fiscal and monetary policies to achieve stability is difficult because economic relations are more _____ than the theory suggests, the economic relations are hard to _____ and the economy also persues _____ goals.

7. The Keynesian position is that while both fiscal and monetary policies affect the level of economic activity, _____ policy is a more effective means of stabilizing the economy.

8. Monetarists:

a. argue that because the _____ for money is stable, the _____ of money is also stable; and that the _____ of money determines the level of activity in the economy;

b. would have the supply of money increase at the same annual rate as the potential rate of growth of _____, a rate of from _____ to _____ percent a year.

9. The New Economic Policy announced in August 1971 was designed to increase _____ _____ exports and _____ in the economy and to limit the rate of _____ _____

10. The New Economic Policy:

a. imposed a temporary freeze on _____, _____, and _____

b. proposed that investment and consumption be increased by

(1) _____

(2) _____

(3) _____

c. put a surcharge on _____ and ended the fixed relation between the dollar and _____

■ PROBLEMS AND PROJECTS

1. Assume that the economy engages in no international trade—that its exports and imports are both zero; that government expenditures for goods and services are $50; that net taxes are also $50; and that the consumption schedule of the economy *before* taxes is that shown in the table below.

NNP	C	C'	S'	i	I
$200	$190	___	___	5.0%	$ 0
250	230	___	___	4.5	10
300	270	___	___	4.0	20
350	310	___	___	3.5	30
400	350	___	___	3.0	40
450	390	___	___	2.5	50
500	430	___	___	2.0	60
550	470	___	___	1.5	70
600	510	___	___	1.0	80

a. Assume that all taxes are personal taxes. Given the marginal propensities to consume and to save evident in the consumption schedule, compute saving and consumption *after* taxes at each level of NNP and enter them in the table.

b. Assume that the level of investment in the economy depends only upon the rate of interest according to the table. Recalling that the government spends $50 for goods and services, what is the equilibrium level of NNP if the rate of interest happens to be 5 percent?

c. Now compute the equilibrium NNP at each of the other eight rates of interest given in the table; and enter the equilibrium NNPs opposite the appropriate rate of interest in the table below. (*Hint:* After computing NNP at 5 percent, the other NNPs can be determined by using the multiplier.)

d. Plot the schedule obtained in (c) on the graph at the right. Place *i* on the vertical axis and NNP on the horizontal axis; and label the curve *IS* (because planned Investment and Saving are equal at the rates of interest and NNPs indicated by the curve).

e. Using your knowledge of the multiplier,

what would be the effect—increase (+) or de-

i	Equilibrium NNP
5.0%	___
4.5	___
4.0	___
3.5	___
3.0	___
2.5	___
2.0	___
1.5	___
1.0	___

crease (−)—on the equilibrium NNP at any given rate of interest of each of the following:
  (1) A tax increase? ___ A tax decrease?

___

  (2) An increase in government expenditures? ___ A decrease in government expenditures?

___

  (3) An increase in the amount of investment at each rate of interest? ___ A decrease in investment demand at each rate of interest? ___

  (4) An increase in the consumption schedule (that is, an increase in consumption at

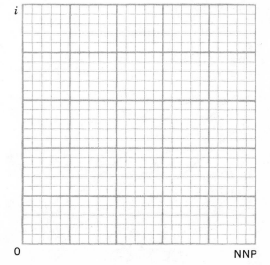

i

0   NNP

each level of NNP)? _____ A decrease in the consumption schedule? _____

f. Utilizing your answers in (e) immediately above, how would each of the following affect—increase (+) or decrease (−)—the entire i-equilibrium NNP schedule you calculated in (c)? (An increase in the schedule means that NNP at each i increases; a decrease means that NNP at each i decreases.)

(1) A tax increase? _____ A tax decrease? _____

(2) An increase in government expenditures? _____ A decrease? _____

(3) An increase in investment demand? _____ A decrease? _____

(4) An increase in the consumption schedule? _____ A decrease? _____

g. How would each of the eight changes listed in (f) above affect the IS curve? Assuming that the initial IS curve in the diagram below is IS_2, which four of the eight changes would move it to IS_1? _____

_____

Which four would move it to IS_3? _____

_____

2. Assume that the total supply of money (M) in the economy is equal to $100. Suppose also that the total demand for money (L) depends upon both the level of NNP and the

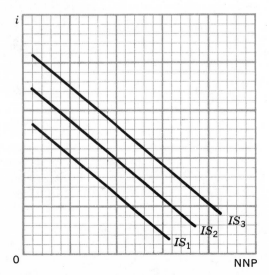

prevailing rate of interest (i) in the economy.

The quantity of money demanded for *transaction* purposes (L_t) depends upon the level of NNP and is shown in the schedule below. The quantity of money demanded for *speculative* purposes (L_s) depends upon the rate of interest and is also shown in the table below. The total demand for money (L) equals the transactions demand plus the speculative demand ($L_t + L_s$).

NNP	L_t	i	L_s
$200	$20	5.0%	$40
250	25	4.5	45
300	30	4.0	50
350	35	3.5	55
400	40	3.0	60
450	45	2.5	65
500	50	2.0	70
550	55	1.5	75
600	60	1.0	80

a. The greater the NNP of the economy, the _____ (greater, smaller) is the quantity of money demanded for transaction purposes; and vice versa.

b. The higher the rate of interest in the economy, the _____ (greater, smaller) is the quantity of money demanded for speculative purposes; and vice versa.

c. If NNP were $200,

(1) L_t would be equal to _____
(2) In order that the supply of money ($100) equal the *total* demand for money ($L_t + L_s$), the speculative demand (L_s) would have to be equal to _____.

and the rate of interest equal to _____ (*Hint:* Subtract L_t from $100 to determine L_s; and then examine the schedule to discover what i must be to cause this L_s). Enter this rate of interest opposite the NNP of $200 in the table on page 131.

d. Now repeat the process followed in (c) above for NNPs from $250 through $600. Determine for each of these NNPs:

(1) The transactions demand (L_t) for money at this NNP.
(2) The amount of money from the total money supply (of $100) remaining to satisfy the speculative demand for money (L_s).
(3) What the rate of interest (i) would have

to be in order that the L_s be the amount indicated in (2); and enter this i opposite the appropriate NNP in the table.

i	Equilibrium NNP
_____	$200
_____	250
_____	300
_____	350
_____	400
_____	450
_____	500
_____	550
_____	600

e. Plot the schedule obtained in (d) above on the graph below. Place i on the vertical axis and NNP on the horizontal axis; and label the curve LM because the quantity of money demanded and the supply of money are equal at the rates of interest and NNPs indicated by the curve).

f. If the supply of money (M) should:

(1) Increase from $100 to $105; the i opposite every NNP would _____

(increase, decrease) by _____ percentage points.

(2) Decrease from $100 to $95, the i opposite every NNP would _____

by _____ percentage points.

g. Using the knowledge gained in (f) above concerning the effects of a change in the supply of money upon the LM schedule; and using the LM_2 curve given in the diagram below, draw:

(1) An LM curve that would result from an increase in the money supply and label it LM_3

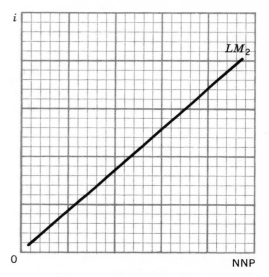

(2) An LM curve that would result from a decrease in the money supply and label it M_1

3. Assume the following: the existence of the consumption and investment schedules given in question 1 above; the existence of the transactions and speculative demand for money schedules given in question 2 above; that government expenditures for goods and services are $50; that net taxes are $50; and that the supply of money is $100.

a. Using the tables which you completed in questions (1 c) and (2 d) above, what NNP and what rate of interest will ensure both that the aggregate quantity of goods and services demanded equals the aggregate quantity supplied; and that the total quantity of money demanded equals the supply of money? (Hint: At what i is the NNP the same in both schedules? Or at what NNP is the i the same in both schedules?)

(1) NNP: $_____

(2) i: _____ percent

b. Plot both the *IS* and the *LM* curves on the following graph. These curves cross at an

(1) NNP of $_____

(2) *i* of _____ percent

c. Look back to your answers to questions (1 *f*) and (2 *g*) above. What would be the effect—increase (+), decrease (−), no change (0), or indeterminate (?)—upon NNP, *i*, *C*, and *I* of each of the following?

	Effect upon			
	NNP	*i*	*C*	*I*
(1) An increase in government expenditures for goods and services	___	___	___	___
(2) An increase in net taxes	___	___	___	___
(3) An increase in the money supply	___	___	___	___
(4) A decrease in the investment schedule	___	___	___	___
(5) An increase in the consumption schedule	___	___	___	___

d. If the NNP of the economy consistent with both full employment and the absence of inflation were $450, what monetary and fiscal measures might be taken to bring the economy's NNP to this level? _____

e. If the NNP of the economy consistent with both full employment and the absence of inflation were $350, what monetary and fiscal measures might be taken to bring the economy's NNP to this level? _____

■ SELF-TEST

Circle the T if the statement is true, the F if it is false.

1. Inappropriate levels of aggregate demand are not the only causes of inflation and unemployment.   **T   F**

2. Keynesians believe that monetary policy cannot be used to lessen inflationary pressures.   **T   F**

3. A budget deficit, according to Keynesians, will bring about a rise in interest rates unless the money supply increases.   **T   F**

4. The chief proponent of the Monetarist position is Milton Friedman.   **T   F**

5. According to the Monetarists, the money supply is the single most important factor affecting output, employment, and prices.   **T   F**

6. From the Monetarist viewpoint, the economy is in equilibrium when the amount of money people want to hold is equal to the supply of money.   **T   F**

7. From the Monetarist way of looking at the economy, increasing *M* will increase *Q* in the equation of exchange.   **T   F**

8. Keynesians contend that the velocity of money is unstable.   **T   F**

9. In August 1971 President Nixon established the Office of Emergency Preparedness to develop policies that would maintain economic growth without promoting inflation.   **T   F**

10. Were the value of the dollar to fall relative to foreign currencies, American made goods would become less expensive to foreigners and foreign made goods would become more expensive for Americans.   **T   F**

Underscore the letter that corresponds to the best answer.

1. Which of the following is *not* one of the difficulties encountered in achieving full employment without inflation? (a) the pursuit of noneconomic goals; (b) the inability to quantify economic relationships; (c) the nonoperational character of the policy implications of the theory of employment; (d) the looseness of the cause-effect relations in macroeconomic theory.

2. Expansion of the money supply, according to Keynesians, would dampen the impact of (or would not be congenial with) (a) a decrease in personal income tax rates; (b) a reduction in government expenditures; (c) increased government transfer payments; (d) a budget deficit.

3. If the demand for money is stable and equal to 25 percent of national income, a $10 billion increase in the money supply will increase the national income by (a) $20 billion; (b) $30 billion; (c) $40 billion; (d) $50 billion.

4. Were the demand for money a stable 12.5 percent of national income and the level of national income at which full employment without inflation is achieved $480 billion, the appropriate money supply, according to the Monetarists would be (a) $40 billion; (b) $50 billion; (c) $60 billion; (d) $80 billion.

5. Suppose the stable demand for money is 20 percent of national income, the actual national income is $600 billion, and the money supply is $100 billion. From the viewpoint of the Monetarists, national income would tend to (a) increase; (b) decrease; (c) remain unchanged; (d) be unstable.

6. Were the Federal government to incur a budget surplus to fight inflation and use the surplus to retire (or buy back) government securities owned by the public, the price level, in the opinion of Monetarists, would (a) not be affected; (b) rise more slowly; (c) rise more rapidly; (d) decrease.

7. The monetary rule suggested by the Monetarists is that the money supply should increase at the same rate as (a) the price level; (b) the real output of the economy; (c) the velocity of money; (d) none of the above.

8. Keynesians believe that adherence to the monetary rule of the Monetarists would result in (a) inflation; (b) unemployment; (c) economic instability; (d) an unstable velocity of money.

9. Which of the following was not a part of President Nixon's New Economic Policy? (a) a reduction in personal income tax rates; (b) a surcharge on all imports subject to tariffs; (c) a proposal to reduce the excise tax on automobiles; (d) severance of the fixed relation between the dollar and foreign currencies.

10. The New Economic Policy of President Nixon (a) was at the time favorably received by most economists; (b) froze interest rates and dividends; (c) was criticized by business leaders who felt it benefited labor and consumers; (d) was designed to prevent inflation by reducing the foreign demand for American goods.

■ DISCUSSION QUESTIONS

1. Explain as briefly as possible what determines the level of national output in the American economy.

2. Distinguish between fiscal and monetary policy and explain how we may use each of them to achieve reasonably full employment and relatively stable prices.

3. What complications and problems are encountered in using monetary and fiscal policy to eliminate inflationary and deflationary gaps.

4. What is the Keynesian position in their controversy with the Monetarists?

5. Why has interest in the role of money as a determinant of the level of economic activity revived in recent years?

6. Explain the Monetarist position. Include in your explanation (a) their analysis of the demand for money and the equilibrium level of national income, (b) the evidence they use to support their position, (c) their analysis of fiscal policy, and (d) their monetary rule.

7. What criticisms do the Keynesians make of the Monetarist position?

8. What three problems prompted President Nixon to announce a New Economic Policy in August 1971?

9. What actions taken by the President and what proposals to Congress were included in the New Economic Policy? Why did the President set up the Cost of Living Council?

10. Why was the President's New Economic Policy criticized?

THE SIMPLE ANALYTICS OF ECONOMIC GROWTH

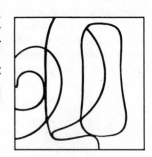

This is the first of three chapters dealing with the important and controversial topic of economic growth. Chapter 20 presents the *theory* of growth, Chapter 21 the *history* of economic growth in the United States, and Chapter 22 the current *problems and policies* relating to American economic growth.

The purpose of Chapter 20 is to explain what makes economic growth possible. After briefly defining and pointing out the significance of growth, the text analyzes the six factors that make growth possible. The four *supply* factors increase the output potential of the economy. Whether the economy actually produces its full potential—that is, whether the economy has both full employment and full production—depends upon two other factors: the level of aggregate demand (the *demand* factor) and the efficiency with which the economy reallocates resources (the *allocative* factor).

The crucial thing to note about the supply factors is that when labor increases more rapidly than natural resources, or capital, or both of these, the economy will be subject to diminishing returns and eventually to decreasing output per person and to a declining standard of living. This will breed the misery and poverty forecast by Malthus 170 years ago. Diminishing returns can, however, be offset—and more than offset—by increasing the amount of capital the economy possesses, by technological progress, and by improving the quality of the labor force at a more rapid rate. This is the way to achieve growth, and diminishing returns have been *more* than offset by those nations which have experienced economic growth. The nations which have not experienced growth have found the force of diminishing returns too great for them: their improvements in technology, capital, and labor just barely offset the effect of diminishing returns. And in some nations, these improvements were so weak that diminishing returns were dominant and the standard of living actually fell.

Probably the most important principle or generalization developed in the chapter employs the theory of output and employment already presented in Chapter 13. Here we discover that the maintenance of full employment in an economy whose productive capacity is increasing annually requires that investment increase annually to ensure a sufficient aggregate demand for the expanding full-employment output. And because investment increases an economy's productive capacity, not only must investment increase from year to year, but it must also increase by increasing amounts to assure the production of the full-employment output. The student must be sure he understands the "why" of this principle, because it is fundamental to an understanding of full employment without inflation in the growing economy.

Actually, Chapter 20 contains very little that is really new. It uses a few of the ideas, terms, and theories found in earlier chapters in order to explain what makes an economy capable of growing (that is, what increases the size of its full-employment or capacity output) and what is necessary if it is actually to grow (that is, if it is to produce all which its expanding capacity allows). With careful reading the student should have little or no trouble with Chapter 20, providing he has done a good job on the earlier chapters and providing he keeps in mind the fundamental distinction between the supply factors and the demand and allocative factors. However, he must be sure he understands the material in this chapter if he is to be ready for the discussion in Chapters 21 and 22 of the history, the problems, and the costs of promoting economic growth in the United States.

■ CHAPTER OUTLINE

1. While modern employment theory is concerned with the short run and an economy with a given productive capacity, growth economics deals with the long run and changes in productive capacity over time.
a. Economic growth means an increase in either the total or the per capita real output of an economy.
b. Economic growth is important because it lessens the burden of scarcity: it provides the means of satisfying existing wants more fully and of fulfilling new needs.
c. One or two percentage point differences in the rate of growth result in substantial differences in annual increases in the economy's output.

2. Whether economic growth can occur depends upon four supply factors; and whether it will occur depends upon the demand factor and the allocative factor.

3. The amount by which total output can increase depends upon the amount and the proportion in which resources are increased.
a. In an economy where the quantities of land and capital are relatively fixed, the law of diminishing returns operates so that increases in the quantity of labor employed eventually result in declining increases in total output per additional unit of labor.
b. A proportionate increase in all resources moves the production possibilities curve to the right in the same proportion. But a dispro-

portionate increase in resources moves it to the right by a percentage less than the percentage by which the most expanded resource has increased.
c. When diminishing returns set in and the marginal product of labor declines, the average product of labor will eventually decline.
d. The optimum population is the population at which the average product of labor (or real output per capita) is at a maximum.
e. Because of diminishing returns and the tendency for population to increase, Malthus predicted widespread poverty as time passed.
f. But growth can occur and poverty can be avoided if diminishing returns are offset by the increases in the productivity of workers that are brought about by more capital, better methods, and an improved labor force.

4. The higher the level of aggregate demand, the closer the economy will be to producing the output which the supply factors make it possible to produce.
a. With the potential full-employment level of output expanding, the volume of net investment must also increase if the economy is to remain in equilibrium at its full-employment level because the volume of saving increases as output rises.
b. An expanding volume of net investment also increases the full-employment output by increasing amounts, and thereby increases by increasing amounts the net investment necessary to maintain full employment.

5. For economic growth to be possible, the economy must also be capable of reallocating its resources with reasonable speed and completeness.

■ IMPORTANT TERMS

Economic growth
Supply factor
Demand factor
Allocative factor
Law of diminishing returns
Marginal product
Average product

Increasing returns
Optimum population
Income-creating aspect of investment
Capacity-creating aspect of investment
Capital-output ratio

■ FILL-IN QUESTIONS

1. Keynesian (or modern) employment theory assumes the productive capacity of the economy is _____; while growth economics is concerned with an economy whose productive capacity _____ _____ over time.

2. Economic growth can mean an increase in either the _____ or the _____ of an economy.

3. An increase in output per capita _____ _____ the standard of living and _____ the burden of scarcity in the economy. It also enables the economy to satisfy _____ more fully and to satisfy _____

4. The four supply factors in economic growth are _____, _____, _____, and _____.

The other two growth factors are the _____ _____ factor and the _____ factor.

5. Assume an economy has a GNP of $600 billion. If the growth rate is 5%, GNP will increase by $_____ billion a year; but if the rate of growth is only 3%, the annual increase in GNP will be $_____ billion. A two percentage point difference in the growth rate results in a $_____ billion difference in the annual increase in GNP.

6. If there are no diseconomies or economies of scale and if *all* resources expand by 8%, the productive capacity of the economy will increase by _____%.

7. The law of diminishing returns says that when additional equal quantities of one resource are used along with fixed quantities of other resources, total output (beyond some point) will _____ by _____ amounts.

8. Assume an economy employs only two resources. One of these increases by 10% and the other increases by 3%. Technology and the quality of the resources are fixed. If this economy is subject to diminishing returns, its productive capacity will increase by less than _____%.

9. When an economy is subject to diminishing returns and the marginal product of labor decreases, the _____ product of labor will sooner or later _____

10. The population size which results in the maximum output per capita (or the maximum average product of labor) is the _____ _____

11. Malthus predicted that because of diminishing returns and the tendency for the _____ of an economy to increase, the standard of living would _____ _____

12. The tendency for the standard of living to fall as the population increases can be lessened or even overcome by increasing the ____ _____ of workers.

13. If the economy is to maintain a given *rate* of economic growth, the *volume* of investment must _____ by _____ amounts.

14. Expenditures for new capital goods both increase _____ and add to the _____ of the economy; the amount by which investment expenditures expand the latter depend upon the volume of investment expenditures and the _____ _____

15. To have the economic growth which the

supply and demand factors make possible, an economy must also be able to _____ its resources from one use to another with

_____

and _____

■ PROBLEMS AND PROJECTS

1. The table below shows the total production of an economy as the quantity of labor employed increases. The quantities of all other resources employed are constant.

Units of labor	Total production	Marginal product of labor	Average product of labor
0	0		0
1	80	_____	_____
2	200	_____	_____
3	330	_____	_____
4	400	_____	_____
5	450	_____	_____
6	480	_____	_____
7	490	_____	_____
8	480	_____	_____

a. Compute the marginal products of the first through the eighth unit of labor and enter them in the table.

b. There are increasing returns to labor from the first through the _____ unit of labor and decreasing returns from the _____ through the eighth unit.

c. When total production is increasing, marginal product is (positive, negative) _____ _____ and when total production is decreasing, marginal product is _____

_____

d. Now compute the average products of the various quantities of labor and enter them in the table.

e. When the marginal product of labor is greater than the average product, average

product is (increasing, decreasing) _____ _____; and when the marginal product is less than the average product, average product is _____

f. The optimum population in this economy would be _____ units of labor, because with this many units of labor the _____

_____

of labor is _____

2. Column 1 of the table below lists the various quantities of labor an economy might employ. Columns 2 and 3 show total production and the average product of labor for each quantity of labor.

(1) Quantity of labor	(2) Total production	(3) Average product of labor	(4) New total production	(5) New average product of labor
0	0	0	0	0
1	80	80	100	_____
2	200	100	220	_____
3	330	110	360	_____
4	400	100	500	_____
5	450	90	600	_____
6	480	80	660	_____
7	490	70	700	_____
8	480	60	720	_____

a. Assume the economy has and employs 4 units of labor. The average product of labor is

_____

b. Now suppose the total productivity of workers increases from the figures shown in column 2 to those given in column 4. Compute the new average products of labor and enter them in column 5.

c. If the economy continued to employ 4 units of labor, the average productivity of labor would have increased by _____%.

d. This increase in the productivity of workers could be due to more _____

_____, improved _____, better _____, or any two or three of these.

e. As a result of this increase in productivity the optimum population for this economy has

_____ from 3 to _____ units of labor.

f. If, while the productivity of workers increased, the number of units of labor this economy had, and employed, increased from 4 to:

(1) 5, the average product of labor would have (increased, decreased) _____

from 100 to _____

(2) 7, the average product of labor would have _____

(3) 8, the average product of labor would have _____

3. Assume that in a certain hypothetical and governmentless economy the marginal propensity to consume is 0.8, that in "year 1" the economy is producing a full-employment level of output of $200, and that the real net national product is capable of increasing by $40 every year.

a. Complete the table below by computing how much consumption and saving would be in each year if the maximum (full-employment) output of the economy were actually produced, and the amount of investment which would be required for the economy to achieve a full-employment level of output.

b. The economy is capable of increasing its

output _____

percent in year 2 if investment increases by

_____

percent.

c. The economy is capable of increasing its

output _____

percent in year 6 if investment increases by

_____

percent.

d. The *rate* at which investment must increase if full employment and maximum output are to be maintained is equal to _____

_____

e. The amount by which investment must increase in any year to maintain full employment and maximum output is equal to the increase in net national product *possible* multiplied by _____

4. This problem is much like problem 3 above; but it is a little more difficult because it does not ignore the capacity-creating aspect of investment as problem 3 did.

Assume that in a governmentless economy the marginal propensity to consume is 0.7, that the capital-output ratio is 3.0, and that in year 1 the economy is producing a full-employment output of $300.

a. Complete the table at the top of page 139 by computing

(1) The full-employment output of the economy in years 2, 3, and 4. (*Hint:* The full-employment output in any year is the full-employment output of the previous year *plus* the investment of the previous year multiplied by the reciprocal of the capital-output ratio.)

Year	Full-employment net national product	Full-employment consumption	Full-employment saving	Investment required to achieve full employment
1	$200	$ 160	$ 40	$ 40
2	240	_____	_____	_____
3	280	_____	_____	_____
4	320	_____	_____	_____
5	360	_____	_____	_____
6	400	_____	_____	_____

Year	Full-employment net national product	Full-employment consumption	Full-employment saving	Investment required to achieve full employment
1	$ 300	$ 210	$ 90	$ 90
2	_____	_____	_____	_____
3	_____	_____	_____	_____
4	_____	_____	_____	_____

(2) The amounts of consumption and saving in each year if the full-employment output is produced.

(3) The amount of investment required in each year to achieve the full-employment level of output.

b. This hypothetical economy's full-employment output is growing at a rate of _____% per year; full employment will be achieved if investment grows by _____% each year.

c. To achieve full employment, investment must increase by _____ amounts; and full-employment output will increase by _____ amounts.

d. In this economy the *average* propensity to save is a constant _____ and the reciprocal of the capital-output ratio is _____; the former figure multiplied by the latter is _____%, which is also _____

■ SELF-TEST

Circle the T if the statement is true, the F if it is false.

1. Growth economics is concerned with an economy in which productive capacity is not fixed.   (T) F

2. The best of the two definitions of economic growth is an increase in the per capita real output of the economy.   T (F)

3. Suppose two economies both have GNPs of $500 billion. If the GNPs grow at annual rates of 3% in the first and 5% in the sec-

ond economy, the difference in their amounts of growth in one year is $10 billion.   (T) F

4. The demand factor in economic growth refers to the ability of the economy to expand its production as the demand for products grows.   T (F)

5. The allocative factor in economic growth refers to the ability of the economy to move resources from one use to another as the productive capacity of the economy grows.   (T) F

6. Diminishing returns for a resource are the eventual result of increasing the employment of that resource by larger percentages than the employment of other resources is increased.   (T) F

7. The effect of diminishing returns to labor upon the standard of living is overcome whenever the average productivity of labor is increased.   T (F)

8. When average product is falling, marginal product is greater than average product. T (F)

9. When marginal product is negative, total production (or output) is decreasing.   (T) F

10. If the volume of investment expands more rapidly than is necessary to keep the full-employment output of the economy expanding at the rate which the supply factors allow, the result will be unemployment. T (F)

11. Other things being constant, the productive capacity of an economy will increase by an amount equal to net investment multiplied by the capital-output ratio.   T (F)

12. One of the requirements for allocative efficiency is the reasonably rapid and complete employment of the new workers in the labor force.   (T) F

Underscore the letter that corresponds to the best answer.

1. Which of the following is *not* one of the benefits of economic growth to a society? (a) everyone enjoys a greater real income; (b) the standard of living in that society increases; (c) the burden of scarcity decreases; (d) the society is better able to meet new needs.

2. Suppose an economy has a GNP of $700 billion and an annual growth rate of 5%. Over a *two*-year period GNP will increase by: (a) $14 billion; (b) $35 billion; (c) $70 billion; (d) $71¾ billion.

3. If the production possibilities curve of an economy moves from *AB* to *CD* on the graph below, and the economy changes the combination of goods it produces from *X* to *Y*, there has been: (a) improvement in both the supply and the other growth factors; (b) an improvement in only the supply factor; (c) an improvement in only the demand and allocative growth factors; (d) an improvement in the level of total employment in the economy.

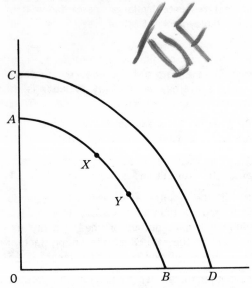

4. Which of the following is *not* a supply factor in economic growth? (a) an expansion in purchasing power; (b) an increase in the economy's stock of capital goods; (c) more natural resources; (d) technological improvements.

For questions 5 and 6 use the data given in the table below.

Units of labor	Total production
0	0
1	50
2	110
3	160
4	200
5	230
6	250
7	260
8	265

5. The marginal product of the fifth unit of labor is: (a) 40; (b) 30; (c) 20; (d) 10.

6. The average product of 4 units of labor is: (a) 70; (b) 60; (c) 50; (d) 40.

7. The law of diminishing returns says that as increased quantities of one resource are added to fixed quantities of other resources, there will eventually be a decrease in: (a) total production; (b) marginal product; (c) average product; (d) the optimum population.

8. The "optimum population" of an economy is: (a) the largest population the resources of that economy are capable of supporting; (b) the level of population which enables the economy to produce the largest possible output; (c) the level of population which enables the economy to produce the largest possible per capita output; (d) the level of population which results in the greatest amount of natural resources and capital equipment per capita in the economy.

9. Which of the following will *not* usually increase the average product of labor? (a) technological improvements; (b) an expanded labor force; (c) an increase in the amount of capital per worker; (d) better-educated workers.

10. If an economy is to maintain a constant *rate* of economic growth, assuming that the marginal propensity to consume is constant: (a) the volume of investment spending must increase at a more rapid rate; (b) the volume of investment spending must increase at the same rate; (c) the volume of investment spending need only remain constant; (d) the volume of investment spending must increase by the same amount that the output of the economy increases.

■ DISCUSSION QUESTIONS

1. What is meant by economic growth? Why should the citizens of the United States be concerned with economic growth?

2. How does growth economics differ from the theory of employment (or the theory of national income determination)?

3. What are the six basic ingredients of economic growth? What is the essential difference between the supply factors and the other two factors? Is there any relationship between the strength of the supply factor and the strength of the demand factor?

4. State the law of diminishing returns. What is the cause of diminishing returns?

5. What does an expansion in the quantity of resources employed do to the production possibilities curve if: (a) all resources expand proportionally and (b) all resources do not expand proportionally?

6. Define the marginal and the average product of labor. If marginal product at first increases and then decreases as more labor is employed, what will happen to the average product? Why will average product behave this way?

7. What is an optimum population? Why is this concept important?

8. What predictions did Malthus make for the economic future of mankind? On what bases did he make this prediction?

9. What can be done to offset or overcome the tendency for the average product of labor and the standard of living to decline as the employment of labor and the population increase?

10. Explain why an increasing volume of net investment is necessary in an economy whose productive capacity is increasing if full employment is to be maintained. What is the connection between investment and increases in productive capacity? Why does the maintenance of full employment require that investment increase by increasing amounts?

11. In addition to expanding aggregate demand, what else is necessary in an economy if it is to experience economic growth at the rate which the supply factors allow?

12. What is meant by allocative efficiency? Why is this kind of efficiency important if there is to be economic growth?

ECONOMIC GROWTH: THE AMERICAN EXPERIENCE

Chapter 21 is the second of the three chapters concerned with economic growth. It uses the theory of growth—the explanation of what makes economic growth possible—presented in Chapter 20 to explain why the American economy has grown in the past sixty or so years.

That it has grown in this period is fairly obvious. Using the two different definitions of growth found in Chapter 20, Chapter 21 begins by describing how much and how fast the American economy has grown. Real GNP has increased 6 times in the past six decades, and per capita real GNP has expanded 2½ times. Since 1870, real GNP has increased, on the average, by 3.6 percent per year and real GNP per capita, again on the average, has increased 1.9 percent annually. This is the record. The important question to ask about this record is whether, in recent years, it might not have been a better record—whether the economy has grown as rapidly as it was able.

Why has the United States grown economically? Because the six growth factors explained in Chapter 20 have made growth possible. The four supply factors in economic growth have increased the productive capacity of the economy more rapidly than the population has expanded. More capital, a larger and better labor force, additional natural resources, and technological advance all have contributed to increased productive capabilities. In addition, aggregate demand has ex-

panded sufficiently to bring about most of the actual growth that the supply factors made possible. And the economy has been able to reallocate its resources with enough speed and completeness to realize the better part of the growth which the supply and demand factors gave the economy power to achieve.

All this is not to say that the growth record of the American economy has been perfect. The record is impressive; but at times aggregate demand has not increased enough, so that the economy has suffered unemployment and a slower growth rate. (At other times there have been increases in aggregate demand which were too large and resulted in inflation.) There have been and still are barriers to allocative efficiency. And the economy's additions to its capital, improvements in the quality of its labor force, and advances in its technology have not been all that they might. The results as far as growth is concerned have been less overall growth than was possible, as well as an uneven rate of growth. But these are topics for the next chapter: the problems associated with growth and the policies that might be applied to speed up growth in the United States.

■ CHAPTER OUTLINE

1. Over the last 60 years the economic growth of the American economy has been impressive, but the rate of growth has varied from

one period to another and has been lower than the growth rate in other developed nations.

2. Four supply factors have contributed to the increased productive potential of the American economy.

a. Natural resources have been generally abundant; when particular scarcities have developed, technology and imports have aided in the relief of these scarcities, and the price system has fostered conservation.

b. The human resources of the economy have increased rapidly in size and improved in quality.

c. Technological progress—research and innovation—has increased the efficiency with which natural, human, and capital resources are employed.

d. Capital formation has increased the American economy's stock of capital goods and thereby provided the American worker with more tools, equipment, and machinery with which to work.

3. Of the supply factors, increases in the quantities of labor and capital have accounted for 40 to 65 percent of the increases in the total output of the American economy; improvements in technology and the quality of the labor force, along with economies of mass production, have accounted for the remaining growth.

4. Variations in the rate of economic growth and a growth rate less than what the supply factors make possible are largely the result of insufficient increases in aggregate demand. The unemployment and GNP gap which accompany insufficient increases in aggregate demand lessen future expansion in the productive capacity of the economy.

5. The social, political, and cultural environment surrounding the economy has been conducive to economic change. It has encouraged new products, new production processes, and new capital equipment; and the economy has been sufficiently flexible to provide for the reallocation of resources required by these changes.

■ IMPORTANT TERMS

Invention   **R and D**
Innovation

■ FILL-IN QUESTIONS

1. Over the last sixty years in the United States:

   a. Real GNP has increased _____ fold.

   b. Real GNP per capita has increased _____ _____ fold.

2. Since 1870 the rates of growth in real GNP and per capita real GNP have, on the average, been _____% and _____%, respectively.

3. In the 1960–1967 period the growth rates in the United States were less than the growth rates in such nations as the U.S.S.R., _____, _____ _____, and _____

4. Figures showing the real GNP and the per capita real GNP of the United States over the past sixty years fail to take account of ___ _____ and _____

5. If a shortage of a raw material develops, its price will tend to _____; this encourages users of the material to _____ _____ and prompts producers of the material to ___ _____. In addition, the supply of raw materials may be augmented by raw materials from _____ _____

6. Technology has helped in the elimination of shortages of raw materials by _____ _____, _____, and _____

7. The size of the nation's labor force depends basically upon the _____ while the quality of the labor force seems to depend upon such factors as its _____

_____ ,

_____ ,

_____ ,

and _____

8. Technological advance means the development and production of _____

_____

and the development and use of _____

_____

9. The amount of innovation which takes place in the American economy depends upon many factors, the most important of which is

_____

10. The average American manufacturing worker has about $_____ worth of capital equipment with which to work; and about _____% of GNP in the United States goes for gross private domestic investment.

11. Since 1929 about _____% of American economic growth has been due to increases in the quantities of capital and labor; the remainder has been due to _____

_____ ,

_____ ,

and _____

12. When aggregate demand does not increase as much as the productive capacity of the economy increases, the result is _____

_____ ;

and when aggregate demand increases by more than the increases in productive capacity, the result is _____

13. The social environment of a society must meet two requirements if there is to be economic growth in that society; these requirements are that _____

and _____ ;
reallocation in the United States has been accomplished by the _____

14. The social environment of the United States has generally been favorable to economic growth because the United States has had _____ ,

_____ ,

and _____

15. Two general impediments to the reallocation of resources which must be overcome if there is to be economic growth are _____

_____

and _____

■ PROBLEMS AND PROJECTS

1. Suppose the real GNP and the population of an economy in seven different years were those shown in the table below.

Year	Population, millions	Real GNP, billions of dollars	Per capita real GNP
1	30	$ 9	$_____
2	60	24	_____
3	90	45	_____
4	120	66	_____
5	150	90	_____
6	180	99	_____
7	210	105	_____

  a. How large would the real per capita GNP of the economy be in each of the seven years? Put your figures in the above table.
  b. What would have been the size of the optimum population of this economy? _____
  c. What was the *amount* of growth in:
  (1) Real GNP between year 1 and year 2?

$_____
  (2) Real GNP per capita between year 2 and year 3? $_____
  d. What was the *rate* of growth in:
  (1) Real GNP between year 3 and year 4?

_____%

(2) Real GNP per capita between year 4 and year 5? _____%

2. Column 2 of the table below gives the productive capacities of an economy *in constant dollars* during the four different years shown in column 1. Productive capacity is growing at a constant rate of 10%.

(1) Year	(2) Productive capacity*	(3) Aggregate demand*	(4) Output of economy*
1	$200.0	$200.0	$_____
2	220.0	210.0	_____
3	242.0	265.0	_____
4	266.2	266.2	_____

* In billions of constant dollars.

a. Aggregate demand, also *in constant dollars*, during these four years is shown in column 3. Given that an economy will produce an output equal to the level of aggregate demand up to the limits of the productive capacity of the economy, what were the *actual* outputs of this economy *in constant dollars* in each of the four years? Place these outputs in column 4.

b. Between year 1 and year 2 the rate of growth in output was _____%. This rate of growth was (more, less) _____ than the rate of growth of productive capacity, because _____

c. In year 2:
(1) The economy had an unused productive capacity of _____ billion constant dollars.
(2) About _____% of its productive capacity was idle.
d. Between years 2 and 3:
(1) The economy had an increase in productive capacity equal to _____ billion constant dollars.
(2) Aggregate demand increased by _____ billion constant dollars.
(3) The increase in aggregate demand was (more, less) _____ than the combined

increase in productive capacity and the idle productive capacity in year 2.
(4) The actual rate of growth in output was about _____%.
(5) The price level would tend to _____ _____ because _____

(6) How could output increase by more than the increase in productive capacity? _____

e. In year 4:
(1) Aggregate demand was _____ than in year 3 and was _____ the productive capacity of the economy.
(2) The price level would tend to _____

(3) There (would, would not) _____ be full employment and the absence of unused productive capacity.

■ SELF-TEST

Circle the T if the statement is true, the F if it is false.

1. Real GNP has tended to increase more rapidly than per capita GNP in the United States.   (T) F

2. Growth and rates of growth estimates generally do not attempt to take account of changes in the quality of goods produced and in the amount of leisure members of the economy enjoy.   (T) F

3. The rate of growth in real GNP in the United States since 1960 has been more rapid than it was on the average in earlier years.   (T) F

4. Since 1960 rates of growth in Japan and the United Kingdom have been greater than in the United States.   T (F)

5. In general, the United States has changed from being an exporter of raw materials to an importer of raw materials.   (T) F

6. The population of the United States has increased by 300 percent since 1900.   T (F)

7. About 11 percent of the gross national product of the United States is devoted to gross private domestic investment.   (T) F

8. The lapse of time between scientific discovery and innovation has tended to decrease over the years.   (T) F

9. Since 1909 improved technology has accounted for a little over 30 percent of the growth of total real output in the United States.   T (F)

10. Changes in the supply factors do not cause changes in the demand factor, and vice versa.   T (F)

Underscore the letter that corresponds to the best answer.

1. Since 1909 real GNP and real GNP per capita in the United States have increased, respectively, about: (*a*) 3- and 1-fold; (*b*) 4- and 1½-fold; (*c*) 5- and 2-fold; (*d*) 6- and 2½-fold.

2. Since about 1870 the total output of the American economy has increased at an average *annual* rate of about: (*a*) ½ of 1%; (*b*) 2%; (*c*) 3½%; (*d*) 5%.

3. Total output per capita in the United States since 1909 has increased at an average annual rate of about: (*a*) 1%; (*b*) 2%; (*c*) 3%; (*d*) 4%.

4. Technology has played an important role in lessening shortages of raw materials in *all but one* of the following ways: (*a*) by developing methods of producing the same product with smaller quantities of raw materials; (*b*) by finding new raw materials which can be used to replace scarce ones; (*c*) by importing raw materials in scarce supply from abroad; (*d*) by devising improved methods of recovering existing raw materials.

5. There are in the American labor force approximately how many million workers? (*a*) 75; (*b*) 85; (*c*) 93; (*d*) 205.

6. Approximately what percentages of the labor force have completed high school and four years college; (*a*) 45% and 8%; (*b*) 45% and 13%; (*c*) 60% and 8%; (*d*) 65% and 13%.

7. The United States currently spends about what percentage of its gross national product on research? (*a*) 2%; (*b*) 2.5%; (*c*) 2.8%; (*d*) 5%.

8. About what percentage of the increase in the total output of the American economy since 1929 was due to increases in the quantities of capital and labor employed? (*a*) 30%; (*b*) 40%; (*c*) 50%; (*d*) 60%.

9. Which of the following is *not* one of the consequences when aggregate demand increases by less than the productive capacity of the economy? (*a*) inflation; (*b*) a GNP gap; (*c*) a slower rate of economic growth; (*d*) unemployed labor.

10. Which of the following is *not* an artificial impediment to economic growth? (*a*) labor union restrictions on the size of their membership; (*b*) government-supported prices for agricultural products; (*c*) the existence of machinery which is suited to the production of a limited number of different goods; (*d*) unfair competition by firms in an industry to prevent the entry of new firms into the industry.

■ DISCUSSION QUESTIONS

1. What has been our economic growth record since 1909? How have American growth rates varied since 1870? Compare recent American growth rates with those in other nations.

2. When shortages of a particular raw material develop, how can the price system help to eliminate the shortage and to conserve the raw material? What role does technology play in eliminating such shortages? How else can shortages of raw materials be reduced?

3. What long-run changes have occurred in the size of the American population and labor force? What qualitative changes have occurred?

4. How large will the American population be in the future? What might cause the population to increase at a slower rate?

5. Why are technological advance and capital formation closely related processes?

6. What is the difference between invention

and innovation? What seem to be the factors that determine the amount of invention taking place in an economy? What determines the amount of innovation occurring in an economy?

7. What have been the sources of the economic growth which the United States has experienced since 1909 and since 1929?

8. What are the economic consequences if aggregate demand increases more than the productive capacity of the economy increases? If aggregate demand increases less than productive capacity increases?

9. What role does the price-market system play in promoting the reallocation of scarce resources? What impediments are there in the United States to the reallocation of resources which must occur if there is to be economic growth?

10. In what ways has the American social environment been conducive to economic growth?

GROWTH IN AMERICAN CAPITALISM: COSTS, PROBLEMS, AND POLICIES

Chapter 22 is the third of the three chapters dealing with economic growth. It is concerned with economic growth in the United States today. However, it deals not only with the current growth of the economy but also with three other contemporary and closely related problems: (1) the problem of automation and technological unemployment, (2) the problem of reallocating labor from old jobs to new ones in a changing economy, and (3) the problem of inflation in an economy producing less than its full-employment output. In studying these interrelated problems, the chapter builds on material studied in earlier chapters, especially in Chapters 20 and 21.

The chapter begins by examining the question of whether further economic growth is desirable in the already affluent American economy. The controversy over whether growth should be a social goal with a high priority has, of course, two sides to it. The case for and the case against growth are both considered. The student will have to decide for himself which case is the stronger and whether the social benefits from growth are worth the costs. Assuming that growth is desirable, what can the Federal government do to promote it? The policies that might be used to promote growth are explained in detail in the second section of the chapter.

But along with more rapid growth come other economic problems. For hundreds of years people have worried about being put out of work by machines. This fear exists in the United States today: the fear that rapid technological advance and the accompanying automation will reduce the number of job opportunities and create technological unemployment. Are technological advances and automation consistent with full employment? How much is there to fear from automation? Professor McConnell presents both the "alarmist" and the "more realistic" viewpoints. His conclusion is that we can avoid technological unemployment if we increase aggregate demand as rapidly as technology increases the productivity of labor. The failure to increase aggregate demand at a sufficient rate will result in unemployment. But there is no need for us to have technological unemployment if we use our monetary and fiscal tools to expand aggregate demand by the right amount.

Technological progress is not, however, the only source of unemployment connected with economic growth in the United States today. The shift in the kinds of labor employers wish to hire is another source. As the economy has grown, employers have increasingly wanted more white-collar workers to fill "brain" jobs and fewer blue-collar workers to fill "brawn" jobs. But many workers whose jobs have disappeared because of this shift are unable to qualify for the new job openings; they lack the skills, the education, or the ability to move. To help them qualify for these new jobs and to decrease unemployment, the Federal government follows an "active" manpower policy. This policy consists of a set of programs designed to create employment for the unemployed worker.

Still another problem associated with economic growth is the problem of inflation. Inflation in an advanced industrial economy that is also suffering from more than normal unemployment was not generally believed possible by most economists. Nonetheless, the American economy has experienced just such an inflation in recent years. As a consequence, economists have had to abandon the contention that this was a demand-pull inflation and to develop new theories to explain the new—or premature—inflation. Here it is important for the student to be able to distinguish between the new cost-push and structural theories and the older theory of inflation. It is also important to see the kind of dilemma this creates for the American people. The dilemma is that we cannot have full employment without inflation and we cannot have stable prices without unemployment. We can choose full employment and considerable inflation, or significant unemployment and stable prices, or some intermediate combination of inflation and unemployment. But we have to choose. A convenient device for understanding the choices open to us is the Phillips curve, a curve showing the rates of unemployment and price inflation that go along with each other. To control or limit the amount of inflation, past administrations attempted to establish wage-price guideposts. These guideposts simply suggested to business firms and labor unions the size of the annual wage increases that would not result in inflation. To make these guideposts effective, the government has relied upon moral suasion and the voluntary restraint of firms and unions. But to limit wage and price increases and so control inflation, the government might also attempt to reduce the market power of firms and unions, take a more direct part in setting wage rates and prices, or levy an excess wage settlement tax. As yet the problem of inflation has not been solved, and it remains one of the major problems faced by the American economy.

■ CHAPTER OUTLINE

1. Once taken for granted in the United States, interest in economic growth revived in the 1960s; and today Americans debate whether it is or is not desirable.

a. Those in favor of rapid growth argue that it increases the standard of living, provides the means of alleviating domestic social problems, and improves the image of the United States and of capitalism in the underdeveloped nations.

b. Those opposed to giving growth a high national priority contend that it imposes great spillover costs on society; is not needed to resolve domestic problems; makes people more anxious and insecure; and, while providing more goods and services, does not result in a better life.

2. Those who argue that economic growth is beneficial contend that government policy can be used to promote growth.

a. Four government policies advanced as a means to greater growth are the maintenance of full employment, increased investment, increased expenditures for basic research, and increased expenditures for education.

b. Those who favor the latter two policies contend they have large spillover benefits.

3. Whether rapid technological progress and automation are consistent with full employment is debatable.

a. One view is that automation reduces employment opportunities and thereby decreases GNP and the rate of economic growth.

b. The other view is that automation has been gradual, has not been widespread, and has not had a significant impact on employment or growth.

c. Automation and full employment are consistent with each other if aggregate demand increases at the same rate as the productivity of labor.

4. Economic growth involves changes in technology, the structure of consumer demand, and the geographical location of firms and industries, and requires that the labor supply be fitted into changing job opportunities.

a. Labor demand has shifted from blue- to white-collar workers (and from brawn to brain jobs), and workers who are no longer needed in one job are not always able to fill new job openings.

b. To solve this problem, the Federal government pursues a manpower policy designed to educate and train workers, to provide information about employment opportunities and the availability of workers, to rehabilitate distressed areas, and to reduce such obstacles to employment as discrimination.

5. Inflation in modern economies has traditionally been viewed as caused by an excess of total demand (the demand-pull theory).

a. More recently economists have advanced two new theories to explain inflation: the cost-push theory and the theory of structural inflation.

b. If cost pushes and changes in the structure of demand result in inflation before the economy reaches full employment, the nation faces a dilemma: full employment without premature inflation and price stability without unemployment are impossible, and a choice must be made between inflation and unemployment.

c. To prevent wage-rate increases from leading to premature inflation, the United States government has suggested wage-price guideposts: wage increases are to be no greater than the overall rate of increase in the productivity of labor. Labor and management might be made to follow this rule by moral suasion, by limiting their market power, or by more direct government participation in the establishment of prices and wages.

■ IMPORTANT TERMS

Automation
(cybernation)

Technological
unemployment

Demand-pull theory
of inflation

The new inflation

Premature inflation

Cost-push theory
of inflation

Theory of structural
inflation

Phillips curve

Wage-price
guideposts

Excess wage settle-
ment tax

■ FILL-IN QUESTIONS

1. Those who favor economic growth for the American economy argue that it will improve the _____, make more resources available for solving _____, and improve the _____ of American capitalism abroad.

2. Influential economists arguing against the need for growth in the United States believe that growth has adverse _____, does not lead to the solution of _____ _____, breeds _____ and _____, and does not result in the _____

3. If the rate of growth in the United States is to be increased, the four conditions that seem to be absolutely necessary to achieve this goal are _____, _____, _____, and _____

4. If the American economy is to have continual full employment, _____ must increase at a rate which equals the rate at which the economy's productive capacity expands.

5. At a time of full employment, to increase investment and decrease consumption requires a(n) _____ money policy and a(n) _____ fiscal policy.

a. The purpose of this money policy is to decrease _____ and thereby increase _____ in the economy.

b. This fiscal policy is achieved by decreasing _____ taxes, increasing _____ taxes, and possibly _____ government expenditures.

6. To increase the growth of the economy by promoting technological advance it is necessary to _____ expenditures for _____

7. Supporters of government expenditures for basic research and education contend that these expenditures produce _____, are for _____, or both.

8. The "alarmist" view in the automation debate is that rapid technological progress will cause _____. A "more realistic" view is that automation has been _____

_____, that it has so far not caused any decreases in employment, and that there is really very little automation in the economy because _____

and _____

9. Automation will not cause unemployment if the rate of increase in _____

_____

is equal to the rate of increase in the _____

_____

10. In a dynamic and growing economy, shifts in the structure of _____

make it difficult for _____

to obtain employment in _____

11. To help solve the manpower problems of the economy the Federal government has pursued an "active" policy. This policy includes the following:

a. _____

b. _____

c. _____

d. _____

12. According to the demand-pull theory of inflation, if the economy is operating at less than full employment a change in the structure of total demand will increase prices in

the sectors of the economy in which _____

_____,

decrease prices in the sectors in which _____

_____,

and leave the _____
unaffected. If there is full employment, an increase in total demand will cause no change in

_____

and increase the _____
This theory does not explain periods of inflation during which there is _____

_____ in the economy.

13. The cost-push theory explains inflation as follows: labor unions possessing consider-

able _____ are able to obtain wage increases from employers who also possess considerable _____

during periods in which there is _____

_____ in the economy; these wage increases plus _____

are passed on to buyers in the form of _____

_____

14. The structural theory of inflation assumes that prices and wages are flexible _____

_____ but not _____;
a change in the structure of demand will cause

prices and wages to _____
in those sectors of the economy in which demand increases, to _____
in the sectors in which demand decreases,

and to _____ overall.

15. The secondary effects of structural inflation are increased prices and wages in those sectors of the economy in which demand has not increased. In those other sectors, unions

ask for and receive higher wages because _____

_____

and firms there have higher material costs if

_____

16. The policy dilemma faced by the American economy is that to have full employment

it must also have _____,

and to have stable prices it must tolerate _____

_____

17. The wage-price guideposts for curbing

cost-push inflation are to limit _____
to the overall rate of increase in the nation's

_____

If employers and labor unions abide by these

guideposts there will be no increases in _____

_____

18. Four proposed policies that might cause employers and labor unions to abide by the

wage-price guideposts are _____,

_____ ,

_____ ,

and _____

■ PROBLEMS AND PROJECTS

1. Below is a Phillips curve.

a. At full employment (a 3% unemployment rate) the price level would rise by _____% each year.

b. If the price level were stable (increasing by 0% a year) the unemployment rate would be _____%.

c. Which of the combinations along the Phillips curve would you choose for the economy? _____ Why would you select this combination? _____

_____

2. Suppose the size of the labor force is constant and it is initially fully employed. Assume now that the productivity of labor increases by 6% annually. If aggregate demand increases by:

a. 5% a year, the result will be _____

b. 7% a year, the result will be _____

c. 6% a year, the result will be _____

3. Indicate whether each of the following events is an example of: demand-pull (D), cost-push (C), structural (S) inflation; or some combination thereof.

a. With less than full employment in the economy, the demand for and the price of aluminum increases at the same time that the demand for copper decreases and the price of copper remains constant; the result is an increase in the price level in the economy. ____

b. With full employment in the economy, the demand for and the prices of both aluminum and copper increase, resulting in an increase in the economy's price level. _____

c. As a result of the events in (a), workers in the aluminum industry ask for and receive a wage increase; workers in the copper industry, patterning their wage requests on wage rates in the aluminum industry, ask for and receive a wage increase. _____

d. As a result of the events in (c), the price of copper is increased even though there is excess capacity and unemployment in the copper industry. _____

e. Firms using copper in the electrical appliance industry find the price of copper increased as a result of the events in (d); they increase the prices of their products by an amount that more than compensates them for their increased material costs. _____

f. Workers in the electrical appliance industry discover that profits in the industry have increased as a result of (e) and that they are able to obtain a wage increase. _____

g. With full employment in the economy, aggregate demand increases at the same time that the demand for metal for automobiles shifts from steel to aluminum; the results are higher prices in the steel and aluminum industries and in the economy. _____

4. Assume that the overall rate of increase in the productivity of labor in the economy is 4 percent per year.

a. The general level of wages in the economy can increase by _____ percent a year without increasing unit labor costs and inducing cost-push inflation.

b. If the wage rate were increased by this percentage,

(1) In an industry in which the productivity of labor had increased 3 percent, labor costs per unit would _____; and the price of the product produced by this industry would _____

(2) In an industry in which the productivity of labor had increased 5 percent, labor costs per unit would _____; and the price of the product would _____

(3) In an industry in which the productivity of labor had increased 4 percent, labor costs per unit would _____; and the product price would _____

c. Granting all workers in the economy this same percentage increase in wages regardless of the rate of productivity increase in their industry means that

(1) The general level of prices in the economy will _____

(2) Prices in the various industries will ____

_____, _____, or _____ depending upon whether productivity increases in these industries were less than, greater than, or the same as the economy's rate of productivity increase.

(3) The economy's productivity increase is shared relatively (equally, unequally) _____ _____ by all workers in the economy.

■ SELF-TEST

Circle the T if the statement is true, the F if it is false.

1. Interest in economic growth revived in the United States during the period of rapid growth in the 1950s.   **T** **(F)**

2. Elimination of unemployment in the present is not altogether desirable because it decreases the rate at which real GNP can be expanded in the future.   **T** **(F)**

3. Other things remaining the same, technological progress and automation increase employment opportunities for the labor force.   **T** **(F)**

4. The actual extent of automation and the possibilities for still more automation in the American economy are both very great.   **T** **(F)**

5. The "new inflation" refers to cost-push inflation but not to structural inflation.   **T** **(F)**

6. "Administered price" inflation is another name for cost-push inflation.   **(T)** **F**

7. The theory of structural inflation concludes that prices and wages may rise in industries which have experienced no change or a decrease in the demand for their products.   **(T)** **F**

8. The three different theories of inflation may be used simultaneously and are not mutually exclusive in explaining inflation.   **(T)** **F**

9. The wage-price guideposts for preventing cost-push inflation are to limit wage increases to the overall rate of increase in productivity in the economy.   **(T)** **F**

10. Application of the antitrust laws has proved effective in the past in curbing the market power of big business; and so it is the most promising technique for fighting the new inflation.   **T** **(F)**

11. Voluntary restraint by business and labor leaders is not apt to be effective in preventing price and wage increases because such restraint requires them to abandon their major goals.   **(T)** **F**

12. The excess wage settlement tax would impose a 3% surtax on the personal incomes of union members who receive inflationary wage increases.   **T** **(F)**

Underscore the letter that corresponds to the best answer.

1. Which of the following is *not* a part of the case for economic growth? (*a*) Growth lessens the unlimited wants-scarce resources problem; **(b)** growth lessens the extent of anxiety and insecurity; (*c*) growth improves the reputation of American capitalism among the underdeveloped nations; (*d*) growth increases the resources available for the solution of domestic socioeconomic problems.

2. Which of the following is *not* a part of the case against economic growth? (*a*) Growth produces pollution and other adverse spillovers; **(b)** growth impedes the increased production of consumer goods; (*c*) growth prevents the attainment of a better life; (d) growth is not needed to provide us with the means of solving domestic social problems.

3. To increase real investment in an economy already at full employment without creating inflationary pressures requires: (a) expansionary monetary and fiscal policies; (b) an expansionary monetary and a contractionary fiscal policy; (c) a contractionary monetary and an expansionary fiscal policy; (d) contractionary monetary and fiscal policies.

4. If technological progress and automation are not to result in technological unemployment and inflation, it is necessary for aggregate demand to: (a) increase at a rate greater than the rate of increase in the productivity of labor; (b) increase at a rate equal to the rate of increase in the productivity of labor; (c) increase by an amount less than the increase in the average productivity of labor; (d) increase by an amount equal to the increase in the average productivity of labor.

5. If the expenditures of a business firm for basic research increase the technical knowledge not only of the firm but also of others: (a) the expenditures are said to be for a social good; (b) the expenditures will result in greater profit for the firm; (c) the expenditures will produce spillover benefits; (d) the expenditures represent the social cost of research.

6. One of the reasons for the failure of a dynamic economy to reemploy unemployed workers is a relative decrease in the number of jobs available in: (a) the service-producing industries; (b) the goods-producing industries; (c) the industries employing white-collar workers; (d) the industries employing skilled workers.

7. Which of the following is *not* one of the acts connected with the active manpower policy of the Federal government? (a) the Employment Act of 1946; (b) the Economic Opportunity Act of 1964; (c) the Civil Rights Act of 1964; (d) the Area Redevelopment Act of 1961.

8. If inflation is explained solely by the demand-pull theory, then: (a) price changes occur only if there is full employment; (b) inflation is the result of chronic unemployment; (c) inflation is the result of wage increases

obtained by labor monopolies; (d) an increase in the level of prices results only from an increase in aggregate demand when the total output of the economy is fixed.

9. If inflation during periods of less than full employment is to be explained by the cost-push theory, it must be assumed that: (a) only unions possess considerable market power; (b) only employers possess considerable market power; (c) both unions and employers possess considerable market power; (d) neither unions nor employers possess considerable market power.

10. The condition that makes structural inflation possible is: (a) the flexibility of prices and wages both upward and downward; (b) the inflexibility of both prices and wages upward and downward; (c) the flexibility of prices and wages downward but not upward; (d) the inflexibility of prices and wages downward but not upward.

11. The public policy dilemma illustrated by a Phillips curve is the mutual inconsistency of: (a) more employment and price stability; (b) a higher unemployment rate and price stability; (c) inflation and more employment; (d) inflation and a lower unemployment rate.

12. Which one of the following proposals for fighting inflation is aimed more at demand-pull inflation than at the new inflation? (a) restriction of total spending; (b) restriction of the market power of labor unions; (c) restriction of the market power of business firms; (d) restriction by public authority of price and wage increases.

■ DISCUSSION QUESTIONS

1. What arguments can be presented on both sides of the question of whether growth in the United States is desirable?

2. Assuming that the United States does wish to accelerate its rate of growth, what four policies seem to be crucial if the growth rate is to be expanded? What seem to be the major difficulties in putting these policies into effect?

3. In what ways do Federal expenditures for research and education result in spillover benefits or produce social goods?

4. Explain the opposing viewpoints of the two sides in the "great automation debate." When will technological progress and automation bring about technological unemployment? What is necessary to prevent rapid technological advances from creating unemployment?

5. What is the microeconomic problem that results from changes in technology, in the structure of consumer demand, and in the geographical location of industry? How is this problem reflected in the changes in the structure of the demand for labor which have occurred?

6. What manpower policies will help to solve the microeconomic problems associated with the employment and reemployment of labor?

7. What does the traditional demand-pull theory of inflation regard as the *condition* that makes inflation possible and the *cause* of in-flation? What monetary and fiscal policies will prevent this type of inflation?

8. Explain briefly the cost-push theory of inflation. Include in your answer the *conditions* necessary for this type of inflation and the *cause* of such inflation.

9. Explain briefly the structural theory of inflation. Include in your answer the *conditions* necessary for this type of inflation to occur, the cause of inflation, and the secondary effects of the original price and wage increases.

10. What is a Phillips curve? What is the public policy dilemma illustrated by this curve?

11. Explain the wage-price guideposts for preventing cost-push inflation. Why would following these guideposts prevent increases in labor costs in the economy? What policies might be employed to induce compliance with the guideposts? What are the drawbacks to each of these policies?

THE MARKET STRUCTURES OF AMERICAN CAPITALISM

In this chapter the text shifts from the study of macroeconomics to the study of microeconomics; from an analysis of national output and the price level to an analysis of the output and prices of firms and industries; and from an examination of the economy as a whole to an examination of the parts of the economy. In addition, the central question to be answered is no longer what will be the level of resource employment, but how are resources allocated among different products, by whom and by what methods will these products be produced, and how will the income generated in their production be distributed among the owners of various resources.

It has been pointed out more than once that price and the price system are the particular devices which American capitalism employs to answer these questions, and that price depends upon the supply of and the demand for the different products. If the operation of the economy and the method by which it answers the basic economic questions are to be understood, it is necessary to discover what determines supply and demand. The supply of products depends basically upon two factors: the cost of producing the product, and the characteristics of the market in which the product is sold. Chapter 23 focuses attention upon the different market structures under which products are sold. Because demand is also influenced by the characteristics of the market in which goods and services are purchased, some attention is paid to the relationship between demand and the character of the market.

Chapter 23's first major section describes four market situations from the point of view of sellers. Although these four situations are no more than generalized categories into which almost all real market situations can be placed, the student should concentrate his attention upon the five major characteristics of each of the four market situations. Most of the analysis in later chapters is based on an understanding of these categories and their characteristics. To facilitate the learning process, a table is provided in the summary at the end of the chapter.

The second section of the chapter describes four generalized market situations from the buyers' side of the market. Each of these situations is defined solely in terms of the number of buyers—one, few, fairly many, or very many—and they are, therefore, quite easy to learn and remember.

The third section of the chapter points out that the degree of competitiveness or noncompetitiveness of a market depends not only upon the five characteristics of each market category but also upon the geographic size of the market, how much competition there is between firms and products in *different* industries, the extent of nonprice competition, and how much competition there is *over time* from new products, processes, and firms. In evaluating the competitiveness of any market the reader will do well to keep these four factors in mind.

The final topic with which the chapter is concerned is the reasons why any industry or market becomes the type of market or industry it is. Four general factors are suggested as causes for the actual development of a market into one of the four categories.

■ CHAPTER OUTLINE

1. On the sellers' side of the market, markets fall into one of four categories: pure competition, pure monopoly, monopolistic competition, and oligopoly. The distinction between market categories depends upon the number of sellers, the type of product, the degree of control which one seller has over price, the ease of entry into the market, and the extent of nonprice competition.

2. On the buyers' side of the market, markets also fall into one of four categories: pure competition, pure monopsony, monopsonistic competition, and oligopsony; the distinction between market categories depends solely upon the number of buyers.

3. How competitive these markets are depends upon four additional elements: the geographic extent of the market and the amount of interindustry, nonprice, and technological competition.

4. The type of market which develops for the exchange of any good or service depends upon such things as the government's laws, regulations, and policies; the practices and behavior of the firms in the market; the technology employed in producing the product; and the institutions of the capitalistic economy.

■ IMPORTANT TERMS

Pure competition	**Monopsony**
Pure monopoly	**Monopsonistic competition**
Monopolistic competition	
	Oligopsony
Oligopoly	**Bilateral monopoly**
Standardized product	**Quality competition**
Nonprice competition	**Interindustry competition**
Product differentiation	

■ FILL-IN QUESTIONS

1. List the five chacateristics of pure competition:

a. _____

b. _____

c. _____

d. _____

e. _____

2. Oligopoly is a market model viewed from the _____ side of the market and monopsonistic competition is a model viewed from the _____ _____ side.

3. The efficient management of economic resources requires that the resources be both _____ and _____ the present chapter begins the study of the (latter, former) _____ aspect of the efficient use of resources.

4. The products produced by purely competitive firms are _____ while those produced by monopolistically competitive firms are _____; the product produced by the pure monopolist has no _____

5. A pure monopolist has no close rivals or competitors because _____

6. The advertising done by a pure monopolist tends to be of a _____ or _____ nature.

7. Monopolistic competition is like pure competition because _____ and _____, but like pure monopoly because _____ _____

8. List the five characteristics of pure monopoly:

a. _____

b. _____

c. _____

d. _____

e. _____

9. In order for the number of firms in a monopolistically competitive industry to be considered "large," it is necessary that _____

_____

10. List the five characteristics of monopolistic competition:

a. _____

b. _____

c. _____

d. _____

e. _____

11. Pure competition and monopolistic competition differ chiefly because _____

_____

12. The product produced by the firms in an oligopoly may be either _____

or _____

13. Oligopolistic firms which produce a standardized product are typically found in those industries which produce either _____

_____

or _____

14. The number of firms in an oligopoly is

_____

and each firm supplies _____
of the total market supply.

15. The degree of control which an oligopolistic firm possesses over the price of its product depends upon two factors: _____

_____

and _____

16. In column (1) of the table below, list the four market models viewed from the buyers' side of the market. In column (2) opposite each of the four market models, list their distinguishing characteristic.

(1) Market model	(2) Distinguishing characteristic
_____	_____
_____	_____
_____	_____
_____	_____

17. In addition to the type of product, the number of sellers, the ease of entry, and the degree of control over price, the competitiveness or noncompetitiveness of a market depends upon _____,

_____,

_____,

and _____

18. The four factors that have been important determinants of market structure in the United States are:

a. _____

b. _____

c. _____

d. _____

■ PROBLEMS AND PROJECTS

1. Employing the following set of terms, complete the table on page 159 by inserting the appropriate letter or letters in the blanks.

a. one   h. considerable
b. few   i. very easy
c. many   j. blocked
d. a very large number k. fairly easy
e. standardized   l. fairly difficult
f. differentiated   m. none
g. some

2. If the buyers' side and the sellers' side of the market are combined so as to employ the four models for each side of the market used

Market characteristics	Market situation			
	Pure competition	Pure monopoly	Monopolistic competition	Oligopoly
Number of firms	_____	_____	_____	_____
Type of product	_____	_____	_____	_____
Control over price	_____	_____	_____	_____
Entry	_____	_____	_____	_____
Nonprice competition	_____	_____	_____	_____

in the text, there are sixteen market models which take into account both sides of the market. In column (1) of the table below, list these sixteen models. In column (2) give an example of each. The first one is given to get you started.

3. Listed below are several firms or types of firms. In the blanks, indicate (1) into what market type—from the sellers' side of the market—this firm falls and (2) the chief reason(s) for placing it in this classification.

a. A local dry-cleaning firm _____

b. A manufacturer of toothpaste _____

c. A farmer raising pigs _____

d. The Ford Motor Company _____

(1) Market models	(2) Example
pure competition–pure competition	_____
_____	_____
_____	_____
_____	_____
_____	_____
_____	_____
_____	_____
_____	_____
_____	_____
_____	_____
_____	_____
_____	_____
_____	_____

e. A used-car dealer _____

_____

f. A steel producer _____

_____

4. Indicate for each of the following industries whether its firms compete in any significant way with firms in other industries and what the competing industries are.

a. Airlines _____

b. Silk _____

c. Plastics _____

d. Television sets _____

e. Copper _____

■ SELF-TEST

Circle the T if the statement is true, the F if it is false.

1. Every industry in the American economy falls clearly into one of four market models.　　**T** ⓕ

2. The definition of competition is one of the very few economic concepts upon which the layman and the economist find it easy to agree.　　**T** ⓕ

3. Although no individual purely competitive firm is able to influence the market price of the product which it produces, all the firms in a purely competitive industry can influence the market price.　　ⓣ **F**

4. A large number of sellers does not necessarily mean that the industry is purely competitive.　　ⓣ **F**

5. Only in a purely competitive industry do individual firms have no control over the price of their product.　　ⓣ **F**

6. Because he is the sole supplier of a product, the pure monopolist cannot affect the market price of his product.　　**T** ⓕ

7. Insofar as pure monopoly is concerned, the industry and the firm are one and the same.　　ⓣ **F**

8. There are no substitutes for the product produced by the pure monopolist.　　**T** ⓕ

9. The monopolistic competitor has only a limited amount of control over the price of his product.　　ⓣ **F**

10. Entry into the monopolistically competitive industry is usually quite difficult.　　**T** ⓕ

11. The greater the degree of product differentiation in an oligopoly, the larger will be the amount of control a firm has over the price of its product.　　ⓣ **F**

12. If an oligopolistic firm is producing a differentiated product, it is more likely to engage in advertising and sales promotion than a firm producing a standardized product.　　ⓣ **F**

13. The existence of just two sellers in a market is called "bilateral monopoly."　　**T** ⓕ

14. The policies of the Federal government have been consistently directed at preventing or eliminating monopoly and at encouraging competition.　　**T** ⓕ

15. The economics of mass production and the role of research in the development of new products and techniques of production generally lead to an increase in the number of firms in an industry and a decrease in the size of these firms.　　**T** ⓕ

Underscore the letter that corresponds to the best answer.

1. Which of the following is *not* one of the four market models as viewed from the sellers' side of the market? (a) pure competition; (b) monopoly; (c) monopolistic competition; ⓓ oligopsony.

2. Which of the following is characteristic of monopolistic competition? (a) standardized product; (b) very few firms; ⓒ entry is fairly easy; (d) very little nonprice competition.

3. Which of the following is *not* characteristic of pure competition? (a) large number of sellers; ⓑ differentiated product; (c) easy entry; (d) no advertising.

4. If the product produced by an industry is standardized, the market structure can be: (a) pure competition or monopolistic competition; ⓑ pure competition or oligopoly; (c) monopolistic competition or oligopoly; (d) pure competition, monopolistic competition, or oligopoly.

5. Into which of the following industries is entry least difficult? *(a)* pure competition; *(b)* pure monopoly; *(c)* monopolistic competition; *(d)* oligopoly.

6. Which of the following industries comes *closest* to being purely competitive? *(a)* wheat; *(b)* shoes; *(c)* retailing; *(d)* farm implements.

7. Which of the following is the *best* example of a pure monopoly? *(a)* the local telegraph company; *(b)* the local water company; *(c)* the Aluminum Company of America; *(d)* the United States Steel Corporation.

8. With respect to which of the following characteristics are purely competitive industries and monopolistically competitive industries most similar? *(a)* type of product; *(b)* number of firms; *(c)* difficulty of entry; *(d)* extent of nonprice competition.

9. Which of the following industry classifications encompasses the greatest number of actual market situations in the American economy? *(a)* pure competition; *(b)* pure monopoly; *(c)* monopolistic competition; *(d)* oligopoly.

10. Which of the following is an example of an oligopoly producing a differentiated product? *(a)* automobiles; *(b)* steel; *(c)* shoes; *(d)* women's dresses.

11. From the buyers' side of the market, the market for automobile workers in Detroit would be: *(a)* purely competitive; *(b)* monopsonistic; *(c)* monopsonistically competitive; *(d)* oligopsonistic.

12. Under which of the following pairs of conditions would the oligopolistic firm have the greatest degree of control over the price of its product? *(a)* no collusion between firms in the industry and a standardized product; *(b)* no collusion between firms in the industry and a differentiated product; *(c)* collusion between firms in the industry and a standardized product; *(d)* collusion between firms in the industry and a differentiated product.

■ DISCUSSION QUESTIONS

1. What does it mean when it is said that "the purely competitive firm is at the mercy of the market"? Why?

2. Why do purely competitive firms do little advertising? Why do monopolistically competitive firms do so much?

3. Explain in what sense the monopolistically competitive firm is competitive and in what sense it is monopolistic.

4. What seems to be the most important factor in preventing rivals from developing to compete with pure monopolists?

5. What are the barriers to entry typically found in oligopolistic markets?

6. How has the Federal government contributed to the formation of monopolies? In what ways has it attempted to limit their formation or to regulate them?

7. Why might an industry which at first glance seems to be purely competitive or monopolistically competitive because of its large number of firms at second glance turn out to be monopolistic or oligopolistic?

8. What determines whether an oligopolist will engage in extensive advertising and other forms of sales promotion?

9. What are the four market models as seen from the buyers' side of the market and their distinguishing characteristics?

10. In assessing the competiveness or noncompetitiveness of a market, what factors should be considered?

11. How does competition *over time* differ from competition *at a point in time*?

12. What factors are important in determining the type of market or industry a particular group of firms will become?

13. Why is it dangerous to employ just four market models—from the sellers' side of the market—in classifying and analyzing American industries?

14. What limits the ability of a monopolistically competitive firm to control the price of its product?

15. Why is entry into a monopolistically competitive industry more difficult than into a purely competitive industry?

16. "Clear-cut mutual interdependence" is one of the characteristics peculiar to oligopoly. What does this mean?

DEMAND, SUPPLY, AND ELASTICITY: SOME APPLICATIONS

Before the student begins to read Chapter 24, he is urged (he would be commanded if this were possible) to read and study Chapter 4 again. It is absolutely necessary that the student have mastered Chapter 4 if the new material of this chapter is to be understood and digested.

As might be guessed, Chapter 24 is, in a sense, a continuation of Chapter 4. In the earlier part of the book it was necessary for the student to have only an elementary knowledge of supply and demand. Now the economic principles, problems, and policies to be studied require a more detailed examination and analysis of supply and demand principles. Of particular importance and value in studying much of the material found in the remainder of the text is the concept of elasticity, to which the major portion of Chapter 24 is devoted.

With respect to the concept of elasticity of demand, it is essential for the student to understand (1) what elasticity measures; (2) how the price-elasticity formula is applied to measure the elasticity of demand precisely; (3) the difference between elastic, inelastic, and unitary elasticity of demand; (4) how total revenue varies in each of the three cases; and (5) the meaning of perfect elasticity and perfect inelasticity. In addition to the analysis of the concept of elasticity of demand, the student will find a discussion of the principal factors which influence the elasticity of demand

and several examples of the importance of this concept in practical economic questions.

When the student has become thoroughly acquainted with the elasticity of demand concept, he will find he has very little trouble understanding the elasticity of *supply* and that the transition requires no more than the substitution of the words "quantity supplied" for the words "quantity demanded." Here attention should be concentrated upon the meaning of elasticity of supply, its measurement, and its principal determinant.

In the final section of the chapter three topics are discussed. The first of these topics is legal price ceilings and minimums. The student should note that these ceilings and minimums prevent supply and demand from determining the equilibrium price of a commodity and from determining the quantity of the commodity which will be bought and sold in the market. The consequences will be shortages or surpluses of the commodity.

The incidence of a sales or excise tax is the second topic. Incidence means "who ends up paying the tax." The most important thing the student will learn is that the elasticities of demand and of supply determine how much of the tax will be paid by buyers and how much of it will be paid by sellers. The student should be especially careful to learn and to understand how the two elasticities affect the incidence of a tax.

The third topic introduces the student to several important new revenue concepts. These concepts are a necessary part of the analysis of the behavior of the business firm under the four sets of market conditions discussed in Chapters 27 through 30, and the student should master them now if he is to understand what follows. Here it is important to distinguish between the way in which the individual pure competitor sees the demand for his product and the way in which the imperfect competitor sees the demand for the product of his firm. After this distinction is understood, the further distinction between the nature of the demand, total-revenue, average-revenue, and marginal-revenue schedules confronting the pure competitor and those confronting the imperfect competitor needs to be made. First learn the revenue concepts, and then learn the difference between the ways in which the pure and the imperfect competitor see them.

■ CHAPTER OUTLINE

1. It is necessary to review the analysis of supply and demand and the concepts found in Chapter 4 before studying this chapter.

2. Price elasticity of demand is a measure of the sensitivity of quantity demanded to changes in the price of the product.

  a. The exact degree of elasticity can be measured by using a formula to compute the elasticity coefficient. Demand is either elastic, inelastic, or of unitary elasticity.

  b. The way in which total revenue changes (increases, decreases, or remains constant) when price changes is a test of the elasticity of demand for a product.

  c. The elasticity of demand for a product depends upon the number of good substitutes the product has, its relative importance in the consumer's budget, whether it is a necessity or a luxury, its durability, and the period of time under consideration.

  d. Elasticity of demand is of great practical importance in matters of public policy and in the setting of prices by the individual business firm.

  e. Price elasticity of supply is a measure of the sensitivity of quantity supplied to changes in the price of the product; while there is no total-revenue test, the formula used to meas-

ure elasticity of demand can also be used to measure elasticity of supply.

3. Supply and demand analysis and the elasticity concepts have many important applications.

  a. Legal price ceilings and price minimums prevent price from performing its rationing function and result in either shortages or surpluses.

  b. The imposition of a sales or excise tax on a commodity decreases the supply of the commodity and increases its price. The amount of the price increase is the portion of the tax paid by the buyer; the seller pays the rest.

  (1) The more elastic (inelastic) the demand for the commodity, the greater (smaller) is the portion paid by the seller.

  (2) The more elastic (inelastic) the supply of the commodity, the greater (smaller) is the portion paid by the buyer.

  c. The way in which the individual firm sees the demand for its product depends upon whether the firm is a pure competitor or an imperfect competitor.

  (1) Under conditions of pure competition, it sees demand as perfectly elastic, average revenue and marginal revenue as equal and constant at the fixed market price, and total revenue as constantly increasing as the firm's output increases.

  (2) Under conditions of imperfect competition, it sees demand as less than perfectly elastic, marginal revenue as less than average revenue, both decreasing as the firm's output increases, and total revenue as increasing at first but then decreasing as its output increases.

■ IMPORTANT TERMS

Review

Demand	Rationing function of prices
Supply	
Law of demand	Change in demand
Law of supply	Change in supply
Equilibrium price	Change in quantity demanded
Equilibrium quantity	
Competition (competitive market)	Change in quantity supplied

New

Price elasticity of demand	Elastic supply
	Inelastic supply
Elastic demand	Market period
Inelastic demand	Short run
Total-revenue test	Long run
Elasticity coefficient	Price ceiling
Elasticity formula	Price support
Unitary elasticity	Tax incidence
Perfect inelasticity of demand	Total revenue
	Average revenue
Perfect elasticity of demand	Marginal revenue
Price elasticity of supply	Imperfect competition

Note: Before answering the Fill-in, Self-test, and Discussion questions and working out the Problems and Projects, the student should return to Chapter 4 in this study guide and review the terms and concepts, answer the questions, and rework the problems.

■ FILL-IN QUESTIONS

1. If a relatively large change in price results in a relatively small change in quantity demanded, demand is _____;
if a relatively small change in price results in a relatively large change in quantity demanded, demand is _____

2. When demand is elastic, buyers are relatively (sensitive, insensitive) _____ to change in the price of the product; when demand is inelastic, they are relatively _____

_____
to changes in price.

3. If demand is elastic, price and total revenue are _____ related; if demand is inelastic, they are _____

_____ related.

4. Complete the summary table.

If demand is	The elasticity coefficient is	If price rises, total revenue will	If price falls, total revenue will
Elastic	_____	_____	_____
Inelastic	_____	_____	_____
Of unitary elasticity	_____	_____	_____

5. If a change in price causes no change in quantity demanded, demand is _____

_____;
if an extremely small change in price results in an increase in quantity demanded from zero to the total quantity available, demand is ____

_____.
When the former is graphed, the demand curve is _____;
a graph of the latter demand curve is _____

_____

6. If the price of a commodity declines,
a. When demand is inelastic the loss of revenue due to the lower price is _____

_____ the gain in revenue due to the greater quantity demanded.
b. When demand is elastic the loss of revenue due to the lower price is _____

_____ the gain in revenue due to the greater quantity demanded.
c. When demand is of unitary elasticity the loss of revenue due to the lower price is ____

_____ the gain in revenue due to the greater quantity demanded.

7. List five determinants of the elasticity of demand:

a. _____

b. _____

c. _____

d. _____

e. _____

8. The most important factor affecting the elasticity of supply is _____

9. If the demand and supply schedules for a certain product are as given in the table, answer the following questions.

Quantity demanded	Price	Quantity supplied
12,000	$10	18,000
13,000	9	17,000
14,000	8	16,000
15,000	7	15,000
16,000	6	14,000
17,000	5	13,000
18,000	4	12,000

a. The equilibrium price of the product is $_____ and the equilibrium quantity is _____

b. If the government imposes a price ceiling of $5 on this product, there would be a _____

of _____
units.

c. If the government imposes a minimum price of $8, there would be a _____

of _____
units.

10. Price ceilings imposed by the United States government have usually occurred during _____

periods, result in _____
of the commodities, and require that the government institute _____
to prevent this.

11. Price ceilings and price minimums prevent prices from performing their _____ function.

12. The two most common examples of government-imposed minimum prices are _____

_____

and _____

13. A minimum price imposed by the government on a commodity causes a _____
of the commodity and requires that the government either _____

or _____
to eliminate this.

14. An individual firm which is purely competitive finds that as it increases its output, the price it must charge to sell this output ___

_____,
while the imperfectly competitive firm finds that the price it must charge to sell a larger output _____;
for this reason the purely competitive firm finds that marginal revenue is _____
average revenue, and the imperfectly competitive firm finds that marginal revenue is _____

_____
average revenue.

15. On the demand schedule which is less than perfectly elastic, the elasticity of demand typically varies with price. Demand tends to be _____

in the upper range of prices, _____
in the lower range, and of unitary elasticity at a price between the two ranges.

16. When a sales or excise tax is levied on a commodity, the amount of the tax borne by buyers of the commodity is equal to _____

_____.
The incidence of such a tax depends on the elasticity of demand and of supply.

a. The buyer's portion of the tax is larger the (more, less) _____ elastic the demand and the _____
elastic the supply.

b. The seller's portion of the tax is larger the _____ elastic the demand and the _____ elastic the supply.

■ PROBLEMS AND PROJECTS

1. If the supply and demand schedules for a certain product are as given in the table, answer the following questions.

Quantity demanded	Price	Quantity supplied
300	$1.00	800
400	.90	700
500	.80	600
600	.70	500
700	.60	400
800	.50	300
900	.40	200

a. The equilibrium price of the product will

be between $_____ and $_____

or approximately $_____
b. The equilibrium quantity of the product

will be between _____

and _____

or approximately _____
c. In the following table, using the demand data given, complete the table by computing total revenue at each of the seven prices and the six elasticity coefficients between each of the seven prices, and indicate whether demand is elastic, inelastic, or of unitary elasticity between each of the seven prices.

Price	Quantity de- manded	Total revenue	Elasticity coeffi- cient	Character of demand
$1.00	300	$_____		
.90	400	_____		
.80	500	_____		
.70	600	_____		
.60	700	_____		
.50	800	_____		
.40	900	_____		

d. Using the supply data derived from the schedules above, complete the following table by computing the six elasticity-of-supply coefficients between each of the seven prices, and indicate whether supply is elastic, inelastic, or of unitary elasticity.

Price	Quantity supplied	Elasticity coefficient	Character of supply
$1.00	800		
.90	700		
.80	600		
.70	500		
.60	400		
.50	300		
.40	200		

e. If the government imposed a:
(1) Price ceiling of $.60, there would be a

_____

of _____
units of the product in the market.
(2) Price minimum of $1, there would be a

_____

of _____
units of the product in the market.

2. On the graph below are three different supply curves (S_1, S_2, and S_3) for a product bought and sold in a competitive market.

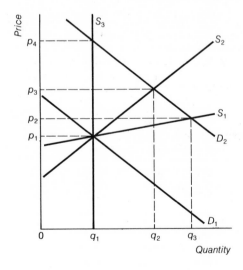

a. The supply curve for the:

(1) market period is the one labeled _____

(2) short run is the one labeled _____

(3) long run is the one labeled _____

b. No matter what the period of time under consideration, if the demand for the product were D_1, the equilibrium price of the product would be _____ and the equilibrium quantity would be _____.

c. Were demand to increase from D_1 to D_2:
(1) in the market period. the equilibrium price would increase to _____ and the equilibrium quantity would _____
(2) in the short run the price of the product would increase to _____ and the quantity would increase to _____
(3) in the long run the price of the product would be _____ and the quantity would be
_____

d. The longer the period of time allowed to sellers to adjust their outputs the (more, less) _____ elastic is the supply of the product.

e. The more elastic the supply of a product, the (greater, less) _____ is the effect on equilibrium price and the _____ is the effect on equilibrium quantity of an increase in demand.

3. In the table below are the demand and supply schedules for copra in the New Hebrides Islands.
a. Before a tax is imposed on copra, its equilibrium price is $_____

b. The government of the New Hebrides now imposes an excise tax of $.60 per pound on copra. Complete the after-tax supply schedule in the right-hand column of the table below.

c. After the imposition of the tax, the equilibrium price of copra is $_____

d. Of the $.60 tax, the amount borne by
(1) the buyer is $_____ or _____%
(2) the seller is $_____ or _____%

4. Below are two graphs.
a. On the first graph draw a perfectly elastic demand curve and a normal upsloping supply curve for a commodity.
(1) Now impose an excise tax on the com-

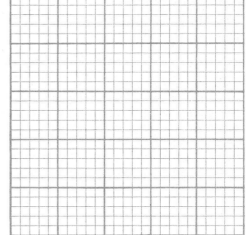

0

Quantity demanded (pounds)	Price (per pound)	Before-tax quantity supplied (pounds)	After-tax quantity supplied (pounds)
150	$4.60	900	_____
200	4.40	800	_____
250	4.20	700	_____
300	4.00	600	_____
350	3.80	500	_____
400	3.60	400	_____
450	3.40	300	0
500	3.20	200	0
550	3.00	100	0

modity, and draw the new supply curve that would result.

(2) As a consequence of the tax, the price

of the commodity has _____

(3) It can be concluded that when demand

is perfectly elastic, the buyer bears _____

of the tax and the seller bears _____
of the tax.

(4) Thus the *more* elastic the demand, the

_____ is the portion of the tax

borne by the buyer and the _____
is the portion borne by the seller.

(5) But the *less* elastic the demand, the

_____ is the portion borne by

the buyer and the _____ is the
portion borne by the seller.

b. On the second graph draw a perfectly elastic supply curve and a normal downsloping demand curve.

(1) Again impose an excise tax on the commodity and draw the new supply curve.

(2) As a result of the tax, the price of the

commodity has _____

(3) From this it can be concluded that when supply is perfectly elastic, the buyer

bears _____ of the tax and

the seller bears _____ of the tax.

(4) Thus the *more* elastic the supply, the

_____is the portion of the

0

tax borne by the buyer and the _____
is the portion borne by the seller.

(5) But the *less* elastic the supply, the ____

_____ is the portion borne by

the buyer and the _____ is the
portion borne by the seller.

5. If the demand schedule confronting an individual firm is as shown in the table below, complete the following questions.

a. Complete the table by computing average revenue, total revenue, marginal revenue, and the coefficient of the price elasticity of demand.

b. Is this firm operating in a market which

Price	Quantity demanded	Average revenue	Total revenue	Marginal revenue	Elasticity coefficient
$11	0	$_____	$_____		
10	1	_____	_____	$_____	_____
9	2	_____	_____	_____	_____
8	3	_____	_____	_____	_____
7	4	_____	_____	_____	_____
6	5	_____	_____	_____	_____
5	6	_____	_____	_____	_____
4	7	_____	_____	_____	_____
3	8	_____	_____	_____	_____
2	9	_____	_____	_____	_____

is purely or imperfectly competitive? _____

How can you tell? _____

c. On the graph below plot the demand schedule, average revenue, total revenue, and marginal revenue; label each of these curves. (*Note*: Plot marginal revenue at ½, 1½, 2½, etc., units of output rather than at 1, 2, 3, etc.)

d. By examination of the total-revenue, marginal-revenue, and price elasticity of demand coefficients, it can be seen that:

(1) Where total revenue is increasing as price falls, demand is _____

and marginal revenue is _____

(2) Where total revenue is decreasing as price falls, demand is _____

and marginal revenue is _____

(3) Where total revenue is constant as price falls, demand is _____

and marginal revenue is _____

e. Using the tables above, explain why marginal revenue is less than average revenue.

_____

_____

6. Below is another demand schedule for an individual firm.

Price	Quantity demanded	Average revenue	Total revenue	Marginal revenue
$10	0	$_____	$_____	
				$_____
10	1	_____	_____	
				_____
10	2	_____	_____	
				_____
10	3	_____	_____	
				_____
10	4	_____	_____	
				_____
10	5	_____	_____	
				_____
10	6	_____	_____	

a. Complete the table by computing average revenue, total revenue, and marginal revenue.

b. Is this firm operating in a market which is purely or imperfectly competitive? _____

How can you tell? _____

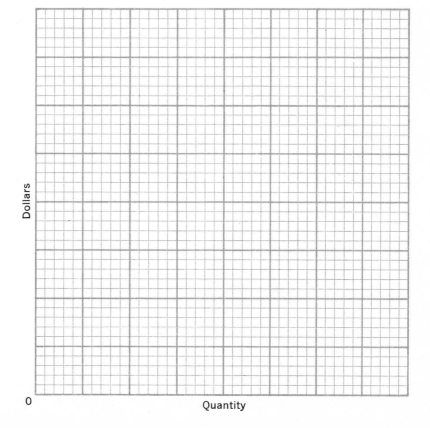

Dollars

0   Quantity

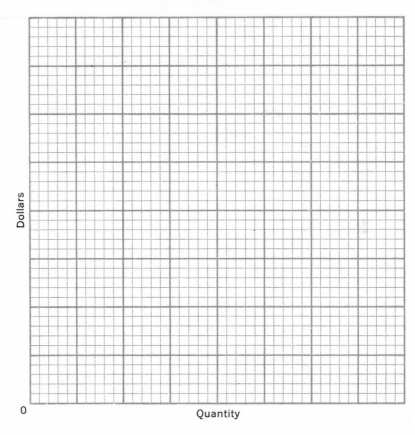

Dollars

0

Quantity

c. On the graph above plot the demand schedule, average revenue, total revenue, and marginal revenue; label each of these curves. (*Note:* Plot marginal revenue at ½, 1½, 2½, etc., units of output rather than 1, 2, 3, etc.)

d. The coefficient of the price elasticity of demand is the same between every pair of quantities demanded. How much is it? _____

e. What relationship exists between average revenue and marginal revenue? _____

■ SELF-TEST

Circle the T if the statement is true, the F if it is false.

1. Demand tends to be inelastic at high prices and elastic at low prices.   T (F)

2. Total revenue will not change if the elasticity of demand is unitary.   (T) F

3. If the relative change in price is greater than the relative change in quantity demanded, the elasticity coefficient is greater than one.   T (F)

4. Elasticity of demand and the slope of the demand curve are two different things. (T) F

5. The demand for most agricultural products is inelastic. Consequently, an increase in supply will reduce the total income of producers of agricultural products.   (T) F

6. If an increase in product price results in no change in the quantity supplied, supply is perfectly elastic.   T (F)

7. If the government imposes a price ceiling above what would be the free-market price of a commodity, a shortage of the commodity will develop and the government will be forced to ration it.   T (F)

8. The purely competitive firm views an average-revenue schedule which is identical to its marginal-revenue schedule.   (T) F

9. As an imperfectly competitive firm increases its output, it finds that its total revenue at first decreases, and that after some output level is reached, its total revenue begins to increase.   T Ⓕ

10. In the range of prices in which demand is inelastic, marginal revenue is a negative amount.   Ⓣ F

11. When an excise tax is placed on a product bought and sold in a competitive market, the portion of the tax borne by the seller equals the amount of the tax less the rise in the price of the product due to the tax. Ⓣ F

12. The more elastic the demand for a good, the greater will be the portion of an excise tax on the good borne by the seller.   Ⓣ F

Underscore the letter that corresponds to the best answer.

1. If when the price of a product rises from $1.50 to $2, the quantity demanded of the product decreases from 900 to 1,000, the elasticity of demand coefficient is: (a) 3.00; (b) 2.71; Ⓒ 0.37; (d) 0.33.

2. If a 1 percent fall in the price of a commodity causes the quantity demanded of the commodity to increase 2 percent, demand is: (a) inelastic; Ⓑ elastic; (c) of unitary elasticity; (d) perfectly elastic.

3. Which of the following is *not* characteristic of a commodity the demand for which is elastic? Ⓐ the elasticity coefficient is less than unity; (b) total revenue decreases if price rises; (c) buyers are relatively sensitive to price changes; (d) the relative change in quantity is greater than the relative change in price.

4. Which of the following is *not* characteristic of a good the demand for which is inelastic? Ⓐ there are a large number of good substitutes for the good; (b) the buyer spends a small percentage of his total income on the good; (c) the good is regarded by consumers as a necessity; (d) the period of time for which demand is given is very short.

5. If a 5 percent fall in the price of a commodity causes quantity supplied to decrease by 8 percent, supply is: (a) inelastic; (b) of unitary elasticity; Ⓒ elastic; (d) perfectly inelastic.

6. If supply is inelastic and demand decreases, total revenue will: (a) increase; Ⓑ decrease; (c) decrease only if demand is elastic; (d) increase only if demand is inelastic.

7. If the government sets a minimum price for a commodity and this minimum price is less than the equilibrium price of the commodity, the result will be: (a) a shortage of the commodity; (b) a surplus of the commodity; Ⓒ neither a shortage nor a surplus of the commodity; (d) an increase in total receipts from the sale of the commodity if demand is inelastic.

8. The demand schedule or curve confronted by the individual purely competitive firm is: (a) perfectly inelastic; (b) inelastic but not perfectly inelastic; Ⓒ perfectly elastic; (d) elastic but not perfectly elastic.

9. The imperfectly competitive firm finds that marginal revenue is: Ⓐ less than average revenue; (b) greater than average revenue; (c) equal to average revenue; (d) sometimes greater and sometimes less than average revenue.

10. The chief determinant of the elasticity of supply of a product is: (a) the number of good substitutes the product has; Ⓑ the length of time producers have to adjust to a change in price; (c) whether the product is a luxury or a necessity; (d) whether the product is a durable or a nondurable good.

11. In a competitive market the portion of an excise tax borne by a buyer is equal to: Ⓐ the amount the price of the product rises as a result of the tax; (b) the amount of the tax; (c) the amount of the tax less the amount the price of the product rises as a result of the tax; (d) the amount of the tax plus the amount the price of the product rises as a result of the tax.

12. Which of the following statements is correct? (a) the more elastic the supply, the greater the portion of an excise tax borne by the seller; Ⓑ the more elastic the demand, the greater the portion of an excise tax borne by the seller; (c) the more inelastic the supply, the greater the portion of an excise tax borne by the buyer; (d) the more inelastic the demand, the greater the portion of an excise tax borne by the seller.

■ DISCUSSION QUESTIONS

1. Define and explain the elasticity of demand concept in terms of each of the following: (a) the relative sensitiveness of quantity demanded to changes in price; (b) the behavior of total revenue when price changes; (c) the elasticity coefficient; (d) the relationship between the relative (percentage) change in quantity demanded and the relative (percentage) change in price.

2. In computing the elasticity coefficient, it usually makes a considerable difference whether the higher price and lower quantity or the lower price and higher quantity are used as a point of reference. What have economists done to eliminate the confusion which would arise if the elasticity of demand coefficient varied and depended upon whether a price rise or price fall were being considered?

3. Why does the government from time to time impose price ceilings and minimum prices on certain goods and services? What are the consequences of these ceilings and minimums if they are not set at the price which would prevail in the free market?

4. Explain what determines the elasticity of supply of an economic good or service.

5. What are the important factors which affect the elasticity of demand for a product?

6. Of what practical importance is the concept of elasticity of demand?

7. Explain the basic difference between the way in which purely competitive and imperfectly competitive individual firms see the demand for their products in terms of (a) price elasticity of demand; (b) the relation of average to marginal revenue; and (c) the behavior of total, average, and marginal revenue as the output of the firm increases.

8. Explain why marginal revenue is always less than average revenue when demand is less than perfectly elastic and how marginal revenue can be computed.

9. What is meant by perfectly elastic demand? By perfectly inelastic demand? What does the demand curve look like when demand is perfectly elastic and when it is perfectly inelastic?

10. When the price of a commodity declines, the quantity demanded of it increases. When demand is elastic, total revenue is greater at the lower price; but when demand is inelastic, total revenue is smaller. Explain why total revenue will sometimes increase and why it will sometimes decrease.

11. Explain the effect which the imposition of a sales or excise tax has upon the supply of a commodity bought and sold in a competitive market. How do you find what part of the tax is passed on to the buyer and what part is borne by the seller? What determines the division of the tax between buyer and seller?

12. What is the relationship between the elasticity of demand for a commodity and the portion of a sales or excise tax on a commodity borne by the buyer and by the seller? What is the relationship between the elasticity of supply and the incidence of the tax?

FURTHER TOPICS IN THE THEORY OF CONSUMER DEMAND

In several earlier chapters it was pointed out that consumers typically buy more of a product as its price decreases and less of it as its price increases. Chapter 25 looks behind this law of demand and explains why consumers behave this way. Two explanations are presented. One, developed in terms of the income effect and the substitution effect, is a general and simple explanation. The other, developed in terms of the concept of marginal utility, is a more detailed explanation and is more difficult to understand.

The marginal-utility explanation requires that the student first understand the concepts and assumptions upon which this theory of consumer behavior rests, and second, do some rigorous reasoning using these concepts and assumptions. It is an exercise in logic, but be sure that you follow the reasoning. To aid you, several problems are provided so that you can work things out for yourself.

Of course no one believes that consumers actually perform these mental gymnastics before they spend their incomes or make a purchase. But the marginal-utility approach to consumer behavior is studied because consumers behave "as if" they made their purchases on the basis of very fine calculations. Thus, this approach explains what we do in fact observe, and makes it possible for us to forecast with a good deal of precision how consumers will react to changes in their incomes and in the prices of products. Several criticisms of the marginal-utility theory are set down in the text. However, before you discard the theory as unrealistic or overly cumbersome, ask yourself whether it "works," that is, whether it enables us to envision the way consumers will behave and their reasons for behaving this way.

■ CHAPTER OUTLINE

1. The law of consumer demand can be explained by employing either the income-effect and substitution-effect concepts, or the concept of marginal utility.

a. Consumers buy more of a commodity when its price falls because their money income will go further (the income effect) and because the commodity is now less expensive relative to other commodities (the substitution effect).

b. The essential assumption made in the alternative explanation is that the more the consumer buys of any commodity, the smaller becomes the marginal (extra) utility he receives from it.

2. The assumption (or law) of diminishing marginal utility is the basis of the theory that explains how a consumer will spend his income.

a. The typical consumer, it is assumed, is rational, knows his marginal-utility schedules for the various goods available, has a limited money income to spend, and must pay a price to acquire each of the goods which give him utility.

b. Given these assumptions, the consumer maximizes the total utility he receives when the marginal utility of the last dollar spent on a commodity is the same for all commodities.

c. Algebraically, his total utility is a maximum when the marginal utility of the last unit of a commodity purchased divided by its price is the same for all commodities.

3. To find a consumer's demand for a product the utility-maximizing rule is applied to determine the amount of the product he will purchase at different prices, his income and tastes and the prices of other products remaining constant.

■ IMPORTANT TERMS

Income effect	**Rational**
Substitution effect	**Budget restraint**
Utility	**Utility-maximizing**
Marginal utility	**rule**
Law of diminishing marginal utility	

■ FILL-IN QUESTIONS

1. A fall in the price of a product tends to

_____

the *real* income of a consumer, and a rise in

its price tends to _____

his real income. This is called the _____

_____

effect.

2. When the price of a product increases, the

product becomes relatively (more, less) _____

_____

expensive than it was and the prices of other

products become relatively (higher, lower) ___

_____

than they were; the consumer will, therefore,

buy (less, more) _____

of the product in question and _____

of the other products. This is called the _____

effect.

3. The marginal-utility theory of consumer

behavior assumes that the consumer is _____

_____

and that he has certain _____
for various goods.

4. A consumer cannot buy all he wishes of every good and service because his income is

_____

and goods and services have _____ ;

these facts are often called the _____

_____

5. When the consumer is maximizing the utility which his income will obtain for him,

the _____

is the same for all the products he buys.

6. The two factors (other than the price of the product and the tastes of the consumer) which determine how much of a particular product a consumer will buy are:

a. _____

b. _____

7. If the marginal utility of the last dollar spent on one product is greater than the marginal utility of the last dollar spent on another

product, the consumer should _____

his purchases of the first and _____
his purchases of the second.

8. The law of diminishing marginal utility

is that _____ will _____
as the consumer increases his consumption of a particular commodity.

■ PROBLEMS AND PROJECTS

1. Suppose that when the price of bread is 25 cents per loaf, the Robertson family buys six loaves of bread in a week.

a. When the price of bread falls to 20 cents, the Robertson family will increase their bread consumption to seven loaves.

(1) Measured in terms of bread, the fall in

Good A			Good B			Good C		
Quantity	Utility	Marginal utility	Quantity	Utility	Marginal utility	Quantity	Utility	Marginal utility
1	21	_____	1	7	_____	1	23	_____
2	41	_____	2	13	_____	2	40	_____
3	59	_____	3	18	_____	3	52	_____
4	74	_____	4	22	_____	4	60	_____
5	85	_____	5	25	_____	5	65	_____
6	91	_____	6	27	_____	6	68	_____
7	91	_____	7	28.2	_____	7	70	_____

the price of bread will _____

their real income by _____ loaves. (*Hint:* How many loaves of bread *could* they now buy without changing the amount they spend on bread?)

(2) Is the Robertsons' demand for bread elastic or inelastic? _____

b. When the price of bread rises from 25 to 30 cents per loaf, the Robertson family will decrease their bread consumption to four loaves.

(1) Measured in terms of bread, this rise in the price of bread will _____

their real income by _____ loaves.

(2) Is the Robertsons' demand for bread elastic or inelastic? _____

2. Assume that Palmer is confronted with three goods, A, B, and C, and that the amounts of utility which their consumption will yield him are as shown in the table above. Compute the marginal utilities for successive units of A, B, and C and enter them in the appropriate columns.

3. Using the marginal-utility data for goods A, B, and C which you obtained in problem 2, assume that the prices of A, B, and C are $5, $1, and $4, respectively, and that Palmer has an income of $37 to spend.

a. Complete the table below by computing the *marginal utility per dollar* for successive units of A, B, and C.

b. Palmer would not buy 4 units of A, 1 unit of B, and 4 units of C because _____

_____

c. Palmer would not buy 6 units of A, 7 units of B, and 4 units of C because _____

_____

d. When Palmer is maximizing his utility he

Good A		Good B		Good C	
Quantity	Marginal utility per dollar	Quantity	Marginal utility per dollar	Quantity	Marginal utility per dollar
1	_____	1	_____	1	_____
2	_____	2	_____	2	_____
3	_____	3	_____	3	_____
4	_____	4	_____	4	_____
5	_____	5	_____	5	_____
6	_____	6	_____	6	_____
7	_____	7	_____	7	_____

will buy: (1) _____ units of A, (2) _____ units of B, (3) _____ units of C; his total utility will be _____ _____ and the marginal utility of the last dollar spent on each wood will be ___

_____

e. If Palmer's income increased by $1, he would spend it on good _____, assuming he can buy fractions of a unit of a good, because

_____

4. In the table below are Thompson's marginal-utility schedules for goods A, B, C, and D and for saving.

a. Assume that the prices of A, B, C, and D are $3, $2, $4, and $5, respectively. Compute the marginal utility per dollar (MU/$) for the four goods and saving. (Hint: The price of saving $1 is $1.)

b. If Thompson's income is $69, to maximize his utility he will purchase: (1) _____ units of A, (2) _____ units of B, (3) _____ units of C, (4) _____ units of D, and save $_____. His total utility will be _____

c. Suppose that instead of good A being priced at $3, its price is one of those listed below. How much of good A will Thompson purchase at each of these prices, his income and the prices of other goods remaining constant? (Hint: It will be necessary for you to compute marginal utility per dollar spent on A at each of these four prices.) The different prices are: (1) $6: _____ units of A, (2) $4: _____ units of A, (3) $2: _____ units of A, (4) $1.50: _____ units of A.

d. Combine the information you have obtained concerning the amounts of A that Thompson would purchase at various prices in the graph and table below. What is this relationship between price and quantity called?

_____

Price of A / Quantity of A

Price of A	Quantity of A demanded
$_____	_____
_____	_____
_____	_____
_____	_____
_____	_____

Unit of good or saving	Good A MU	Good A MU/$	Good B MU	Good B MU/$	Good C MU	Good C MU/$	Good D MU	Good D MU/$	Saving MU	Saving MU/$
1	45	____	12	____	40	____	40	____	6	____
2	30	____	11	____	36	____	34	____	5	____
3	20	____	10	____	32	____	30	____	4	____
4	15	____	9	____	28	____	27	____	3	____
5	12	____	8	____	24	____	25	____	2	____
6	10	____	7	____	20	____	23	____	1	____
7	9	____	6	____	16	____	20	____	½	____
8	7½	____	5	____	12	____	15	____	¼	____

■ SELF-TEST

Circle the T if the statement is true, the F if it is false.

1. An increase in the real income of a consumer will result from an increase in the price of a product which the consumer is buying.
   T (F)

2. Utility and usefulness are not synonymous.
   (T) F

3. All consumers are subject to the budget restraint.
   (T) F

4. When the consumer is maximizing his total utility, the marginal utilities of the last unit of every product he buys are identical.   T (F)

5. Because utility cannot actually be measured, the marginal-utility theory cannot really explain how consumers will behave.   T (F)

6. To find a consumer's demand for a product, the price of the product is varied while his tastes and income and the prices of other products remain unchanged.   (T) F

Underscore the letter that corresponds to the best answer.

1. The reason the substitutions effect works to encourage a consumer to buy more of a product when its price decreases is: (a) the real income of the consumer has been increased; (b) the real income of the consumer has been decreased; (c) the product is now relatively less expensive than it was; (d) other products are now relatively less expensive than they were.

2. Which of the following best expresses the law of diminishing marginal utility? (a) the more a person consumes of a product, the smaller becomes the utility which he receives from its consumption; (b) the more a person consumes of a product, the smaller becomes the utility which he receives as a result of consuming an additional unit of the product; (c) the less a person consumes of a product, the smaller becomes the utility which he receives from its consumption; (d) the less a person consumes of a product, the smaller becomes the utility which he receives as a result of consuming an additional unit of the product.

3. Which of the following is *not* an essential assumption of the marginal-utility theory of consumer behavior? (a) the consumer has a small income; (b) the consumer is rational; (c) goods and services are not free; (d) goods and services yield decreasing amounts of marginal utility as the consumer buys more of them.

4. Assume a consumer has the marginal utility schedules for goods X̄ and Y given below, that the prices of X and Y are $1 and $2, respectively, and that the income of the consumer is $9. When the consumer is maximizing the total utility he receives, he will buy (a) 7X and 1Y; (b) 5X and 2Y; (c) 3X and 3Y; (d) 1X and 4Y.

Good X		Good Y	
Quantity	MU	Quantity	MU
1	8	1	10
2	7	2	8
3	6	3	6
4	5	4	4
5	4	5	3
6	3	6	2
7	2	7	1

5. When the consumer in multiple-choice question 4 above purchases the combination of X and Y that maximizes his total utility, his utility is (a) 36; (b) 45; (c) 48; (d) 52.

6. Suppose that the prices of A and B are $3 and $2, respectively, that the consumer is spending his entire income and buying 4 units of A and 6 units of B, and that the marginal utility of both the 4th unit of A and the 6th unit of B is 6. It can be concluded that: (a) the consumer is in equilibrium; (b) the consumer should buy more of A and less of B; (c) the consumer should buy less of A and more of B; (d) the consumer should buy less of both A and B.

■ DISCUSSION QUESTIONS

1. Explain, employing the income-effect and substitution-effect concepts, the reasons consumers buy more of a product at a lower price than at a higher price, and vice versa.

2. Why is utility a "subjective concept"? How does the subjective nature of rationality limit

the practical usefulness of the marginal-utility theory of consumer behavior?

3. What essential assumptions are made about consumers and the nature of goods and services in developing the marginal-utility theory of consumer behavior? What is meant by "budget restraint"?

4. When is the consumer in equilibrium and maximizing his total utility? Explain why any deviation from this equilibrium will decrease the consumer's total utility.

5. Using the marginal-utility theory of consumer behavior, explain how an individual's demand schedule for a particular consumer good can be obtained. Why does a demand schedule obtained in this fashion almost invariably result in an inverse or negative relationship between price and quantity demanded?

THE COSTS OF PRODUCTION

In previous chapters the factors which influence the demand for any product purchased by consumers have been examined in some detail. Chapter 26 turns to the other side of the market and begins the investigation of the forces which determine the amounts of any particular product a business firm will offer to sell at various prices. In short, this chapter looks behind supply. The examination of supply is not completed in this chapter, however. One of the factors affecting the supply of any product is the type of market in which the product is sold, and in the next four chapters supply is examined in four different types of product market.

The most important determinant of the supply of any product is the cost of producing the product. Chapter 26 is simply an examination of the way in which the costs of the firm change as the output of the firm changes. This chapter is extremely important if the chapters which follow it are to be understood. For this reason it is necessary for the student to master the material dealing with the costs of the firm.

The student will probably find that he has some difficulty with the new terms and concepts. Particular attention, therefore, should be given to them. These new terms and concepts, which are listed below, are used in the explanation of the costs of the firm and will be used over and over again in later chapters. If the student will try to learn them in the order in which he encounters them he will have little difficulty because the later terms build on the earlier ones.

After the new terms and concepts are well fixed in the student's mind, understanding the generalizations made about the relationships between cost and output will be much simpler. Here the important things to note are: (1) that the statements made about the behavior of costs are *generalizations* (they do not apply to any particular firm or enterprise, but are more or less applicable to every business firm); and (2) that the generalizations made about the relationships between particular types of cost and the output of the firm are fairly precise generalizations. When attempting to learn these generalizations, the student will find it worthwhile to draw rough graphs (with cost on the vertical and output on the horizontal axis) which describe the cost relationships. Try it especially with the following types of costs: short-run fixed cost, short-run variable cost, short-run total cost, short-run average fixed cost, short-run average variable cost, short-run average total cost, short-run marginal cost, and long-run average cost.

One last cue: In addition to learning *how* the costs of the firm vary as its output varies, be sure to understand *why* the costs vary the way they do. In this connection note that the behavior of short-run costs is closely linked to the law of diminishing returns and that the behavior of long-run costs is influenced solely by the economies and diseconomies of scale.

■ CHAPTER OUTLINE

1. Because resources are scarce and may be employed to produce many different products, the cost of using resources to produce any one of these products is the amount of other products that cannot be produced.

   a. In money terms, the costs of employing resources to produce a product are the payments a firm must make to the owners of resources to attract these resources away from their best alternative opportunities for earning incomes; they may be either explicit or implicit.

   b. Normal profit is an implicit cost for a firm.

   c. Economic or pure profit is any income which a firm receives in excess of all its economic (explicit plus implicit) costs.

   d. The firm's economic costs vary as the firm's output varies; and the way in which costs vary with output depend upon the type of changes (that is, short-run or long-run) the firm is able to make in the amounts of resources it employs.

2. In the short run the firm cannot change the size of its plant and can vary its output only by changing the quantities of the variable resources it employs.

   a. The law of diminishing returns is the most important factor influencing the manner in which the costs of the firm change as it changes its output in the short run.

   b. The total short-run costs of a firm are partly fixed and partly variable costs; the former are costs which do not change and the latter are costs which do change as the firm's output changes.

   c. Average fixed, variable, and total cost are equal, respectively, to the firm's fixed, variable, and total costs divided by the output of the firm.

   d. Marginal cost is the extra cost involved in producing one additional unit of output.

3. In the long run all the resources employed by the firm are variable resources, and all its costs, therefore, are variable costs.

   a. As the firm expands its output by increasing the size of its plant, average cost tends to fall at first because of the economies of large-scale production; but as this expansion continues, sooner or later, average cost begins to rise because of the diseconomies of large-scale production.

   b. The economies and diseconomies encountered in the production of different goods are important factors influencing the size of firms and the number of firms actually found in various industries.

■ IMPORTANT TERMS

Economic cost	Variable resources
Alternative (opportunity) cost doctrine	Fixed cost
	Total cost
Explicit cost	Variable cost
Implicit cost	Average fixed cost
Normal profit	Average variable cost
Economic (pure) profit	Average (total) cost
	Marginal cost
Short run	Economies of large scale
Long run	
Law of diminishing returns	Diseconomies of large scale
Fixed resource	

■ FILL-IN QUESTIONS

1. The cost of producing a particular product is the quantity of _____ that cannot be produced. This way of looking at costs is called the _____ or the _____ cost doctrine.

2. The money cost of producing a product is the amount of money the firm must pay to resource owners to _____ from alternative employments. These costs may be either _____ or _____ costs.

3. Normal profit is an _____ cost because it is the payment the firm must make to obtain _____; but economic profit is the amount by which a firm's total receipts exceed its _____ costs, the sum of its _____ and _____ costs.

4. In the short run the firm can change its output by changing the _____ it employs, but it cannot change _____

5. In the long run firms can _____ or _____ an industry, but in the short run the number of firms in an industry is _____

6. The law of diminishing returns states that as successive units of a _____ are added to a _____, beyond some point the _____ attributable to each additional unit of the ___

_____

will _____

7. The short-run costs of a firm are either

_____

costs or _____ costs, but in the long run all costs are _____

_____

costs.

8. In the short run, variable costs at first ___

_____

by _____ amounts, but after some level of output is reached, they _____ by _____ amounts.

9. On the graph at the top of the next column sketch the manner in which fixed cost, variable cost, and total cost vary with the output the firm produces in the short run.

10. The law of diminishing returns causes a firm's _____

cost, _____

cost, and _____ cost to decrease at first and then to increase as the output of the firm increases. On the next graph sketch these three cost curves in

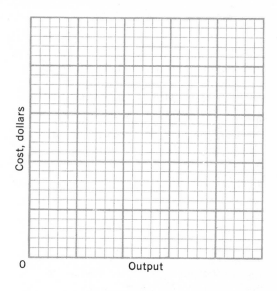

such a way that their proper relationship to each other is shown.

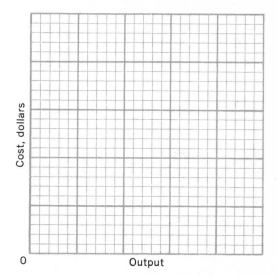

11. Marginal cost is the increase in either

_____

cost or _____ which occurs when the firm increases its output by one unit.

12. If marginal cost is less than average variable cost, average variable cost will be ___

_____,

but if average variable cost is less than marginal cost, average variable cost will be _____

13. The long-run average cost of producing a product is equal to the lowest of the short-run costs of producing that product after the

firm has _____ .
Below are the short-run average-cost curves of producing a product with three different sizes of plants, plant 1, plant 2, and plant 3. Draw the firm's long-run average-cost curve.

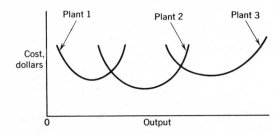

14. List below four important types of economy of large scale:

a. _____

b. _____

c. _____

d. _____

15. The factor which gives rise to diseconomies of large scale is _____

■ PROBLEMS AND PROJECTS

1. Below is a production-possibilities table for an economy. Employing the doctrine of alternative or opportunity cost:

Good X	0	1	2	3	4	5	6	7	8	9	10
Good Y	55	54	52	49	45	40	34	27	19	10	0

a. What is the *total* cost of producing 5 units of X? _____

b. If 2 units of good X are produced, what in the *average* cost of a unit of X? _____

c. Were the economy to increase its output of good X from 6 to 7 units, the *marginal* cost of the additional unit of X would be

_____

2. Assume that a firm has a plant of fixed size and that it can vary its output only by varying the amount of labor it employs. The table below shows the relationship between the amount of labor employed and the output of the firm.

a. Compute the ten marginal products of labor and enter these figures in the table.

b. Assume each unit of labor costs the firm $10. Compute the total cost of labor for each quantity of labor the firm might employ, and enter these figures in the table.

c. Now determine the marginal cost of the firm's product as the firm increases its output.

Quantity of labor employed	Total output	Marginal product of labor	Total cost of labor	Marginal cost of product
0	0		$_____	
1	5	_____	_____	$_____
2	11	_____	_____	_____
3	18	_____	_____	_____
4	24	_____	_____	_____
5	29	_____	_____	_____
6	33	_____	_____	_____
7	36	_____	_____	_____
8	38	_____	_____	_____
9	39	_____	_____	_____
10	39½	_____	_____	

Output	Fixed cost	Variable cost	Total cost	Average fixed cost	Average variable cost	Average total cost	Marginal cost
$ 0	$200	$ 0	$_____				
1	200	50	_____	$_____	$_____	$_____	$_____
2	200	90	_____	_____	_____	_____	_____
3	200	120	_____	_____	_____	_____	_____
4	200	160	_____	_____	_____	_____	_____
5	200	220	_____	_____	_____	_____	_____
6	200	300	_____	_____	_____	_____	_____
7	200	400	_____	_____	_____	_____	_____
8	200	520	_____	_____	_____	_____	_____
9	200	670	_____	_____	_____	_____	_____
10	200	900	_____	_____	_____	_____	_____

Divide the *increase* in total labor cost by the *increase in total output* to find the marginal cost. Enter these figures in the table.

  d. When the marginal product of labor:

  (1) Increases, the marginal cost of the firm's product _____

  (2) Decreases, the marginal cost of the firm's product _____

3. In the table above you will find a schedule of a firm's fixed cost and variable cost.

  a. Complete the table by computing total cost, average fixed cost, average variable cost, average total cost, and marginal cost.

  b. On the small graph below, plot and label fixed cost, variable cost, and total cost.

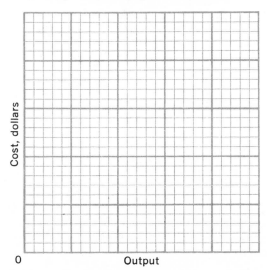

Cost, dollars

0   Output

c. On the large graph (at the top of page 184), plot average fixed cost, average variable cost, average total cost, and marginal cost; label the four curves.

4. Below are the short-run average-total-cost schedules for three plants of different size which a firm might build to produce its product. Assume that these are the only possible sizes of plants which the firm might build.

Plant size A		Plant size B		Plant size C	
Output	ATC	Output	ATC	Output	ATC
10	$ 7	10	$17	10	$53
20	6	20	13	20	44
30	5	30	9	30	35
40	4	40	6	40	27
50	5	50	4	50	20
60	7	60	3	60	14
70	10	70	4	70	11
80	14	80	5	80	8
90	19	90	7	90	6
100	25	100	10	100	5
110	32	110	16	110	7
120	40	120	25	120	10

a. Complete the *long-run* average-cost schedule for the firm on page 184.

b. For outputs between:

(1) _____ and _____, the firm should build plant A.

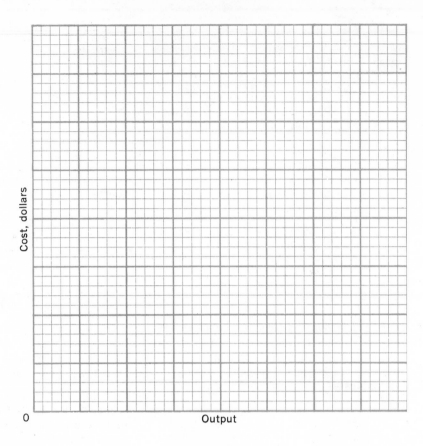

Cost, dollars

0 Output

(2) _____ and _____, the
firm should build plant B.

(3) _____ and _____, the
firm should build plant C.

Output	Average cost
10	$_____
20	_____
30	_____
40	_____
50	_____
60	_____
70	_____
80	_____
90	_____
100	_____
110	_____
120	_____

■ SELF-TEST

*Circle the T if the statement is true, the F if it
is false.*

1. Economic or pure profit is an explicit cost,
while normal profit is an implicit cost. **T F**

2. The economic costs of a firm are the payments it must make to resource owners to
attract their resources from alternative employments. **T F**

3. In the short run, firms are unable to enter
an industry or to leave it. **T F**

4. The law of diminishing returns states that
as successive amounts of a variable resource
are added to a fixed resource, beyond some
point total output will diminish. **T F**

5. The larger the output of a firm, the smaller
is the fixed cost of the firm. **T F**

6. If the fixed costs of a firm should increase
while its variable costs remain unchanged,
marginal cost will also remain unchanged.
T F

7. Marginal cost is equal to average variable cost at the output at which average variable cost is a minimum.   **T   F**

8. When the marginal product of a variable resource increases, the marginal cost of producing the product will decrease; and when marginal product decreases, marginal cost will increase.

9. One of the explanations of why the long-run average-cost curve of a firm rises after some level of output has been reached is the law of diminishing returns.

10. A firm can avoid the diseconomies of large scale by becoming a multiplant firm.   **T   F**

Underscore the letter that corresponds to the best answer.

1. In the following production-possibilities table the *average* cost of 5 units of good B is: (a) 4 units of A; (b) 5 units of A; (c) 7 units of A; (d) 9 units of A.

Good A	0	11	21	30	38	45	51	56	60	63	65
Good B	10	9	8	7	6	5	4	3	2	1	0

2. Using the same production-possibilities data given in question 1, the *marginal* cost of the second unit of B is: (a) 2 units of A; (b) 3 units of A; (c) 4 units of A; (d) 5 units of A.

3. Which of the following is most likely to be a long-run adjustment for a firm which manufactures jet fighter planes on an assembly-line basis? (a) an increase in the amount of steel the firm buys; (b) a reduction in the number of "shifts" of workers from three to two; (c) a changeover from the production of one type of jet fighter to the production of a later-model jet fighter; (d) a changeover from the production of jet fighters to the production of sports cars.

4. Assume that the only variable resource is labor and that as the amount of labor employed by a firm increases, the output of the firm increases in the way shown in the table. The marginal product of the fourth unit of labor is: (a) 3 units of output; (b) 3¾ units of output; (c) 4 units of output; (d) 15 units of output.

Amount of labor	Amount of output
1	3
2	8
3	12
4	15
5	17
6	18

5. Because the marginal product of a resource at first increases and then decreases as the output of the firm increases: (a) average fixed cost declines as the output of the firm increases; (b) average variable cost at first increases and then decreases; (c) variable cost at first increases by increasing amounts and then increases by decreasing amounts; (d) total cost at first increases by decreasing amounts and then increases by increasing amounts.

For questions 6 and 7 use the data given in the table below. The fixed cost of the firm is $500 and the firm's variable cost is indicated in the table.

Output	Variable cost
1	$ 200
2	360
3	500
4	700
5	1,000
6	1,800

6. The average total cost of the firm when 4 units of output are being produced is: (a) $175; (b) $200; (c) $300; (d) $700.

7. The marginal cost of the sixth unit of output is: (a) $200; (b) $300; (c) $700; (d) $800.

8. In the table on page 186 three short-run cost schedules are given for three plants of different sizes which a firm might build in the long run. What is the *long-run* average cost of producing 40 units of output? (a) $7; (b) $8; (c) $9; (d) $10.

9. Using the data given for question 8, at what output is long-run average cost a minimum? (a) 20; (b) 30; (c) 40; (d) 50.

Plant 1		Plant 2		Plant 3	
Output	ATC	Output	ATC	Output	ATC
10	$10	10	$15	10	$20
20	9	20	10	20	15
30	8	30	7	30	10
40	9	40	10	40	8
50	10	50	14	50	9

10. Which of the following is *not* a factor which results in economies of scale? (*a*) more efficient utilization of the firm's plant; (*b*) more efficient utilization of the firm's by-products; (*c*) greater specialization and division of labor in the management of the firm; (*d*) utilization of more efficient equipment.

■ DISCUSSION QUESTIONS

1. Explain the difference between the opportunity and the money cost of producing a product and the difference between an explicit and an implicit cost. How would you determine the implicit money cost of a resource?

2. What is the difference between normal and economic profit? Why is the former an economic cost?

3. What type of adjustments can a firm make in the long run that it cannot make in the short run? What adjustments can it make in the short run? How long is the short run?

4. Why is the distinction between the short run and the long run important?

5. State precisely the law of diminishing returns. Exactly what is it that diminishes, and why does it diminish?

6. Distinguish between a fixed cost and a variable cost. Why are short-run total costs partly fixed and partly variable costs, and why are long-run costs entirely variable?

7. Why do short-run variable costs increase at first by decreasing amounts and later increase by increasing amounts? How does the behavior of short-run variable costs influence the behavior of short-run total costs?

8. Describe the way in which short-run average fixed cost, average variable cost, average total cost, and marginal cost vary as the output of the firm increases.

9. Why is marginal cost "a very strategic concept"? What is the connection between marginal product and marginal cost? How will marginal cost behave as marginal product decreases and increases?

10. What is the precise relationship between marginal cost and minimum average variable cost and between marginal cost and minimum average total cost? Why are these relationships necessarily true?

11. What does the long-run average-cost curve of a firm show? What relationship is there between long-run average cost and the short-run average total-cost schedules of the different-sized plants which a firm might build?

12. Why is the long-run average-cost curve of a firm U-shaped?

13. What is meant by an economy of large scale? What are some of the more important types of such an economy?

14. What is meant by and what causes diseconomies of large scale?

15. Why are the economies and diseconomies of scale of great significance, and how do they influence the size of firms in an industry and the number of firms in an industry?

PRICE AND OUTPUT DETERMINATION: PURE COMPETITION

Chapter 27 is the first of four chapters which bring together a specific market model and the study of production costs found in Chapter 26. Each of these four chapters analyzes and draws conclusions for a different market situation. The questions which are analyzed and for which *both short-run and long-run* answers are sought are the following: given the costs of the firm, what output will it produce; what will be the market price of the good; what will be the output of the entire industry; what will be the profit received by the firm; and what relationships will exist between market price, average total cost, and marginal cost.

In addition to finding the answers to these questions the student should attempt to discover *why* the questions are answered the way they are in each of the market models and in what way the answers obtained in one model *differ* from those obtained in the other models.

Actually, the answers are obtained by applying relatively simple logic to different sets of assumptions. It is important, therefore, to note specifically how the assumptions made in one model differ from those of other models. Each model assumes that every firm is guided in making its decisions solely by the desire to maximize its profits, and that the costs of the firm are not materially affected by the type of market in which it *sells* its output. The important differences in the models which account for the differing answers involve (1) the characteristics of the market,

such as the number of sellers, the ease of entry into and exodus from the industry, and the kind of product (standardized or differentiated) being produced; and (2) the way in which the *individual firm* sees the demand for *its* output.

A few special words need to be said about Chapter 27. It begins by noting that there are several good reasons for studying pure competition, not the least of which is that in the long run, pure competition—subject to certain exceptions—results in an ideal or perfect allocation of resources. After obtaining the answers to the questions mentioned in the first paragraph above, the author returns at the end of the chapter to explain in what sense competitive resource allocation is ideal and in what cases it may be less than ideal. In Chapters 28 and 29, which concern monopoly and monopolistic competition, respectively, it will be found that in these market situations resource allocation is less than ideal. The student, therefore, should pay special attention in Chapter 27 to what is meant by an ideal allocation of resources and why perfect competition results in this perfect allocation.

Several other hints might be given to help the student with the material in Chapter 27.

1. The output the firm will produce in order to maximize its profits is analyzed in both the short run and the long run. Be sure that you understand exactly what is meant by these two terms.

2. Be aware that the output the firm will

produce, its costs and profits, and the market price of the product may be different in the long run from what they are in the short run.

3. Remember that the sole principle which it is assumed governs the behavior of the firm in both the short run and the long run is its desire to maximize its total profits.

4. The two approaches which are employed to examine the behavior and decisions of the firm result in exactly the same conclusions.

5. The individual firm's short-run supply curve is obtained from the firm's short-run marginal-cost curve, and the market supply curve is the sum of all the individual firms' supply curves.

6. Short-run market supply and market demand determine the price and the output of the purely competitive industry in the short run.

7. Three *specific* cases are employed in each approach in order to obtain a general principle about the firm's most profitable output.

8. It is the entry and exit of firms which forces a competitive industry to produce an ideal output in the long run.

9. Whether an increased demand for the product of a competitive industry results in a constant or higher market price depends upon whether the entry of new firms increases or does not affect the cost curves of the firms in the industry.

■ CHAPTER OUTLINE

1. Pure competition is a situation in which a large number of independent firms, no one of which is able by itself to influence market price, sell a standardized product in a market which firms are free to enter and which firms are free to leave in the long run. Although pure competition is rare in practice, there are at least three good reasons for studying this "laboratory case."

2. There are two complementary approaches to the analysis of the output that the purely competitive firm will produce in the short run.

a. Employing the total-revenue–total-cost approach, the firm will produce that output at which total profit is the greatest or total loss is the least, provided that the loss is less than the firm's fixed costs (that is, provided that total revenue is greater than total variable cost). If the firm's loss is greater than its fixed cost, it will lessen its loss by producing no output.

b. Employing the marginal-revenue–marginal-cost approach, the firm will produce that output at which marginal revenue (or price) and marginal cost are equal, provided price is greater than average variable cost. If price is less than average variable cost, the firm will shut down to minimize its loss. The short-run supply curve of the individual firm is that part of its short-run marginal-cost curve which is above average variable cost, and the supply curve of the entire industry is the sum of the supply curves of the individual firms.

c. Given the short-run supply curve of the industry and the total demand for the product, the equilibrium price of the product in the short run will be that price at which total quantity supplied and total quantity demanded are equal; equilibrium quantity will equal quantity supplied and quantity demanded at the equilibrium price; and the firms in the industry may be either prosperous or unprosperous.

3. In the long run the price of a product produced under conditions of pure competition will equal the minimum average total cost, and firms in the industry will neither receive profits nor suffer losses.

a. If profits are being received in the industry during the short run, firms will enter the industry in the long run (attracted by the profits), increase total supply, and thereby force price down to the minimum average total cost.

b. If losses are being suffered in the industry during the short run, firms will leave the industry in the long run (seeking to avoid losses), reduce total supply, and thereby force price up to the minimum average total cost.

c. If an industry is a constant-cost industry, the entry of new firms will not affect the average-total-cost schedule or curve of firms in the industry. Hence an increase in demand will result in no increase in the long-run equilibrium price, and the industry will be able to supply any quantity of output at a constant price.

d. If an industry is an increasing-cost industry, the entry of new firms will raise the average-total-cost schedule or curve of firms in the industry. Hence an increase in demand will result in an increase in the long-run equilibrium price, and the industry will supply larger quantities only at higher prices.

4. In the long run, each purely competitive firm is compelled by competition to produce that output at which price (or marginal revenue), average total cost, and marginal cost are equal and average total cost is a minimum.

a. An economy in which all industries were purely competitive would tend to result in a more or less ideal or perfect allocation of resources.

(1) Goods are most efficiently produced when the average total cost of producing them is a minimum; and buyers benefit most from this efficiency when they are charged a price just equal to minimum average total cost.

(2) Goods are produced in such quantities that the total satisfaction obtained from the economy's resources is a maximum when the price of every good is equal to its marginal cost.

b. Even in a purely competitive economy, resource allocation may be somewhat less than ideal because of four possible deterrents to allocative efficiency.

■ IMPORTANT TERMS

Total-receipts–total-cost approach	The competitive industry's short-run supply curve (schedule)
Marginal-revenue–marginal-cost approach	Short-run competitive equilibrium
The profit-maximizing case	Long-run competitive equilibrium
Break-even point	Constant-cost industry
The loss-minimizing case	Increasing-cost industry
The close-down case	Long-run supply
MR = MC rule	Ideal allocation of resources
P = MC rule	
The firm's short-run supply curve (schedule)	

■ FILL-IN QUESTIONS

1. What are the four specific conditions which characterize pure competition?

a. _____

b. _____

c. _____

d. _____

2. Economic profit is equal to _____

_____

3. The two approaches which may be used to determine the most profitable output for any firm are the _____

approach and the _____
approach.

4. A firm should produce in the short run if

_____;

it should produce that output at which _____

_____,

or, said another way, that output at which ___

_____

5. A firm is willing to produce at a loss in the short run if the price which sellers receive is greater than _____

6. In the short run the individual firm's supply curve is _____;

the short-run market supply curve is _____

_____

7. The short-run equilibrium price for a product produced by a purely competitive industry is the price at which _____

_____

and _____

are equal; the equilibrium quantity is _____

_____

8. In the short run in a purely competitive industry, the number of firms in the industry and the sizes of their plants are _____,

while in the long run they are _____

9. When the purely competitive industry is in long-run equilibrium _____

and _____

and _____

of the individual firm are equal to the long-run average total cost of the firm, and long-run average total cost is _____

10. Firms tend to enter an industry in the long run if _____ and leave it if _____

11. If the entry of new firms into an industry tends to raise the costs of all firms in the industry, the industry is said to be a(n) ____

_____

industry.

12. An industry is apt to be a constant-cost industry if _____ or if _____

13. If resources are "ideally" allocated in an economy, _____ is a maximum; this occurs in a purely competitive economy, it is contended, because the goods which the economy produces are those which _____, and these goods are produced in _____ way.

14. The most efficient method of production, it is argued, means that:

a. _____ technology is used.

b. _____ and _____ are equal.

c. the only costs involved are those which

_____

d. each firm produces that output at which its average total cost is a _____

15. The "right" goods (the goods consumers want most) are produced in an economy if the

_____

and the _____
of each good are equal.

16. A purely competitive economy does *not* allocate resources most efficiently if:

a. _____

b. _____

c. _____

d. _____

■ PROBLEMS AND PROJECTS

1. Assume that a purely competitive firm has the schedule of costs given in the table below.
   a. Complete the first table on page 191 showing the total revenue and total profit of the firm at each level of output the firm might produce, assuming market prices of $55, $120, and $200.
   b. Indicate what output the firm would produce and what its profits would be at a:

   (1) Price of $55: output of _____
   and profit of _____
   (2) Price of $120: output of _____
   and profit of _____
   (3) Price of $200: output of _____
   and profit of _____

Output	TFC	TVC	TC	AFC	AVC	ATC	MC
0	$300	$ 0	$ 300				
1	300	100	400	$300	$100	$400	$100
2	300	150	450	150	75	225	50
3	300	210	510	100	70	170	60
4	300	290	590	75	73	148	80
5	300	400	700	60	80	140	110
6	300	540	840	50	90	140	140
7	300	720	1,020	43	103	146	180
8	300	950	1,250	38	119	156	230
9	300	1,240	1,540	33	138	171	290
10	300	1,600	1,900	30	160	190	360

Output	Market price = $55		Market price = $120		Market price = $200	
	Revenue	Profit	Revenue	Profit	Revenue	Profit
0	$_____	$_____	$_____	$_____	$_____	$_____
1	_____	_____	_____	_____	_____	_____
2	_____	_____	_____	_____	_____	_____
3	_____	_____	_____	_____	_____	_____
4	_____	_____	_____	_____	_____	_____
5	_____	_____	_____	_____	_____	_____
6	_____	_____	_____	_____	_____	_____
7	_____	_____	_____	_____	_____	_____
8	_____	_____	_____	_____	_____	_____
9	_____	_____	_____	_____	_____	_____
10	_____	_____	_____	_____	_____	_____

c. Complete the supply schedule of a firm in the table below and indicate what the profit of the firm will be at each price.

Price	Quantity supplied	Profit
$360	_____	$_____
290	_____	_____
230	_____	_____
180	_____	_____
140	_____	_____
110	_____	_____
80	_____	_____
60	_____	_____

d. If there are 100 firms in the industry and all have the same cost schedule:

(1) Complete the market supply schedule in the table in the next column.

(2) Using the demand schedule given in (1): (a) what will the market price of the product be? $_____; (b) what quantity will the individual firm produce? _____;

(c) how large will the firm's profit be? $_____;

(d) will firms tend to enter or leave the indus-

Quantity demanded	Price	Quantity supplied
400	$360	_____
500	290	_____
600	230	_____
700	180	_____
800	140	_____
900	110	_____
1,000	80	_____

try in the long run? _____ Why?

_____

2. If the total costs assumed for the individual firm in problem 1 were long-run total costs and if the industry were a constant-cost industry:

a. What would be the market price of the product in the long run? $_____

b. What output would each firm produce when the industry is in long-run equilibrium?

_____

c. Approximately how many firms will there be in the industry in the long run, given the present demand for the product? _____

d. If the following were the market demand

schedule for the product, how many firms would there be in the long run in the industry?

Price	Quantity demanded
$360	500
290	600
230	700
180	800
140	900
110	1,000
80	1,100

e. On one graph draw the long-run supply curve of this industry. On the second graph draw a long-run supply curve for an increasing-cost industry.

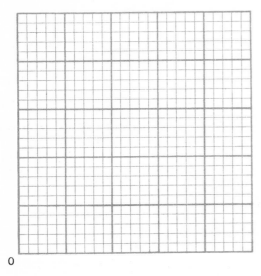

0

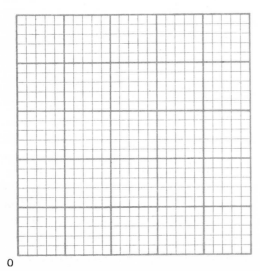

0

■ SELF-TEST

Circle the T if the statement is true, the F if it is false.

1. One of the reasons for studying the pure competition model is that many industries are almost purely competitive.   **T F**

2. A firm will produce in the short run that output at which marginal cost and marginal revenue are equal provided that the price of the product is greater than its average variable cost of production.   **T F**

3. If a firm is producing an output less than its profit-maximizing output, marginal revenue is greater than marginal cost at that output.   **T F**

4. The short-run supply curve tends to slope upward from left to right because of the law of diminishing returns.   **T F**

5. A firm wishing to maximize its profits will always produce that output at which marginal cost and marginal revenue are equal.   **T F**

6. Because the individual purely competitive firm is unable to influence the market price of the product it produces, the market price will change only if the demand for the product changes.   **T F**

7. When firms in an industry are earning profits which are less than normal, the supply of the product will tend to decrease in the long run.   **T F**

8. Given the short-run costs of firms in a purely competitive industry, the profits of these firms depend solely upon the level of the total demand for the product.   **T F**

9. Pure competition, if it could be achieved in all industries in the economy, would result in the most efficient allocation of resources.   **T F**

10. Under conditions of pure competition firms are forced to employ the most efficient production methods available to them if they are to earn no more than normal profits.   **T F**

11. The marginal costs of a firm in producing a product are society's measure of the marginal worth of alternative products.   **T F**

Underscore the letter that corresponds to the best answer.

1. In a purely competitive industry: (*a*) each of the firms will engage in various forms of nonprice competition; (*b*) new firms find no obstacles to entering the industry in the short run; (*c*) the individual firms do not have a "price policy"; (*d*) each of the firms produces a differentiated (nonstandardized) product.

2. A firm will be willing to produce at a loss in the short run if: (*a*) the loss is no greater than its total fixed costs; (*b*) the loss is no greater than its average fixed costs; (*c*) the loss is no greater than its total variable costs; (*d*) the loss is no greater than its average variable cost.

3. The MC $= P$ rule *cannot* be used to determine the most profitable output of a firm: (*a*) when price and marginal revenue are equal; (*b*) in purely competitive industries; (*c*) when demand is perfectly elastic; (*d*) when average revenue is greater than marginal revenue.

4. The individual firm's short-run supply curve is that part of its marginal-cost curve lying above its: (*a*) average-total-cost curve; (*b*) average-variable-cost curve; (*c*) average-fixed-cost curve; (*d*) average-revenue curve.

5. If a single purely competitive firm's most profitable output in the short run were an output at which it was neither receiving a profit nor suffering a loss, one of the following would *not* be true. Which one? (*a*) marginal cost and average total cost are equal; (*b*) marginal cost and average variable cost are equal; (*c*) marginal cost and marginal revenue are equal; (*d*) marginal cost and average revenue are equal.

6. Which one of the following statements is true of a purely competitive industry in short-run equilibrium? (*a*) price is equal to average total cost; (*b*) total quantity demanded is equal to total quantity supplied; (*c*) profits in the industry are equal to zero; (*d*) output is equal to the output at which average total cost is a minimum.

7. When a purely competitive industry is in long-run equilibrium, one of the following statements is *not* true. Which one? (*a*) firms in the industry are earning normal profits; (*b*) price and long-run average total cost are equal to each other; (*c*) long-run marginal cost is at its minimum level; (*d*) long-run marginal cost is equal to marginal revenue.

8. Increasing-cost industries find that their costs rise as a consequence of an increased demand for the product because of: (*a*) the diseconomies of scale; (*b*) diminishing returns; (*c*) higher resource prices; (*d*) a decreased supply of the product.

9. Which one of the following is *most likely* to be a constant-cost industry? (*a*) agricultural and extractive industries; (*b*) an industry in the early stages of its development; (*c*) an industry which employs a significant portion of the total supply of some resource; (*d*) the steel and oil industries.

10. It is contended that which of the following triple identities results in an ideal allocation of resources? (*a*) $P = AC = MC$; (*b*) $P = AR = MR$; (*c*) $P = MR = MC$; (*d*) $AC = MC = MR$.

11. An economy is producing the goods most wanted by society when, for each and every good, their: (*a*) price and average cost are equal; (*b*) price and marginal cost are equal; (*c*) marginal revenue and marginal cost are equal; (*d*) price and marginal revenue are equal.

■ DISCUSSION QUESTIONS

1. Explain exactly what the economist means by pure competition.

2. If pure competition is so rare in practice, why are students of economics asked to study it?

3. Why is a firm willing to produce at a loss in the short run if the loss is no greater than the fixed costs of the firm?

4. Explain how the short-run supply of an individual firm and of the purely competitive industry are determined.

5. What determines the equilibrium price and quantity of a purely competitive industry in the short run? Will economic profits in the industry be positive or negative?

6. Why do the MC $=$ MR rule and the MC $=$

P rule mean the same thing under conditions of pure competition?

7. What are the important distinctions between the short run and the long run and between equilibrium in the short run and in the long run in a competitive industry?

8. When is the purely competitive industry in long-run equilibrium? What forces the purely competitive firm into this position?

9. What is a constant-cost industry? What is an increasing-cost industry? Under what economic conditions is each likely to be found? What will be the nature of the long-run supply curve in each of these industries?

10. What is meant by an ideal or the most efficient allocation of resources? Why is it said that a purely competitive economy results in this type of allocation.

11. What did Adam Smith mean when he said that self-interest and competition bring about results which are in the best interest of the economy as a whole without government regulation or interference?

12. Even if an economy is purely competitive, the allocation of resources may not be ideal. Why?

13. Does pure competition *always* promote both the use of the most efficient technological methods of production and the development of better methods?

PRICE AND OUTPUT DETERMINATION: PURE MONOPOLY

Chapter 28 is the second of the four chapters which deal with specific market models and is concerned with what economists call pure monopoly. Like pure competition, pure monopoly is rarely found in the American economy. But there are industries which are very close to being pure monopolies, and an understanding of pure monopoly is helpful in understanding the more realistic situations of monopolistic competition and oligopoly.

It is only possible for pure monopoly, approximations of pure monopoly, and oligopoly to exist if firms are prevented in some way from entering an industry in the long run. Anything which tends to prevent entry is referred to as a "barrier to entry." The first part of Chapter 28 is devoted to a description of the more important types of barriers to entry. Remember that barriers to entry not only make it possible for monopoly to exist in the economy but also explain why so many markets are oligopolies. These barriers to entry should be recalled by the student when he begins his study of Chapter 30.

Like the preceding chapter, this chapter tries to answer certain questions about the firm. These are: what output will the firm produce; what price will it charge; what will be the profit received by the firm; and what will be the relationships between price, average total cost, and marginal cost. In answering these questions for the monopoly firm and in comparing pure competition and pure monopoly note the following:

1. Both the competitive and monopoly firm try to maximize profits by producing that output at which marginal cost and marginal revenue are equal.

2. The monopolist *is* the industry, and the competitor is but one of many firms in the industry.

3. The individual competitor sees a perfectly elastic demand for his product at the going market price, which it cannot influence by itself; the monopolist sees a demand schedule which is less than perfectly elastic. The former, therefore, has *only* an output policy, while the latter is able to determine the price at which it will sell its output (that is, the output it decides to sell will determine the price at which it can sell, or the price at which it decides to sell will determine the size of the output it will be able to sell).

4. When demand is perfectly elastic, price is equal to marginal revenue and is constant; but when demand is less than perfectly elastic, marginal revenue is less than price and both decrease as the output of the firm increases.

5. Because entry is blocked in the long run, firms cannot enter a monopolistic industry to compete away profits as they can under conditions of pure competition.

Chapter 28 also assesses resource allocation under monopoly conditions by comparing it with resource allocation under purely competitive conditions. Here it is important to see that (with one exception) under monopoly conditions the price of the product will be greater than both the minimum long-run average cost and marginal cost. For these reasons the output of the monopolist will be neither efficiently produced nor produced in an amount which efficiently allocates resources.

Because monopoly does cause a misallocation of resources, many of the natural monopolies are public utilities. Public utilities have the maximum prices they may charge set by agencies of government. The aim of regulation is a better allocation of the economy's resources. The final section of Chapter 28 introduces the student to the problem of determining the maximum price a monopolist may charge. The dilemma of regulation is that setting the ceiling price equal to *marginal* cost improves resource allocation but may force the monopolist to suffer economic losses (and government to subsidize him); and that setting price equal to *average* cost eliminates the losses of the monopolist, but results in a less efficient allocation of resources.

■ CHAPTER OUTLINE

1. Pure monopoly is a market situation in which a single firm sells a product for which there are no close substitutes. While it is rare in practice, the study of monopoly provides an understanding of firms which are "almost" monopolies and is useful in understanding monopolistic competition and oligopoly.

2. Pure monopoly (and oligopoly) can exist in the long run only if potential competitors find there are barriers which prevent their entry into the industry. There are at least six types of entry barriers, but they are seldom perfect in preventing the entry of new firms. Efficient production may, in some cases, require that firms be prevented from entering an industry.

3. The pure monopolist employs his cost and demand data to determine his most profitable output and the price he will charge.

a. Unlike the pure competitor, the monopolist has a price policy. Because he is the sole supplier, the price he charges will determine the amount of the product he can sell (or the amount he decides to produce and sell will determine the price at which he can sell it). Consequently, marginal revenue is less than

price (or average revenue), and both decrease as the output of the monopolist increases.

b. Monopoly power in the sale of a product does not by itself affect the prices the monopolist pays or his costs of production.

c. The monopolist produces that output at which marginal cost and marginal revenue are equal; he charges that price at which this profit-maximizing output can be sold.

d. It is not true that a monopolist charges as high a price as is possible, and it is not true that his profit per unit is as large as it might be; a monopoly, in fact, may not be profitable at all.

4. Pure monopoly is likely to have the following economic effects:

a. Because it produces smaller outputs and charges higher prices than would result from conditions of pure competition and because price will be greater than both average total and marginal cost, resources are misallocated.

b. Monopoly contributes to income inequality in the economy.

c. Monopolists may or may not use more efficient (less costly) methods of production, and they may or may not inhibit technological progress.

5. The prices charged by monopolists are often regulated by governments to reduce the misallocation of resources.

a. A ceiling price determined by the intersection of the marginal-cost and demand schedules improves the allocation of resources.

b. This ceiling price may force the firm to produce at a loss; and so government may set the ceiling at a level determined by the intersection of the average-cost and demand schedules to allow the monopolist a fair return.

c. The dilemma of regulation is that the ceiling price which results in the more efficient allocation of resources may cause losses for the monopolist, and that a fair-return price results in a less efficient allocation.

■ IMPORTANT TERMS

Pure monopoly
Barrier to entry
Natural monopoly
Tying agreement
Unfair competition

The economies of being established
Fair-return price
Dilemma of regulation

■ FILL-IN QUESTIONS

1. The study of pure monopoly is important

because some industries are _____
of pure monopoly and because it enables the

student better to understand _____

_____

and _____

2. How would you characterize (weak, non-existent, strong, or strongest) the long-run barriers to entry into each of the following?

a. Pure competition: _____

b. Pure monopoly: _____

c. Monopolistic competition: _____

d. Oligopoly: _____

3. What are the six most important types of barrier to entry?

a. _____

b. _____

c. _____

d. _____

e. _____

f. _____

4. If there are substantial economies of scale in the production of a product, a small-scale firm will find it difficult to enter into and survive in such an industry because _____

_____

and a firm will find it difficult to start out on

a large scale in the industry because _____

_____

5. Public utility companies tend to be _____

_____

monopolies, and they receive their franchises

from and are _____
by governments.

6. If a company with a patent on a certain product agrees to sell the product only to those who buy from it other products on which

it does not have a patent, there is a _____

between the company with the patent and those who buy from it.

7. Unfair methods of competition (or cut-throat tactics) such as _____,

_____, _____,

and _____
may force a firm's rivals from an industry or prevent the establishment of new firms in the industry.

8. If there are economies of being established, this means that established firms have

_____

which may be due to _____,

_____, _____,

or _____

9. The demand schedule confronting the pure

monopolist is _____
perfectly elastic; this means that marginal

revenue will be _____
than average revenue and that both marginal

revenue and average revenue _____
as output increases.

10. When the profits of a monopolist are being maximized _____

and _____
are equal and price (or average revenue) is

_____

than marginal cost.

11. Three common fallacies about the pure monopolist are that:

a. He charges the _____
price.

b. His average (or per unit) profit is _____

_____

c. He always receives a _____

12. A monopolist may refuse to set his price and output at the level that would maximize

his profits in order to prevent _____

and _____

13. In the long run the price charged by a monopolist is not forced down to the level of average cost because there is no _____

_____
to force price downward.

14. The output produced by a monopolist is inefficiently produced because the average total cost of producing the product is not ____

_____,
and resources are not efficiently allocated because _____

is greater than _____

15. Resources can definitely be said to be more efficiently allocated by pure competition than by pure monopoly only if the _____

_____
of the purely competitive firm and the monopolist are the same; they will not be the same if the monopolist, by virtue of being a large

firm, enjoys _____
not available to the pure competitor.

16. Monopoly seems to result in a greater inequality of income than there would be

otherwise because _____

17. Monopoly is, on the one hand, conducive to technological advance because monop-

olists have the _____
to finance research and development and their

monopoly position will protect _____

_____ that results
from the introduction of new products and techniques. On the other hand, the absence of competitors means that there is no _____

_____ to technological advance.

18. In an economy in which technological progress is important, the economic efficiency

of pure competition can be said to be _____

_____

19. The misallocation of resources that re-

sults from monopoly can be *eliminated* if a ceiling price for the monopolist's product is

set equal to _____;
such a price is, however, usually less than

_____

20. If a regulated monopolist is allowed to earn a fair return, the ceiling price for his

product is set equal to _____;
such a price reduces but does not eliminate

■ PROBLEMS AND PROJECTS

1. The demand schedule for the product produced by a monopolist is given in the table below.

a. Complete the table by computing total revenue at each of the eleven prices and the ten marginal revenue figures.

b. Using the table of costs given in problem 1 of Chapter 27:

(1) What output will the monopolist produce? _____

(2) What price will the monopolist charge?
$_____

(3) What total profit will the monopolist receive? $_____

(4) What average profit will the monopolist receive? $_____

Price	Quantity demanded	Total revenue	Marginal revenue
$700	0	$_____	
			$_____
650	1	_____	
			_____
600	2	_____	
550	3	_____	_____
500	4	_____	_____
450	5	_____	_____
400	6	_____	_____
350	7	_____	_____
300	8	_____	_____
250	9	_____	_____
200	10	_____	_____

c. Using the same table of costs and demand schedule, how large a total profit would the monopolist receive if he produced the outputs listed in the table below?

Output	Profit	Output	Profit
1	_____	6	_____
2	_____	7	_____
3	_____	8	_____
4	_____	9	_____
5	_____	10	_____

2. Again employing the cost schedule given in problem 1, Chapter 27, and the demand schedules given in the following table, complete the second table below for each set of demand data.

Demand schedule 2		Demand schedule 3	
Price	Quantity demanded	Price	Quantity demanded
$210	0	$80	0
190	1	75	1
170	2	70	2
150	3	65	3
130	4	60	4
110	5	55	5
90	6	50	6
70	7	45	7
50	8	40	8
30	9	35	9
10	10	30	10

	Demand 2	Demand 3
Output of the firm	_____	_____
Price it will charge	_____	_____
Total profit	_____	_____
Average profit	_____	_____

3. In the next column are cost and demand data for a pure monopolist.

a. An unregulated monopolist would produce _____ units of his product, sell it at a price of _____, and receive a total profit of _____

Quantity demanded	Price	Marginal revenue	Average cost	Marginal cost
0	$17.50			
1	16.00	$16.00	$24.00	$24.00
2	14.50	13.00	15.00	6.00
3	13.00	10.00	11.67	5.00
4	11.50	7.00	10.50	7.00
5	10.00	4.00	10.00	8.00
6	8.50	1.00	9.75	8.50
7	7.00	-2.00	9.64	9.00
8	5.50	-5.00	9.34	9.25
9	4.00	-8.00	9.36	9.50

b. If this monopolist were regulated and the maximum price he would charge were set equal to marginal cost, he would produce _____ units of his product, sell it at a price of _____, and receive a total profit of _____. Such regulation would either _____ the firm or require that the regulating government _____ the firm.

c. If the monopolist were regulated and allowed to charge a fair-return price, he would produce _____ units of product, charge a price of _____, and receive a profit of _____

d. From which situation—a, b, or c—does the most efficient allocation of resources result? _____ From which situation does the least efficient allocation result? _____ In practice, government would probably select situation _____

■ SELF-TEST

Circle the T if the statement is true, the F if it is false.

1. The pure monopolist produces a product for which there are no substitutes.   **T   F**

2. The weaker the barriers to entry into an industry, the more competition there will be in the industry, other things being equal.   **T   F**

3. The dilemma of monopoly regulation is that the production by a monopolist of an output that causes no misallocation of resources may force the monopolist to suffer an economic loss.   **T   F**

4. Monopoly is always undesirable unless it is regulated by government.   **T   F**

5. The monopolist can increase the sale of his product only if he charges a lower price.
                                             T   F

6. The monopolist determines his profit-maximizing output by producing that output at which marginal cost and marginal revenue are equal and sets his product price equal to marginal cost and marginal revenue at that output.   **T   F**

7. When a monopolist is maximizing his total profit he is also producing that output at which his per unit (or average) profit is a maximum.   **T   F**

8. A monopolist may refrain from maximizing his total profits in order to discourage the entry of new firms into the industry.   **T   F**

9. Resources are misallocated by a monopoly because price is not equal to marginal cost.
                                             T   F

10. In a society in which technology is not changing and the economies of scale can be employed by both pure competitors and monopolists, the purely competitive firm will use the more efficient methods of production.
                                             T   F

Underscore the letter that corresponds to the best answer.

1. Which of the following is the *best* example of a pure monopoly? (*a*) your neighborhood grocer; (*b*) the telephone company in your community; (*c*) the manufacturer of a particular brand of toothpaste; (*d*) the only airline furnishing passenger service between two major cities.

2. Which of the following is *not* an important characteristic of a natural monopoly? (*a*) substantial economies of scale are available; (*b*) very heavy fixed costs; (*c*) it is a public utility; (*d*) competition is impractical and/or would be very expensive for the consumer.

3. A monopolist who is limited by the imposi-

tion of a ceiling price to a fair return sells his product at a price equal to: (*a*) average total cost; (*b*) average variable cost; (*c*) marginal cost; (*d*) average fixed cost.

4. Monopoly can probably exist over a long period of time only if: (*a*) it is based on the control of raw materials; (*b*) it controls the patents on the product; (*c*) cut-throat competition is employed to eliminate rivals; (*d*) government assists the monopoly and prevents the establishment of rival firms.

5. Which of the following is *not* true with respect to the demand data confronting a monopolist? (*a*) marginal revenue is greater than average revenue; (*b*) marginal revenue decreases as average revenue decreases; (*c*) demand is less than perfectly elastic; (*d*) average revenue (or price) decreases as the output of the firm increases.

6. Assume the cost and demand data for a pure monopolist as given in the table below. How many units of output will the firm produce? (*a*) 1; (*b*) 2; (*c*) 3; (*d*) 4.

Output	Total cost	Price
0	$ 500	$1,000
1	520	600
2	580	500
3	700	400
4	1,000	300
5	1,500	200

7. If the monopolist for whom cost and demand data are given in question 6 above were forced to produce the socially optimum output by the imposition of a ceiling price, the ceiling price would have to be: (*a*) $200; (*b*) $300; (*c*) $400; (*d*) $500.

8. When the monopolist is maximizing his total profits *or* minimizing his losses: (*a*) total revenue is greater than total cost; (*b*) average revenue is greater than average total cost; (*c*) average revenue is greater than marginal cost; (*d*) average total cost is less than marginal cost.

9. A monopolist does not *produce* his product as efficiently as is possible because: (*a*) the average total cost of producing it is not a minimum; (*b*) the marginal cost of producing the last unit is less than its price; (*c*) he is earning a profit; (d) average revenue is greater than the cost of producing an extra unit of output.

10. Over time monopoly *may* result in greater technological improvement than would be forthcoming under conditions of pure competition for several reasons. Which of the following is *not* one of these reasons? (a) technological advance will lower the costs and enhance the profits of the monopolist, and these increased profits will not have to be shared with rivals; (b) technological advance will act as a barrier to entry and thus allow the monopolist to continue to be a monopolist; (c) technological advance requires research and experimentation, and the monopolist is in a position to finance them out of his profits; (d) technological advance is apt to make existing capital equipment obsolete, and the monopolist can reduce his costs by speeding up the rate at which his capital becomes obsolete.

■ DISCUSSION QUESTIONS

1. What is pure monopoly? Why is it studied if it is so rare in practice?

2. What is meant by a barrier to entry? What kinds of such barriers are there? How important are they in pure competition, pure monopoly, monopolistic competition, and oligopoly?

3. Why are the economies of scale a barrier to entry?

4. Why are most natural monopolies also public utilities? What does government hope to achieve by granting exclusive franchises to and regulating such natural monopolies?

5. What is meant by unfair competition? What kinds of unfair competition are there? How is unfair competition used to create monopolies and to bar the entry of new firms into industries?

6. Why is it said that the "monopoly power achieved through patents may well be cumulative"?

7. What advantage does the going, established firm have over the new, immature firm in an industry?

8. Compare the pure monopolist and the individual pure competitor with respect to: (a) their demand schedule; (b) their marginal-revenue schedule; (c) the relationship between marginal revenue and average revenue; (d) their price policy; (e) their ability to administer price.

9. What output will the monopolist produce? What price will he charge?

10. Why does the monopolist not charge the highest possible price for his product? Why does the monopolist not set the price for his product in such a way that his average profit is a maximum? Why are some monopolies unprofitable?

11. Why would any monopolist refrain from setting his price and producing an output that would maximize his total profits?

12. In what sense is resource allocation and production more efficient under conditions of pure competition than under monopoly conditions? Does pure competition *always* result in greater efficiency?

13. How does monopoly affect the distribution of income in an economy?

14. Does monopoly, when compared with pure competition, result in more rapid or less rapid technological progress? What are the arguments on *both* sides of this question? What evidence is there to support the two views?

15. Explain under what conditions you would prefer monopoly to pure competition.

16. How do public utility regulatory agencies attempt to eliminate the misallocation of resources that results from monopoly? Explain the dilemma that almost invariably confronts the agency in this endeavour; explain also why a fair-return price only reduces but does not eliminate the misallocation.

PRICE AND OUTPUT DETERMINATION: MONOPOLISTIC COMPETITION

Chapter 29 is the third of the four chapters which deal with specific market situations. As its name implies, monopolistic competition is a blend of pure competition and pure monopoly; and one of the reasons for studying those relatively unrealistic market situations was to prepare the student for the more realistic study of monopolistic competition. It must be pointed out that monopolistic competition is not a realistic description of all markets; but the study of it does help the student to understand the many markets which are nearly monopolistically competitive. It also helps him to understand why oligopoly is prevalent in the American economy and how oligopoly differs from monopolistic competition.

The first task is to learn exactly what is meant by monopolistic competition. Next the student should examine the demand curve which the monopolistically competitive firm sees for its product and note how and why it differs from the demand curves faced by the purely competitive firm and by the monopolist. In this connection it is important to understand that as the individual firm changes the character of the product it produces or changes the extent to which it promotes the sale of its product, both the costs of the firm and the demand for the product may change. A firm confronts a different demand curve every time it alters its product or its promotion of that product.

With the product and promotional campaign of the firm *given*, the price-output analysis of the monopolistic competitor is relatively simple. In the short run this analysis is identical with the analysis of the price-output decision of the pure monopolist in the short run. It is only in the long run that the competitive element makes itself apparent: The entry (or exit) of firms forces the price the firm charges down (up) *toward* the level of average cost. This price is not equal either to *minimum* average cost or to marginal cost, and consequently monopolistic competition, on these two scores, can be said to be less efficient than pure competition.

A relatively large part of Chapter 29 is devoted to a discussion of nonprice competition. This is done for very good reasons. In monopolistically competitive industries much of the competitive effort of individual firms is given over to product differentiation, product development, and product advertising. Each firm has three things to manipulate—quantity or price, product, and advertising—in trying to maximize its profits. While monopolistic competition may not be as economically efficient as pure competition in terms of a *given* product and the promotion of it, when all the economic effects—good and bad—of differentiation, development, and advertising are considered this shortcoming may or may not be offset. Whether it is actually offset is an unanswerable question. If Chapter 29 has one central idea it is this: Monopolistic competition cannot be compared with pure competition solely on the basis of prices charged at any given moment of time; it must also be judged in terms of whether it results in better products, in a wider variety of products, in better-informed consumers, in lower-priced radio and television programs, magazines, and newspapers, and other redeeming features.

In short, the study of monopolistic competition is a realistic study and for that reason it is a difficult study. Many factors have to be considered in explaining how such a group of firms behaves and in appraising the efficiency with which such an industry allocates scarce resources.

■ CHAPTER OUTLINE

1. A monopolistically competitive industry is one in which a fairly large number of independent firms produce differentiated products, in which both price and various forms of nonprice competition occur, and into which entry is relatively easy in the long run. While there are many industries which approximate monopolistic competition, many more industries are blends of monopolistic competition and oligopoly.

2. Assume—for this part of the anlysis only—that the products the firms in the industry are producing and the amounts of promotional activity in which they are engaged are given.

a. The demand curve confronting each firm will be highly but not perfectly elastic because each firm has many competitors who produce close but not perfect substitutes for the product it produces.

b. In the short run the individual firm will produce that output at which marginal cost and marginal revenue are equal and charge the price at which that output can be sold; either profits or losses may result in the short run.

c. In the long run the entry and exodus of firms will tend to change the demand for the product of the individual firm in such a way that profits are eliminated (price and average cost are made equal to each other).

3. Monopolistic competition among firms producing a given product and engaged in a given amount of promotional activity results in less economic efficiency and more waste than does pure competition. Although average cost and

price are equal, the individual firm produces an output smaller than the output at which marginal cost and price are equal and smaller than the output at which average cost is a minimum.

4. In addition to setting its price and output so that its profit is maximized, each individual firm also attempts to differentiate its product and to promote (advertise) it in order to increase the firm's profit; these additional activities give rise to nonprice competition among firms.

a. Product differentiation and product development, as devices which firms employ in the hope of increasing their profit, may offset the wastes of monopolistic competition to the extent that they result in a wider variety and better quality of products for consumers.

b. Whether the advertising of differentiated products results in economic waste or in greater economic efficiency is debatable; there are good arguments on both sides of this question and there is no clear answer to it.

c. The monopolistically competitive firm tries to adjust its price, its product, and the promotion of its product so that the amount by which the firm's total revenue exceeds the total cost of producing and promoting a product is a maximum.

■ IMPORTANT TERMS

Monopolistic competition

Product differentiation

Nonprice competition

Informative advertising

Competitive advertising

■ FILL-IN QUESTIONS

1. In a monopolistically competitive market a _____ number of producers sell _____ products; these producers do not _____ _____ and they engage in both _____ and _____ competition. In the long run, entry into the industry is _____

2. The fact that monopolistically competitive firms sell differentiated products results in each firm having _____ control over the price of its product and _____ _____ between the firms.

3. Given the product being produced and the extent to which that product is being promoted, in the *short run:*

a. The demand curve confronting the monopolistically competitive firm will be _____ _____ elastic than that facing a monopolist and ____ _____ elastic than that facing a pure competitor.

b. The elasticity of this demand curve will depend upon _____ and _____

c. The firm will produce that output at which _____ and _____ are equal.

4. In the long run, the *entry* of new firms into a monopolistically competitive industry will _____ the demand for the product being produced by each firm in the industry and _____ _____ the elasticity of that demand.

5. In the long run, *given* the product and the amount of product promotion, the price being charged by the individual firm will tend to _____, its economic profits will tend to _____ _____ and its average cost will be _____ than the minimum average cost of producing and promoting the product.

6. Given the product and the extent of product promotion, monopolistic competition is wasteful because _____ and because _____

7. In the long run, the monopolistic competitor cannot protect and increase his profits by varying his product's price or output, but he can try to protect and increase his profits through _____ and _____

8. Product differentiation and product development tend to result in the consumer's being offered _____ at any given moment of time and _____ _____ over a period of time.

9. Advertising which accurately describes the price and qualities of products is called ____ _____ advertising, while that which makes unsubstantiated claims for products is _____ _____ advertising.

10. Those who argue that advertising expenditures are socially desirable contend that advertising (a) increases the _____ _____ of consumers; (b) supports _____; (c) promotes the development of _____ _____; (d) results in lower _____; (e) induces a high level of _____ which leads to greater total employment.

11. The critics of advertising argue (a) that most advertising is persuasive but not _____ _____; (b) that advertising _____ resources; (c) that it entails significant _____ which are not paid by advertisers; (d) that it does not lower _____;

(e) that it does not really increase _____

_____ in the economy;
(f) that advertising expenditures are a significant _____
into many industries.

12. In attempting to maximize his profits the monopolistic competitor will vary his price,

his _____,

and the _____
of his product until he feels that no further change in these three variables will result in greater profits.

■ PROBLEMS AND PROJECTS

1. Listed below are several industries. Indicate in the space to the right of each whether you believe it is monopolistically competitive (MC) or not monopolistically competitive (N). If you indicate the latter, explain why you think the industry is not a monopolistically competitive one.

a. The production of automobiles in the United States. _____

_____

b. The retail distribution of automobiles in the United States. _____

c. Grocery supermarkets in a city of 500,000 people. _____

_____

d. The retail sale of gasoline in a city of 500,000 people. _____

_____

e. The production of low-priced shoes in the United States. _____

_____

f. The mail-order sale of men's clothes.

_____

_____

2. Assume that the short-run cost and demand data given in the table below confront a monopolistic competitor selling a given product and engaged in a given amount of product promotion.

a. Compute the marginal cost and marginal revenue of each unit of output and enter these figures in the table.

b. In the short run the firm will (1) produce _____ units of output, (2)

sell its product at a price of $_____,

and (3) have a total profit of $_____

c. In the long run, (1) the demand for the firm's product will _____,

(2) until the price of the product equals _____

_____

and (3) the total profits of the firm are _____

_____

Output	Total cost	Marginal cost	Quantity demanded	Price	Marginal revenue
0	$ 50		0	$120	
1	80	$_____	1	110	$_____
2	90	_____	2	100	_____
3	110	_____	3	90	_____
4	140	_____	4	80	_____
5	180	_____	5	70	_____
6	230	_____	6	60	_____
7	290	_____	7	50	_____
8	360	_____	8	40	_____
9	440	_____	9	30	_____
10	530	_____	10	20	_____

■ SELF-TEST

Circle the T if the statement is true, the F if it is false.

1. Monopolistic competitors have no control over the market price of their products. **T   F**

2. The smaller the number of firms in an industry and the greater the extent of product differentiation, the greater will be the elasticity of the individual seller's demand curve. **T   F**

3. One reason why monopolistic competition is wasteful, given the products the firms are producing and the extent to which they are promoting them, is that the average cost of producing the product is greater than the minimum average cost at which the product could be produced. **T   F**

4. If advertising expenditures fluctuate directly (or positively) with total spending in the economy, they will be countercyclical and lead to greater stability in employment and the price level. **T   F**

5. Those who contend that advertising contributes to "social imbalance" argue that there is an overproduction of private goods partly as a result of persuasive advertising. **T   F**

6. A firm will improve the quality of its product only if it expects that the additional revenue which it will receive will be greater than the extra costs involved. **T   F**

7. There tends to be rather general agreement among both critics and defenders of advertising that advertising increases the average cost of producing and promoting the product. **T   F**

8. Empirical evidence clearly indicates that advertising reduces competition and makes entry into an industry more difficult. **T   F**

Underscore the letter that corresponds to the best answer.

1. Which of the following is *not* characteristic of monopolistic competition? (a) product differentiation; (b) a relatively large number of firms; (c) a feeling of interdependence among the firms; (d) relatively easy entry in the long run.

2. Given the following short-run demand and cost schedules for a monopolistic competitor, what output will the firm produce? (a) 2; (b) 3; (c) 4; (d) 5.

Price	Quantity demanded	Total cost	Output
$10	1	$14	1
9	2	17	2
8	3	22	3
7	4	29	4
6	5	38	5
5	6	49	6

3. Assuming the short-run demand and cost data in question 2 above, *in the long run* the number of firms in the industry: (a) will be less than in the short run; (b) will be the same as in the short run; (c) will be greater than in the short run; (d) cannot be determined from the available information.

4. Given the product the firm is producing and the extent to which the firm is promoting it, *in the long run:* (a) the firm will produce that output at which marginal cost and price are equal; (b) the elasticity of demand for the firm's product will be less than it was in the short run; (c) the number of firms in the industry will be greater than it was in the short run; (d) the profits being earned by the firms in the industry will tend to equal zero.

5. Which of the following is *not* one of the features of monopolistic competition which may offset the wastes associated with such a market structure? (a) a wider variety of products is offered to consumers; (b) advertising tends to be of the competitive type; (c) the quality of products improves over time; (d) consumers are better informed of the availability and prices of products.

6. Which of the following would probably be the best example of "competitive advertising"? (a) a "for sale" ad in the classified section of a newspaper; (b) one of the twice-weekly full-page advertisements of a grocery supermarket in a newspaper; (c) the advertisement for a particular brand of aspirin in a monthly magazine; (d) the national television advertisement of a drugstore chain announcing a "one-cent sale."

7. Which of the following would *not* be characteristic of a monopolistically competitive firm when it is in long-run equilibrium? (a) no further increase in the firm's output will decrease the firm's average revenue more than it decreases average cost; (b) no further decrease in the firm's price will increase the firm's total revenue more than it increases total costs; (c) no further variation in the firm's product will reduce total costs less than it reduces total revenue; (d) no further change in the firm's advertising campaign will increase total revenue more than it increases total costs.

8. Which of the following can be fairly concluded with respect to the economic effects of advertising? (a) advertising helps to maintain a high level of aggregate demand in the economy; (b) consumers benefit less from advertising expenditures than they do from expenditures for product development; (c) advertising in the American economy is more informative than competitive; (d) lower unit costs and lower prices result when a firm advertises because advertising increases the size of the firm's market and promotes economies of scale.

■ DISCUSSION QUESTIONS

1. What are the chief characteristics of a monopolistically competitive market? In what sense is there competition and in what sense is there monopoly in such a market?

2. What is meant by product differentiation? By what methods can products be differentiated? How does product differentiation affect the kind of competition in and inject an element of monopoly into markets?

3. Comment on the elasticity of the demand curve faced by the monopolistically competitive firm in the short run, assuming that the firm is producing a given product and is en-

gaged in a given amount of promotional activity. What two factors determine just how elastic that demand curve will be?

4. What output will the monopolistic competitor produce in the short run, and what price will he charge for his product? What determines whether the firm will earn profits or suffer losses in the short run?

5. In the long run what level of profits will the individual monopolistically competitive firm *tend* to receive? Why is this just a tendency? What forces profits toward this level, and why will the firm produce a long-run output which is smaller than the most "efficient" output? (Again assume, in answering this question, that the firm is producing a given product and selling it with a given amount of promotional activity.)

6. In what two senses is monopolistic competition wasteful or a misallocation of resources?

7. What methods, other than price cutting, can an individual monopolistic competitor employ to attempt to protect and increase his profits in the long run?

8. To what extent and how do product differentiation and product development offset the "wastes" associated with monopolistic competition?

9. Does advertising result in a waste of resources, or does it promote a more efficient utilization of resources? What arguments can be presented to support the contention that it is wasteful and detrimental, and what claims are made to support the view that it is beneficial to the economy? What empirical evidence is there?

10. When is a monopolistic competitor in long-run equilibrium not only with respect to the price he is charging but also with respect to the product he is producing and the extent to which he is promoting his product?

PRICE AND OUTPUT DETERMINATION: OLIGOPOLY

This last of the four chapters dealing with specific market situations is in a way the most difficult. Oligopoly is one of those areas of economic study where economists have found it impossible to reach definite conclusions. Under conditions of pure competition, pure monopoly, and monopolistic competition fairly definite conclusions regarding market prices and the outputs of individual firms are reached, but such conclusions are not easily drawn from an analysis of oligopoly. This is why the study of oligopoly is difficult—the generalizations are vague—and this is unfortunate but also unavoidable.

Oligopoly is probably the most realistic market situation which the student will examine, and many economists believe it is the type of market most prevalent—or at least, most important—in the American economy. Because it is so realistic its study is all the more difficult. Chapter 30 is little more than an introduction to this very complex market situation. There are, however, certain things the student can and should learn about it.

What oligopoly *is* is fairly simple to understand. The *consequences* of "fewness" and the "mutual interdependence" and feeling of uncertainty to which it gives rise are not quite so easy to grasp, but they are of the greatest importance. For these reasons the student should make every attempt to learn exactly *what is meant* by mutual interdependence and

uncertainty and *why they exist* in an oligopoly. If he can do this, he is well on the road to understanding why specific and definite conclusions cannot be reached concerning market prices and the outputs of individual firms. He will also see why oligopolists are loath to engage in price competition and why they frequently resort to collusion to set prices and to nonprice competition to determine market shares.

Chapter 30 employs several devices to explain the two major behavioral characteristics of oligopoly: the tendency for the prices charged by oligopolists to be rigid, and the tendency for oligopolists to determine what price to charge by collusion. The kinked demand curve is one of these devices. It explains why, in the absence of collusion, oligopolists will not raise or lower their prices even when their costs change. But the kinked demand curve does not explain what price oligopolists will set; it only explains why price, once set, will be relatively inflexible. To set price, oligopolists often resort to some form of collusion (such as a cartel, gentlemen's agreement, or price leadership). Collusion reduces the uncertainty each firm has about the prices rivals will charge and enables it to increase its profits. It also enables the industry as a whole to increase its joint profit. The results of collusion are a price and output which are the same as would prevail if the industry were a pure monopoly. But collusion is seldom perfect because there are so many obstacles to collusion. As a result of these obstacles, price may be somewhat less and output somewhat greater than those which would be set by a monopolist.

Another device used to explain the behavior of oligopolists is the theory of games and the profits-payoff table. Using this table, we can again understand why noncolluding oligopolists will tend to keep their price unchanged. The table also helps us see why oligopolists will find it more profitable either to set price collusively or to merge their firms.

The final section of the chapter poses the question of whether oligopolies efficiently allocate resources. As with the same question with respect to monopolistic competition, there is only a tentative answer. There are, however, several reasons to believe that over the years oligopoly may have beneficial results for society as a whole, even though it may not appear at any given moment to be allocating resources efficiently.

■ CHAPTER OUTLINE

1. An oligopoly is an industry composed of a few mutually interdependent firms selling either a standardized or a differentiated product. The existence of such industries is usually the result of economies of scale and the advantages of merger.

2. The economic analysis of oligopoly is difficult for two reasons: The term "oligopoly" actually covers many different market situations; and the individual oligopolist, because of the uncertainty which accompanies mutual interdependence, is seldom able to estimate his own demand curve. Important characteristics of oligopoly are inflexible prices and simultaneous price changes.

3. An examination of two oligopoly models helps to explain price rigidity and the price-output behavior of oligopolists.

a. Under conditions of noncollusive oligopoly, an oligopolist believes that when he lowers his price his rivals will lower their prices, and that when he increases his price his rivals will not increase their prices. He is therefore reluctant to change his price at all for fear of

decreasing his profits and beginning a price war.

b. Because of the uncertainties of noncollusive oligopoly, oligopolists may collude to maximize their joint profit by setting their price and joint output at the same levels at which a pure monopolist would set them.

c. Joint-profit maximization by collusive oligopolists is only a tendency because of several obstacles to collusion.

4. The theory of games and a profits-payoff table help us understand the behavior of oligopolists. A profits-payoff table:

a. Shows the different prices two oligopolists might charge and their profits for every combination of prices.

b. Demonstrates their mutual interdependence: the price one firm should set to maximize its profits depends upon the price charged by the other firm.

c. Illustrates price rigidity and explains why each firm is reluctant either to raise or to lower its price.

d. Indicates how both firms may gain by setting a collusive price or may increase their joint profits by merging.

5. Oligopolistic firms avoid price competition but engage in nonprice competition to determine each firm's market share (sales).

6. Whether oligopoly is economically efficient is almost impossible to determine.

a. At a given moment of time oligopoly probably results in restricted outputs, economic profits, and higher costs and prices.

b. Over a period of time, oligopoly may be progressive and result in larger outputs, lower costs, and technological progress.

(1) Technological competition among firms that have both the means and the incentives to improve their products and production techniques will result in economic progress.

(2) The evidence suggests that while many oligopolies have been progressive, many others have not engaged in any significant research and have failed to develop better products and processes.

c. Countervailing power may also limit the restrictive power of oligopolies.

d. Oligopoly, *if* it results in technological progress or in economies of scale or *if* it is curbed by countervailing power, may be as efficient in allocating resources as competition.

■ IMPORTANT TERMS

Oligopoly	Gentlemen's agreement
Fewness	Price leadership
Mutual inter-dependence	Price break
Price rigidity	Theory of games
Noncollusive oligopoly	Profits-payoff (price-profits) table
Collusive oligopoly	Duopoly
Kinked demand curve	Restrictive oligopoly
Joint-profit maximization	Progressive oligopoly
Cartel	Countervailing power

■ FILL-IN QUESTIONS

1. In an oligopoly a _____ firms produce either a _____ or a _____ product, and entry into such an industry is _____

2. Because oligopoly consists of a small number of firms, they are necessarily _____; this means that each firm must consider _____ when setting the price of its product; the monopolist does not face this problem because he has _____ rivals, and the pure competitor does not face it because he has _____ rivals.

3. The two major underlying causes of oligopoly are _____ and _____

4. Formal economic analysis cannot be easily used to explain the prices and outputs of oligopolists because _____ and _____

5. Oligopoly prices tend to be _____ and oligopolists tend to change their prices when they change them.

6. There tends to be very little _____ competition and a great deal of _____ _____ competition in oligopolies.

7. The kinked demand curve which the individual oligopolist sees for his product is highly _____ at prices above the current or going price and tends to be only slightly _____ or _____ below that price.

8. The kinked demand curve for an oligopolist is drawn on the assumption that if the oligopolist raises his price his rivals will _____ and if he lowers his price his rivals will _____ _____

9. Because the oligopolist who confronts a kinked demand curve finds that there is a _____ _____ in his marginal-revenue curve, small changes in the marginal-cost curve do not change the _____ _____

10. When oligopolists collude to maximize joint profits, the price they set and their combined output are the same as _____

11. Four obstacles to the tendency of collusive oligopolists to maximize joint profits are:

a. _____

b. _____

c. _____

d. _____

12. A cartel is a written or oral agreement either to _____ or to _____

13. A gentlemen's agreement is a _____

agreement on _____;
each firm's share of the market is determined

by _____

_____

The firm that sets the price which the other

firms in the industry follow is the _____

14. In a profits-payoff (or price-profits) table

the _____ are

along the top and the _____
are along the left side. The two figures in each

box (or cell) in the table are the _____

_____

15. The profits-payoff table demonstrates that:
a. The most profitable price for one firm to

charge depends upon _____
b. In most cases either a price increase or a

decrease by one firm will _____
that firm's profit, because when it raises price

its rival will _____

and when it lowers price its rival will _____

_____

c. The two firms can increase their joint

profit either by _____ or _____

16. Oligopolists use nonprice competition to
determine each firm's share of the market be-

cause _____

and _____

17. Oligopolists typically have both the means
and the incentives to effect technological ad-

vances; the means are _____

_____

and the incentives are:

a. _____

b. _____

c. _____

d. _____

18. Such evidence as is available makes it
clear that most oligopolies (have, have not)

_____ been progres-

sive in developing new products and techniques; their expenditures for research and

development have been _____
and a large percentage of such expenditures

of oligopolists have been _____

_____

19. Countervailing power tends to develop for
both defensive and offensive reasons. The

defensive reason is the desire of _____

and _____

to protect themselves from _____

_____

and the offensive reason is the desire to _____

_____

20. Oligopoly may be more efficient in allocating resources than competition if it has

lower _____, produces

a _____ product, or is curbed

by _____; in the
absence of these conditions it will produce

_____ outputs and charge

_____ prices than a competitive industry.

■ PROBLEMS AND PROJECTS

1. The kinked demand schedule which an oligopolist believes confronts him is given in
the table on page 212.
a. Compute the oligopolist's total revenue at
each of the nine prices, and enter these figures in the table.
b. Also compute marginal revenue and the
coefficient (arc) of elasticity of demand between the nine prices, and enter these figures
in the table.
c. What is the current, or going, price for

the oligopolist's product? $_____

How much is he selling? _____
d. On the graph on page 212 plot the oligopolist's demand curve and marginal-revenue
curve. Connect the demand points and the

Price	Quality demanded	Total revenue	Marginal revenue	Elasticity of demand
$2.90	100	$_____		
2.80	200	_____	$_____	$_____
2.70	300	_____	_____	_____
2.60	400	_____	_____	_____
2.50	500	_____	_____	_____
2.40	525	_____	_____	_____
2.30	550	_____	_____	_____
2.20	575	_____	_____	_____
2.10	600	_____	_____	

marginal-revenue points with as straight a line as possible. *Be sure* to plot the marginal-revenue figures at the average of the two quantities involved, that is, at 150, 250, 350, 450, 512½, 537½, 562½, and 587½.

e. Assume that the marginal-cost schedule of the oligopolist is given in columns (1) and (2) of the table on page 213. Plot the mar-

ginal-cost curve on the graph on which demand and marginal revenue are plotted.

(1) Given demand and marginal cost, what price should the oligopolist charge to maxi-

mize his profits? $_____

How many units of product will he sell at this

price? _____

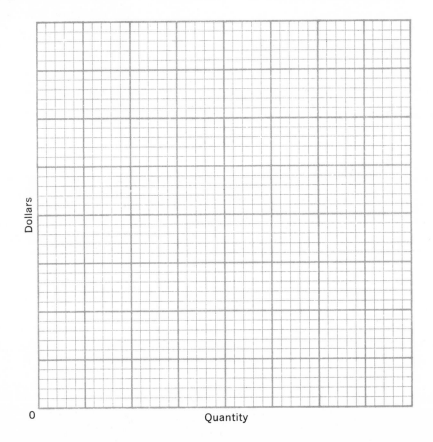

Dollars

0   Quantity

(1) Output	(2) MC	(3) MC′	(4) MC″
150	$1.40	$1.90	$.40
250	1.30	1.80	.30
350	1.40	1.90	.40
450	1.50	2.00	.50
512½	1.60	2.10	.60
537½	1.70	2.20	.70
562½	1.80	2.30	.80
587½	1.90	2.40	.90

(2) If the marginal-cost schedule changed from that shown in columns (1) and (2) to that shown in columns (1) and (3), what price should he charge? $_____ What level of output will he produce? _____ How have his profits changed as a result of the change in costs? _____ Plot the new marginal-cost curve on the graph.

(3) If the marginal-cost schedule changed from that shown in columns (1) and (2) to that shown in columns (1) and (4), what price should he charge? $_____ What level of output will he produce? _____ How have his profits changed as a result of the change in costs? _____ Plot the new marginal-cost curve on the graph.

2. An oligopoly producing a homogeneous product is composed of three firms. Assume that these three firms have identical cost schedules. Assume also that if any one of these firms sets a price for the product, the other two firms will follow and charge the same price. As long as they all charge the same price they will share the market equally: the quantity demanded of each will be the same.

Below is the total-cost schedule of one of these firms and the demand schedule that confronts it when the other two firms charge the same price as this firm.

a. Complete the marginal-cost and marginal-revenue schedules facing the firm.

b. What price would this firm set if it wished to maximize its profits? $_____

c. How much would:

(1) It sell at this price? _____

(2) Its profits be at this price? $_____

d. What would be the industry's:

(1) Total output at this price? _____

(2) Joint profits at this price? $_____

e. Is there any other price this firm can set, assuming that the other two firms will charge the same price, which would result in a greater joint profit for them? _____ If so, what is that price? $_____

f. If these three firms colluded (or merged) in order to maximize their joint profit, what price would they charge? $_____

3. On page 214 is a profits-payoff (or price-profits) table.

Output	Total cost	Marginal cost	Price	Quantity demanded	Marginal revenue
0	$ 0		$140	0	
1	30	$_____	130	1	$_____
2	50	_____	120	2	_____
3	80	_____	110	3	_____
4	120	_____	100	4	_____
5	170	_____	90	5	_____
6	230	_____	80	6	_____
7	300	_____	70	7	_____
8	380	_____	60	8	_____

Firm Y's prices

X \ Y	$4	$3	$2
$4	$50 / $49	$57 / $40	$60 / $32
$3	$39 / $50	$44 / $44	$42 / $38
$2	$30 / $48	$35 / $46	$40 / $42

(Firm X's prices shown on the left axis)

a. If firm X charges a price of $3, for Y to maximize its profits it should charge a price of

$_____. But if firm Y sets a price of $3, the most profitable price for X to charge is

$_____. And if X charges $2, the most

profitable price for Y is $_____.

b. Assume both firm X and firm Y are initially charging a price of $3.

(1) If X increased its price from $3 to $4,

Y (would or would not) _____

increase its price to $4 because _____

_____

(2) Knowing that Y would not follow a price increase from $3 to $4, X (would, would

not) _____ increase its price to

$4 because _____

_____

(3) If X decreased its price from $3 to $2,

Y (would, would not) _____ de-

crease its price to $2 because _____

(4) Knowing that Y would follow a price decrease from $3 to $2, X (would, would not)

_____ decrease its price to $2

because _____

c. If X and Y colluded to maximize their joint profit:

(1) Firm X would set a price of $_____

and have a profit of $_____

(2) Firm Y would set a price of $_____

and have a profit of $_____

(3) Firms X and Y would have a joint profit

of $_____

■ SELF-TEST

Circle the T if the statement is true, the F if it is false.

1. The element of "uncertainty" which exists in oligopolies is the uncertainty faced by each firm on how its rivals will react if it changes its price.   **T   F**

2. Price competition between firms is an important characteristic of oligopoly.   **T   F**

3. The kinked demand curve is an economic tool which can be used to explain how the current market price of a product is determined.   **T   F**

4. A cartel is usually a written agreement among firms which sets the price of the product and determines each firm's share of the market.   **T   F**

5. The practice of price leadership is almost always based on a formal written or oral agreement.   **T   F**

6. Whenever oligopoly exists, firms will collude to maximize their joint profit.   **T   F**

7. Nonprice competition is the typical method of determining each oligopolist's share of the total market.   **T   F**

8. It is often argued that oligopolists typically possess both the means and the incentives to technological progress, and that the means are the substantial profits received by them.   **T   F**

9. Almost all the important technological advances in the United States since 1900 can be attributed to the research and development activities of large business firms.   **T   F**

10. Oligopoly may be socially desirable if it results in lower production costs or in better products than would be obtainable under more competitive conditions.   **T   F**

Underscore the letter that corresponds to the best answer.

1. "Mutual interdependence" means that: (a) each firm produces a product similar but not identical to the products produced by its rivals; (b) each firm produces a product identical to the products produced by its rivals; (c) each firm must consider the reactions of its rivals when it determines its price policy; (d) each firm faces a perfectly elastic demand for its product.

2. The demand curve confronting an oligopolist tends to be: (a) elastic; (b) of unitary elasticity; (c) inelastic; (d) one which depends upon the prices charged by his rivals.

3. If an individual oligopolist's demand curve is "kinked," it is necessarily: (a) inelastic below the going price; (b) inelastic above the going price; (c) elastic above the going price; (d) of unitary elasticity at the going price.

4. In the next column is the demand schedule confronting an oligopolist. Which one of the eight prices seems to be the "going" price of the product produced by the firm? (a) $4.50; (b) $4; (c) $3.50; (d) $3.

5. When oligopolists collude to maximize their joint profit, the results are generally: (a) greater output and higher price; (b) greater output and lower price; (c) smaller output and lower price; (d) smaller output and higher price.

Price	Quantity demanded
$5.00	10
4.50	20
4.00	30
3.50	40
3.00	42
2.50	44
2.00	46
1.00	48

6. Which of the following constitutes an obstacle to collusion among oligopolists? (a) a general business recession; (b) a small number of firms in the industry; (c) a homogeneous product; (d) the patent laws.

7. Which of the following is *not* a means of colluding? (a) a cartel; (b) a price break; (c) a gentlemen's agreement; (d) price leadership.

8. Which of the following does *not* contribute to the existence of oligopoly? (a) the economies of large-scale production; (b) the gains in profits that result from mergers; (c) low barriers to entry into an industry; (d) extensive sales promotion activities by the established firms in an industry.

9. A profits-payoff (or price-profits) table is used to explain all but one of the following: (a) mutual interdependence; (b) the advantages of collusion; (c) price rigidity; (d) product differentiation.

10. Countervailing power means that: (a) new firms enter oligopolistic industries to compete with and to lower the profits of the firms in the industry; (b) oligopolists restrict their profits for fear the government will investigate their pricing policy and for fear of adverse public opinion; (c) technological advance results over time in lower prices, improved products, and larger outputs in oligopolies; (d) resource suppliers and customers of oligopolists tend to become oligopolists themselves in order to protect themselves and to share in the oligopolists' profits.

■ DISCUSSION QUESTIONS

1. What are the essential characteristics of an oligopoly? How does it differ from monopolistic competition?

2. How prevalent is oligopoly in the American economy? Is it more or less prevalent than monopolistic competition?

3. What do "mutual interdependence" and "uncertainty" mean with respect to oligopoly? Why are they special characteristics of oligopoly?

4. What are the underlying causes of oligopoly?

5. Why is it difficult to employ formal economic analysis to explain the prices charged by and the outputs of oligopolists?

6. To what extent are oligopoly prices flexible and to what extent is there price competition among oligopolistic firms?

7. Explain what the kinked demand curve is, its most important characteristics, the assumptions upon which it is based, and the kind of marginal-revenue curve to which it gives rise. How can the kinked demand curve be used to explain why oligopoly prices are relatively inflexible? Under what conditions will oligopolists acting independently raise or lower their prices even though their demand curves may be kinked?

8. Explain the difference between (a) collusive and noncollusive oligopoly, (b) restrictive and progressive oligopoly, and (c) homogeneous and differentiated oligopoly.

9. Why do oligopolists find it advantageous to collude? What are the obstacles to collusion?

10. Explain (a) a cartel, (b) a gentlemen's agreement, and (c) price leadership.

11. Why do oligopolists engage in extensive nonprice competition?

12. Explain what a profits-payoff (or price-profits) table is and how it is used to demonstrate (a) mutual interdependence, (b) price rigidity, and (c) the advantages of collusion and merger.

13. Is oligopoly economically efficient and beneficial to society? Explain why your answer depends upon whether a short-run or a long-run view is taken.

14. What is meant when it is said that oligopolists have both the means and the incentives for technological improvements?

15. Explain precisely what is meant by countervailing power. How does it differ from the more traditional view that the self-interest of firms is regulated by "same-side-of-the-market" competition? What shortcomings does it have as a regulatory force?

PRODUCTION AND THE DEMAND FOR ECONOMIC RESOURCES

Chapter 31 is the first of a group of three chapters which examine the markets for resources. A resource market is simply a market in which demand and supply determine the prices (called wages, rent, interest, and profit) of resources and the quantities of these resources that will be hired. Just as Chapters 23 through 30 have looked behind demand and supply in product markets, Chapters 31 through 33 look behind demand and supply in resource markets.

The demanders of resources are business firms who employ resources to produce their products. Chapter 31 begins the examination of resource markets by looking at the business firm and the demand side of the resource market. The material in this chapter is *not* an explanation of what determines the demand for a *particular* resource—such as labor, land, capital, or entrepreneurial ability—but is rather an explanation of what determines the demand for *any* resource. In Chapters 32 and 33 the supply sides of the resource market and particular resources are examined in detail.

The list of important terms for Chapter 31 is relatively short, but included in the list are two very important concepts—marginal revenue product and marginal resource cost—which the student must grasp if he is to understand how much of a resource a firm will hire. These two concepts are similar to but not identical with the marginal-revenue and marginal-cost concepts employed in the study of product markets and in the explanation of how large an output a firm will produce. Marginal revenue and marginal cost are, respectively, the change in the firm's total revenue and the change in the firm's total cost when it produces and sells an additional unit of *output;* marginal revenue product and marginal resource cost are, respectively, the change in the firm's total revenue and the change in the firm's total cost when it hires an additional unit of an *input.* (*Note:* The two new concepts deal with changes in revenue and costs as a consequence of hiring more of a *resource.*)

When a firm wishes to maximize its profits, it produces that *output* at which marginal revenue and marginal cost are equal. But how much of each resource does it hire if it wishes to maximize its profits? It hires that amount of each *resource* at which the marginal revenue product and the marginal resource cost of that resource are equal.

There is still another similarity between the output and the input markets insofar as the firm is concerned. You will recall that the competitive firm's *supply* curve is a portion of its *marginal-cost* curve. The competitive firm's *demand* curve for a resource is its *marginal-revenue-product* curve. Just as cost is the important determinant of supply, the revenue derived from the use of a resource is the important factor determining the demand for that resource.

■ CHAPTER OUTLINE

1. The study of what determines the prices of resources is important because resource prices influence the size of individual incomes and the distribution of income; and they ration scarce resources.

2. Economists generally agree upon the basic principles of resource pricing, but the complexities of different resource markets make these general principles difficult to apply.

3. The demand for a single resource depends upon (or is derived from) the demand for the goods and services it can produce.

a. Because resource demand is a derived demand, the demand for a single resource depends upon the marginal productivity of the resource and the price of the good or service it is used to produce. Marginal revenue product combines these two factors—the marginal physical product of a resource and the value of the product it produces—into a single useful tool.

b. A firm will hire a resource up to the point where the marginal revenue product of the resource is equal to the marginal resource cost; and the firm's marginal-revenue-product schedule for a resource is that firm's demand schedule for the resource.

c. If a firm sells its output in an imperfectly competitive market, the more the firm sells the lower becomes the price of the product. This causes the firm's marginal-revenue-product (resource demand) schedule to be less elastic than it would be if the firm sold its output in a purely competitive market.

d. The market (or total) demand for a resource is the sum of the demand schedules of all firms employing the resource.

4. Changes in the demand for the product being produced, changes in the productivity of the resource, and changes in the prices of other resources will tend to change the demand for a resource.

5. The elasticity of the demand for a particular resource depends upon the rate at which the marginal physical product of that resource declines, the extent to which other resources can be substituted for the particular resource, the elasticity of demand for the product being produced, and the importance of the total cost of the resource relative to the total costs of the firm.

6. Firms typically employ more than one resource in producing a product.

a. The firm is hiring resources in the most profitable combination, if it hires resources in a competitive market, when the marginal revenue product of each resource is equal to the price of the resource. (If it employs resources in imperfectly competitive markets, it is employing resources in the most profitable combination when the marginal revenue product of each resource is equal to its marginal resource cost.)

b. The firm employing resources in perfectly competitive markets is hiring resources in the least-cost combination when the ratio of the marginal physical product of a resource to its price is the same for all the resources the firm hires. (If it hires resources in imperfectly competitive markets it is employing them in the least-cost combination when the ratio of the marginal physical product to the marginal resource cost is the same for all resources.)

■ IMPORTANT TERMS

Derived demand	**Output effect**
Marginal revenue product	**Profit-maximizing combination of resources**
Marginal resource cost	
MRP = MRC rule	**Least-cost combination of resources**
Substitution effect	

■ FILL-IN QUESTIONS

1. Resource prices ration _____ and are one of the factors that determine the

_____

of households; they are also one of the deter-

minants of the _____ of business firms.

2. The demand for a resource is a _____

_____

demand and depends upon the _____

_____

and the _____

3. A firm will find it profitable to hire additional units of a resource up to the point at

which the _____

and the _____
of the resource are equal; if the firm hires the resource in a purely competitive market, the

_____

and the _____
of the resource are necessarily equal.

4. A firm's demand schedule for a resource

is the firm's _____
schedule for that resource because both indi-

cate the _____
of the resource the firm will hire at various

resource _____

5. A producer who sells his product in an imperfectly competitive market finds that the

more of a resource he hires, the _____

_____

becomes the price at which he can sell his product. As a consequence the marginal-reve-nue-product (or demand) schedule for the re-

source is _____
elastic than it would be if the output were sold in a purely competitive market.

6. A firm can hire 4 units of a resource and produce 20 units of a product which sells for $6 per unit; if it were to hire 5 units of the resource, it would be able to produce 27 units of product which would sell for $5 per unit. The marginal revenue product of the 5th unit

of the resource is $_____, which is equal

to _____ × $_____

minus _____ × $_____

7. The market demand curve for a resource

is obtained by _____

_____

8. The demand for a resource will change if

the demand for the _____

changes, if the _____

of the resource changes, or if the _____

_____

of other resources change.

9. In the space to the right of each of the following, indicate whether the change would tend to increase (+), decrease (−), or have no effect (0) upon a firm's demand for a particular resource:

a. An increase in the price of the firm's

product _____

b. A decrease in the amounts of all other

resources the firm employs _____

c. An increase in the efficiency of the re-

source _+_

d. An increase in the price of a substitute

resource _____

e. A decrease in the price of a complemen-

tary resource _____

10. Other things being equal, a decrease in the price of resource A will induce the firm

to hire _____ of resource

A and _____ of other resources;

this is called the _____ effect.
But if the decrease in the price of A results in lower total costs and an increase in output,

the firm may hire _____

of other resources; this is called the _____

_____ effect.

11. Four determinants of the elasticity of demand for a resource are the rate at which

the _____
of the resource decreases, the degree to which

other resources can be _____

for the resource, the _____
for the product which it is used to produce,

and the _____

_____

12. A firm that hires resources in purely competitive markets is employing the combination of resources which will result in maximum profits for the firm when the _____ of every resource is equal to its _____

13. Suppose a firm employs resources in purely competitive markets. If the firm wishes to produce any given amount of its product in the least costly way, the ratio of the _____ _____ of each resource to its _____ must be the same for all resources.

14. When the marginal revenue product of a resource is equal to the price of that resource, the marginal revenue product of the resource divided by its price is equal to _____

_____

15. Assume that a firm employs resources in imperfectly competitive markets. The firm is:
  a. Employing the combination of resources that maximizes its profits when the _____ of every resource is equal to its _____ (or when the _____ each resource divided by its _____ is equal to _____).
  b. Employing the combination of resources that enables it to produce any given output in the least costly way when the _____ of every resource divided by its _____ is the same for all resources.

■ PROBLEMS AND PROJECTS

1. The bottom table shows the total product a firm will be able to obtain if it employs varying amounts of resource A, the amounts of the other resources the firm employs remaining constant.
  a. Compute the marginal physical product of each of the seven units of resource A and enter these figures in the table.
  b. Assume the product the firm produces sells in the market for $1.50 per unit. Compute the total revenue of the firm at each of the eight levels of output and the marginal revenue product of each of the seven units of resource A. Enter these figures in the table.
  c. On the basis of your computations complete the firm's demand schedule for resource A in the table below by indicating how many units of resource A the firm would employ at the given prices.

Price of A	Quantity of A demanded
$21	_____
18	_____
15	_____
12	_____
9	_____
6	_____
3	_____
1	_____

Quantity of resource A employed	Total product	Marginal physical product of A	Total revenue	Marginal revenue product of A
0	0		$_____	
1	12	_____	_____	$_____
2	22	_____	_____	_____
3	30	_____	_____	_____
4	36	_____	_____	_____
5	40	_____	_____	_____
6	42	_____	_____	_____
7	43	_____	_____	_____

Quantity of resource B employed	Marginal physical product of B	Total product	Product price	Total revenue	Marginal revenue product of B
0		_____		$ 0.00	
1	22	_____	$1.00	_____	$_____
2	21	_____	.90	_____	_____
3	19	_____	.80	_____	_____
4	16	_____	.70	_____	_____
5	12	_____	.60	_____	_____
6	7	_____	.50	_____	_____
7	1	_____	.40	_____	_____

2. In the table at the top of this page you will find the marginal-physical-product data for resource B. Assume that the quantities of other resources employed by the firm remain constant.

a. Compute the total product (output) of the firm for each of the eight quantities of resource B employed and enter these figures in the table.

b. Assume that the firm sells its output in an imperfectly competitive market and that the prices at which it can sell its product are those given in the table. Compute and enter in the table:

(1) Total revenue for each of eight quantities of B employed.

(2) The marginal revenue product of each of the seven units of resource B.

c. How many units of B would the firm employ if the market price of B were:

(1) $25: _____

(2) $20: _____

(3) $15: _____

(4) $9: _____

(5) $5: _____

(6) $1: _____

3. In the table below are the marginal-physical- and marginal-revenue-product schedules for resource C and resource D. Both resources are variable and are employed in purely competitive markets. The price of C is $2 and the price of D is $3.

a. The least-cost combination of C and D that would enable the firm to produce:

(1) 64 units of its product is _____ C and _____ D.

Quantity of resource C employed	Marginal physical product of C	Marginal revenue product of C	Quality of resource D employed	Marginal physical product of D	Marginal revenue product of D
1	10	$5.00	1	21	$10.50
2	8	4.00	2	18	9.00
3	6	3.00	3	15	7.50
4	5	2.50	4	12	6.00
5	4	2.00	5	9	4.50
6	3	1.50	6	6	3.00
7	2	1.00	7	3	1.50

(2) 99 units of its product is _____ C

and _____ D.

b. The profit-maximizing combination of C

and D is _____ C and _____ D.

c. When the firm employs the profit-maximizing combination of C and D, it is also employing C and D in the least-cost combination

because _____

equals _____

d. Examination of the figures in the table

reveals that the firm sells its product in a ___

_____ competitive market at

a price of $_____

e. Employing the profit-maximizing combination of C and D, the firm's:

(1) Total output is _____

(2) Total revenue is $_____

(3) Total cost is $_____

(4) Total profit is $_____

■ SELF-TEST

Circle the T if the statement is true, the F if it is false.

1. The prices of resources are an important factor in the determination of the supply of a product.   (T) F

2. A resource which is highly productive will always be in great demand.   T (F)

3. A firm's demand schedule for a resource is the firm's marginal-revenue-product schedule for the resource.   (T) F

4. A producer's demand schedule for a resource will be more elastic if he sells his product in a purely competitive market than it would be if he sold the product in an imperfectly competitive market.   (T) F

5. If two resources are "complementary," an increase in the price of one of them will reduce the demand for the other.   (T) F

6. An increase in the price of a resource will cause the demand for the resource to decrease.   T (F)

Use the following information as the basis for answering questions 7 and 8. The marginal revenue product and price of resource A are $12 and a constant $2, respectively, and the marginal revenue product and price of resource B are $25 and a constant $5, respectively. The firm sells its product at a constant price of $1.

7. The firm should decrease the amount of A and increase the amount of B it employs if it wishes to decrease its total cost without affecting its total output.   T (F)

8. If the firm wishes to maximize its profits, it should increase its employment of both A and B until their marginal revenue products fall to $2 and $5, respectively.   (T) F

Underscore the letter that corresponds to the best answer.

1. The study of the pricing of resources tends to be complex because: (a) supply and demand do not determine resource prices; (b) economists do not agree on the basic principles of resource pricing; (c) the basic principles of resource pricing must be varied and adjusted when applied to particular resource markets; (d) resource pricing is essentially an ethical question.

Use the total-product and marginal-physical-product schedules for a resource found below to answer questions 2, 3, and 4. Assume that the quantities of other resources the firm employs remain constant.

Units of resource	Total product	MPP
1	8	8
2	14	6
3	18	4
4	21	3
5	23	2

2. If the product the firm produces sells for a constant $3 per unit, the marginal revenue product of the 4th unit of the resource is: (a) $3; (b) $6; (c) $9; (d) $12.

3. If the firm's product sells for a constant $3 per unit and the price of the resource is a constant $15, the firm will employ how many units of the resource? (a) 2; (b) 3; (c) 4; (d) 5.

4. If the firm can sell 14 units of output at a price of $1 per unit and 18 units of output at a price of $0.90 per unit, the marginal revenue product of the 3rd unit of the resource is: (a) $4; (b) $3.60; (c) $2.20; (d) $0.40.

5. Which of the following would increase a firm's demand for a particular resource? (a) an increase in the prices of complementary resources used by the firm; (b) a decrease in the demand for the firm's product; (c) an increase in the productivity of the resource; (d) a decrease in the price of the particular resource.

6. Which of the following would result in an increase in the elasticity of demand for a particular resource? (a) an increase in the rate at which the marginal physical product of that resource declines; (b) a decrease in the elasticity of demand for the product which the resource helps to produce; (c) an increase in the percentage of the firm's total costs accounted for by the resource; (d) a decrease in the number of other resources which are good substitutes for the particular resource.

7. A firm is allocating its expenditure for resources in a way that will result in the least total cost of producing any given output when: (a) the amount the firm spends on each resource is the same; (b) the marginal revenue product of each resource is the same; (c) the marginal physical product of each resource is the same; (d) the marginal physical product per dollar spent on the last unit of each resource is the same.

8. A firm that hires resources in competitive markets is *not necessarily* maximizing its profits when: (a) the marginal revenue product of every resource is equal to 1; (b) the marginal revenue product of every resource is equal to its price; (c) the ratio of the marginal revenue product of every resource to its price is equal to 1; (d) the ratio of the price of every resource to its marginal revenue product is equal to 1.

■ DISCUSSION QUESTIONS

1. Why is it important to study resource pricing?

2. Why is resource demand a derived demand, and upon what two factors does the strength of this derived demand depend?

3. Explain why firms that wish to maximize their profits follow the MRP = MRC rule.

4. What constitutes a firm's demand schedule for a resource? Why?

5. Why is the demand schedule for a resource less elastic when the firm sells its product in a noncompetitive market than when it sells it in a purely competitive market?

6. What determines the total, or market, demand for a resource?

7. Explain what will cause the demand for a resource to increase and what will cause it to decrease.

8. Explain the difference between the "substitution effect" and the "output effect."

9. What determines the elasticity of the demand for a resource? Explain the exact relationship between each of these determinants and elasticity.

10. Assuming a firm employs resources in purely competitive markets, when is it spending money on resources in such a way that it can produce a given output for the least total cost?

11. When is a firm that employs resources in purely competitive markets utilizing these resources in amounts that will maximize the profits of the firm?

12. Were a firm to employ resources in *imperfectly* competitive markets, what would your answers to questions 10 and 11 be?

THE PRICING AND EMPLOYMENT OF RESOURCES: WAGE DETERMINATION

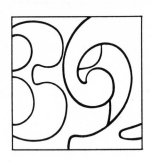

In the preceding chapter the text explained what determines the demand for *any* particular resource. Chapter 32 builds upon this explanation and applies it to the study of a very particular resource, labor, and to the price paid for the use of labor, the wage rate.

As was learned in Chapters 27 through 30, it takes more than an understanding of supply and demand to explain prices and the outputs of firms and industries. An understanding of the type of market in which products are bought and sold is also required. For this reason purely competitive, monopolistic, monopolistically competitive, and oligopolistic markets were examined in some detail. The same tends to be true of labor markets: Different types of labor markets must be examined if the factors which determine wage rates are to be understood.

Following some brief comments on the meanings of certain terms, the general level of wages, and the reasons for the high and increasing general wage level in the United States, Chapter 32 explains how supply and demand determine wage rates in particular types of labor markets. Four kinds of labor markets are studied: (1) the competitive market in which the number of employers is large and labor is nonunionized; (2) the monopsony market in which a single employer hires labor under competitive (nonunion) conditions; (3) markets in which unions control the supply of labor and the number of employers is large; and (4) bilateral monopoly markets, in which a single employer faces a labor supply controlled by a single union.

It is, of course, important for the student to learn the characteristics of and the differences between each of these labor markets. It is also important that he study each of them carefully to see *how* supply and demand are affected by the characteristics of the market and to see what wage rate will tend to be paid in these markets. In the first two types of market the wage rate which will be paid is quite definite, and here the student should learn exactly what level of wages and employment will prevail.

When unions control the supply of labor, wage and employment levels are less definite. If the demand for labor is competitive, the wage rate and the amount of employment will depend upon how successful the union is in increasing the demand for labor, in restricting the supply of labor, or in setting a wage rate which employers will accept. If there is but a single employer, wages and employment will fall within certain limits; exactly where they occur within these limits will depend upon the bargaining strength of the union and the firm. The student should, however, know what the limits are.

The sections explaining wages in particular labor markets are probably the most important parts of the chapter. But the sections which examine the effects of minimum wage laws on employment and wage rates, the effect of unionization upon wage rates in the United

States, the reasons why different workers receive different wage rates, and the effect of investment in human capital are also important. The minimum wage laws, the author concludes, tend to reduce the level of employment in labor markets affected by the law; and so workers who lose their jobs because of minimum wage legislation are hurt. But those workers who retain their jobs at an increased wage benefit. The organization of workers into unions has resulted in higher wages for and has benefited these workers; but has decreased the wages of and has hurt the unorganized workers in the economy. Overall, the average wage of workers, organized and unorganized, has not been increased by unionization.

Aside from the unionization of workers, workers receive different wage rates because the workers are different, the jobs they do are different, and workers do not and cannot always move from one job to another even if there is a strong economic motive to do so. The differences among workers and the differences in their mobility, the author explains in the last section of the chapter, are largely the result of the different amounts spent by the worker, by his family, and by society to educate him, to improve his health, and to increase his mobility. Each of these three kinds of expenditure is an investment in human capital. The amounts invested in human capital explain wage differentials among the races, among the sexes, among geographic regions, and among individual workers; they also explain the historic increases in the average level of real wages in the American economy.

■ CHAPTER OUTLINE

1. A wage (or wage rate) is the price paid per unit of time for any type of labor and can be measured either in money or in real terms. Earnings are equal to the wage multiplied by the amount of time worked.

2. The general level of wages in the United States is the highest in the world; this is due to the high productivity of American labor and, therefore, the strong demand for labor relative to the supply of labor.

3. The wage rate received by a specific type of labor depends upon the demand for and the supply of that labor and upon the characteristics of the market in which labor is hired.

a. In a purely competitive and nonunionized labor market the total demand for and the total supply of labor determine the wage rate; from the point of view of the individual firm the supply of labor is perfectly elastic at this wage rate (that is, the marginal labor cost is equal to the wage rate) and the firm will hire that amount of labor at which the marginal revenue product of labor is equal to the marginal labor cost.

b. In a monopsonistic and nonunionized labor market the firm's marginal labor costs are greater than the wage rates it must pay to obtain various amounts of labor, and it hires that amount of labor at which marginal labor cost and the marginal revenue product of labor are equal. Both the wage rate and the level of employment are less than they would be under purely competitive conditions.

c. In labor markets in which unions control the supply of labor, they attempt to increase wage rates by increasing the demand for labor, by limiting the supply of labor, or by imposing upon employers wage rates in excess of the equilibrium wage rate which would prevail in a purely competitive market.

d. In a labor market characterized by bilateral monopoly, the wage rate depends, within certain limits, on the relative bargaining power of the union and the employer.

e. Whether minimum wage laws reduce poverty is a debatable question; but the evidence suggests that while they increase the incomes of employed workers they also reduce the number of workers employed.

f. The unionization of workers has increased the wages received by union members slightly above what they would have received in the absence of unionization; but these wage increases have been at the expense of unorganized workers and unionization has not increased the average real wages of all workers.

4. Not all labor receives the same wage. Wage differentials exist because the labor force consists of noncompeting groups, because jobs vary in difficulty and attractiveness, and because laborers are not perfectly mobile.

5. Differences in wages received are to a great extent the result of differences in the amounts invested in human capital: the amounts expended to improve the education, the health, and the mobility of workers. Investment in human capital increases the productivity of a worker and, as a consequence, the wages and income he receives.

■ IMPORTANT TERMS

Wage	Inclusive unionism
Wage rate	Industrial union
Earnings	Bilateral monopoly
Money wage	Wage differential
Real wage	Noncompeting groups
Marginal labor cost	Equalizing differences
Monopsony	Immobility
Oligopsony	Investment in human capital
Exclusive unionism	
Craft union	

■ FILL-IN QUESTIONS

1. A wage rate is the price paid for labor per _____ and the earnings of labor are equal to _____ _____; money wages are an amount of money, while real wages are _____

2. American labor tends to be highly productive, among other reasons, because of the large amounts of _____ and _____ in the economy relative to the size of the labor force and because of the _____ _____ and _____ methods employed.

3. In a competitive market the supply curve for a particular type of labor tends to slope upward from left to right because _____ _____; the wage rate in the market will equal the rate at which the _____ and the _____

are equal. Demand here is the sum of the _____ of all firms hiring this type of labor.

4. Insofar as an individual firm hiring labor in a competitive market is concerned, the supply of labor is _____ elastic because _____

5. The individual employer who hires his labor in a competitive market hires that quantity of labor at which the _____ of labor is equal to the _____ or the _____

6. A monopsonist employing labor in a market which is competitive on the supply side will hire that amount of labor at which _____ _____ and _____ are equal; because _____ is always greater than _____ in such a market, he will pay a wage which is less than _____ and _____

7. When compared with a competitive labor market, a market dominated by a monopsonist results in _____ wage rates and_____ employment.

8. The basic objective of labor unions is to _____; they attempt to accomplish this goal either by _____, by _____, or by _____

9. Craft unions typically try to increase wages by _____ while industrial unions try to increase wages by _____; if they are successful, employment in the craft or industry affected is _____

10. In a bilateral monopoly labor market, the monopsonist will not pay a wage greater

than _____ ;
the union will ask for some wage greater than

the _____ ;
within these limits the wage rate will depend

on _____

11. The imposition of effective minimum wage rates, ignoring any shock effects, in:

a. competitive labor markets is to _____

the wage rate and to _____ employment.

b. monopsonistic labor markets is to _____

_____ the wage rate and to _____
employment.

c. the economy as a whole seems to have

been to _____ the wage rate and to _____
employment.

12. The effect of the unionization of workers

in the American economy has been to _____

_____ wage rates in the organized indus-

tries, to _____ them in the unorganized

industries, and to _____
the average level of wages of organized and unorganized workers.

13. Actual wage rates received by different workers tend to differ because workers are not

_____ ,

because jobs differ in _____ ,

and because labor markets are _____

_____

14. The total labor force is composed of a

number of _____
groups of workers. Within each of these groups some workers receive higher wages than others, and these wage differentials are called

_____

because _____

15. Workers performing identical jobs often receive different wages; these differences are

due to _____

of three basic types: _____ ,

_____ ,

and _____

16. Investment in human capital:

a. consists of expenditures for _____

_____ , _____ , and _____

b. increases the _____ and

_____ of workers.

c. explains a good part of the increases in

the level of _____ in the United States.

d. and accounts for much of the difference in wages and incomes among different indi-

viduals and among different _____

■ PROBLEMS AND PROJECTS

1. Suppose a single firm has for a particular type of labor the marginal revenue product schedule given in the following table.

Number of units of labor	MRP of labor
1	$15
2	14
3	13
4	12
5	11
6	10
7	9
8	8

a. There are 100 firms with the same marginal-revenue-product schedules for this particular type of labor. Compute the total or market demand for this labor by completing column 1 in the table at the top of page 228.
b. Using the supply schedule for labor given in columns 2 and 3:
(1) What will be the equilibrium wage rate?

$ _____
(2) What will be the total amount of labor

hired in the market? _____
c. The individual firm will:

(1) have a marginal labor cost of $_____

(2) employ _____ units of labor.

(1) Quantity of labor demanded	(2) Wage rate	(3) Quantity of labor supplied
_____	$15	850
_____	14	800
_____	13	750
_____	12	700
_____	11	650
_____	10	600
_____	9	550
_____	8	500

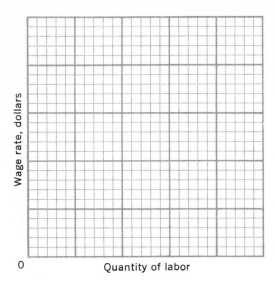

Wage rate, dollars

0   Quantity of labor

(3) pay a wage of $_____

d. On the graph at the right plot the market demand and supply curves for labor and indicate the equilibrium wage rate and the total quantity of labor employed.

e. On the graph at the top of page 229 plot the individual firm's demand curve for labor, the supply curve for labor, and the marginal-labor-cost curve which confronts the individual firm; indicate the quantity of labor the firm will hire and the wage it will pay.

f. The imposition of a $12 minimum wage rate would change the total amount of labor

hired in this market to _____

2. In the table below, assume a monopsonist has the marginal-revenue-product schedule for a particular type of labor given in columns 1 and 2 and that the supply schedule for labor is that given in columns 1 and 3.

a. Compute the firm's total labor costs at each level of employment and the marginal labor cost of each unit of labor, and enter these figures in columns 4 and 5.

b. The firm will:

(1) hire _____ units of labor.

(2) pay a wage of $_____
(3) have a marginal revenue product for

labor of $_____
for the last unit of labor employed.

c. Plot the marginal revenue product of labor, the supply curve for labor, and the mar-

(1) Number of labor units	(2) MRP of labor	(3) Wage rate	(4) Total labor cost	(5) Marginal labor cost
0		$ 2	$_____	
1	$36	4	_____	$_____
2	32	6	_____	_____
3	28	8	_____	_____
4	24	10	_____	_____
5	20	12	_____	_____
6	16	14	_____	_____
7	12	16	_____	_____
8	8	18	_____	_____

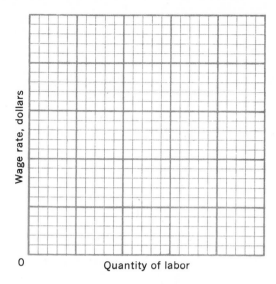

0   Quantity of labor

a. In the table below compute the supply schedule for labor which now confronts the monopsonist by completing column 2.

(1) Number of labor units	(2) Wage rate	(3) Total labor cost	(4) Marginal labor cost
1	$_____	$_____	$_____
2	_____	_____	_____
3	_____	_____	_____
4	_____	_____	_____
5	_____	_____	_____
6	_____	_____	_____
7	_____	_____	_____
8	_____	_____	_____

ginal-labor-cost curve on the graph below; indicate the quantity of labor the firm will employ and the wage it will pay.

b. Compute the total labor cost and the marginal labor cost at each level of employment, and enter these figures in columns 3 and 4.

c. The firm will:

(1) hire _____ units of labor.

(2) pay a wage of $_____

(3) pay total wages of $_____

d. As a result of unionization the wage rate

has _____,

the level of employment has _____,

and the earnings of labor have _____

e. On the graph below plot the firm's mar-

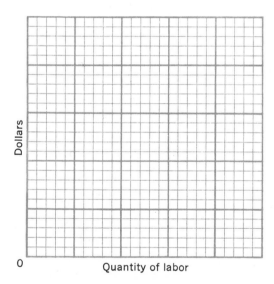

0   Quantity of labor

d. If this firm hired labor in a competitive

labor market, it would hire at least _____

units and pay a wage of at least $_____

3. Assume that the employees of the monopsonist in problem 2 organize a union. The union demands a wage rate of $16 for its members, and the monopsonist decides to pay this wage because a strike would be too costly for him.

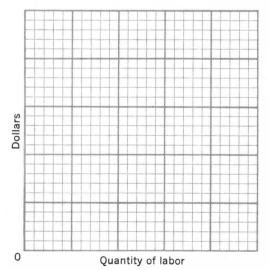

0   Quantity of labor

ginal revenue product of labor schedule, the labor supply schedule, and the marginal-labor-cost schedule. Indicate also the wage rate the firm will pay and the number of workers it will hire.

■ SELF-TEST

Circle the T if the statement is true, the F if it is false.

1. The general level of real wages is higher in the United States than in foreign countries because the supply of labor is great relative to the demand for it.   T (F)

2. If an individual firm employs labor in a competitive market, it finds that its marginal labor cost is equal to the wage rate in that market.   (T) F

3. Both monopsonists and firms hiring labor in competitive markets hire labor up to the point where the marginal revenue product of labor and marginal labor cost are equal. (T) F

4. A monopsonist is also a monopolist in the product market.   T (F)

5. Restricting the supply of labor is a means of increasing wage rates more commonly used by craft unions than by industrial unions.
                                          (T) F

6. The imposition of an above-equilibrium wage rate will cause employment to fall off more when the demand for labor is inelastic than it will when the demand is elastic. T (F)

7. If a labor market is competitive, the imposition of an effective minimum wage will increase the wage rate paid and decrease employment in that market.   (T) F

8. Actual wage rates received in different labor markets tends to differ because the demands for particular types of labor relative to their supply differ.   (T) F

9. "Ben Robbins is a skilled artisan of a particular type, is unable to obtain membership in the union representing that group of artisans, and is, therefore, unable to practice his trade." This is an example of labor immobility.   (T) F

10. Given a firm's demand for labor the lower the wage it must pay the more workers it will hire.   (T) F

Underscore the letter that corresponds to the best answer.

1. Real wages would decline if the: (a) prices of goods and services rose more rapidly than money wage rates; (b) prices of goods and services rose less rapidly than money wage rates; (c) prices of goods and services and wage rates both rose; (d) prices of goods and services and wage rates both fell.

2. The individual firm which hires labor under competitive conditions faces a supply curve for labor which: (a) is perfectly inelastic; (b) is of unitary elasticity; (c) is perfectly elastic; (d) slopes upward from left to right.

3. A monopsonist pays a wage rate which is: (a) greater than the marginal revenue product of labor; (b) equal to the marginal revenue product of labor; (c) equal to the firm's marginal labor cost; (d) less than the marginal revenue product of labor.

4. Compared with a competitive labor market, a monopsonistic market will result in: (a) higher wage rates and a higher level of employment; (b) higher wage rates and a lower level of employment; (c) lower wage rates and a higher level of employment; (d) lower wage rates and a lower level of employment.

5. Higher wage rates and a higher level of employment are the usual consequences of: (a) inclusive unionism; (b) exclusive unionism; (c) an above-equilibrium wage rate; (d) an increase in the productivity of labor.

6. Which of the following has been a consequence of unionization? (a) higher wage rates for unionized workers; (b) greater employment of unionized workers; (c) greater employment of the workers in the labor force; (d) a higher level of real wages in the economy.

7. Industrial unions typically attempt to increase wage rates by: (a) imposing an above-equilibrium wage rate upon employers; (b) increasing the demand for labor; (c) decreasing the supply of labor; (d) forming a bilateral monopoly.

8. The fact that a star baseball player receives a wage of $125,000 a year can *best* be explained in terms of: (a) noncompeting labor groups; (b) equalizing differences; (c) labor immobility; (d) imperfections in the labor market.

9. The fact that unskilled construction workers received higher wages than gas station attendants is *best* explained in terms of: (a) noncompeting labor groups; (b) equalizing differences; (c) labor immobility; (d) imperfections in the labor market.

10. Which of the following is *not* true? (a) investment in human capital increases the productivity of workers; (b) expenditures for health, education, and mobility are investments in human capital; (c) whether to invest in real capital is a decision similar to the decision of whether to invest in human capital; (d) differences in the amounts invested in human capital explain the equalizing differences in wage rates.

■ DISCUSSION QUESTIONS

1. Why is the general level of real wages higher in the United States than in foreign nations? Why has the level of real wages continued to increase even though the supply of labor has continually increased?

2. Explain why the productivity of the American labor force is so high. In what way has the labor force itself contributed to this high productivity?

3. In the competitive model what determines the market demand for labor and the wage rate? What kind of supply situation do all firms as a group confront? Why? Under what economic conditions would a group of firms in a competitive market not confront such a supply schedule? What kind of supply situation does the individual firm confront? Why?

4. In the monopsony model what determines the market demand for labor and the wage rate? What kind of supply situation does the monopsonist face? Why? How does the wage rate paid and the level of employment compare with what would result if the market were competitive?

5. In what sense is a worker who is hired by a monopsonist "exploited" and one who is employed in a competitive labor market "justly" rewarded for his labor? Why do monopsonists wish to restrict employment?

6. When supply is less than perfectly elastic, marginal labor cost is greater than the wage rate. Why?

7. What basic methods do labor unions employ to try to increase the wages received by their members? If these methods are successful in raising wages, what effect do they have upon employment?

8. When labor unions attempt to restrict the supply of labor to increase wage rates, what devices do they employ to do this for the economy as a whole and what means do they use to restrict the supply of a given type of worker?

9. How do industrial unions attempt to increase wage rates, and what effect does this method of increasing wages have upon employment in the industry affected?

10. What is bilateral monopoly? What determines wage rates in a labor market of this type?

11. What is the effect of minimum wage laws upon wage rates and employment in (a) competitive labor markets; (b) monopsony labor markets; (c) the economy as a whole?

12. How has the unionization of workers affected the wage rates and the employment of (a) unionized workers; (b) nonunionized workers; (c) workers in general?

13. Why are the wage rates received by workers in different occupations, by workers in the same occupations, and by workers in different localities different?

14. Explain what is meant by investment in human capital and why the decision to invest in human capital is like the decision to invest in real capital. What is the effect of investment in human capital upon the productivity, the wage rates, and the income of workers?

15. Using the concept of investment in human capital, explain (a) the differences in wage rates among the races and geographic regions and the differences between the sexes; and (b) the historic rise in real wages in the American economy.

THE PRICING AND EMPLOYMENT OF RESOURCES: RENT, INTEREST, AND PROFITS

Chapter 33 concludes the study of the prices of resources by examining rent, interest, and profits. Compared with the study of wage rates in Chapter 32, each of the three major sections in Chapter 33 is considerably briefer and a good deal simpler. The student might do well to treat this chapter as if it were actually three very short chapters.

There is nothing especially difficult about Chapter 33. By now the student should understand that the marginal revenue product of a resource determines the demand for that resource and that this understanding can be applied to the demand for land and capital. It will be on the supply side of the land and capital markets that the student will encounter whatever difficulties there are. The supply of land is unique because it is perfectly *inelastic:* changes in rent do not change the quantity of land which will be supplied. Demand, given the quantity of land available, is thus the sole determinant of rent. Of course land varies in productivity and can be used for different purposes, but these are merely the factors which explain why the rent on all land is not the same.

Capital, as the economist defines it, means capital equipment. Is the rate of interest, then, the price paid for the use of capital equipment? No, not quite. Capital is not one kind of equipment; it is many different kinds. In order to be able to talk about the price paid for the use of capital equipment there must be a common denominator, a simple way

of adding up different kinds of capital equipment. The common denominator is money. Interest (or the rate of interest) is the price paid for the use of money. *Businessmen* hire money in order to purchase capital equipment, but households and governments also hire money, and for different purposes. The total demand for money is derived, therefore, not only from the *expected* marginal revenue product of additional capital equipment but also from the demands of households and governments for money.

On the supply side of the money (or loanable funds) market it is sufficient to determine who has money to loan, to determine how much money they *could* loan, and to determine how much they *will* loan. Here it is particularly important to note that savers are the principal suppliers of loanable funds, that they have motives for *not* loaning their money, and that the supply of loanable funds depends upon the strength of these motives. Interest is the reward which must be paid to overcome their desire not to lend their money.

When it comes to profits, supply and demand analysis fails the economist. Profits are not merely a wage for a particular type of labor; rather they are rewards for taking risks and the gains of the monopolist. Such things as "the quantity of risk taken" or "the quantity of effort required to establish a monopoly" simply can't be measured; consequently it is impossible to talk about the demand for or the supply of them.

Nevertheless, profits are important in the economy. They are largely rewards for doing things that have to be done if the economy is to allocate resources efficiently and to progress and develop; they are the lure or the bait which makes men willing to take the risks that result in efficiency and progress.

■ CHAPTER OUTLINE

1. Economic rent is the price paid for the use of land or natural resources whose supply is perfectly inelastic.

  a. Demand is the active determinant of economic rent because changes in the level of economic rent do not change the quantity of land supplied; economic rent is, therefore, a payment which in the aggregate need not be paid to ensure that the land will be available.

  b. Some people have argued that land rents are unearned incomes and that either land should be nationalized or rents should be taxed away. The single tax advocated by Henry George would have no effect upon resource allocation. While critics have pointed out the disadvantages of such a tax, there is a renewed interest in taxing land values to improve the equity and efficiency of local tax systems.

  c. Economic rents on different types of land vary because land differs in its productivity and because it has alternative uses; hence rent is a cost to a firm because it must compete to lure superior land away from alternative employments.

2. Interest is the price paid for the use of money (loanable funds), and the rate of interest is determined by the demand for and the supply of loanable funds.

  a. Businesses, households, and governments are the demanders, while the potential suppliers of loanable funds are households, businesses, and commercial banks; the actual supply of loanable funds may be less than the potential supply because households and businesses have motives for liquidity.

  b. The rate of interest tends to be an administered price because government is both a large demander and a large supplier (through the banking system) of loanable funds relative to the size of the market.

  c. The interest rate performs two important functions: It determines the total amount of investment in the economy, and it rations the investment among different firms and industries.

3. Economic profit is what remains for the firm after all its explicit and implicit opportunity costs have been paid.

  a. Profit is a payment for entrepreneurial ability, which involves combining and directing the use of resources in an uncertain and innovating world.

  b. Profits are rewards for assuming the risks in an economy in which the future is uncertain and subject to change and for assuming the risks and the uncertainties inherent in innovation. They are also surpluses which business firms obtain from the exploitation of monopoly power.

  c. The expectation of profits motivates business firms to innovate, and profits (and losses) guide business firms to produce products and to use resources in the way desired by society.

■ IMPORTANT TERMS

Economic rent	**Precautionary motive**
Incentive function	**Speculative motive**
Single-tax movement	**Economic (pure) profit**
Loanable funds	
The (or pure) rate of interest	**Static economy**
	Insurable risk
Liquidity preference	**Uninsurable risk**
Transactions motive	

■ FILL-IN QUESTIONS

1. Rent is the price paid for the use of _____

_____

and _____

and their total supply is _____

2. _____

is the active determinant of rent, while _____

_____

is passive. Because rent does not perform an

_____

function, economists consider it to be a _____

_____,

a payment that need not be made to ensure that the land will be made available to the economy.

3. Socialists argue that land rents are _____

_____

incomes and that land should be _____

_____

so that these incomes can be used for the good of society as a whole. Proponents of ___

_____

argue that economic rent could be completely taxed away without affecting the amount of land available for productive purposes.

4. Rents on different pieces of land are not

the same because _____

_____.

And while rent from the viewpoint of the economy as a whole is a surplus, rent is a

cost to _____
users of land which must be paid because

land has _____

5. Interest is the price paid for the use of

_____

or _____
which are not economic resources but which

business firms are willing to hire because ___

_____

6. Interest rates on different loans tend to

differ because of differences in _____,

_____,

and _____,

and because of _____

7. The greatest percentage of loanable funds

is borrowed by _____
and the amount they are willing to borrow

depends basically upon _____

8. The relationship between the quantity of loanable funds demanded and the rate of in-

terest is a _____

one, but the demand for loanable funds tends

to be _____

9. The potential sources of loanable funds

are the _____

and _____

saving of _____

and _____

and the money _____

by _____

and _____

10. Savers have three principal motives for holding money rather than securities; these

are the _____,

_____,

and _____
motives.

11. The rate of interest tends to be an _____

_____
price, yet it performs two important functions for the economy: The rate of interest helps to

determine how much _____ will occur in

the economy and then _____

_____ it among various firms and industries in the economy.

12. Economic profits are a payment for the

resource called _____,

which involves combining _____

and making _____

with regard to their use and _____

in an _____
environment.

13. When the future is _____,
businessmen necessarily assume risks, some

of which are _____

and some of which are _____.
The risks which businessmen cannot avoid

arise either because the _____

_____

is changing or because the firm itself deliberately engages in _____

14. Profits are important in the American economy because the expectation of profits stimulates firms to innovate, and the more innovation there is, the higher will be the levels

of _____,

_____,

and _____

in the economy.

15. Profits and losses promote the efficient

_____

of resources in the economy unless the profits

are _____ profits.

■ PROBLEMS AND PROJECTS

1. Assume that the quantity of a certain type of land available is 300,000 acres and the demand for this land is that given in the table below.

Pure land rent, per acre	Land demanded, acres
$350	100,000
300	200,000
250	300,000
200	400,000
150	500,000
100	600,000
50	700,000

a. The pure rent on this land will be $_____
b. The total quantity of land rented will be

_____ acres.
c. On the graph to the right plot the supply and demand curve for this land and indicate the pure rent for land and the quantity of land rented.
d. If landowners were taxed at a rate of $250 per acre for their land, the pure rent on

this land after taxes would be $_____

and the number of acres rented would be ___

2. What effect—increase (+), decrease (−), or indeterminate (?)—will each of the follow-

0   Number of acres

ing have upon the rate of interest in the economy?
a. Increases in the amounts of money commercial banks are willing to lend at any given

rate of interest. _____
b. An increase in the economy's NNP. _____
c. An increase in the amount of all business done on a "charge it until the first of the

month" basis. _____
d. The belief that interest rates will decline

in the near future. _____
e. A deficit in the budget of the Federal

government. _____
f. An increase in the profits which business firms expect to realize from the purchase of

new capital goods. _____
g. A technological breakthrough which makes much of the capital equipment in the economy

obsolete. _____
h. A belief on the part of households *only* that a depression is over and prosperity is

"just around the corner." _____

■ SELF-TEST

Circle the T if the statement is true, the F if it is false.

1. Rent is the price paid for the use of land and other property resources. **T** (F)

2. Rent is a surplus because it does not perform an incentive function.   (T) F

3. The demand for loanable funds is inelastic.   (T) F

4. The rate of interest tends to be an administered price because government is both a heavy demander of and an important supplier of loanable funds.   (T) F

5. The potential supply of loanable funds is usually greater than the actual supply because savers often prefer to have demand deposits or cash rather than securities which pay interest.   (T) F

6. If the economists' definition of profits were used, total profits in the economy would be greater than they would be if the businessman's definition were used.   T (F)

7. The expectation of profits is the basic motive for innovation, while actual profits and losses aid in the efficient allocation of resources.   (T) F

Underscore the letter that corresponds to the best answer.

1. The supply of land is: (a) perfectly inelastic; (b) of unitary elasticity; (c) perfectly elastic; (d) elastic but not perfectly elastic.

2. Which of the following is *not* characteristic of the tax proposed by Henry George? (a) it would be equal to 100 percent of all land rent; (b) it would be the only tax levied by government; (c) it would not affect the supply of land; (d) it would reduce rents paid by the amount of the tax.

3. The smaller the *rate* of interest on a loan: (a) the greater the risk involved; (b) the shorter the length of the loan; (c) the smaller the amount of the loan; (d) the greater the imperfections in the money market.

4. Given the demand for loanable funds, the higher will be the rate of interest: (a) the more new money commercial banks are creating; (b) the less the economy needs money for transaction purposes; (c) the greater the number of savers who expect the rate of interest to rise in the future; (d) the fewer the number of savers who find it necessary to take precautions against unfavorable financial contingencies in the future.

5. Changes in the rate of interest do *not:* (a) affect the total amount of investment in the economy; (b) affect the amount of investment occurring in particular industries; (c) guarantee that the demand for and the supply of loanable funds will be equal; (d) guarantee that there will be full employment in the economy.

6. Which of the following would *not* be a function of the entrepreneur? (a) the introduction of a new product on the market; (b) the making of decisions in a static economy; (c) the incurring of unavoidable risks; (d) the combination and direction of resources in an uncertain environment.

7. The monopolist who earns an economic profit is able to do so because: (a) he is an innovator; (b) all his risks are insurable; (c) uncertainty has been reduced to the minimum; (d) most of his decisions are nonroutine.

■ DISCUSSION QUESTIONS

1. Explain what determines the economic rent paid for the use of land. What is unique about the supply of land?

2. Why is land rent a "surplus"? What economic difficulties would be encountered if the government adopted Henry George's single-tax proposal as a means of confiscating this surplus? What arguments are used to support the renewed interest in the heavy taxation of land values?

3. Even though land rent is an economic surplus it is also an economic cost for the individual user of land. Why and how can it be both an economic surplus and an economic cost?

4. What is interest? What determines the rate of interest in the economy?

5. Why are there actually many different rates in the economy at any given time?

6. Who are the demanders of loanable funds? Why do they wish to borrow? Who are the potential suppliers, and what motives do potential suppliers have for remaining liquid (that is, for retaining possession of their money rather than exchanging it for interest-bearing securities)?

7. Upon what does the amount of loanable funds which business firms wish to borrow primarily depend?

8. What two important functions does the rate of interest perform in the economy? How well does it perform these functions?

9. What are economic profits? For what resource are they a payment, and what tasks does this resource perform?

10. Why would there be no economic profits in a purely competitive static economy?

11. "The risks which an entrepreneur assumes arise because of uncertainties which are external to the firm and because of uncertainties which are developed by the initiative of the firm itself." Explain.

12. What two important functions do profits or the expectation of profits perform in the economy? How does monopoly impede the effective performance of these functions?

13. Monopoly results in profits and reduces uncertainty. Is it possible that monopolists may undertake more innovation as a result? Why?

GENERAL
EQUILIBRIUM:
THE PRICE SYSTEM
AND ITS OPERATION

Chapter 34 provides a conclusion to the previous eleven chapters, tying together many of the things the student has already learned about microeconomics. By this time he has read a large amount of material concerning the operation of supply and demand in product and resource markets under different market conditions. He may have lost sight of the fact—emphasized in Chapter 5—that the American economy is a *system* of markets and prices. This means that *all* prices and *all* markets are linked together.

The chief purpose of Chapter 34 is to help the student understand why and how these markets are linked together, connected, and interrelated. The theory which explains the relationships between different markets and different prices is called *general* equilibrium analysis. (By way of contrast, the theory which explains a single product or resource market and the price of the one good or service bought and sold in that market is called *partial* equilibrium analysis.) An understanding of general equilibrium is necessary in order to understand how the price system as a whole operates to allocate its scarce resources.

The author employs three approaches to enable the student to grasp the essentials and the importance of general equilibrium analysis. He first explains in words the effects of an increase in the demand for automobiles. Then, using graphs and curves, he explains in more detail the effects of an increase in the demand for a hypothetical product X accom-

panied by a decrease in the demand for product Y. Both of these explanations include not only the short- and long-run effects upon the products involved but also the effects upon the markets in which the producers employ resources, upon the markets for complementary and substitute products, upon the markets in which the resources used to produce these other products are employed, and upon the distribution of income in the economy. Finally, to help the student understand the interrelationships between the different sectors of the economy, the author employs an input-output table.

Having examined these market and price interrelationships, the student next should note this. Given the distribution of income among consumers, and subject to several important exceptions, a price system in which all markets are purely competitive will bring about an ideal allocation of the economy's resources. It will maximize the satisfaction of consumer wants and thereby maximize economic welfare in the economy. The American economy, of course, is *not* made up of purely competitive markets. And because of these imperfectly competitive markets, the allocation of resources is actually less than ideal and economic welfare is somewhat less than a maximum.

In addition—and these are important exceptions—even a purely competitive price system does not allocate resources to allow for the spillover costs and the spillover benefits of the products it produces; and it does not produce social goods in sufficient quantities. Hence government seems to be needed (remember the fourth economic function of government in Chapter 6) to adjust output for spillover costs and benefits and to provide society with social goods.

Also, a price system that allocates resources ideally does not necessarily distribute its total output (or income) in accordance with our ethical standards. Economists don't and probably never will know which of the many possible distributions of income is ideal. But according to society's notions of what is right and wrong (just and unjust), it is wrong to have highly unequal distributions of incomes, or incomes below a certain minimum level. Hence the third economic function of government: the redistribution of income and wealth.

Chapter 34 ends by reemphasizing the importance of general equilibrium analysis. Interrelations between markets and prices do exist, and they can be extremely important in tracing through the economy the *total effect* of an economic policy or the *full consequences* of changes in consumers' tastes, the availability of resources, and technology. At the conclusion of this chapter the student should be ready to examine several of the trouble spots that concern the operation of the price system and the way in which we allocate our scarce resources. These trouble spots are examined in the next seven chapters which make up Part 6 of the text.

■ CHAPTER OUTLINE

1. Partial equilibrium analysis is the study of equilibrium prices and quantities in the specific product and resource markets which form the price-market system. General equilibrium analysis is the study of the interrelations between these markets.

2. Any change in tastes, in the supply of resources, or in technology will not only have an immediate effect upon equilibrium price and quantity in a specific market, but will also have secondary effects in other markets and upon other equilibrium prices and quantities.

3. To understand the effects of an increase in consumer demand for product X accompanied by a decrease in consumer demand for

product Y, imagine that the industry producing X uses only type A labor and that the industry producing Y uses only type B labor.

a. Assume also that the demand for each product is negative because of diminishing marginal utility and the supply is positive because of increasing marginal cost; and assume that the demand for each type of labor is negative because of diminishing marginal product and the supply is positive because of the work-leisure preferences of workers.

b. Beginning with all markets in long-run equilibrium, the short-run effects are an increased (decreased) output and price and economic profits (losses) in industry X (Y), an increased (decreased) derived demand for type A (type B) labor, and increased (decreased) wage rates and employment for type A (type B) labor.

c. The long-run adjustments are the entry (exit) of firms in industry X (Y); an increase (decrease) in the supply of X (Y); a higher (lower) price than existed initially in industry X (Y), assuming increasing-cost industries; an increase (decrease) in the supply of A (B); and higher (lower) wage rates for A (B) than initially existed.

d. In addition to these adjustments there will also be:

(1) An increase (decrease) in the demand for and the prices and outputs of products which are substitutes (complements) for X or complements (substitutes) for Y; and an increased (decreased) demand for the resources used to produce those products whose output increases.

(2) An increase (decrease) in the demand for the other resources used along with A (B).

(3) A redistribution of income from workers and entrepreneurs in Y to those in X.

4. Given the distribution of consumer income, purely competitive product and resource markets result in an allocation of an economy's resources and the output of those goods and services which maximize the satisfaction of wants.

5. To the extent that product and resource markets in the real world are imperfectly competitive, the satisfaction of wants will be less than a maximum, and adjustments to changes will be less complete and slower. But this may be offset by more rapid technological progress and greater product variety.

6. For two reasons, even an economy in which all markets are perfectly competitive may not allocate resources efficiently.

a. The price system does not take spillover costs and spillover benefits into account and does not automatically produce social goods.

b. The price system may not distribute the economy's income ideally or optimally.

7. The input-output table indicates the specific relationships that exist between the outputs of the various sectors of the economy.

a. Any change in the output of a particular sector alters the quantities of inputs it employs; and these inputs are the outputs of other sectors.

b. A change in a particular sector's output will, therefore, initiate a series of changes in output in many other sectors of the economy.

8. General equilibrium analysis is important because it provides a wider understanding of the effects of any economic change or policy upon the economy.

■ IMPORTANT TERMS

Price system

Partial equilibrium analysis

General equilibrium analysis

Input-output analysis

Input-output table

■ FILL-IN QUESTIONS

1. Partial equilibrium analysis is concerned with prices and outputs in _____ markets in the economy, and general equilibrium analysis is concerned with the _____

_____

between markets and prices.

2. A change in the demand for product Z will affect not only the equilibrium price and quantity of product Z but may also affect the equilibrium price and quantity of:

a. _____

b. _____

c. _____

d. _____

3. General equilibrium exists in an economy where there is _____

in all the _____ and _____ markets in the economy.

4. Economic changes or disturbances which may result not only in "big splashes" but also in little waves and ripples are of three basic types: changes in _____,

changes in _____,

and changes in _____

5. When studying the markets for products and for resources, we assume that the demand curves slope _____ and the supply curves slope _____

a. The slope of the demand curve for:

(1) Products is due to _____

(2) Resources is due to _____

b. The slope of the supply curve for:

(1) Products is due to _____

(2) Resources is due to _____

6. Assume the demand for consumer good P increases while the demand for consumer good Q decreases. In the short run:

a. The price and output of P will _____

_____ and the price and output of

Q will _____

b. Profits in industry _____ will increase and profits in industry _____ will decrease.

c. If the only resource used in industry P is type C labor and the only resource used in industry Q is type D labor, the demand for C

will _____ and the demand for

D will _____

d. Wage rates and the quantity of labor employed in the market for _____ will

increase while those in the market for _____ will decrease.

7. Using the same assumptions made in 6 above, if the two industries are increasing-cost industries, the increase in the demand for P along with the decrease in the demand for Q will in the long run:

a. Cause firms to enter industry _____ and to leave industry _____

b. _____ the supply of P and _____ the supply of Q.

c. _____ the price of P and _____ the price of Q from what they were originally.

d. Increase the supply of type _____ labor and decrease the supply of type _____ labor.

e. _____ the employment of type C labor and _____ the employment of type D labor.

8. Still using the assumptions made in 6 and 7 above, the increase in the demand for P and the decrease in the demand for Q will:

a. Increase the demand for products which are (substitutes, complements) _____ for P and decrease the demand for _____

b. _____ the demand for those resources used along with type C labor and _____ the demand for those resources used along with type D labor.

c. Redistribute income from workers and entrepreneurs in industry _____ to those in industry _____

9. Given the distribution of income, purely competitive product and resource markets bring about the production of a combination of goods and services which _____ of consumers because:

a. The _____ of each good or service is equal to its _____

b. The average cost of each product is a _____

c. The utility of the last dollar spent by a consumer on each good or service is _____

for all goods and services.

10. Product and resource markets in the real world are actually _____ competitive. As a result the allocation of resources is _____ and adjustments to changes in tastes, technology, and the availability of resources are _____ _____ and _____

11. Two potential offsets to imperfectly competitive markets are more rapid _____ _____ and greater _____

12. The ability of a purely competitive price system to allocate resources efficiently is open to question for two reasons.

a. It fails to take into account the _____ _____ and the _____ of the goods and services produced and it neglects or ignores the production of _____

b. It does not necessarily result in an ideal _____ of _____

13. The _____ sectors of the economy are listed down the left side of an input-output table and the _____ sectors across the top of the table. The _____ _____ of any sector in the table is a(n) _____ of other sectors of the economy.

14. Assuming constant returns to scale, if industry X sells 30 percent of its product to industry Y and if industry Y decides to increase its production by 25 percent, then industry X will have to increase its production by _____ percent.

15. An understanding of general equilibrium analysis is important if one is to evaluate the overall _____, to understand specific _____, and to formulate _____

■ PROBLEMS AND PROJECTS

1. Listed below are three types of economic change which can occur in the economy. In the spaces allotted following each change, indicate what you think the effect will be—increase (+), decrease (−), no change (0), or an indeterminate change (?)—on demand or supply, price, and output or employment in the markets affected by the initial change.

No answers to this problem will be found in the "Answers" section because the answer to each question depends upon such things as whether the short run or the long run is considered, whether the industry is an increasing- or constant-cost industry, and whether the student considers only the "immediate-secondary effect" or considers also the "secondary-secondary effect" of the initial change. The purpose of this exercise is simply to get the student to *attempt* to trace through the economy the full effect of an initial change and to see the extent and complexity of price-market interrelations.

a. Decrease in the demand for consumer good X but no *initial* change in the demand for other consumer goods.

(1) Effect on the price of and the quantity of X produced. _____

(2) Effect on the demand for, the price of, and the output of goods which are substitutes for good X. _____

(3) Effect on the demand for, the price of, and the output of goods which are complements for good X. _____

(4) Effect on the demand for, the price of, and the employment of resources used in the production of good X. _____

(5) Effect on the supply of, the price of, and the output of goods which employ the same resources used in the production of good X. _____

(6) Effect on the demand for, the price of, and the employment of resources which are substitutes for the resources used to produce X. _____

b. Increase in the supply of resource Y.

(1) Effect on the price of and the employment of resource Y. _____

(2) Effect on the supply of, the price of, and the output of goods which employ resource Y in the production process. _____

(3) Effect on the demand for, the price of, and the employment of resources which are complementary to resource Y. _____

(4) Effect on the demand for, the price of, and the output of those goods which are substitutes for the goods produced with resource Y. _____

(5) Effect on the demand for, the price of, and the output of those goods which are complements for the goods produced with resource Y. _____

(6) Effect on the demand for, the price of, and the employment of resources which are substitutes for resource Y. _____

c. Improvement in the technology of producing good Z.

(1) Effect on the supply of, the price of, and the output of good Z. _____

(2) Effect on the demand for, the price of, and the output of goods which are substitutes for good Z. _____

(3) Effect on the demand for, the price of, and the output of goods which are complements for good Z. _____

(4) Effect on the demand for, the price of, and the employment of resources used to produce good Z. _____

(5) Effect on the supply of, the price of, and the output of those goods which also employ the resources used to produce good Z. _____

2. Below is an incomplete input-output table for an economy with five sectors. All the figures in the table are physical units rather than dollars.

Producing sectors	Using sectors					Total outputs
	A	B	C	D	E	
A	100	150	75	—	25	425
B	30	20	70	80	200	—
C	10	60	—	20	20	110
D	205	35	40	10	—	300
E	—	140	60	35	80	390

a. Complete the table by computing (by addition or subtraction) the missing input-output figures.

b. Assume that sector B wishes to expand its output by 100 units. By what percentage does sector B wish to expand its output?

_____%

c. Assuming constant returns to scale in all sectors of the economy, by how many *units* will each of the following sectors of the economy have to expand their outputs if sector B is to expand its output by 100 units?

(1) Sector A: _____

(2) Sector C: _____

(3) Sector D: _____

(4) Sector E: _____

d. By what *percentage* will each of these sectors have to expand their outputs?

(1) Sector A: _____%

(2) Sector C: _____%

(3) Sector D: _____%

(4) Sector E: _____%

e. What further adjustments in the outputs of the various sectors of the economy will follow those given in (c) and (d) above?

_____

_____

■ SELF-TEST

Circle the T if the statement is true, the F if it is false.

1. General equilibrium analysis is the same thing as macroeconomics.   **T (F)**

2. The study of the effect of an increase in the demand for product C, other things remaining equal, upon the price and the output of product C is an example of partial equilibrium analysis.   **(T) F**

3. The supply curve for a product slopes upward in the short run because of the diminishing marginal productivity of variable resources.   **(T) F**

Use the following data for the three questions below and for multiple choice questions

6 and 7. Initially there is general equilibrium, and then the demand for consumer good W increases and the demand for consumer good Z decreases. Both industries are increasing-cost industries in the long run. Industry W employs only type G labor, and Z employs only type H labor.

4. In the short run, price, output, and profits will increase in industry Z and decrease in industry W.   **T (F)**

5. In the long run, the quantity of type G labor employed will increase and the quantity of type H labor employed will decrease.   **(T) F**

6. Income will be redistributed from workers and entrepreneurs in industry Z to those in industry W.   **(T) F**

7. Given the distribution of income in the economy, purely competitive product and resource markets lead to the production of a collection of products which maximizes the satisfaction of consumer wants.   **(T) F**

8. In the real world, product and resource markets tend to be purely competitive. **T (F)**

9. A purely competitive price system results in an ideal or optimal distribution of income.   **T (F)**

10. General equilibrium analysis gives a broader picture of the economic consequences of economic changes and economic policies than partial equilibrium analysis even though some of these consequences turn out to be insignificant.   **(T) F**

Underscore the letter that corresponds to the best answer.

1. If the demand for consumer good A increased, which one of the following would *not* be a possible consequence? (a) increase in the price of A; (b) increase in the demand for resources used to produce A; (c) increase in the supply of those goods which are substitutes for A; (d) increase in the prices of other goods which employ the same resources used to produce A.

2. If the supply of resource B increased, which one of the following would *not* be a possible consequence? (a) decrease in the price of B; (b) decrease in the demand for those goods produced from B; (c) decrease in the demand for those resources which are substitutes for resource B; (d) decrease in the demand for those goods which are substitutes for the goods produced with resource B.

3. The price system produces approximately what percentage of the output and employs about what percentage of the resources of the American economy? (a) 70%; (b) 80%; (c) 90%; (d) 100%.

4. The downward slope of the demand curve for a product is the result of: (a) diminishing marginal utility; (b) diminishing marginal productivity; (c) increasing marginal cost; (d) the work-leisure preferences of workers.

5. The upward slope of the supply curve of labor is the result of: (a) diminishing marginal utility; (b) diminishing marginal productivity; (c) increasing marginal cost; (d) the work-leisure preferences of workers.

Use the data preceding True-False question 4 to answer the following two questions.

6. When the new long-run general equilibrium is reached: (a) the wage rate for type G labor will be higher than it was originally; (b) the wage rate for type G labor will be lower than it was originally; (c) wage rates in both labor markets will be the same as they were originally; (d) it is impossible to tell what will have happened to wage rates.

7. As a result of the changes in the demands for W and Z: (a) the demand for products which are substitutes for Z will have increased; (b) the demand for products which are complements for W will have decreased; (c) the demand for products which are substitutes for Z will have decreased; (d) the demand for products which are complements for Z will have decreased.

8. Which of the following is not the result of purely competitive product and resource markets? (a) the distribution of income among consumers maximizes the satisfaction of wants in the economy; (b) the average cost of producing each product is a minimum; (c) the price of each product is equal to its marginal cost; (d) the marginal utility of every product divided by its price is the same for all products purchased by an individual consumer.

9. All but one of the following is the result of imperfectly competitive product and re-

source markets. Which one? (a) resources are allocated less efficiently than under purely competitive conditions; (b) the price system is less responsive to changes in tastes, technology, and the availability of resources than a purely competitive price system; (c) there is a smaller variety of products than in a purely competitive system; (d) monopoly drives prices above and monopsony drives them below their competitive levels.

10. Which of the following is a disadvantage of a purely competitive price system? (a) underallocates resources to those products whose production entails a spillover cost; (b) overallocates resources to those products whose consumption entails spillover benefits; (c) underallocates resources to the production of social goods and services; (d) fails to distribute income optimally.

Use the following input-output table to answer questions 11 and 12 below.

Producing sectors	Using sectors					Total outputs
	A	B	C	D	E	
A	20	15	35	25	60	155
B	45	55	90	10	20	220
C	40	15	80	10	5	150
D	65	10	25	20	40	160
E	100	75	80	45	10	310

11. If sector C were to decrease its output by 50 units, and assuming constant returns to scale in all sectors, the initial impact on sector B would be a decrease in its output of: (a) 5 units; (b) 13⅓ units; (c) 26⅔ units; (d) 30 units.

12. If sector C is to increase its output by 20%, and assuming constant returns to scale, sector E's output will have to increase initially by: (a) 5.2%; (b) 19.4%; (c) 20%; (d) 37.5%.

■ DISCUSSION QUESTIONS

1. Explain the difference between partial equilibrium and general equilibrium analysis.

2. Why is general equilibrium analysis so important?

3. Suppose the demand for television sets decreases at the same time that the demand for airline travel increases. What would be (a) the short-run effects of these changes in the markets for television sets and airline travel and in the markets for television-set production workers and airline workers; (b) the long-run effects in these markets; (c) the long-run effects in the markets for complementary and substitute products and in the markets for other resources; and (d) the effect upon the distribution of income?

4. Imagine that the availability of iron ore used to produce steel increased or the technology of steel making improved. What would be the short- and long-run effects upon (a) the steel industry; (b) steelworkers; (c) the automobile industry; (d) the aluminum industry; (e) the machine tool industry; and (f) the coal industry?

5. Why is a purely competitive price system "conducive to an efficient allocation of resources"?

6. When a price system is less than purely competitive, what are the economic consequences?

7. What costs, benefits, and goods does even a purely competitive price system neglect or ignore? What are the economic results of this neglect?

8. What is meant by an ideal or optimal distribution of income? Why can't economists determine what the optimal distribution of income is?

9. Explain precisely what an input-output table is and the kind of information it contains.

10. In addition to indicating the interrelationships between the various sectors of the economy, an input-output table can be used for what other purposes?

THE MONOPOLY PROBLEM: THE SOCIAL CONTROL OF INDUSTRY

This is the first of seven chapters which deal with specific trouble spots in the American economy and is one of the two chapters which concern the monopoly problem. Chapter 35 examines the monopoly problem in output markets, and Chapter 39 examines the monopoly problem in the labor market. It should be noted that the term "monopoly" as used here does *not* mean pure or absolute monopoly; it means, instead, control of a large percentage of total supply by one or a few suppliers. Actually there is no such thing as pure monopoly.

Whether big business and industrial monopolies are a real threat to efficient resource allocation and technological progress in the United States is certainly a debatable question. It is a question that will be argued from time to time by the American people and their representatives in Congress. Chapter 35 does not attempt to answer the question. It is important, however, for students to see that it is a debatable question, to see that there are good and plausible arguments on both sides of the question, and to see that the empirical evidence is very tentative.

A part of Chapter 35 is devoted to an examination of the ways in which the Federal government has attempted to prevent the formation of business monopolies and to limit the use of monopoly power. In addition, the chapter examines the ways in which this same government has—either intentionally or unintentionally—promoted and fostered monopoly. In these sections the student will find a discussion of a rather large number of Federal laws, and the question which the student almost always raises is, "Am I expected to know all these laws?" The answer is yes, he should have a general knowledge of these laws. If the student is to understand how government has restricted and promoted monopoly, he should know (1) what the major pieces of Federal legislation with these aims and/or results have been; (2) what the main provisions of each of these laws were; and (3) how successful each of these laws was in accomplishing its aims.

Another question which the student often raises with respect to these laws is, "What good is there in knowing them anyway?" In examining any important current problem it is important to know how the problem arose, what steps have already been taken to solve it, how successful the attempts were, and why the problem is still not solved. A more general answer to the same question is that an informed citizenry is necessary if a democracy is to solve its problems. And most of these laws continue in force and are enforced; many students will work for business firms which are subject to their provisions.

Two final points: In studying the ways in which government has promoted business monopoly, the student should again note specific laws. In addition, three possible future policies which the government might adopt with respect to business monopoly are listed, and the student should learn what arguments proponents of these policies advance to support their proposals.

■ CHAPTER OUTLINE

1. The term "monopoly," as used in this chapter, means a situation in which a small number of firms control all or a substantial percentage of the total output of a major industry. Business firms may be large in either an absolute or a relative sense, and in many cases they are large in both senses. Chapter 35 is concerned with firms large in both senses.

2. Whether business monopoly is beneficial or detrimental to the American economy is debatable. A case can be made *against* business monopoly and *for* it.

3. Many argue that while competition is not perfect in many industries it is "workable"; that big business is able to realize the economies of mass production; that it is conducive to a rapid rate of technological change; that business investment and pricing policies are a stabilizing influence in the economy; and that socially responsible business leaders do not abuse their monopoly power.

4. Others argue, however, that monopoly power results in restricted outputs, higher prices, misallocation of resources, greater income inequality, a slow rate of technological progress, economic instability, and a threat to political freedom.

5. Government policies toward business monopoly have not been clear and consistent; legislation and policy have at various times both restricted and promoted monopoly power.
   a. Following the Civil War, the expansion of the American economy brought with it the creation of trusts (or business monopolies) in many industries; and the fear of the trusts resulted in the establishment of regulatory agencies and the enactment of antitrust legislation.
   b. Where natural monopoly existed and competition was not economic (as in the railroad industry) regulatory agencies were empowered to control and limit monopoly power.
   c. Such antitrust legislation as the Sherman Act, the Clayton Act, the Federal Trade Commission Act, and other laws have attempted to restrain the growth and use of monopoly power.
   d. Yet numerous exemptions to and suspensions of the antitrust laws have been made and various pieces of legislation have directly promoted monopoly.

6. There are at least three proposals (with supporting arguments) which have been suggested as future government policies for dealing with business monopoly: maintenance of the present policy, direct government ownership or regulation of business monopoly, and the restoration of effective competition in monopolistic industries.

■ IMPORTANT TERMS

Monopoly	Tying agreement
Big business	Cease-and-desist order
Absolute bigness	
Relative bigness	Wheeler-Lea Act
Workable competition	Robinson-Patman Act
Regulatory agency	Celler Act
Natural monopoly	Conglomerate
Interstate Commerce Act	Reciprocal selling
	Webb-Pomerene Act
Sherman Act	Resale price maintenance
Clayton Act	
Federal Trade Commission Act	Miller-Tydings Act
	Technological determinism
Interlocking directorate	Effective competition

■ FILL-IN QUESTIONS

1. As used in this chapter, monopoly means that a _____

firms control _____

of the output of a _____
industry; and this chapter is concerned with

firms that are large in both a _____

_____

and an _____
sense.

2. Those who argue the case *for* business monopoly contend that _____ competition regulates big business; that big

firms are able to realize _____;

that big business leads to a _____

of technological change; that the _____

_____

and _____

policies of large firms contribute to economic

stability; and that business leaders have a ___

_____

which prevents abuses of monopoly power.

3. Workable competition includes at least five varieties of competition other than price competition; these are:

a. _____

b. _____

c. _____

d. _____

e. _____

4. Galbraith argues that:
a. the dominant role of the giant corpora-

tion is dictated by _____:

efficient production requires large amounts

of _____, highly sophisticated

_____, and detailed _____

b. the goals of a mature corporation are

_____ and _____; and to

achieve these goals the corporation integrates

_____, finances its expansion ____

_____, controls consumers by _____

and _____, and allies itself with

_____ to manage the economy.

5. Those who argue the case *against* business monopoly assert that monopolists _____

output; _____ prices; _____

resources; contribute to _____

in the distribution of income, to a _____

_____

of technological progress, and to _____

_____

in the economy; and pose serious _____
dangers.

6. Federal legislation and policies have at

times attempted to maintain _____

while at other times they have fostered _____

_____

7. When a single firm is able to supply the entire market at a lower average cost than a

number of competing firms, there is a _____

_____ monopoly. In the United States many of these monopolies are controlled by

regulatory _____ or _____
whose function is to prevent the abuse of monopoly power.

8. The Sherman Antitrust Act of 1890 made

_____

and _____
illegal.

9. The Clayton Act of 1914 prohibited such

practices as _____,

_____,

_____,

and _____

10. The Federal Trade Commission was set up under the act of that name in 1914; the

commission was given the power to _____

_____,

hold _____,

and to issue _____,
but the power of the commission has been

limited by the ruling of _____

that they hold the final authority to _____

_____

11. The _____
Act banned the acquisition of the assets of

one firm by another, and the _____
Act prohibited the acquisition of the stock of

one firm by another when the result would be reduced competition.

12. The _____
Act had the effect of prohibiting false and misleading advertising, and the _____

_____

Act was aimed at eliminating the _____

_____

which large chain stores were able to obtain from their suppliers.

13. Most of the mergers of business firms within the last ten years have been _____

_____ mergers in which a firm in one industry merges with firms in _____

_____

14. Government promotes the growth of monopoly when it _____
certain industries or practices from antitrust prosecution, when it grants _____,

and when it enacts _____

15. Export trade associations and resale price maintenance contracts were exempted from the provisions of the antitrust laws by, respectively, the _____

Act and the _____

Act; in addition, _____

and _____
have been made exempt from the antitrust laws by other Federal legislation.

16. The _____
have the effect of granting inventors legal monopolies on their products, while _____

_____

shelter American producers from foreign competition.

17. Three possible future policy alternatives for dealing with business monopoly are:

a. _____

b. _____

c. _____

18. Effective competition means that the number of producers is large enough that ___

_____,

the absence of _____,

and _____

■ **PROBLEMS AND PROJECTS**

Below is a list of Federal laws. Following this list is a series of provisions found in Federal laws. Match each of the laws with the appropriate provision by placing the appropriate letter after each of the provisions.
A. Sherman Act
B. Clayton Act
C. Federal Trade Commission Act
D. Wheeler-Lea Act
E. Robinson-Patman Act
F. Celler Act
G. Webb-Pomerene Act
H. Miller-Tydings Act
I. Interstate Commerce Act

1. Exempted American exporters from the antitrust laws by permitting them to form export trade associations. _____

2. Established a commission to investigate and prevent unfair methods of competition.

_____

3. Established a commission to regulate the railroads, their rates, and their services. _____

4. Made monopoly and restraint of trade illegal and criminal.

5. Outlawed quantity discounts and unreasonably low prices where their effect is to eliminate competition. _____

6. Prohibited the acquisition of the assets of a firm by another firm when such an acquisition will lessen competition. _____

7. Had the effect of prohibiting false and misleading advertising and the misrepresentation of products. _____

8. Clarified the Sherman Act and outlawed specific techniques or devices used to create monopolies and restrain trade. _____

9. Exempted resale price maintenance contracts from the provisions of the Sherman Act in those states in which state law allows such contracts. _____

■ SELF-TEST

Circle the T if the statement is true, the F if it is false.

1. The term "monopoly" in this chapter is taken to mean a situation in which a single firm produces a unique product and entry into the industry is blocked by impassable barriers. **T (F)**

2. It is clear that on balance, business monopoly is detrimental to the functioning of the American economy. **T (F)**

3. Those who support the case for business monopoly contend that only big business is able to achieve significant economies of scale. **(T) F**

4. Those who emphasize the importance of workable competition as a device for the regulation of big business contend that the competitiveness of any industry should be judged almost solely on the basis of the number of firms in it and the barriers to entry. **T (F)**

5. The Federal government has consistently passed legislation and pursued policies designed to maintain competition. **T (F)**

6. The Federal courts are the final authority in interpreting the antitrust laws. **(T) F**

7. The Robinson-Patman Act was aimed at preventing firms from acquiring the *assets* of other firms where the effect would be to reduce competition. **T (F)**

8. The doctrine of technological determinism is one of the arguments advanced to support the view of those who advocate the restoration of vigorous and effective competition. **T (F)**

9. Those who propose the maintenance of the *status quo* as a policy for dealing with business monopoly argue that workable competition regulates big business. **(T) F**

10. Proponents of public regulation and ownership as a means of controlling business monopoly point to the success of the antitrust laws in limiting the growth of monopoly power. **T (F)**

Underscore the letter that corresponds to the best answer.

1. "Big business" in this chapter refers to which one of the following? (a) firms that are absolutely large; (b) firms that are relatively large; (c) firms that are either absolutely or relatively large; (d) firms that are both absolutely and relatively large.

2. Which of the following is *not* a part of the case *against* business monopoly? (a) monopolists charge higher prices than competitive firms would charge; (b) monopolists earn economic profits which they use for research and technological development; (c) monopoly leads to the misallocation of resources; (d) monopoly leads to greater income inequality.

3. An essential part of the case *for* business monopoly is that the operations of big business are regulated by: (a) pure competition; (b) monopolistic competition; (c) workable competition; (d) effective competition.

4. Which one of the following is *not* a part of the case *for* big business? (a) large firms have lower unit costs because they are able to use their power to depress resource prices; (b) large firms are led by socially responsible business executives who refuse to use their economic power in a way detrimental to the public; (c) large firms result in a more rapid rate of technological progress because they have both the resources and the incentives for research; (d) large firms are effectively regulated by interproduct, technological, and potential competition.

5. Which one of the following laws stated that contracts and conspiracies in restraint of trade, monopolies, attempts to monopolize, and conspiracies to monopolize were illegal? (a) Sherman Act; (b) Clayton Act; (c) Federal Trade Commission Act; (d) Robinson-Patman Act.

6. Insofar as its effect upon competition and monopoly is concerned, which one of the following acts has the least in common with the other three acts? (a) Wheeler-Lea Act; (b) Miller-Tydings Act; (c) Celler Act; (d) Clayton Act.

7. Which one of the following acts specifically outlawed tying contracts and interlocking directorates? (a) Sherman Act; (b) Clayton Act;

57890123457890

(c) Federal Trade Commission Act; (d) Wheeler-Lea Act.

8. Which one of the following acts has given the Federal Trade Commission the task of preventing false and misleading advertising and the misrepresentation of products? (a) Clayton Act; (b) Federal Trade Commission Act; (c) Robinson-Patman Act; (d) Wheeler-Lea Act.

9. Which one of the following is *not* characteristic of the Interstate Commerce Act of 1887? (a) it was based on the supposition that competition was unworkable in the railroad industry; (b) transportation was deemed essential to many individuals, firms, and industries; (c) it substituted government management and operation of the railroads for private management and operation; (d) the Interstate Commerce Commission was established to regulate railroad rates and services.

10. Which one of the following acts amended the Sherman Act to exempt resale price maintenance contracts from the antitrust laws? (a) Webb-Pomerene Act; (b) Miller-Tydings Act; (c) Robinson-Patman Act; (d) Celler Act.

■ DISCUSSION QUESTIONS

1. Explain the difference between the way the term "monopoly" is used in this chapter and the way it is used in Chapter 28. How can "big business" be defined? How is the expression used in this chapter?

2. What are the chief arguments in the case *for* business monopoly?

3. What are the chief arguments in the case *against* business monopoly? What empirical evidence is there to support this case?

4. Explain what is meant by "workable competition." How does it differ from pure competition, and what forms of competition does it include?

5. Against the argument that big business results in economies of scale (that is, mass-production economies) three counterarguments are often presented. What are they?

6. What are the "technological imperatives" that "have brought the corporate giant to a dominant role in the American economy"? What are the goals of the mature corporation and how does it attempt to achieve these goals, according to Galbraith?

7. In what way is the approach of the Interstate Commerce Act to the problem of monopoly different from the approach of the other antitrust laws? Why were the railroads (and later, other industries) subject to this approach?

8. What are the essential provisions of the Sherman Act?

9. The Clayton Act and the Federal Trade Commission Act amended or elaborated the provisions of the Sherman Act, and both aimed at preventing rather than punishing monopoly. What were the chief provisions of each of these acts, and how did they attempt to prevent monopoly? How has the power of the FTC been subsequently limited by the Federal courts?

10. What were the main provisions of each of the following acts? (a) Wheeler-Lea Act; (b) Robinson-Patman Act; (c) Celler Act.

11. How effective has antitrust legislation been in preventing monopoly *and* in restoring competition?

12. In what ways has the Federal government fostered the growth of monopoly? How did each of the following acts contribute to such growth? (a) Webb-Pomerene Act; (b) Miller-Tydings Act; (c) Robinson-Patman Act; (d) the various protective tariffs.

13. How do patent laws contribute to the growth of monopoly power? (In your answer, mention patent pools and tying agreements.)

14. What are the three alternatives which are often suggested as future policies for dealing with business monopoly? What arguments can you present to support each of these policies?

15. Explain the difference between "workable" and "effective" competition.

RURAL ECONOMICS: THE FARM PROBLEM

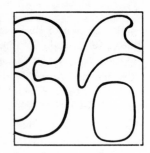

Probably no current economic problem has aroused public interest to the extent and for the number of years that the farm problem has. It has concerned not only those directly engaged in agriculture or living and working in agricultural areas but also every American consumer and taxpayer. Other problems seem to come and go; the farm problem seems always to be with us.

Chapter 36 is devoted exclusively to an examination of rural poverty and the farm problem—the second of the seven specific trouble spots studied in this part of the book. The chapter opens with a brief history of the recent experiences of American farmers. The *symptoms* of the farm problem are declining farm prices, declining farm incomes, farm incomes which are low relative to the incomes of nonfarm families, and a highly unequal distribution of farm income among farm families.

The symptoms of the farm problem, however, are not the same thing as the *causes* of the farm problem. If the problem is to be solved, it is necessary to understand what has occasioned the straits in which agriculture finds itself. In fact, as the author points out, the failure to solve the problem has been brought about by the failure to understand and treat its causes. Actually there are two farm problems, a long-run problem and a short-run problem. Each problem has its own particular causes, and the next major section of the chapter deals with the two problems.

The long-run problem is that farm prices and farm incomes have tended to decline relatively over the years. To understand the causes of this problem, the student is asked to make use of his knowledge of the concept of inelasticity of demand and his knowledge of the effect upon price and total receipts of a large increase in supply and a small increase in demand. Why demand tends to be inelastic for agriculture products and why supply has increased so much more than demand is explained, but it is up to the student to see how these two causes, plus the relative immobility of agricultural resources, give rise to the symptoms of the long-run farm problem.

The short-run farm problem is that farm prices and farm incomes tend to fluctuate sharply from year to year. The cause of this problem is again the inelasticity of demand for agricultural products. Under such conditions relatively small year-to-year changes in either demand or supply will result in relatively large changes in the prices and total income received by farmers. To understand the short-run farm problem, the student is required again to make use of his knowledge of supply and demand.

The policies of the Federal government in dealing with the farm problem (the farm program) have been directed at raising farm incomes by supporting farm prices. In connection with the support of farm prices the student will be introduced to the concept of parity. Parity is not a difficult concept to understand, but it is an important one if the student is to comprehend any of the current discussion which surrounds it.

Once the student understands parity pricing and recognizes that the parity price has been above what the purely competitive price would have been, he will come to some fairly obvious conclusions. At the parity price there is a surplus of the commodity. The Federal government buys this surplus in order to keep the actual market price at the parity-price level. To eliminate these surpluses, government must either increase the demand for or decrease the supply of these commodities. Programs to increase demand and decrease supply have been put into effect, but they have not been entirely successful in reducing the annual surpluses of farm products.

The author concludes the chapter by explaining why the farm program has been unsuccessful and what policies might be adopted to solve the basic problem of excess productive capacity. The program suggested by the Committee for Economic Development is described at the very end of the chapter. The student might compare this program with other possible solutions to the farm problem and note how the CED plan tries to avoid at least one of the pitfalls which has caused previous farm programs to fail.

■ CHAPTER OUTLINE

1. A history of American agriculture in the twentieth century makes it clear that agricultural prices and farm incomes have fluctuated with changes in demand; and that there has been a general tendency for the prices received by farmers and their incomes to decline.

2. The evidence also makes it clear that farmers are, on the average, poorer than people not engaged in farming; that the distribution of income among farmers is highly unequal; and that rural poverty is exceedingly common.

3. The farm problem is both a long-run and a short-run problem. The symptoms of the former are the relative decreases in farm incomes and prices which have occurred over the years; and the symptoms of the latter are the sharp changes in farmers' incomes from year to year.

a. The causes of the long-run problem are the inelastic demand for farm products, the large increases in the supply of these products which have taken place relative to modest increases in the demand for them, and the relative immobility of agricultural resources.

b. The cause of the short-run problem is the inelastic demand for agricultural products: relatively small changes in demand or supply result in relatively large changes in agricultural prices and farm incomes.

c. The long-run problem is, therefore, the result of four factors, and the short-run problem is the result of inelastic demand.

d. Another explanation of the long-run problem is that as the American economy grew and improved its agricultural technology, it reallocated too small an amount of its resources away from agriculture and into the nonagricultural sectors of the economy.

4. Those who represent the farmer claim that he has a special right to assistance from the government.

a. Farmers have been successful in obtaining various forms of public aid, and the policy of the Federal government toward agriculture has included programs designed to raise farm prices and incomes.

b. The parity price of any agricultural product would give the farmer the same real income per unit of output year after year. Parity equals the price of the product in a base year multiplied by the ratio of the index of prices paid currently to the index of prices paid in the base year.

c. The farm program of the government has supported farm prices at some percentage of the parity price. But because the parity price has almost always been above the purely competitive market price, government has had to support the parity price by purchasing and accumulating expensive surpluses of these agricultural commodities.

d. To reduce the annual and accumulated surpluses, government has attempted to reduce supply by means of acreage-allotment and soil bank programs and to expand demand by means of a variety of programs.

e. These programs have been only partially successful in reducing the surpluses held by the Federal government.

5. The farm program has been largely unsuccessful in raising farm prices and incomes because it has failed to move resources out of agriculture, because the major benefits have not been directed toward the low-income families, and because the farm program has not been consistent with other government policies aimed at increasing agricultural production.

6. Three possible solutions to the farm program are the:
  a. free-market solution which would abandon price supports and output restrictions
  b. production controls solution which would set output quotas for all farmers
  c. optimum R & D solution which would restrict the rate of technological progress in agriculture

7. Another program proposed by the Committee for Economic Development offers a unified plan for affecting a permanent solution.

■ IMPORTANT TERMS

Farm problem	Public Law 480
Long-run farm problem	Food for Peace program
Short-run farm problem	Acreage-allotment program
Farm program	Soil bank program
Agricultural Adjustment Act	Committee for Economic Development
Parity	Adaptive approach
Price support	Adjustment price
Parity price	

■ FILL-IN QUESTIONS

1. What was the economic condition—prosperity or depression—of American agriculture in each of the following periods?
  a. 1894 to 1914: _____
  b. 1914 to 1920: _____
  c. 1920 to 1940: _____
  d. 1940 to 1950: _____
  e. 1950 to date: _____

2. The per capita farm income tends to be

_____ than per capita nonfarm income, and the distribution of farm income is _____

3. The long-run farm problem is one of _____

_____

and the short-run farm problem is one of ____

_____

4. The basic causes of the long-run farm problem are _____,

_____,

and _____

5. The demand for farm products tends to be inelastic because _____

6. The supply of farm products has increased rapidly since about the time of World War I

because of _____

7. The demand for agricultural products in the United States has not increased as rapidly as the supply of these products because ____

_____

and _____

8. The price system has failed to reallocate farmers into occupations earning higher incomes because as resources, farmers, their

land, and their capital are highly _____

9. The basic cause of the short-run farm

problem is the _____
demand for agricultural commodities, and this contributes to unstable farm prices and incomes in two ways. Relatively _____
changes in the output of farm products result

in relatively _____
changes in farm prices and incomes, and rela-

tively _____

changes in demand result in relatively _____

_____

changes in prices and incomes.

10. As the American economy has grown and improved its agricultural technology, it has

failed to reallocate _____ from

_____ to _____

11. Two of the reasons advanced to support the farmers' claim to assistance from the Federal government are the contentions that agriculture:

a. Has borne too large a share of the _____

_____

of _____ in the U.S.

b. Sells its products in _____

markets and is unable to control the _____

_____ of these products.

12. The "farm program" is actually a series of programs concerned with (a) farm _____

_____,

_____,

and _____;

(b) _____; (c) _____;

(d) _____; (e) _____;

etc. In practice the principal aim of the farm program has been to _____

13. If a farmer receives a parity price for his product, he is guaranteed that year after year a _____

output will enable him to acquire _____

_____

14. If the government supports farm prices at an above-equilibrium level, the result will be _____ which the government

must _____ in order to maintain prices at their support levels.

15. To bring the equilibrium level of prices in the market up to their support level, government has attempted to _____

the demand for and to _____ the supply of farm products.

16. Two programs employed by the government to reduce agricultural production are the

_____

and the _____

programs. To increase demand it has at-

tempted to find _____

for agricultural commodities, to increase ____

_____,

and to _____

more agricultural products.

17. The farm program has not been successful in solving the farm problem because it has

not _____

resources, because it has mostly benefited

those farmers who _____

_____

and because other government policies have

worked to _____

_____

18. The three policies which government might employ to reduce excess agricultural capacity are:

a. _____

b. _____

c. _____

19. The Committee for Economic Development in its farm plan recommends:

a. _____

b. _____

c. _____

d. _____

e. _____

20. The CED proposes to implement the exodus of human resources from agriculture

by improving the quality _____,
by providing young people in agricultural areas with skills and training they can use to

obtain employment in _____, by

providing better information about _____

_____ to rural people, and by subsidizing

_____

21. The adjustment price of a farm product will permit the total output of the product to

be sold without a _____

and will give to efficiently employed agricultural resources an income equivalent to that earned in _____. This price will be *below* the current _____ price and *above* the competitive price that would prevail if all _____

_____

■ PROBLEMS AND PROJECTS

1. The following table gives the index of prices farmers paid in six different years. The price farmers received in year 1, the base year, for a certain agricultural product was $.35 per bushel. Complete the table by computing the parity prices of the product in year 2 through year 6.

Year	Index of prices farmers paid	Parity price of product
1	100	$.35
2	120	_____
3	175	_____
4	210	_____
5	200	_____
6	230	_____

2. In columns 1 and 2 in the table below is a demand schedule for agricultural product X.

(1) Price	(2) Bushels of X demanded	(3) Bushels of X demanded
$2.00	600	580
1.80	620	600
1.60	640	620
1.40	660	640
1.20	680	660
1.00	700	680
.80	720	700
.60	740	720

a. Is demand elastic or inelastic in the price range given? _____

b. If the amount of X produced should increase from 600 to 700 bushels, the income of producers of X would _____ from $_____ to $_____; an increase of _____% in the amount of X produced would cause income to _____ _____ by _____%.

c. If the amount of X produced were 700 bushels and the demand for X changed from that shown in columns 1 and 2 to that shown in columns 1 and 3, the price of X would

_____

from $_____ to $_____; the income of farmers would _____ from $_____ to $_____

d. Assume that the government supports a price of $1.80, that the demand for X is that shown in columns 1 and 2, and that farmers grow 720 bushels of X. There will be a surplus of _____ bushels of X, and if the government buys this surplus at the support price, the cost to the government will be $_____

e. Assume that instead of supporting a price of $1.80 as it did in (d), the government pays farmers the difference between $1.80 and the price they would receive in a free market. If demand and the output of farmers are the same:

(1) The free-market price will be $_____ and the government will pay farmers $_____ per bushel

(2) The total cost to the government of this program will be $_____

(3) The total cost of this program will be (greater, less) _____ than the cost of the program in (d), but the government will have no problem of _____

(4) The total cost of this program will be greater than the cost of the program in (d) because the demand for the product is _____

_____

3. The demand schedule for agricultural product Y is given in columns 1 and 2 of the following table.

(1) Price	(2) Bales of Y demanded	(3) Bales of Y demanded
$5.00	40,000	41,000
4.75	40,200	41,200
4.50	40,400	41,400
4.25	40,600	41,600
4.00	40,800	41,800
3.75	41,000	42,000
3.50	41,200	42,200

a. If farmers were persuaded by the government to reduce the size of their crop from 41,000 to 40,000 bales, the income of farmers would _____

from $_____ to $_____

b. If the crop remained constant at 41,000 bales and the demand for Y increased to that shown in columns 1 and 3, the income of

farmers would _____

from $_____ to $_____

■ SELF-TEST

Circle the T if the statement is true, the F if it is false.

1. The distribution of the total farm income among farmers in the American economy can be said to be a highly unequal one.   **T   F**

2. Per capita nonfarm income is over one and one-half times the per capita farm income.   **T   F**

3. Most of the recent technological advances in agriculture have been initiated by farmers.   **T   F**

4. The supply of agricultural products has tended to increase more rapidly than the demand for these products in the United States.   **T   F**

5. The size of the farm population of the United States has declined at a more rapid rate than the rate at which agriculture's share of national income has declined.   **T   F**

6. The size of the farm population in the United States has declined in both relative and absolute terms since about 1935.   **T   F**

7. The quantities of agricultural commodities produced tend to be fairly *insensitive* to changes in agricultural prices because a large percentage of farmers' total costs are variable.   **T   F**

8. Application of the parity concept to farm prices causes farm prices to decline and results in agricultural surpluses.   **T   F**

9. The acreage-allotment and soil bank programs are designed to decrease the supply of farm products.   **T   F**

10. Restricting the number of acres which farmers employ to grow agricultural products has not been a very successful method of reducing surpluses because farmers tend to cultivate their land more intensively when the acreage is reduced.   **T   F**

Underscore the letter that corresponds to the best answer.

1. Which one of the following periods has little or nothing in common with the other three insofar as the economic condition of American agriculture in the period is concerned? (a) 1900 to 1914; (b) 1914 to 1920; (c) 1920 to 1940; (d) 1940 to 1950.

2. Which of the following is *not* characteristic of American agriculture? (a) farmers sell their products in highly competitive markets; (b) farmers buy in markets which are largely noncompetitive; (c) the demand for agricultural products tends to be inelastic; (d) agricultural resources tend to be highly mobile.

3. If both the demand for and the supply of a product increase: (a) the quantity of the product bought and sold will increase; (b) the quantity of the product bought and sold will decrease; (c) the price of the product will increase; (d) the price of the product will decrease.

4. Which one of the following is *not* a reason why the increases in the demand for agricultural commodities have been relatively small? (a) the population of the United States has not increased as rapidly as the productivity of agriculture; (b) the increased per capita incomes of American consumers have resulted in less than proportionate increases in their expenditures for farm products; (c) the demand for agricultural products is inelastic;

(d) the standard of living in the United States is well above the level of bare subsistence.

5. The price system has failed to solve the problem of low farm incomes because: (a) the demand for agricultural products is relatively inelastic; (b) the supply of agricultural products is relatively elastic; (c) agricultural products have relatively few good substitutes; (d) agricultural resources are relatively immobile.

6. If the demand for agricultural products is inelastic, a relatively small increase in supply will result in: (a) a relatively small increase in farm prices and incomes; (b) a relatively small decrease in farm prices and a relatively large increase in farm incomes; (c) a relatively large decrease in farm prices and incomes; (d) a relatively large increase in farm prices and a relatively small decrease in farm incomes.

7. Farm parity means that: (a) the real income of the farmer remains constant; (b) a given output will furnish the farmer with a constant amount of real income; (c) the purchasing power of the farmer's money income remains constant; (d) the money income of the farmer will buy a constant amount of goods and services.

8. If the price of a certain farm product were $.75 in the base period when the index of prices paid by farmers was 90, and if the present index of prices paid by the farmer is 150, then the parity price of the farm product today is: (a) $.90; (b) $1.12½; (c) $1.25; (d) $1.50.

9. The necessary consequence of the government's supporting farm prices at an above-equilibrium level is: (a) a surplus of agricultural products; (b) increased consumption of agricultural products; (c) reduced production of agricultural products; (d) the dumping of agricultural products.

10. Which one of the following is *not* a reason why the farm program has been generally unsuccessful in accomplishing its aims? (a) the programs of some government agencies have been designed to increase agricultural efficiency and productivity; (b) restricting agricultural output increases farm prices but reduced farm income when demand is inelastic; (c) the human and nonhuman resources employed in agriculture have not been reduced and reallocated; (d) the principal beneficiaries of government aid have been farmers with high, not low, incomes.

■ DISCUSSION QUESTIONS

1. What was the economic condition of American agriculture: (a) prior to World War I; (b) during World War I; (c) from 1920 to 1940; (d) during World War II; (e) since 1950? Explain the fundamental causes of the condition of agriculture in each of these periods.

2. Comment on (a) the size of farm incomes relative to nonfarm incomes; (b) the recent trend of farm incomes relative to nonfarm incomes; (c) the distribution of total farm income among farmers.

3. What is the long-run farm problem and its specific causes? What is the short-run farm problem and its causes?

4. Why does the demand for agricultural products tend to be inelastic?

5. What have been the specific causes of the large increases in the supply of agricultural products since World War I?

6. Why has the demand for agricultural products failed to increase at the same rate as the supply of these products?

7. Explain why the farm population tends to be relatively immobile. If farmers were more mobile, how would the price system reallocate their labor away from agriculture and into more prosperous occupations?

8. Explain why the inelastic nature of the demand for and the supply of agricultural products results in prices and incomes which change by large amounts as a consequence of small changes in either demand or supply.

9. Why do agricultural interests claim that farmers have a special right to aid from the Federal government?

10. What is meant by "the farm program" in the broad sense? What particular aspect of the farm problem has received the major attention of farmers and their representatives in Congress?

11. Explain what a parity price is and how the parity price of a farm product is computed.

12. What device does the government employ to support above-equilibrium agricultural prices? Why is the result of government-supported prices invariably a surplus of farm commodities?

13. What programs has the government used to try to restrict farm production? Why have these programs been relatively unsuccessful in limiting agricultural production?

14. How has the Federal government tried to increase the demand for farm products? What forces have worked to increase the world demand for American farm products?

15. Why has the farm program not been successful in preventing falling farm prices and incomes, surpluses, and an unequal distribution of farm income?

16. Explain each of the three policy options that would reduce the excess productive capacity of agriculture. In what way do these options constitute a dilemma for government?

17. What are the chief features of the Committee for Economic Development's farm plan? In what ways does this plan differ from the present farm program of the Federal government?

URBAN ECONOMICS: THE PROBLEMS OF THE CITIES

The farmers whose economic problems were examined in the last chapter have tilled the soil since before the beginning of recorded history. Cities and the problems of city living are nearly as old. Cities have been plagued by crowded conditions, crime, disease, poverty, and pollution for as long as cities have existed. Like the problems of the farmers, the problems of the city are not entirely new. What makes the problems of the cities especially important in the United States today is the simple statistic that over two-thirds of the American population now resides in cities. (By way of contrast, only about one-twentieth of the population is engaged in farming.)

While the problems of cities may not be completely new, some of these problems have become more pressing than ever before. Other city problems are new and did not exist in the large cities of early recorded history. It is not possible in a single chapter to examine all the contemporary problems confronting American cities. The author, therefore, focuses his attention on the more crucial of these problems, their causes, and their potential solutions.

Economics is not the only discipline interested in the development of cities and their problems. Other social scientists and natural and physical scientists are concerned and contribute to the analysis of these problems and to their solutions. This is to say that city problems and solutions go well beyond economics. But economics is an essential part of the explanation of the development of cities, their current plight, and the steps necessary to the improvement of city living. And this is the subject matter of this chapter: the economic aspects of urban problems.

The organization of Chapter 37 is relatively simple. Professor McConnell first explains the economic reasons why cities emerge and grow by examining the economies of agglomeration. But as cities grow larger the disadvantages of agglomeration eventually appear. These deglomerative forces lead firms and families to the suburbs where they can enjoy the benefits of urban life without having to contend with its increasing problems. With this flight to suburbia comes political fragmentation and an economic imbalance between the central city and the suburbs. This historical development is the source of many of our current urban problems. The three problems given special attention by the author are transportation, pollution, and the ghetto. Each is examined in some detail and the possible solutions to each problem are considered. The final section of the chapter looks at the financial and institutional changes which may have to be made before any improvement in city living is possible. These changes include the political consolidation of the fragmented local governments, the employment of new methods of financing metropolitan governments, and the creation of entirely new cities.

The problem of the inadequate income of many of those who live in cities, especially in the ghettos, is not examined in great detail in this chapter. Poverty and the economics of inequality in the American economy is the trouble spot examined in Chapter 38.

■ CHAPTER OUTLINE

1. Today over two-thirds of the American population live in urban areas.

2. Economic forces have lead to the development and expansion of cities.

a. Firms can lower the cost of transporting resources and products by locating near their markets and other firms.

b. The increased productivity of agriculture has reduced the number of workers in farming. These excess workers have been drawn to cities where, because of the economies of agglomeration, business firms and jobs are located.

c. Deglomerative forces, sooner or later, limit the growth of central cities and the concentration of firms, and lead to the expansion of the suburbs and to business decentralization.

3. To reap the advantages of urban life and to avoid its disadvantages, firms and households have moved to the suburbs. This flight to suburbia and the resulting suburban sprawl have had at least two important consequences.

a. A large number of separate political units surround the central city.

b. Wealth and income have increased in the suburbs and decreased in the central city; and the central city has experienced a decline in its tax base while its problems and need for public revenue have expanded.

4. The flight to the suburbs has lead to a locational mismatch of jobs and the labor force, automobile congestion and pollution, and the need for a more efficient transportation system.

5. The improvement of urban transportation requires solutions to both a short-run and a long-run problem.

a. To utilize the existing transport facilities more effectively entails the adoption of user charges and peak pricing policies.

b. To build a better transport system entails the development of public mass-transit systems.

6. Because of their high concentrations of population and industry, urban areas have a pollution problem.

a. The dimensions of the problem are well known and the long-run consequences are little short of terrifying.

b. The cause of the pollution problem is the material imbalance between the wastes that result from production and consumption and the ability of the environment to reabsorb these wastes.

c. To reduce pollution requires that the costs of pollution be made private instead of social costs (be transferred from society to the polluter); and this may be accomplished by legislating standards, levying special taxes on polluters, or by creating a market for pollution rights.

7. Another problem characteristic of cities is the central city ghetto of low income, nonwhite, inadequately housed, and poorly educated inhabitants.

a. The poverty of the ghetto can be reduced by providing more and better jobs, income maintenance, and better education and training for those who live there.

b. For a variety of reasons the environment of the ghetto has not yet been improved by subsidized housing and urban renewal.

8. Solutions to the various urban problems require that sufficient financial resources be allocated and that certain institutional changes be made.

a. Consolidation of the many political units would increase the efficiency of decision making and improve equity by putting the needs and the resources within the same governmental unit.

b. To obtain sufficient resources to deal with urban problems may also require Federal revenue sharing, the shifting of some of the burden to the Federal government, and a restructuring of the property tax.

c. Because of the problems currently facing cities and the expected 100 million expansion in the urban population within the next 30 years, entirely new cities may need to be built.

■ IMPORTANT TERMS

Economies of ag-
glomeration

Internal economies

External economies

Infrastructure

Deglomerative forces

User charge

Peak pricing

Materials balance
approach

Emission fees

Political fragmen-
tation

Black capitalism

■ FILL-IN QUESTIONS

1. About _____ million people and _____ percent of the American population live in cities today; and both these figures will prob-ably _____ during the next 30 years.

2. Deciding how to produce goods and serv-ices includes the decision of _____ to produce them. This latter decision is an important one because there are _____ costs involved in moving _____ to the firm and in moving the finished prod-ucts to _____

3. Before cities can develop agriculture must be able to produce _____ food and fiber so that _____ is available to pro-duce nonagricultural goods and services.

4. The economies of agglomeration refer to the lower production and marketing costs which firms realize when they locate _____

_____

The three such principal economies are:

a. _____

b. _____

c. _____

5. The deglomerative forces include all those forces which result in _____ production costs. Some of these are _____ to the firm; and others are _____, are shifted to _____, and are called _____ costs.

6. The flight of people and firms to the sub-urbs enables them to obtain _____

_____

and to avoid _____.
The chief consequences of this movement have been political _____ and economic _____ between the central city and the suburbs.

7. The movement of the higher-income fam-ilies and the wealthier firms to new political units in suburbia has:

a. eroded the _____ tax _____ and brought about increases in tax _____ in the central city;

b. left behind a central city of poor fam-ilies, many of whom are _____ and on _____, living in _____ popu-lated areas for which the cost of providing so-cial facilities and services is _____

8. The flight to the suburbs has also resulted in:

a. a locational mismatch because the _____ of those who live in suburbia are in the cen-tral city and of those who live in the central are in suburbia;

b. the need for a more efficient _____ system;

c. expanded use of the _____, traf-fic _____, and air _____

d. the construction of still more _____ _____, the development of more distant _____, and still more _____ and _____

e. the general deterioration of the _____ _____ systems of the cities

9. It has been suggested that:
a. to relieve highway congestion there be _____ on drivers and that _____ _____ policies should be used on high-ways and mass transit systems;

b. in the long run it will be necessary to rebuild the _____ in urban areas.

10. The materials balance approach to pollution is that the _____ of the residual _____ produced by society has come to exceed the ability of _____ to _____ them. This imbalance is the result of increases in the nation's _____ and _____, changes in _____ and the absence of economic _____ to refrain from pollution.

11. The central city ghetto has developed in major American cities because:

a. the more _____ and better _____ whites have moved to the _____ and left behind obsolete _____
b. their places have been taken by poorly _____, unskilled, and ____-income Negroes from the rural _____
c. job opportunities for the ghetto inhabitants have shifted from the _____ to the _____; and access to these opportunities has been limited by the deterioration of the _____ system and racial _____

12. To alleviate poverty in the ghettos requires that their residents be provided with more and better _____, improved _____ and _____; and that a program of income _____ be instituted.

13. Bringing ghetto residents to the job opportunities in the suburbs will necessitate an improved _____.
One way of creating new job opportunities in the central city is _____

14. The institutional and financial prerequisites to the solution of urban problems are political _____ and an increase in the _____ of urban governments.

15. Political consolidation will result in more efficient _____ making and reduce the disparity between _____ and _____ within urban areas.

16. The larger financial problem of urban areas will be reduced by political consolidation, Federal revenue _____, the shifting of some of the financial burden of cities to _____, and by overhauling the _____ tax so that _____ is taxed more heavily and _____ less heavily.

■ PROBLEMS AND PROJECTS

1. Below is a table showing the average number of motor vehicles traveling each mile of highway in a hypothetical metropolitan area and the estimated cost to society of each vehicle mile traveled during various periods of the day.

Period of the day	Vehicles per highway mile	Cost per vehicle mile	Total cost
7am–9am	500	$ .60	$_____
9am–12n	150	.10	_____
12n–2pm	200	.15	_____
2pm–4pm	100	.10	_____
4pm–6pm	600	.85	_____
6pm–10pm	200	.15	_____
10pm–7am	50	.10	_____

a. In every twenty-four hour period the total number of vehicles traveling each mile of highway is _____ and the total cost for each mile of highway traveled is $_____
b. The average cost to society for a vehicle to travel one mile is $_____

c. Assuming that the number of vehicles per highway mile is not affected by the imposition of a user charge and that the user charge is the same during all periods, the user charge that would enable society to recover the full

cost of the highway system would be $_____ per vehicle mile

d. Imagine now that the imposition of this user charge results in the following change in vehicular traffic during the various periods of the day. The cost per vehicle mile remains the same in each period; and the total cost in each period is shown in the table below.

Period of the day	Vehicles per high-way mile	Total cost	Total revenue
7am–9am	450	$270.00	$_____
9am–12n	135	13.50	_____
12n–2pm	180	27.00	_____
2pm–4pm	90	9.00	_____
4pm–6pm	540	459.00	_____
6pm–10pm	180	27.00	_____
10pm–7am	45	4.50	_____

(1) The total cost per day of each mile of highway is $_____

(2) Compute the total revenue in each period when a 50 cents per mile user charge is made. The total revenue per day on each mile of highway is $_____

(3) In what two periods are the revenues received less than the cost in that period?

_____ and _____

e. If it is desired to reduce the number of vehicles per mile of highway in these two periods to 400; and if each 1 cent increase in the user charge decreases the number of vehicles per mile by 10 vehicles, the user charge in the:

(1) 7am–9am period should be increased to _____ cents per mile

(2) 4pm–6pm period should be increased to _____ cents per mile

2. Assume the atmosphere of Cuyahoga County, Ohio (the Cleveland metropolitan area), is able to reabsorb 1,500 tons of pollutants per year. The schedule below shows the price polluters would be willing to pay for the right to dispose of 1 ton of pollutants per year and the total quantity of pollutants they would wish to dispose of at each price.

Price (per ton of pol-lutant rights)	Total quantity of pollutant rights demanded (tons)
$ 0	4,000
1,000	3,500
2,000	3,000
3,000	2,500
4,000	2,000
5,000	1,500
6,000	1,000
7,000	500

a. If there were no emission fee, polluters would put _____ tons of pollutants in the air each year; and this quantity of pollutants would exceed the ability of nature to reabsorb them by _____ tons.

b. To reduce pollution to the capacity of the atmosphere to recycle pollutants, an emission fee of $_____ per ton should be set.

c. Were this emission fee set, the total emission fees collected would be $_____

d. Were the quantity of pollution rights demanded at each price to increase by 500 tons, the emission fee could be increased by $_____ and total emission fees collected would increase by $_____

3. Describe conditions in the central city ghetto by placing one or more of the adjectives in the list below after each of the following indicators of well-being.

high   crowded
low   grossly inadequate
inadequate   deteriorated
old   deplorable
poor

a. Schools: _____

b. Mortality rates: _____

c. Income levels: _____

d. Medical care: _____

e. Housing: _____

f. Crime rates: _____

g. Sanitation: _____

h. Disease incidence: _____

■ SELF-TEST

Circle the T if the statement is true, the F if it is false.

1. About 150 million Americans live in cities.
  T F

2. External economies of scale shift a firm's average-cost curve downward. T F

3. A deglomerative force increases the cost of producing a product and may be either internal or external to the firm. T F

4. Since 1900 the percentage of the American population living in central cities has increased. T F

5. The flight to the suburbs has involved the migration of families but has not resulted in the movement of business firms. T F

6. The flight to the suburbs has brought about a general improvement in the public mass-transit systems of cities. T F

7. Pollution is caused almost exclusively by profit-seeking business firms. T F

8. An effective antipollution policy requires that the social costs of pollution be turned into private costs. T F

9. Black capitalism entails the development of business firms in ghetto areas which are owned and operated by blacks. T F

10. It has been estimated that improved employment opportunities for its residents will eliminate 90 percent of the ghetto poverty.
  T F

Underscore the letter that corresponds to the best answer.

1. About what percentage of the American population lives in cities? (a) 85%; (b) 75%; (c) 55%; (d) 45%.

2. Deciding where to produce a product is a part of the decision a firm makes when it decides (a) what to produce; (b) how much to produce; (c) how to produce; (d) for whom to produce.

3. Which of the following will result in an internal economy of scale for firm A? (a) the growth of the market for firm A's product; (b) the development of other firms who are able to perform specialized services for firm A; (c) the expansion and improvement of the infrastructure; (d) the improvement of the transportation facilities employed by firm A.

4. The flight to the suburbs has had all but one of the following consequences. Which one? (a) political consolidation; (b) an economic imbalance between the central city and the suburbs; (c) an erosion of the property tax base in the central city; (d) a mismatch between the location of the labor force and the location of job opportunities.

5. Which of the following is *not* generally considered to be a step that would lead to the solution of the urban transportation problem? (a) the imposition of user charges on the highway system; (b) following a peak pricing policy on the public mass-transit systems; (c) the reconstruction and expansion of the mass-transit systems; (d) the construction of more and the expansion of existing highways to connect the central city with the suburbs.

6. Which of the following would do little or nothing to reduce pollution? (a) create a market for pollution rights; (b) charge polluters an emission fee; (c) enact legislation that prohibits pollution and fines polluters; (d) redesign and reconstruct the infrastructure.

7. Which of the following has probably been the most important cause of the emergence of black ghettos? (a) racial discrimination; (b) the flight to the suburbs; (c) the deterioration of public mass-transit systems; (d) high crime rates in the central cities.

8. The unemployment rate among blacks is (a) less than; (b) about the same as; (c) double; (d) triple the rate for whites.

9. Which of the following would do little by itself to solve the problems of the central city? (a) political consolidation; (b) increased use of local income taxes; (c) Federal revenue sharing with the cities; (d) reduced taxation of buildings.

10. The suggestion to overhaul the property tax system has been made (a) because the property tax is proportional; (b) to reduce land values; (c) as an incentive for the construction and improvement of buildings; (d) to increase the supply of land.

■ DISCUSSION QUESTIONS

1. Explain why firms must decide where to produce and why they tend to agglomerate.

2. What is the difference between an internal and an external economy? What are the principal economies which induce firms to locate near other firms?

3. What is a deglomerative force? What are the principal deglomerative forces internal to the firm? What deglomerative forces are external to the firm?

4. Explain the reasons for the flight of families and business firms to the suburbs. What families and kinds of firms have remained in the central city?

5. Explain in detail the two most important consequences of the flight to suburbia.

6. What are the causes of the urban transportation problem and what might be done to improve urban transportation systems? Include in your answer the user charge and peak pricing concepts.

7. Employing the materials balance approach, explain the causes of the pollution problem. What are the three major policies that might be adopted to reduce pollution and what problems would be encountered in applying these policies?

8. Explain why ghettos developed in central cities and describe living conditions in and the characteristics of the typical ghetto. What can be done to change these conditions?

9. What steps has government taken to stimulate the construction of new housing? Why have these programs failed to help low-income families in the central city?

10. What are the institutional and financial requisites to the solution of urban problems? Why are these changes necessary and how might they be accomplished?

THE ECONOMICS OF INEQUALITY AND POVERTY

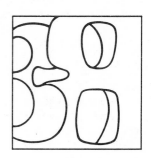

Chapter 38 examines the fourth of the so-called trouble spots in the American economy—the unequal distribution of the total income of the economy among its families and the poverty of many of its families.

The things which the student will learn are (1) the extent and the causes of income inequality in the United States; (2) the degree to which income inequality has changed in the past thirty years and since World War II; (3) why some people contend that income inequality is bad and should be reduced and why others argue that it is beneficial and should not be reduced; (4) how poverty is defined, how many poor there are, where the greatest concentrations of poverty are in the American economy, and what the economic status of nonwhites is; (5) why the poor are invisible; (6) the types of programs that are included within the American social security system; (7) what is meant by the "vicious circle of poverty" and the "paradox of the welfare state"; (8) the two fundamental and opposing philosophies of the cause of poverty; (9) how the economic opportunities of the poor can be expanded to reduce poverty; and (10) the nature of the proposals for reducing poverty by income maintenance or "workfare."

Several ideas are worth repeating here because of their importance to the whole discussion of inequality and poverty. First, the student will recall from Chapter 6 that one of the functions of government in the American economy is to modify the economic results which a *pure* price-market system would yield: it is the price-market system and the institutions of capitalism which bring about an unequal distribution of income, and government in the United States has worked to reduce—but not eliminate—this unequal distribution.

Second, the critics of the price-market system (see Chapter 5), including the socialists and communists, have attacked the system because of the inequality and poverty that it breeds; but capitalism has replied to its critics by reducing these faults and in so doing has maintained the faith of the American people in the price-market system as an efficient method of resource allocation. It is for this reason that the Socialist Party and other groups advocating drastically different economic systems have met with so little success in the United States.

Third, the single most effective method of reducing the importance of income inequality and the extent of poverty in the United States has been the maintenance of full employment and an expanding average standard of living. Other programs have aided in the achievement of this goal, but the best cure has been the high and ever-increasing output of the American economy.

Fourth, very few people advocate an absolutely equal distribution of income; the question to be decided is not one of inequality or equality, but of how much or how little inequality there should be. The question can be looked at either ethically or economically, and the economist has nothing to offer on the ethical question but his own personal value judgment. From the economic point of view the question is what *degree* of income inequality will result in the most efficient allocation and the highest level of employment of resources. The pros and cons of the income-inequality issue represent no more than different opinions on what degree of inequality will bring about full employment and full production.

Finally, while poverty is caused by many forces, it is essentially an economic problem. Any attack on poverty will have to be basically an economic attack. There are reasons why the problem of poverty may not be solved in the United States; but one of these reasons is not that the American economy cannot afford to abolish poverty. The costs of poverty far outweigh the costs of eliminating it; and surely the richest nation in the world can afford what it costs to provide the necessities of life for all of its citizens.

■ CHAPTER OUTLINE

1. The facts concerning the extent of income inequality and of poverty in the United States can be seen by examining distribution-of-income tables.

a. The impersonal price system does not necessarily result in a distribution of income which society deems just; at least five specific factors explain why income inequality exists.

b. Not only has the absolute size of the real income received by various income classes increased since 1929, but the relative distribution of personal income has also changed to reduce the extent of income inequality.

c. Whether income equality is desirable or not is open to debate. Those who attack it contend that it results in reduced consumer satisfaction, lower productivity, fewer occupational opportunities for the lower income groups, and social and political inequality.

d. Income inequality is defended primarily on the grounds that it makes a large volume of saving (and, therefore, investment) possible; that it furnishes incentives to work, produce, and innovate; and that it provides the higher incomes which subsidize the development of new products and cultural progress.

2. Knowing how the economy's income is distributed among its families is the factual background to the poverty problem in the United States.

a. Using the generally accepted definition of poverty, over one-tenth of the people in the American economy live in poverty. These poor tend to be concentrated among poorly educated and trained, aged, agricultural, manless, physically unhealthy, and unemployed families in which there are many children.

b. As a result of a higher incidence of unemployment and various forms of discrimination, there is more poverty among nonwhite than among white families.

c. American poverty is obscured by the general affluence of the economy as a whole and by the fact that much of the poverty is hidden from the eyes of the remainder of society.

d. Poverty also tends to be self-perpetuating: The children of the poor in one generation become the poor families of the next generation.

3. Poverty persists in the American economy despite the existence of a number of social welfare programs.

a. The social security system includes old age, survivors, disability and health insurance; unemployment insurance; and public assistance to the aged and blind, the disabled, and dependent children.

b. It is paradoxical that while the United States has various welfare programs to assist the poor, these programs tend to benefit least those who most need help.

c. There are two fundamental and opposing philosophies regarding the cause of poverty and the policies to deal with it.

(1) One view is that the poor are responsible for their own plight and government should not help them.

(2) The opposing view is that poverty is the result of social forces beyond the control of the individual and that society as a whole must assist the poor.

(3) The evidence indicates that most of those who are poor are unable to help themselves.

4. An antipoverty program for the United States:

a. would increase the economic opportunities of the poor by maintaining a prosperous and growing economy and by expanding the job opportunities open to those with low incomes

b. might include a Federal program that would guarantee a minimum income to all citizens by instituting a negative income tax

c. or might include instead the "Workfare" or family assistance plan proposed by President Nixon

■ IMPORTANT TERMS

Income inequality

Poverty

Old age, survivors, disability, and health insurance

Medicare

Unemployment insurance

Guaranteed income

Negative income tax

■ FILL-IN QUESTIONS

1. It can fairly be said that the extent of income inequality in the United States is _____

_____

2. The important factors which explain income inequality are differences in _____

_____,

and _____,

the unequal distribution of _____,

and the unequal distribution of _____, among the population.

3. The percentage of total personal income received by the highest quintile has _____

_____ since 1929; these changes can fairly be said

to have been _____

4. Since the close of World War II the distribution of personal income in the United

States has _____

5. Those who condemn income inequality contend that it reduces _____,

_____,

and _____;

and that it fosters _____ inequality.

6. The defenders of income inequality argue

that it results in _____,

_____,

and _____

7. Using the more or less official definition of poverty,

a. The poor includes any family of four with

less than _____ and any individual with

less than _____ a year to spend.

b. Approximately _____ percent of

the population and about _____ million people are poor.

8. While there is no "typical" poor family, the families of the nation living in poverty tend to be concentrated among certain groups. These groups are:

a. _____

b. _____

c. _____

d. _____

e. _____

f. _____

g. _____

9. Relative to the size of the two groups, there is more poverty among (whites, non-

whites) _____. This is the re-

sult of a (higher, lower) _____ rate of unemployment among nonwhites which

is due in large part to _____ in employment opportunities and education.

10. What five reasons explain why in the affluent American economy those living in poverty remain hidden or invisible?

a. _____

b. _____

c. _____

d. _____

e. _____

11. The three parts of the social security system in the United States are _____

_____

insurance, _____

insurance, and _____

12. The paradox of the welfare programs of the United States is that these programs tend

to be of _____
benefit to those who need economic assistance

the _____

13. There are two conflicting philosophies regarding the source of poverty. One philosophy contends that poverty is due to _____

_____

_____

and that government should not help the poor; the other argues that the cause of poverty is

_____

and that the poor must be helped by the government.

14. To expand the economic opportunities for low-income groups and reduce poverty it

is necessary to have a _____

and _____ economy.

15. Income maintenance (or a guaranteed annual income) might be achieved either by

making provisions for a _____

tax or by adopting the "_____"
program proposed by President Nixon.

■ PROBLEMS AND PROJECTS

1. The distribution of personal income among consumer units in a hypothetical economy is shown in the table below.
a. Complete the table by computing:
(1) The percentage of all consumer units in each income class and all lower classes; enter these figures in column 4.
(2) The percentage of total income received by each income class and all lower classes; enter these figures in column 5.
b. From the distribution of income data in columns 4 and 5 it can be seen that:
(1) Consumer units with less than $3,000 a

year income constitute the lowest _____%

of all consumer units and receive _____%
of the total personal income.
(2) Consumer units with incomes of $7,500

a year or more constitute the highest ____%

of all consumer units and receive _____%
of the total personal income.

2. On page 271 is a table containing different possible earned incomes for a family of a certain size.
a. Assume that $5,000 is the minimum income desirable for a family of this size. Compute the income deficit at each earned income level and enter them in the table.

(1) Personal income class	(2) Percentage of all consumer units in this class	(3) Percentage of total income received by this class	(4) Percentage of all consumer units in this and all lower classes	(5) Percentage of total income received by this and all lower classes
Under $2,000	18	4	_____	_____
2,000–2,999	12	6	_____	_____
3,000–3,999	14	12	_____	_____
4,000–4,999	17	14	_____	_____
5,000–7,499	19	15	_____	_____
7,500–9,999	11	20	_____	_____
10,000 and over	9	29	_____	_____

Earned income	Income deficit	Income subsidy	Total income
$ 0	$_____	$_____	$_____
1,000	_____	_____	_____
2,000	_____	_____	_____
3,000	_____	_____	_____
4,000	_____	_____	_____
5,000	_____	_____	_____

Earned income	Income deficit	Income subsidy	Total income
$ 0	$_____	$_____	$_____
1,000	_____	_____	_____
2,000	_____	_____	_____
3,000	_____	_____	_____
4,000	_____	_____	_____
5,000	_____	_____	_____

b. Assume the negative income tax rate is 60%. Enter the income subsidy and the total income at each level of earned income in the table.

c. This negative income tax program retains incentives to work because whenever the family earns an additional $1,000 the income subsidy decreases by only $_____ and total income increases by $_____.

d. But this program does not result in a total income of $5,000 for the family unless its earned income is $_____

e. Complete the table below to show the amount of income subsidy the family would have to receive in order to make its total income $5,000. Income subsidies of this size

Earned income	Income subsidy	Total income
$ 0	$_____	$5,000
1,000	_____	$5,000
2,000	_____	$5,000
3,000	_____	$5,000
4,000	_____	$5,000
5,000	_____	$5,000

would ensure the family a minimum income of $5,000; but would destroy incentives to work because whenever the family earns an additional $1,000 its income subsidy would decrease by $_____ and its total income would increase by $_____

f. In the next column is another table showing the different possible earned income levels for a family of a certain size.

(1) Assume that $5,000 is still the minimum income desirable for a family of this size; but that the income deficit is found by subtracting earned income from $8,333⅓. Compute the income deficit at each level of earned income and enter them in the table.

(2) Assume the negative income tax rate is still 60% of the income deficit. Compute the income subsidy at each earned income level; and the total income. Enter these amounts in the table.

(3) This negative income tax program maintains incentives to work because whenever earned income increases by $1,000 the subsidy decreases by $_____ and total income increases by $_____.

(4) It also ensures that the family, no matter what its earned income is, receives a total income of $_____ or more; but results in total incomes in excess of $5,000 if the family has an earned income greater than $_____.

■ SELF-TEST

Circle the T if the statement is true, the F if it is false.

1. According to the author of the text, there is considerable income inequality in the United States. **T F**

2. Since 1929 the percentage of total personal income received by consumer units in the highest income quintile has decreased. **T F**

3. The greater incidence of poverty among nonwhites is, for the most part, attributable to educational and occupational discrimination.   **T   F**

4. Those who defend income inequality contend that it results in a higher level of consumption spending and thereby promotes a higher level of aggregate demand, output, and employment in the economy.   **T   F**

5. Using the semiofficial definition of poverty, some 10 percent of the population of the United States is poor.   **T   F**

6. The incidence of poverty tends to be greater among the unhealthy than the healthy segments of the population.   **T   F**

7. One of the reasons the poor are "invisible" is the relative inexpensiveness of clothing in the American economy.   **T   F**

8. The paradox of the welfare state is that the United States has a higher per capita income than all other nations, but a less developed social security system than most other countries in the world.   **T   F**

9. The "vicious circle of poverty" refers to the fact that poverty tends to be passed on from generation to generation.   **T   F**

10. Of the two philosophies of poverty, one contends that poverty is caused by social forces beyond the control of the individual and the other believes that poverty is due to government interferences with the price-market system.   **T   F**

Underscore the letter that corresponds to the best answer.

1. Approximately what percentage of all American families have personal incomes of over $15,000 annually? (*a*) 5%; (*b*) 10%; (*c*) 15%; (*d*) 20%.

2. Approximately what percentage of all American families have personal incomes of less than $3,000 a year? (*a*) 5%; (*b*) 10%; (*c*) 15%; (*d*) 20%.

3. Which of the following would be evidence of a decrease in income inequality in the United States? (*a*) a decrease in the percentage of total personal income received by the lowest quintile; (*b*) an increase in the percentage of total personal income received by the highest quintile; (*c*) an increase in the percentage of total personal income received

by the four lowest quintiles; (*d*) a decrease in the percentage of total personal income received by the four lowest quintiles.

4. In the post–World War II period there has been: (*a*) a significant decrease in the percentage of total personal income received by the highest quintile; (*b*) a significant increase in the percentage of total personal income received by the lowest quintile; (*c*) a significant increase in the percentage of total personal income received by the middle three quintiles; (*d*) no significant change in the percentage of total personal income received by any of the five quintiles.

5. Which of the following is *not* one of the contentions of those who condemn income inequality? (*a*) it is an obstacle to the maximization of consumer satisfactions; (*b*) it leads to social and political inequality; (*c*) it results in insufficient saving in the economy and thereby causes insufficient investment and an inadequate level of aggregate demand and unemployment; (*d*) it reduces the productivity of the economy's resources.

6. Poverty does not have a precise definition, but the more or less official definition of "poor" is any family of four and any individual with less to spend annually, respectively, than: (*a*) $3,700 and $1,800; (*b*) $4,000 and $2,000; (*c*) $4,000 and $1,500; (*d*) $3,000 and $2,000.

7. Which of the following groups is *least* apt to suffer from poverty? (*a*) farmers living in the South; (*b*) urban families in the North; (*c*) nonwhites with little education; (*d*) families headed either by a woman or an aged person.

8. Which of the following is *not* a cause of the invisibility of the American poor? (*a*) poverty in the cities is not easily seen from the more common means of transportation; (*b*) poverty in rural areas is not easily seen from the more common means of transportation; (*c*) poverty among the old and sick is not easily seen because these people seldom emerge from their dwelling places; (*d*) poverty among the unemployed is more than offset by unemployment compensation.

9. Which of the following is one of the three parts of the American social security system? (*a*) public housing; (*b*) agricultural subsidies;

(c) unemployment insurance; (d) minimum wage laws.

10. A negative income tax would (a) reduce incentives to work; (b) fail to guarantee a minimum income to all people; (c) subsidize people who are not poor; (d) result in at least one but not necessarily all of the above.

■ DISCUSSION QUESTIONS

1. How much income inequality is there in the American economy? Cite figures to support your conclusion. What causes income inequality in American capitalism?

2. Has the distribution of income before taxes changed in the United States during the past 40 years? If it has, in what way, to what extent, and why has it changed? Has income distribution changed in the past 25 or so years?

3. Is income inequality desirable? What are the arguments on both sides of this question?

4. What is the currently accepted and more or less official definition of poverty? How many people and what percentage of the American population are poor if we use this definition of poverty?

5. What characteristics—other than the small amounts of money they have to spend—do the greatest concentrations of the poor families of the nation *tend* to have? Why is there more poverty among nonwhites than whites?

6. Why does poverty in the United States tend to be invisible or hidden?

7. What is meant by the "vicious circle of poverty"?

8. What is the "paradox of the welfare state" in the American economy? What are the three programs embodied in the social security system of the United States? In what ways do these programs contribute to the paradox?

9. Is the problem of poverty primarily a problem to be solved by government or by individuals? What are the two opposing philosophies or viewpoints that would underlie the answer to this question? Which philosophy do you accept and why?

10. If government were to attack the problem of poverty in the United States, what programs or policies might it adopt?

LABOR UNIONS AND COLLECTIVE BARGAINING

Another trouble spot in the American economy is in the area of labor-management relations. It is an area that is almost always in the news for one reason or another—strikes, new legislation, wage increases, union demands, and charges and countercharges by both employers and unions.

The labor union has become an important institution in American capitalism. Labor unions did not always occupy the position in the economy that they now do. The first part of Chapter 39 is devoted to a historical review of their development in the United States and is separated into three periods. The important thing for the student to see is that the growth and power of unions in each of these periods clearly depended upon the rights and recognition given to them by Federal law. At first the law repressed them, then it encouraged them, and finally it has sought to curb and control their greatly increased power.

In Chapter 32 the student learned how unions directly and indirectly seek to influence wage rates. The impact of the union upon its own membership, upon employers, and upon the rest of the economy is more than just a matter of wages, however. The third major section of Chapter 39 examines the contents of a typical contract between a union and an employer. The purpose of this examination is to give the student some idea of the goals which unions seek and other issues over which employers and employees bargain and upon which they must reach an agreement. Another extremely important idea which the student will find in the section is this: labor-management relations mean more than the periodic signing of a contract; they also mean the day-to-day working relations between the union and the employer and the new problems and issues not specifically settled in the contract which must be resolved under the general provisions of that contract.

The question posed in the final section is one that the student has encountered many times in earlier chapters: How does this affect the *allocation* of resources and the *employment* of resources in the American economy? In this particular case the question becomes: How do labor unions affect the allocation and employment of labor? Here is another of those questions for which there is no definite answer. There are, however, opposing views on the economic effect of unions, and the author explains in detail the two *extreme* views. The answer to the question in all probability lies somewhere between the position that unions are very bad for the economy and the position that they are very good for it.

A final word of advice. The list of important terms is long, but the student will find it worthwhile to master it. An understanding of the terms leads to a better understanding of the history and many of the issues and problems of labor-management relations.

■ CHAPTER OUTLINE

1. The history of labor unions in the United States can be divided into three periods or phases.

a. During the repression phase, between 1790 and 1930, the growth of unions was severely limited by the judicial application of the criminal conspiracy doctrine and by the refusal of many firms to recognize and bargain with unions; between 1886 and 1930 the AFL, following the union philosophy of Samuel Gompers, was able to organize many crafts and expand its membership.

b. Between 1930 and 1947, the encouragement phase, labor union membership grew rapidly, encouraged by prolabor legislation; and the CIO was formed to unionize industrial workers.

c. In the intervention phase from 1947 onward, government regulation and control of labor-management relations increased with the passage of the Taft-Hartley and Landrum-Griffin Acts.

d. The merger of the AFL and CIO in 1955 reunited the American labor movement.

e. Since the achievement of labor unity, the labor movement, facing both internal and external obstacles, has been unable to increase its membership by any substantial amount.

2. Collective bargaining and the resulting work agreements are more often than not the result of compromise between labor and management; strikes and violence are actually quite rare.

3. The typical agreement between the employer and the union covers four basic areas. But collective bargaining is more than the periodic negotiation of an agreement; it also involves union and workers' security and day-to-day labor-management relations in an economy which is continually changing.

4. Whether unions and their practices do or do not lead to the efficient allocation of resources and to economic stability and growth is another of those hotly debated economic questions; a case can be made for both points of view.

■ IMPORTANT TERMS

Criminal-conspiracy doctrine

Injunction

Discriminatory discharge

Blacklist

Lockout

Yellow-dog contract

Company union

Business unionism

Norris-La Guardia Act

Wagner (National Labor Relations) Act

National Labor Relations Board

Taft-Hartley (Labor-Management Relations) Act

Jurisdictional strike

Sympathy strike

Secondary boycott

Featherbedding

Closed shop

Union shop

Open shop

Nonunion shop

Right-to-work law

Checkoff

Reopening clause

Landrum-Griffin (Labor-Management Reporting and Disclosure) Act

Preferential hiring

Seniority

Arbitration

American Federation of Labor

Congress of Industrial Organizations

Two terms for review:

Craft unionism

Industrial unionism

■ FILL-IN QUESTIONS

1. Almost _____ million workers belong to labor unions in the United States. This is approximately what percentage of the nonagricultural labor force? _____

2. During the repression phase of labor union history, union growth was slow because

_____

and _____

3. Unions were limited in their growth between 1790 and 1930 by courts which applied

the _____

doctrine to labor unions and issued _____

_____

to prevent strikes, picketing, and boycotts.

4. Employers used the following nonjudicial means of retarding the growth of labor unions

in the repression phase: _____

_____ ,

_____ ,

_____ ,

_____ ,

_____ ,

_____ ,

and _____

5. The philosophy of the AFL under the leadership of Samuel Gompers was _____

_____ ,

_____ ,

and _____

6. In the encouragement phase of labor union history, unions grew as a consequence of such favorable legislation as the _____

_____

and _____

Acts; and the _____

based on the principle of _____

unionism, was formed to organize the _____

workers.

7. The National Labor Relations Act of 1935 guaranteed the "twin rights" of labor: the

right to _____

and the right to _____ ;

in addition it established the _____

and listed a number of _____

8. Three important events that occurred in the history of labor unions after 1946 were

the passage of the _____

and _____

Acts and the _____ .
Some economists contend that in the 1955–1965 period union membership was almost

_____ and that the labor movement

was characterized by _____

9. The four principal sections of the Labor-Management Relations Act of 1947 are:

a. _____

b. _____

c. _____

d. _____

10. The Landrum-Griffin Act of 1959 regulates union _____

and _____

and lists the rights of _____

upon which _____
may not infringe.

11. A typical work agreement between a union and an employer covers four basic areas:

a. _____

b. _____

c. _____

d. _____

12. Labor and management tend to base their arguments for and against higher wages on

four points, namely, _____ ,

_____ ,

_____ ,

and _____

13. Collective bargaining is concerned not only with wage rates but also with the _____

_____

and _____
of unions and their members; and while negotiation of a work agreement is important ___

_____

and _____
the agreement are equally important.

14. Those who argue that labor unionism leads to less than full employment and less than full production contend that unions are

_____

which are able to obtain _____

wage rates and thereby _____
resources. It is also argued that unions con-

tribute to both _____

and _____

and that they should be either _____

or _____

or that _____

or _____
should be substituted for collective bargaining
between labor and management.

15. Unions argue that their monopoly power
is not fully used because the union must con-

sider the effect of its wage demands upon ___

_____

and _____

and because labor leaders are _____.
In addition, it is contended that business firms

limit the power of unions by _____

_____,

that labor markets would not be competitive if

_____,

that union power offsets _____,

and that _____
is more decisive in determining the level of
employment in the economy than the wage
demands of unions.

■ PROBLEMS AND PROJECTS

1. Below is a list of frequently employed
terms, and following the terms is a series
of identifying phrases. Match the term with
the phrase by placing the appropriate letter
after each of the phrases. (*Note:* All the terms
will not be needed.)
  A. Injunction
  B. Blacklist
  C. Lockout
  D. Yellow-dog contract
  E. Company union
  F. Business union
  G. Jurisdictional strike
  H. Sympathy strike
  I. Secondary boycott
  J. Featherbedding
  K. Closed shop
  L. Union shop
  M. Open shop
  N. Nonunion shop
  O. Checkoff
  P. Craft union
  Q. Industrial union

1. A worker must be a member of the union

before he is eligible for employment. _____
2. A worker agrees when employed not to

join a union. _____
3. A union open to all workers employed by

a given firm or in a given industry. _____
4. A union organized and encouraged by an
employer to prevent the formation of a union
which might make "unreasonable" demands.

_____

5. The deduction by an employer on behalf
of the union of a worker's union dues from

his wages. _____
6. A dispute between two unions over whose

members are to perform a certain job. _____
7. A court order which forbids a person or

group of persons to perform some act. _____
8. The closing of the place of employment
by the employer as a means of preventing the

formation of a union. _____
9. Concern of unions with better pay, hours,
and working conditions rather than with ideal-
istic plans for social and economic reform.

_____

10. Payment of workers for work not actu-

ally performed. _____

2. Below is a list of provisions found in four
important pieces of labor legislation. Identify
the act in which the provision is found by
putting either (A) for the Norris-La Guardia
Act, (B) for the Wagner Act, (C) for the Taft-
Hartley Act, or (D) for the Landrum-Griffin
Act in the space following each provision.
  a. Specified that contracts between a union
and an employer must contain a termination

or reopening clause. _____
  b. Established a board to investigate unfair
labor practices and to conduct elections

among workers. _____

c. Guaranteed to workers the right to organize unions and to bargain collectively. _____

d. Declared that yellow-dog contracts were unenforceable and limited the use of injunctions against unions. _____

e. Regulated union elections and finances and guaranteed certain rights to union members in their dealings with the union and its officers. _____

f. Outlawed the closed shop, jurisdictional and certain sympathy strikes, secondary boycotts, and featherbedding. _____

g. Provided a procedure whereby strikes affecting the health and safety of the nation might be delayed. _____

h. Outlawed company unions, antiunion discrimination in hiring and discharging workers, and interfering with the rights of workers to form unions. _____

■ SELF-TEST

Circle the T if the statement is true, the F if it is false.

1. An injunction is a court order which declares that combinations of workmen to raise wages are illegal. **T F**

2. Blacklisting was a device employed by early labor unions to cut off a firm's labor supply. **T F**

3. Union membership has increased in every year since the end of World War II. **T F**

4. The CIO was based on the principle of industrial unionism while the AFL was operated on the craft union philosophy. **T F**

5. The Taft-Hartley Act lists a number of unfair labor practices on the part of management. **T F**

6. Under the provisions of the Labor-Management Relations Act of 1947 the checkoff and featherbedding are prohibited. **T F**

7. The Teamsters and the United Mine Workers are important unions not affiliated with the AFL-CIO. **T F**

8. The four-points criteria employed by unions

in arguing for higher wages can also be used by management to resist higher wages and to argue for decreased wages. **T F**

9. Arbitration means the settlement of a dispute by a third party who renders a decision which the parties to the dispute have agreed in advance to accept. **T F**

10. The case made against the social desirability of labor unions involves the assertion that union practices contribute to both depression and inflation. **T F**

Underscore the letter that corresponds to the best answer.

1. About what percentage of all nonagricultural workers are members of unions? (a) 23%; (b) 28%; (c) 33%; (d) 38%.

2. Which of the following would not be used by an employer to prevent the organization of a genuine union among his employees? (a) lockout; (b) featherbedding; (c) company union; (d) yellow-dog contract.

3. Which one of the following was an essential part of Samuel Gompers' union philosophy? (a) industrial unionism; (b) support of the Democratic Party at the polls; (c) establishment of producer cooperatives operated by labor and management; (d) business unionism.

4. The Norris-La Guardia Act outlawed: (a) yellow-dog contracts; (b) the closed shop; (c) company unions; (d) blacklisting.

5. The Wagner Act outlawed: (a) company unions; (b) the closed shop; (c) the checkoff; (d) injunctions against unions.

6. The Taft-Hartley Act outlawed: (a) the nonunion shop; (b) the open shop; (c) the union shop; (d) the closed shop.

7. Which one of the following is *not* a provision of the Landrum-Griffin Act? (a) allows a worker to sue his union if the union denies the member certain rights; (b) unions are prohibited from making political contributions in elections for Federal offices; (c) requires regularly scheduled union elections and the use of secret ballots; (d) guarantees union members the right to attend union meetings, to vote and to participate in the meeting, and to nominate union officers.

8. If workers at the time they are hired have a choice of joining the union and paying dues or of not joining the union and paying no dues, there exists: (*a*) a union shop; (*b*) an open shop; (*c*) a nonunion shop; (*d*) a closed shop.

9. Which one of the following is not presently an unfair labor practice? (*a*) the refusal of either unions or companies to bargain in good faith; (*b*) the coercion of employees by unions to join and by companies not to join unions; (*c*) the practices of company and business unionism; (*d*) both jurisdictional strikes and secondary boycotts.

10. Which one of the following is *not* a part of the "case for labor unions"? (*a*) unions have to consider the effect of their wage demands upon employment and prices; (*b*) unions offset the monopsony power of producers and thereby increase the efficiency of resource allocation; (*c*) aggregate demand is the basic factor determining employment and prices, not the level of wage rates; (*d*) unions reduce labor mobility and thereby increase the efficiency and productivity of labor.

■ DISCUSSION QUESTIONS

1. What are the three phases in the history of labor unions in the United States? What was the law with respect to unions, what was the extent of unionization, and what were the principal events in each of these periods?

2. How were the courts able to retard the growth of unions between 1790 and 1930? How did employers attempt to limit union growth?

3. Explain the union philosophy of Samuel Gompers.

4. What were the chief provisions of the Norris-La Guardia Act and the Wagner Act?

5. Explain how the principles of the CIO differed from those on which the AFL was based.

6. Contrast the philosophy and policy embodied in the Wagner Act with that found in the Taft-Hartley Act.

7. What are the four main sections of the Taft-Hartley Act? What specific practices are outlawed by the act and what specific things are required of unions, union officers, and bargaining agreements?

8. Explain the major provisions of the Landrum-Griffin Act.

9. What were the forces which resulted in the merger of the AFL and CIO in 1955?

10. What do economists mean when they talk of stagnation in the labor movement in the United States? What evidence is there of stagnation? What are the probable causes of it?

11. Explain what usually constitute the "prerogatives of management."

12. What are the four arguments employed by labor (management) in demanding (resisting) higher wages? Why are these arguments "two-edged"?

13. What is meant by grievance procedure? Why is such a procedure so important in labor-management relations? In the typical labor-management contract found in the text, what are the four steps which may be used in settling grievances?

14. Do unions lead to a better or worse allocation of resources and to a higher or lower level of resource employment? Give the two extreme views on these questions.

15. What are the two extreme views on what the future public policy toward labor unions should be?

16. What is a right-to-work law? What arguments are presented in support of right-to-work laws by those who favor them? What arguments are advanced by labor unions in opposition to them?

THE ECONOMICS OF THE WAR INDUSTRY

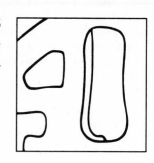

War and national defense require that scarce resources be used to produce military hardware and to staff the armed forces. Because the employment of scarce resources is the subject matter of economics, war and defense are a part of the study of economics. The group of private firms and public agencies that employ resources to produce military goods and services are known as the war industry.

This chapter on the war industry is *not* an examination of the cases for and against the war in Southeastern Asia. It does not debate the issue of whether the United States employs too large or too small a portion of its resources for that war in particular and for national defense in general. Appraising the *benefits* of the Vietnam war and of American defense is beyond the professional competence of economists and the subject matter of economics. All that economists can do is estimate the cost and examine the effects of the war industry upon the economy. And this is the purpose of Chapter 40: to look at the war industry as a user of scarce resources.

There are a variety of things the student should learn from Chapter 40. The more important things he should learn are (1) the size of and the cost to the American economy of the war industry; (2) the ways in which the Department of Defense—the Pentagon—differs from and is like a privately owned business firm; (3) the process employed to procure military hardware in the product markets of the economy and Galbraith's and Melman's

criticisms of this process; (4) the reasons for cost overruns in procuring military goods; (5) the case for and the objections to replacing the draft with a volunteer army; (6) the effects of military expenditures on national output and employment and the price level; (7) the problems of obtaining the peace dividend that would be available to the economy if the United States were to disarm; (8) the arguments offered in defense of the war industry; (9) the nature of the Schultze proposal; and (10) the reasons why two antagonistic nations remain armed even though both would gain economically from mutual disarmament.

■ CHAPTER OUTLINE

1. Current American military expenditures exceed $80 billion a year; and are about 40 percent of all Federal expenditures and 10 percent of the GNP.

2. The opportunity cost of the defense establishment equals the output of civilian goods and services sacrificed and depends upon the level of output the economy would produce if there were no defense expenditures.

3. A military establishment and its expenditures affect the allocation of the economy's resources.

a. Unlike a privately owned business firm, the military establishment does not sell its product in the market, is a nonprofit organization whose existence depends upon the existence of hostile military establishments in other nations, and does not compete in a free market to obtain most of the labor it uses.

b. The Department of Defense buys military hardware from private firms; and it has been suggested that they collude to raise the prices of military supplies and the size of the defense budget.

c. It is also contended that the DOD acts like a central-management office and military goods producers like its subsidiaries; and that motivated by the desire to expand, they have made unwise decisions.

d. The actual cost of procuring military goods often grossly exceeds the estimated cost because the DOD seems unable to control the costs of suppliers.

e. Using conscription to obtain military manpower conflicts with freedom of occupational choice.

f. A volunteer army has been suggested as a means of distributing military manpower costs more equitably, lessening the real cost of the armed forces, and restoring individual freedom of choice.

g. Critics of a volunteer army contend that it will increase the cost of maintaining an army, produce a professional military force to threaten democracy and political freedom, result in racial imbalance in the armed forces, and be too small for a nonnuclear world war.

4. A military establishment and its expenditures affect the stability of the economy.

a. Changes in military spending have contributed to economic instability since World War II; and military expenditures have been closely linked historically with inflation.

b. Should peace come and disarmament occur, the economy would realize a peace dividend if it adopted proper fiscal and monetary policies and planned reconversion efficiently.

5. In defense of the defense establishment it can be argued that:

a. critics of war have laid too much of the blame for the problems of American society on the war industry and some of these criticisms seem unjustified.

b. the military establishment preserves the peace which is necessary to the growth of the economy.

6. The extensive size of the military establishment and the uses to which the resources it employs could be put in solving domestic social problems has led to the suggestion that a new method is needed to determine national priorities.

7. The theory of games can be utilized to explain why nations arm; the dilemma of disarmament; and how longsightedness and third parties might prevent nations from arming.

■ IMPORTANT TERMS

Military–industrial complex

Peace dividend

Cost overrun

Pentagon capitalism

Dilemma of disarmament

■ FILL-IN QUESTIONS

1. In 1970 the military expenditures of the United States were about $_____ billion, about _____ percent of the GNP, and about _____ percent of all Federal expenditures.

2. The opportunity cost of the American defense posture is the _____ the economy foregoes by using resources for military purposes.

3. The military establishment is unlike a private business firm because it:

a. obtains its revenue from _____ and not from _____

b. is a _____ organization rather than a _____ seeking organization

c. depends for its existence upon the existence of _____

d. obtains most of its labor by _____ _____ it rather than by _____ in the labor market to obtain it.

4. The methods employed by the Department of Defense to procure military goods from private business firms have been criticized and it is contended that:

a. the military and weapons suppliers have a common interest in increasing the _____ *b.* the military—industrial complex has become a state-management system in which the Pentagon behaves like a _____ office and military goods producers like its _____; and that the goal of this system is to _____

c. the military is unable to enforce effective _____ controls upon suppliers, extends interest free credit to suppliers in the form of _____, and allows contractors to _____ inventions financed by public money

5. Those who believe in a volunteer army contend that it will more equitably _____ the cost of military manpower, that the cost of this manpower will _____ than the real cost of a conscript army, and that it will result in greater freedom of _____

6. The objections to a volunteer army are that it will increase the _____ of maintaining an army, produce an army of _____, result in _____ imbalance in the armed forces, and will be _____ if a nonnuclear world war must be fought.

7. Defense spending:
a. during wartime almost always results in inflation because governments fail to increase _____ by enough to prevent _____ inflation, and finance the war by _____ newly created _____

b. has contributed to economic _____ since the end of World War II.

8. A peace dividend is the additional _____ _____ an economy would be able to produce if it decreased its production of _____

9. To offset a large reduction in military expenditures requires that government do at least one of the following: _____

net taxes, _____ expenditures for nonmilitary goods, or follow a _____ money policy.

10. In defense of the American military establishment it can be argued that:
a. in a growing economy it is possible to produce both more _____ goods and more _____ **goods**

b. expenditures for space and defense have resulted in significant _____ benefits for the civilian economy

c. cost overruns are found both in the _____ _____ sector of the economy and in the nonmilitary agencies of the public sector; and are probably the _____ consequence of the kinds of products and transactions involved

d. military spending is inflationary only when government fails to employ the proper _____ _____ and _____ policies

e. military expenditures prevent a major military _____ and that this is a prerequisite for economic _____

11. Charles Schultze has proposed that a committee be formed to assess our _____ _____ and to evaluate our _____ and _____ needs.

12. The dilemma of disarmament:
a. is that both nations would _____ from mutual disarmament but each nation would be _____ if it alone disarmed

b. can be solved either by instilling _____ _____ in the two nations; or by having a _____ penalize those nations who arm (or fail to disarm)

■ **PROBLEMS AND PROJECTS**

1. On page 283 is a production possibilities curve showing the different combinations of military and civilian goods and services an economy is capable of producing.

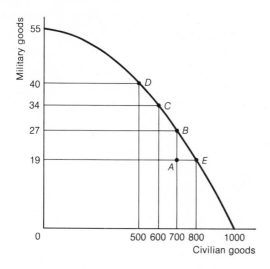

a. If both nations were disarmed, Avisannia could increase its payoff from _____ to _____ if it armed and Hortsylvania did not arm.

b. If Avisannia were armed and Hortsylvania were not, Hortsylvania could increase its payoff from _____ to _____ by arming.

c. If both nations were armed, Avisannia's payoff would decrease from _____ to _____ if it disarmed and Hortsylvania did not disarm.

d. If both nations were armed, mutual disarmament would increase each's payoff from _____ to _____.

e. Were both nations:

(1) disarmed a penalty of more than _____ would prevent each nation from arming

(2) armed a penalty of more than _____ would lead each nation to disarm

a. If the economy were at point *A* and moved to point *B*, the production of military goods would have increased by _____; and the cost of this increased production of military goods would have been _____ civilian goods.

b. If the economy were at point *B* and moved to point *C*, the production of military goods would have increased by _____; and the cost of this increased production of military goods would have been _____ civilian goods.

c. If the economy were at point *D* and disarmament occurred so that the economy could move to point *E*, the peace dividend would be _____ civilian goods.

d. If the economy were at point *D* and the economy moved to point *A* as a result of disarmament, the peace dividend would be only _____ civilian goods.

2. The diagram below shows the gains and losses to two nations, Avisannia and Hortsylvania, from arming and from disarming.

		Avisannia	
		Arm	Disarm
Hortsylvania	Arm	−3 / −3	−6 / +6
	Disarm	+6 / −6	+3 / +3

■ SELF-TEST

Circle the T if the statement is true, the F if it is false.

1. Economists are better able to estimate the benefits than the costs of defense spending.   T F

2. If the economy fully employed its resources in the absence of any military expenditures, the opportunity cost of military preparedness is zero.   T F

3. To prevent a cutback in defense spending from bringing about a recession it would be appropriate to increase taxes and follow a tight money policy.   T F

4. Most military hardware is not produced in government operated arsenals but by privately operated business firms.   T F

5. Galbraith argues that the relationship of the Department of Defense to the giant corporate suppliers of war goods is bilateral monopoly; and that the prices paid are approximately competitive.   T F

6. A volunteer armed force would shift a part of the cost of military manpower from draftees and reluctant volunteers to taxpayers.   T F

7. Since the end of World War II changes in military spending have resulted in economic instability in the American economy.   T F

8. It is not possible for an economy to produce both more military and more civilian goods.   **T F**

9. Defenders of the military argue that without a strong military posture peace is impossible and that without peace economic development and progress are impossible.

T F

10. The dilemma of disarmament is that only one nation benefits from mutual disarmament.

T F

Underscore the letter that corresponds to the best answer.

1. About what percent of the GNP and labor force of the American economy are used for military purposes? (a) 5%; (b) 10%; (c) 15%; (d) 20%.

2. Which of the following results in an over-estimation of the size of the war industry? (a) failure to include the spillover benefits of military expenditures to the civilian economy; (b) the use of conscript labor to staff the greater part of the armed forces; (c) the exclusion of veterans' benefits from the Department of Defense budget; (d) the inclusion of expenditures for space and atomic energy in the budgets of the NASA and the AEC.

3. The military establishment is like a private business firm because they both (a) have a problem in selling their product; (b) are monopolists; (c) are monopsonists; (d) employ labor represented by large labor unions.

4. The notion that the Department of Defense acts like a central-management office and producers of military goods like its subsidiaries is referred to as (a) the war industry; (b) the military–industrial complex; (c) Pentagon capitalism; (d) mutual deterrance.

5. Which of the following is *not* a part of the case for a volunteer army? (a) the monetary cost of a volunteer army would be less; (b) military manpower costs would be more equitably distributed; (c) a volunteer army is more consistent with freedom of occupational choice; (d) young people would make more rational decisions in choosing an occupation.

6. War almost always results in inflation because (a) the production of civilian goods decreases; (b) taxes rise; (c) governments fail to increase taxes; (d) governments borrow newly created money.

7. To prevent unemployment and recession when peace breaks out requires (a) a reduction in net taxes; (b) an increase in government nondefense expenditures; (c) an easy money policy; (d) at least one but not necessarily all of the above.

8. If society wishes to take a peace dividend in the form of more private consumption and investment (a) government nondefense expenditures should be increased; (b) tax rates should be reduced; (c) transfer payments should be reduced; (d) a tight money policy should be followed.

9. Those who would rebut criticism of the military put forth all but one of the following arguments. Which one? (a) military expenditures are always inflationary; (b) military expenditures result in significant spillover benefits for the civilian economy; (c) cost overruns are not peculiar to the military establishment; (d) more military goods and services do not require fewer civilian goods and services.

10. The proposal to establish a committee to assess national priorities came from (a) John Kenneth Galbraith; (b) Seymour Melman; (c) Charles L. Schultze; (d) Robert McNamara.

■ DISCUSSION QUESTIONS

1. Explain why military expenditures have risen from less than 1 percent of national output in the period prior to World War II to almost 10 percent today.

2. In what three ways may the dollar-and-cents figures for military expenditures in the United States understate the overall cost of the war industry? What effects have military spending had upon consumption, industrial concentration, geographic concentration, and research and development activities?

3. What is meant by the opportunity cost of national security? When will this cost be zero and when will it be greater than zero? What does foreign experience suggest about the opportunity cost of the military establishment?

4. In what ways is the military establishment unlike a private business firm? Are they alike in any way?

5. Explain how the Department of Defense procures war goods and why this procurement method has been subject to severe criticism.

6. Explain: (a) Pentagon capitalism; (b) change order; (c) "buy in, get well later"; and (d) progress payment.

7. What is the case for a volunteer army? What are the objections to a volunteer army?

8. Explain (a) why conscription results in a large and discriminatory tax on draftees and how a volunteer armed force would shift this tax to society as a whole; and (b) why the real cost of a volunteer army would be less than a conscripted army of the same size.

9. Does military spending lead to economic instability? Must it also result in inflation?

10. Explain what is meant by a "peace dividend." What fiscal and monetary policies should be followed if a potential peace dividend is to be realized? How does the mix of fiscal and monetary policies chosen determine the form in which this dividend is taken?

11. What are the structural problems that arise as a consequence of demobilization and disarmament? How severe are these problems likely to be?

12. What arguments can be put forth to defend the war industry and the military establishment against its critics?

13. What is the proposal advanced by Charles Schultze and why did he make this proposal?

14. What is meant by the dilemma of disarmament and how can this dilemma be solved?

15. Construct a simple payoff model to show why, when one nation arms, the end result is mutual armament; and why neither nation would disarm unilaterally.

THE SOCIAL IMBALANCE CONTROVERSY

The question of social imbalance is a relatively new one. Among respected economists there is a strong difference of opinion as to whether there is a social imbalance problem at all. But if there is such a problem it might well be *the* most important and serious economic problem the American economy will face in the years to come.

Chapter 41 does try to convince the student that this problem does in fact exist. Rather it tries to explain (1) what is meant by social imbalance; (2) the arguments and evidence presented by those who contend the problem does exist and is serious; (3) the arguments and evidence offered by those who believe that the problem does not exist, is not important, or cannot be solved by our economy without "incurring excessive costs"; and (4) the means which might be employed to eliminate or reduce social imbalance if it does exist. (In addition, the student is advised to give special attention to the alleged economic and political consequences of social imbalance; Wagner's Law; and the reasons why the actual output of social goods and services may not increase as rapidly as the demand for them.)

While the problem of social imbalance can be analyzed by using economic principles (theory), there will be no agreement among economists or students on the existence of the problem. The source of this disagreement will be neither theoretical nor factual but ethical. Those who believe that social imbalance exists believe that the distribution of the economy's scarce resources between the public and private sectors *is not right* and *ought* to allocate more resources to the public sector of the economy. Those who believe there is social imbalance believe that the distribution of resources is *right* and *ought not* to be changed. There is no practical way of measuring the benefits of publicly produced goods and services and of comparing these benefits with the benefits of privately produced goods and services. Whether there is social imbalance or social balance is, therefore, a value judgment—a question of what ought and what ought not to be, rather than a question of what is and what is not. But economists can attempt to explain why different groups have different values and what the political, economic, and social consequences of these different values will be. Describing this is the goal of Chapter 41.

■ CHAPTER OUTLINE

1. Many economists contend that there is a social imbalance in the United States today: too large an output of private goods and too small an output of social goods.

2. They argue that this distortion in the composition of the national output results in a misallocation of resources, economic instability, and a smaller growth rate.

3. Those who believe that this imbalance exists assert that as the American economy has grown and become more affluent the quantity of social goods and services demanded has increased more rapidly than the quantity supplied.

4. The demand for social goods has increased rapidly because of war, population growth, industrialization, urbanization, and the operation of Wagner's Law.

5. The existence of numerous and serious obstacles has prevented the supply of social goods from increasing as rapidly as the demand.

6. Critics of the social imbalance doctrine contend that social imbalance does not really exist; that if it did exist increased public spending would not necessarily help to solve the problem; and that the cost of reducing social imbalance would be substantial and greater than the benefits to be obtained.

7. If social imbalance does exist, what might be done to reduce or eliminate it?
a. The end of hot and cold war and disarmament would free resources for the greater production of nonmilitary public goods.
b. Economic growth would increase the ability of the economy to provide public goods without decreasing the quantities of private goods available.
c. Increased use of the sales tax might be a relatively painless and hidden means of transferring resources from the private to the public sector.

■ IMPORTANT TERMS

Social imbalance
Social balance
Wagner's Law

Balance of interests effect
Tax competition

■ FILL-IN QUESTIONS

1. Social imbalance means that too many resources are allocated to the production of

_____ and too few
to the production of _____;
whether there is social imbalance in the United States today is a(n) _____
questions rather than a factual question.

2. Evidence of the presence of social imbalance in the economy is the fact that the American consumer spent more on _____

_____
in 1970 than government in the United States spent on highways; and that more was spent

on _____,

_____,

and _____
than was spent on research and development.

3. Since 1939 real nondefense government expenditures as a percentage of real nondefense GNP have _____

to _____ percent.

4. Proponents of the social imbalance doctrine contend that social imbalance results in

_____,

_____,

and _____
in the economy.

5. Economists who see social imbalance in the contemporary American economy argue

that the _____ for social goods and services has increased more rapidly than their _____.
The former tends to increase as the real per capita income of the economy increases because consumers want relatively more public goods and relatively fewer private goods; this

is called _____

6. Briefly, what are the six obstacles which prevent the supply of public goods and services from keeping pace with the growing demand for them?

a. _____

b. _____

c. _____

d. _____

e. _____

f. _____

7. Critics of the social imbalance doctrine contend that social imbalance really does not exist. They point out that _____

_____ is not sufficient to allow a large amount of spending for nonessentials, that the output of certain important nondefense public goods

has increased more rapidly than _____

_____,

and that there are certain forces such as ___

_____,

_____,

and _____ which facilitate the expansion of the output of social goods.

8. The critics also argue that:

a. Increased government spending will not reduce social imbalance because:

(1) _____

(2) _____

b. The benefits to be obtained from the reduction of social imbalance would entail substantial costs such as:

(1) _____

(2) _____

(3) _____

9. Two ways in which government spending for goods and services might be increased without reducing the output of private goods

and services would be to obtain _____

_____ and to allocate

all or a large part of the economy's _____

_____

to the increased output of public goods.

10. If the public sector is to increase its relative share of the national output, one method of transferring resources to the public sector will be to increase public revenue

through the increased use of the _____ tax.

■ PROBLEMS AND PROJECTS

1. Since the following questions have no factual answers there are no answers given in the Answer section at the back of the book. The questions are designed to help you find for yourself the answer to the ethical question of social imbalance.

a. List five specific and most important types of social goods and services which you personally believe should be produced in greater quantities:

(1) _____

(2) _____

(3) _____

(4) _____

(5) _____

b. Now list five specific and most important types of private goods and services which you personally believe should be produced in smaller quantities:

(1) _____

(2) _____

(3) _____

(4) _____

(5) _____

c. What would you estimate would be the extra cost involved if the five items in (a) were increased by the amounts you believe neces-

sary? $_____ How do you propose that governments obtain this extra revenue?

_____

d. How do you propose to induce consumers to want less and the economy to produce

fewer of the items you listed in (b)? _____

_____

e. Do you believe that there is an imbalance between the output of social and the output of

private goods? _____ Why do you

believe this? _____

f. Ignoring military expenditures, do you believe that governments supply too much of

some social goods and too few of others? ___

_____ If your answer is yes, which things

would you have government supply less of?

_____

Which more of? _____
g. Do you believe that the private sector of the economy would be better off if it had less of certain private goods and more of some other private goods? _____ If your answer is yes, which private goods should it have less of and which more of? _____

_____

How would you attempt to achieve the greater and the smaller consumption of these items?

_____

■ SELF-TEST

Circle the T if the statement is true, the F if it is false.

1. Those who argue that there is social imbalance in the American economy contend that as the economy has developed the production of private goods has been slighted in favor of public goods.   **T   F**

2. Real nondefense government spending in the United States was approximately the same in 1970 as it was in 1939.   **T   F**

3. Economists who believe social imbalance exists in the United States contend that it decreases the rate at which the economy is able to grow.   **T   F**

4. The alleged cause of social imbalance is the failure of the demand for public goods and services to increase as rapidly as the supply of public goods and services.   **T   F**

5. The characteristic of social goods which impedes their production is that they do not become a part of a this-for-that transaction.   **T   F**

6. Tax competition refers to the attempts of states and communities to attract new firms and employment opportunities by taxing firms at lower rates than other states and communities do.   **T   F**

7. The benefits of social goods and services tend to be remote and uncertain to the individual taxpayer who is not able to select and

pay for only the social goods and services he desires.   **T   F**

8. Inflation, according to those who argue the case of social imbalance, tends to create strong public pressure for reduced government spending and taxes.   **T   F**

9. The critics of the social imbalance thesis point out that the typical individual citizen tends to view an increase in the supply of public goods and services as costless to him.   **T   F**

10. An end to the Vietnam war, disarmament, and economic growth would automatically produce a relative increase in the public sector's share of national output.   **T   F**

Underscore the letter that corresponds to the best answer.

1. Which of the following economists would argue that there is social balance in the United States? (a) John Kenneth Galbraith; (b) Alvin H. Hansen; (c) Francis M. Bator; (d) Henry C. Wallich.

2. In 1970 the nondefense expenditures of government in the United States were approximately what percentage of the nondefense GNP? (a) 7.5; (b) 11; (c) 13.5; (d) 16.

3. Which of the following is *not* one of the alleged results of social imbalance in the United States? (a) the satisfaction (total utility) received from the economy's resources is less than is possible; (b) a rate of economic growth that is impossible for the economy to maintain; (c) unstable consumer spending, employment, and national output; (d) military strength that is less in proportion to GNP than is the military strength of the U.S.S.R.

4. Wagner's Law states that in a growing economy the output of *private* goods and services: (a) increases absolutely and decreases relatively; (b) decreases absolutely and increases relatively; (c) increases both absolutely and relatively; (d) decreases both absolutely and relatively.

5. Which of the following is *not* a factor that would prevent the supply of public goods and services from growing as rapidly as the demand for them? (a) Wagner's Law; (b) the sales promotion (advertising) activities of producers of private goods and services; (c) the effects of inflation; (d) tax competition.

6. The very mechanisms and mores of capitalism, it is alleged, inhibit the expansion of the public sector. Among other considerations, this refers to: (a) the underrepresentation of the urban and industrial segments of the population in the state and national legislatures; (b) the tendency of the population to think of the existing level of taxation as the acceptable level; (c) the tendency of a large part of the population to view public goods as wasteful, as of secondary importance, and as a necessary evil; (d) the attempt of many people to "keep up with the Joneses."

7. Economists who deny the social imbalance thesis offer several counterarguments to the arguments of those who have advanced the thesis. Which of the following is *not* one of the counterarguments? (a) many of the more important "new needs" of society are for private rather than public goods; (b) the transfer of resources from the private to the public sector would be economically depressing; (c) a relative increase in the supply of public goods would be accompanied by a loss of personal freedom; (d) an increase in public and a decrease in private spending will not necessarily result in the substitution of high-priority goods and services for low-priority goods and services.

8. The "balance of interests" effect is used as an argument against increased government spending to redress social imbalance. This effect refers to: (a) the ability of a combination of special interest groups to have their pet low-social-priority projects enacted into law; (b) the tendency of government spending to increase across the board instead of merely increasing for the higher priority projects; (c) the equilibrium that necessarily exists between the public and private sectors of the economy when the political process of a nation is really democratic; (d) the near equality between the rates at which nonmilitary GNP and the expenditures for nonmilitary public goods and services have increased since World War II.

9. Economists who see social imbalance as a serious problem and a relative increase in government expenditures as a corrective force advocate the greater use of what type of tax to finance the increased expenditures? (a) sales tax; (b) personal income tax; (c) corporate income tax; (d) corporate excess profits tax.

■ DISCUSSION QUESTIONS

1. Explain what is meant by social imbalance. Why is the question of whether there is social imbalance an ethical question?

2. What evidence is there that social imbalance does exist in the United States today? What evidence is there that it does not exist?

3. If there is social imbalance in the American economy, why does it "constitute a first-rank economic problem" in the view of some economists?

4. What are the alleged causes of social imbalance in American capitalism? In your answer use the concepts of increasing demand for and increasing supply of public goods and services; and explain why the former tends to increase both relatively and absolutely as the real per capita income of the economy rises.

5. Explain in detail how each of the following tends to impede the increased output of public (social) goods and services; (a) the mechanisms and mores of capitalism; (b) political realities in the United States; (c) the character of social goods and services; (d) tax problems; (e) advertising and emulation; (f) inflation.

6. Why do those economists who do not believe there is social imbalance in the American economy argue that: (a) there is no serious imbalance; (b) increased government spending would not reduce or eliminate it; (c) the costs of achieving balance would be excessive?

7. If there is social imbalance in the United States, what means or policies might be used to narrow the gap between the output of private goods and public goods?

8. Is there or is there not serious social imbalance in the United States today? Justify your conclusion. What should be done *if* serious imbalance does exist? Explain why you advocate this solution.

INTERNATIONAL TRADE AND THE ECONOMICS OF FREE TRADE

This is the first of three chapters dealing with international trade and finance. International trade is a subject with which most students have little firsthand experience. For this reason many of the terms, concepts, and ideas encountered will be unfamiliar and may not be readily grasped. However, most of this material is fairly simple if the student will take some pains to examine it. The ideas and concepts employed are new, but they are not especially complex or difficult.

At the beginning it is essential to recognize that international trade is important to the United States. Exports from and imports into the American economy are both about $60 billion a year. The United States *absolutely* is the greatest exporting and importing nation in the world. In *relative* terms, other nations have exports and imports which are larger percentages of their GNPs. They may export and import more than 40 percent of GNP, while the United States exports and imports only about 4 percent of GNP. It is equally important for the student to understand from the beginning that international trade differs from the trade that goes on within nations. Different nations use different monies, not just one money; resources are less mobile internationally than they are *intra*nationally; and governments interfere more with foreign than they do with domestic trade.

But while foreign trade differs from domestic trade in these three ways, nations trade for the same basic reason that people within a nation trade: to take advantage of the benefits of specialization. The student has already examined the gains that result when there is specialization based on comparative advantage; he is urged to review pages 44 through 46 in Chapter 3. To supplement this review, the author of the text reexamines specialization and trade between two nations. This is the most important section of Chapter 42. The student should be sure he understands (1) what comparative advantage is, (2) why nations gain when they specialize in commodities for whose production they have a comparative advantage, meanwhile trading these commodities for the commodities in which other nations specialize, (3) what is meant by the terms of trade, and (4) how increasing costs limit but do not halt specialization and trade between nations.

The result of specialization and trade is a better allocation of the world's resources—a higher standard of living in all nations. Assuming trade is not restricted by tariffs, quotas, and other barriers, and ignoring transportation costs, there is also a tendency for the prices of products and of resources to be the same in every country. This is the case for free trade: every nation gets more output from its resources than it could if it did not specialize and trade. The case for protection —for barriers, quotas, and the like—is most eagerly advanced by those who will benefit from trade barriers even though their nations and economies will suffer. Those who favor protection advance a number of arguments to support their case. The student should examine the five arguments for protection which conclude the chapter in order to find the fallacies and inaccuracies in them.

■ CHAPTER OUTLINE

1. Trade between nations is large enough and unique enough to warrant special attention.

a. While the relative importance of international trade to the United States is less than it is to other nations, this country's imports and exports are both about 4 per cent of its GNP and $59 and $63 billion a year, respectively. This trade provides both important raw materials and markets for finished goods; and net exports have a multiplier effect.

b. International trade has three characteristics which distinguish it from domestic trade.

2. Specialization based on comparative advantage and trade between nations are advantageous because the world's resources are not equally distributed and the efficient production of different commodities necessitates different methods and combinations of resources.

3. A simple hypothetical example explains comparative advantage and the gains from trade.

a. Suppose the world is composed of only two nations, who are each capable of producing two different commodities and whose production possibilities curves are different straight lines (whose cost ratios are fixed and unequal).

b. With different cost ratios, each nation will have a comparative advantage in the production of one of the two products. And each nation finds that if it specializes entirely in that product, it can obtain the other product by trading at a cost lower than its own production cost.

c. The ratio at which one product is traded for another—the terms of trade—lies between the cost ratios of the two nations.

d. Each nation gains from this trade because specialization permits a greater total output from the same resources and a better allocation of the world's resources.

e. If costs ratios in the two nations are not constant, specialization may not be complete.

4. The major effects of international trade and specialization are:

a. A more efficient use of world resources.

b. A tendency toward equal prices for each product throughout the world.

c. A tendency toward equal prices for each resource throughout the world.

5. Nations may retard international trade by erecting artificial barriers.

a. Tariffs and import quotas, established for a variety of reasons, are the principal barriers to trade.

b. The argument for free trade is that it leads to a better allocation of resources and a higher standard of living in the world.

c. There are several arguments for protection, most of which are fallacious or based on half-truths.

■ IMPORTANT TERMS

Review

Comparative advantage	**Terms of trade**
Net exports	**Production possibilities curve**
Specialization	

New

Labor-(land-, capital-) intensive commodity	**Tariff**
	Revenue tariff
Cost ratio	**Protective tariff**
Trading possibilities line	**Import quota**

■ FILL-IN QUESTIONS

1. Special attention is devoted to international trade because resources are _____ between nations than within a nation, because every nation employs a different _____ and because international trade is subject to more _____ than domestic trade.

2. The imports and exports of the United States amount to about _____% of the economy's GNP or between $_____ and $_____ billion.

3. Ranked in order of their importance the three principal exports of the United States are

_____,

_____,

and _____;

the three most important imports are _____

_____,

_____,

and _____

4. The nations of the world tend to specialize in those goods in the production of which

they have a _____,
to export these goods, and to import those goods in the production of which they have a

_____

5. Nations specialize and trade because it is more efficient: it enables each nation to obtain

_____

from the same quantity of _____;

and because the distribution of _____

in the world is _____ and the efficient production of different products re-

quires _____

6. If the cost ratio in country X is 4 Panama hats equal 1 pound of bananas, while in country Y, 3 Panama hats equal 1 pound of bananas:

a. Hats are relatively (expensive, inexpen-

sive) _____ in country X and

bananas relatively _____

b. Hats are relatively _____ in

country Y and bananas relatively _____

c. X has a comparative advantage and should

specialize in the production of _____

_____ and Y has a comparative advantage and should specialize in the pro-

duction of _____

d. When X and Y specialize and trade, the terms of trade will be somewhere between

_____ and _____ hats for each pound of

bananas; and will depend upon _____

_____

e. When the actual terms of trade turn out to be 3½ hats for 1 pound of bananas, the cost of obtaining:

(1) 1 Panama hat has been decreased from

_____ to _____ pounds of bananas in Y

(2) 1 pound of bananas has been decreased

from _____ to _____ Panama hats in X

7. International specialization is not com-

plete because the _____

of producing a good _____
as a nation produces more of that good.

8. The economic effects of international trade and specialization are:

a. The more _____ use of the world's resources.

b. A tendency for the _____ of a product to be the same in all nations.

c. A tendency for the price of a _____
to be the same in all nations.

9. The two most widely employed barriers to

international trade are _____

and _____,

which nations establish in order to _____

_____,

_____,

_____,

and _____

10. The basic argument for free trade is that

it results in _____

and _____;
five arguments for protection are:

a. _____

b. _____

c. _____

d. _____

e. _____

■ PROBLEMS AND PROJECTS

1. Shown below are the production possibilities curves for two nations: the United States and Chile. Suppose these two nations do not currently engage in international trade and specialization, and suppose that points A and a show the combinations of wheat and copper they now produce and consume.

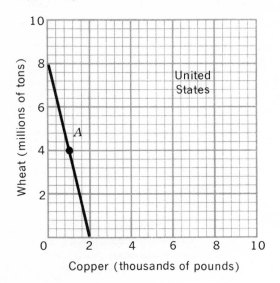

Copper (thousands of pounds)

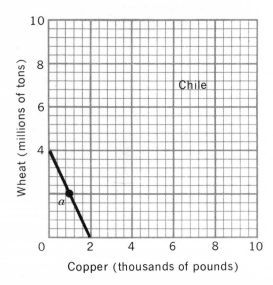

Copper (thousands of pounds)

a. The straightness of the two curves indicates that the cost ratios in the two nations are

_____

b. Examination of the two curves reveals that the cost ratio in:

(1) The United States is _____ million tons of wheat for _____ thousand pounds of copper.

(2) Chile is _____ million tons of wheat for _____ thousand pounds of copper.

c. If these two nations were to specialize and trade wheat for copper,

(1) The United States would specialize in the production of wheat because _____

_____

(2) Chile would specialize in the production of copper because _____

d. The terms of trade, if specialization and trade occur, will be greater than 2 and less than 4 million tons of wheat for 1 thousand pounds of copper because _____

_____

e. Assume the terms of trade turn out to be 3 million tons of wheat for 1 thousand pounds of copper. Draw in the trading possibilities curve for the United States and Chile.

f. With these trading possibilities curves, suppose the United States decides to consume 5 million tons of wheat and 1 thousand pounds of copper while Chile decides to consume 3 million tons of wheat and 1 thousand pounds of copper. The gains from trade to:

(1) The United States are _____ million tons of wheat and _____ thousand pounds of copper.

(2) Chile are _____ million tons of wheat and _____ thousand pounds of copper.

2. Imagine that France and the United States do not specialize or trade. Wine is relatively inexpensive in France and chicken is relatively expensive. In the United States, however, wine is relatively expensive and chicken is relatively inexpensive. This is the result of the relative scarcity and high price of resources used to produce chicken in France and of the relative scarcity and high price of wine-producing resources in the United States.

a. When these two nations begin to specialize and trade, the total demand for:

(1) French-produced wine will (increase, decrease) _____ and French-produced chicken will _____

(2) American-produced wine will _____ and American-produced chicken will _____

b. As a result of these changes in demand,

(1) The price of wine in France will (rise, fall) _____ and the price of wine in the United States will _____ until these two prices are _____

(2) The price of chicken in France will ____ _____ and the price of chicken in the United States will _____ until these two prices are _____

c. Because the demand for resources is a derived demand,

(1) The demand for resources used in France to produce the wine will _____ and the demand for resources used to produce chicken in France will _____

(2) The demand for resources used in the United States to produce wine will _____ and the demand for resources used to produce chicken in the United States will _____

d. These changes in the demands for resources cause the prices paid:

(1) In France for wine-producing resources to _____ and for chicken-producing resources to _____ until they are _____

(2) In the United States for wine-producing resources to _____ and for chicken-producing resources to _____ until they are _____

e. The result is that:

(1) France will shift resources from the production of _____ to the production of _____

(2) The United States will shift resources from the production of _____ to the production of _____

■ SELF-TEST

Circle the T if the statement is true, the F if it is false.

1. Nations tend to produce and export those goods in the production of which they have a comparative advantage.   (T) F

2. The principal import of the United States is nonferrous metals.   T (F)

3. The principal export of the United States is machinery.   (T) F

Use the following production possibilities to answer questions 4, 5, and 6 below and to answer multiple-choice questions 4 and 5.

NEPAL PRODUCTION POSSIBILITIES TABLE

Product	Production alternatives					
	A	B	C	D	E	F
Yak fat	0	4	8	12	16	20
Camel hides	40	32	24	16	8	0

KASHMIR PRODUCTION POSSIBILITIES TABLE

Product	Production alternatives					
	A	B	C	D	E	F
Yak fat	0	3	6	9	12	15
Camel hides	60	48	36	24	12	0

4. In Kashmir the cost of 1 camel hide is 3 units of yak fat.   T (F)

5. Nepal has a comparative advantage in producing camel hides.   T (F)

6. With specialization and trade, the trading possibilities curves of both nations would move to the right of their production possibilities curves.   (T) F

7. Increasing production costs tend to prevent specialization among trading nations from being complete.   Ⓣ F

8. The case for free trade is that it will result in the more efficient use of the world's resources and greater world output.   Ⓣ F

Underscore the letter that corresponds to the best answer.

1. International trade is a special and separate area of economic study for several reasons. Which one of the following is *not* one of these reasons: Ⓐ international trade is based on the principle of comparative advantage; (b) resources are less mobile internationally than domestically; (c) countries engaged in international trade use different monies; (d) international trade is subject to a greater number of political restrictions than domestic trade.

2. In 1970 the imports of the United States amounted to approximately what percentage of the United States's GNP? (a) 2%; Ⓑ 4%; (c) 6%; (d) 8%.

3. Nations would not need to engage in trade if: (a) all products were produced from the same combinations of resources; (b) world resources were evenly distributed among nations; (c) world resources were perfectly mobile; Ⓓ all of the above.

Use the tables preceding true-false question 4 to answer the following two questions.

4. If Napal and Kashmir engage in trade, the terms of trade will be: Ⓐ between 2 and 4 camel hides for 1 unit of yak fat; (b) between ⅓ and ½ units of yak fat for 1 camel hide; (c) between 3 and 4 units of yak fat for 1 camel hide; (d) between 2 and 4 units of yak fat for 1 camel hide.

5. If Nepal and Kashmir, in the absence of trade between them, both produced combination C, the gains from trade would be: Ⓐ 6 units of yak fat; (b) 8 units of yak fat; (c) 6 units of yak fat and 8 camel hides; (d) 8 units of yak fat and 6 camel hides.

6. Which of the following is *not* one of the effects when nations begin to specialize and trade? Ⓐ a shift of resources away from the production of commodities in which nations have comparative advantages; (b) a fall in the prices of resources which were relatively expensive; (c) a rise in the prices of products which were relatively inexpensive; (d) an increased demand for relatively inexpensive products and resources.

7. Which one of the following is characteristic of tariffs? (a) they prevent the importation of goods from abroad; (b) they specify the maximum amounts of specific commodities which may be imported during a given period of time; Ⓒ they often protect domestic producers from foreign competition; (d) they enable nations to reduce their exports and increase their imports during periods of depression.

8. Which one of the following arguments for protection is the least fallacious and most pertinent in the United States today? Ⓐ the military self-sufficiency argument; (b) the increase-domestic-employment argument; (c) the protect-high-wages argument; (d) the infant-industry argument.

■ DISCUSSION QUESTIONS

1. Why do nations specialize in certain products and export their surplus production of these foods at the same time that they are importing other goods? Why do they not use the resources employed to produce the surpluses which they export to produce the goods which they import?

2. In what ways is international specialization and trade limited? In what ways is international trade different from the trade which takes place within a nation?

3. In relative and absolute terms, how important is international trade to the United States? What are the principal exports and imports of the American economy? What commodities used in the economy come almost entirely from abroad, and what American industries sell large percentages of their output abroad?

4. What two facts—one dealing with the distribution of the world's resources and the other related to the technology of producing different products—are the basis for trade among nations?

5. Explain (a) the theory or principle of comparative advantage; (b) what is meant by and what determines the terms of trade; and (c) the gains from trade.

6. What effects does the commencement of specialization and trade among nations have upon (a) the allocation of the trading nations'

resources, (b) resource prices in the trading nations, and (c) the prices of products in the nations that trade?

7. How are tariffs and import quotas used to restrict international trade? Why do nations wish to restrict trade?

8. What is the "case for free trade"? What is the "case for protection"? How valid and pertinent to the United States is each of the five basic arguments for protection?

THE BALANCE
OF PAYMENTS
AND EXCHANGE RATES

In the last chapter the student learned *why* nations engage in international trade. In Chapter 43 he will learn *how* nations using different monies are able to trade among themselves. The means they employ to overcome the difficulties that result because of the use of different monies is fairly simple. When a nation wishes to buy a good or service, make a loan, or present a gift in another nation, it *buys* some of the money used in the foreign nation. It pays for the foreign money with some of its own money. In other words, the nation exchanges its own money for foreign money. And when a nation sells a good or service abroad or receives a loan or a gift from abroad and obtains foreign money, it *sells* this foreign money—often called foreign exchange—in return for some of its own money. That is, it exchanges foreign money for its own money. The price a country pays for or is paid for foreign exchange is the foreign exchange rate. And like most prices, the foreign exchange rate is determined by the demand for and the supply of foreign money.

As the student knows from the last chapter, nations buy and sell large quantities of goods and services across national boundaries. But nations also make and receive gifts and loans abroad, buy and sell gold internationally, and own foreign bank accounts and foreign currency. At the end of a year, nations summarize their foreign sales and purchases of goods and services, their gifts and loans, and the changes in the amounts of gold and for-

eign money they own. This summary is a nation's international balance of payments: a record of how it obtained foreign exchange during the year and what it did with that money. Of course, all foreign money obtained was used for some purpose—it did not evaporate—and consequently the balance of payments *always* balances. The international balance of payments is an extremely important and useful device for understanding the amounts and kinds of international transactions in which a nation engages. But it also enables us to understand such things as international equilibrium and disequilibrium, balance of payments surpluses and deficits, and gold gains and losses, as well as the causes of these problems and how to deal with them.

Probably the most difficult sections of the chapter are concerned with what economists call international disequilibrium and the means by which international disequilibrium can be eliminated. Here the student should pay particular attention to: (1) exactly what is meant by international equilibrium and disequilibrium; (2) how foreign exchange rates which fluctuate will help to correct disequilibrium; (3) the disadvantages of freely fluctuating exchange rates; (4) how changing price and income levels help to eliminate disequilibrium; (5) the advantages and disadvantages of changing price and income levels as a device for correcting disequilibrium; (6) how nations may obtain international equilibrium through government regulation; and (7) the advantages and disadvantages of government controls.

One last word for the student. This chapter is filled with new terms. Some of these are just special words used in international economics to mean things with which the student is already familiar. Be very sure you learn what all of the new terms mean. It will simplify your comprehension of this chapter and enable you to understand more readily the international economic and financial problems and policies examined in the next chapter.

■ CHAPTER OUTLINE

1. Trade between two nations differs from domestic trade because the monies of both nations are used.

a. For example, American exports create a demand for dollars and a supply of foreign money. They increase the number of dollars owned by Americans (or decrease the amount of foreign money owned by foreigners). American exports earn the monies to pay for American imports.

b. American imports create a supply of dollars and a demand for foreign money. They decrease the number of dollars owned by Americans (or increase the amount of foreign money owned by foreigners). American imports use up the monies obtained by exporting.

2. The international balance of payments for a nation is a record of its sales to and purchases from all other nations in the world. It contains eight major sections.

a. The first three sections record a nation's exports of goods and services, its imports of these things, and the difference between exports and imports—its balance of trade.

b. The next three sections record net remittances (private gifts), net governmental transactions (loans and gifts), and net capital movements (loans and investments).

c. The seventh section records the amount due to or from other nations as a result of the transactions in the first six sections.

d. The last section indicates how the amount due to or from other nations was financed or balanced: with gold or with changes in the amounts of one nation's money owned by foreign nations (international monetary reserves).

e. A nation may lose gold or money to other nations even if it has exported more goods and services than it has imported (that is, even if it has a balance of trade surplus). This occurs when the amounts it gives and invests abroad exceed the size of its balance of trade surplus.

3. A nation has a disequilibrium in its international balance of payments when the gold and international reserves it owns increase or decrease. An increase is a balance of payments surplus and a decrease is a deficit.

a. Just like an individual family, a nation has a surplus or deficit when it spends, gives, and invests less or more than its income.

b. The autonomous transactions are recorded in the first six sections of the international balance of payments and the accommodating transactions in the last section. The latter must make (or accommodate) themselves to the former.

4. When a nation has a payments surplus or deficit and there is international disequilibrium, one of three kinds of adjustments take place to bring about equilibrium.

a. Freely fluctuating exchange rates tend to increase (decrease) a nation's outpayments and decrease (increase) its inpayments if it began with a payments surplus (deficit).

b. Price and income levels in a nation with a payments surplus (deficit) tend to rise (fall), increase (decrease) outpayments, and decrease (increase) inpayments to restore equilibrium.

(1) Such adjustments affect price levels, the level and distribution of real income, and employment in the nations involved; and these effects may be unwanted by the nations.

(2) The international gold standard was one example of a system which worked in this way and kept exchange rates relatively stable.

c. Public controls are often employed by a nation to eliminate its payments deficit.

(1) The nation may reduce the price of its money to foreigners—devalue its money—and thus increase the price of foreign monies to its citizens in order to increase inpayments and decrease outpayments.

(2) It may also use tariffs, quotas, and subsidies to expand exports (inpayments) and reduce imports (outpayments) without changing exchange rates.

■ IMPORTANT TERMS

Rate of exchange
(foreign exchange
rate)

International balance
of payments

Balance of trade

(Balance of) trade
surplus

(Balance of) trade
deficit

Remittance

Net capital movement

Financing (balancing)
transactions

(Balance of) pay-
ments deficit

(Balance of) pay-
ments surplus

International mone-
tary reserves

International
equilibrium

International
disequilibrium

Autonomous
transactions

Accommodating
transactions

Freely fluctuating
exchange rate

Exchange rate
depreciation

Exchange rate
appreciation

International gold
standard

Gold export point

Gold import point

Foreign exchange
control

Currency devaluation

Currency depreciation

Trade controls

■ FILL-IN QUESTIONS

1. The rate of exchange for the French franc

is the number of _____

which an American must pay to obtain _____

_____

2. When the rate of exchange for the Ger-
man mark is 25 cents, the rate of exchange

for the dollar is _____ marks.

3. American _____ or foreign

_____ create a demand for for-
eign money and a supply of dollars; American

_____ or foreign _____
create a demand for dollars and a supply of
foreign money.

4. American exports and foreign imports (in-

crease, decrease) _____ the
amount of foreign money owned by Americans

or _____ the number of dollars

owned by foreigners, and _____
the money supply in the United States while

it _____
the money supply in foreign nations.

5. The eight principal sections in a nation's
international balance of payments are:

a. _____

b. _____

c. _____

d. _____

e. _____

f. _____

g. _____

h. _____

6. The balance of trade is the difference be-

tween a nation's exports and imports of _____

_____,

_____,

and _____.
If a nation's exports of these items are greater
than its imports of them, it has a balance of

trade _____

7. Net capital movements record the _____

_____ and _____
which one nation makes in other nations. The
financing (or balancing) transactions record

the changes in a nation's holdings of _____

_____ and _____
and in the amount of its money owned by
foreigners.

8. A nation has a balance of payments sur-

plus (deficit) when its _____

(_____) exceeds its _____

(_____), and when it gains (loses)

_____ and/or _____
and the amount of its money owned by for-

eigners _____ (_____).

9. A nation is in international disequilibrium

when it has either a payments _____

or payments _____ and is in
equilibrium when it has neither.

10. A country can have a trade surplus *and* a payments deficit if it _____, _____, and _____ more abroad than its trade surplus.

11. The accommodating transactions are gains and losses of _____, _____, and _____. Other transactions in the international balance of payments are _____ transactions.

12. The three mechanisms for eliminating international disequilibrium are _____, _____, and _____

13. If foreign exchange rates fluctuate freely and a nation has a balance of payments surplus, the price of that nation's money in the foreign exchange market will tend to _____

and the price of foreign exchange in that nation will tend to _____. As these changes take place, the nation's inpayments will _____ and its outpayments will _____ to reduce the surplus.

14. There are three problems which arise when foreign exchange rates fluctuate freely: The _____ associated with flexible rates tend to _____

_____

trade, a nation's _____ can be worsened, and fluctuating exports and imports can affect _____ and _____ in an economy.

15. A nation is on the gold standard when it _____ and _____

16. If the nations of the world are on the gold standard, rates of exchange will depend

upon _____ and _____; and the rate will only fluctuate between the _____ and the _____

17. Assuming exchange rates are stable and a nation has a balance of payments deficit:
a. The money supply and price level in that nation will _____
b. This will make things bought at home (more, less) _____ expensive and things bought abroad _____ expensive.

c. As a result this country will _____ the amount it buys and _____ the amount it sells in the rest of the world.

d. This, in turn, _____ this country's outpayments and _____ its inpayments, thereby reducing or eliminating its balance of payments deficit.

18. The principal advantage of using changing price and income levels to correct balance of payments deficits or surpluses is _____

_____.
The chief disadvantage is that nations must also accept changes in _____,

_____,

and _____ in order to have international equilibrium.

19. When a nation with a payments deficit employs exchange controls to obtain international equilibrium, the government of that nation _____ the rate of exchange in order to reduce the

_____

of that nation to the level of its _____ and the government will also have to _____

_____

foreign exchange; _____

and _____

tend to increase in those nations which employ exchange controls and to decrease in other nations.

20. Nations may also attempt to eliminate a balance of payments deficit by placing _____

_____ and _____

on imports and by _____ exports.

■ PROBLEMS AND PROJECTS

1. Use the hypothetical international balance of payments data for the United States given in the table below.

	Dollars (in billions)
Net remittances	−1.5
¹ Income from U.S. investments abroad	+7.3
³ Capital outflow	−10.2
⁴ Increase in liquid dollar balances held by foreigners	+3.9
² Imports of goods	−31.1
² Income from foreign investments in the United States	−1.8
⁴ Decrease in United States holdings of gold and foreign currencies	+0.7
² Imports of services	−6.2
³ Capital inflow	+3.0
¹ Exports of goods	+32.5
¹ Exports of services	+8.1
Net government transactions	−4.7

a. Compute with the appropriate sign (+ or −):

(1) United States exports: $ +47.9

(2) United States imports: $ −39.1

(3) Net capital movements: $ −7.2

(4) Financing transactions: $ +4.6

b. Using the data and your computations in (a), complete the United States balance of international payments below. (Use Table 43–1 in the text as a model and assume that there are no errors or omissions.)

(1) U S exports $ 47.9
(1a) Goods 32.5
(1b) Services 8.1
(1c) Inc. from Invest. 7.3
(2) U S Imports −39.1
(2a) Goods −31.1
(2b) Services −6.2
(2c) Inc. from foreign Inv. −1.8
(3) Net balance due +8.8
(4) Net remittances −1.5
(5) Net govern. transact. −4.7
(6) Net Capital movements −7.2
(6a) US capital outflow −10.2
(6b) Foreign capital inflow +3.0
(7) Balance due US tor. −4.6
(8a) Decrease in US holdings +0.7
(8b) Increase in Liquid dollars +3.9

c. The United States had a balance of payments deficit of $ 4.6

d. The autonomous transactions amounted to (use the proper sign) $ +4.6 and the accommodating transactions to $ −4.6

2. Below are a series of foreign exchange rates for the British pound. For each of these rates compute the rate of exchange for the American dollar:

$2.00: £ 1/2 $4.00: £ 1/4
$2.50: £ 2/5 $4.50: £ 3/9
$3.00: £ 1/3 $5.00: £ 1/5
$3.50: £ 2/7

It can be seen that the higher the rate of exchange for the pound, the lower is the rate of exchange for the dollar.

3. Assume that both the United States and Great Britain are on the gold standard. The United States defines the dollar as being worth $1/35$ of an ounce of gold and Great Britain defines the pound as being worth $1/5$ of an ounce of gold. Assume that the cost of packing, insuring, and shipping *one ounce* of gold between the United States and Great Britain is $0.21.

a. Ignoring the packing, insuring, and shipping charges, £1 is worth $_____

and $1.00 is worth £_____

b. In the United States the gold export point will be $_____ and the gold import point will be $_____

c. In Great Britain the gold export point will be £_____ and the gold import point will be £_____
(Carry your answers to three decimal places.)

4. (This is a more difficult problem, but try it to see how close you come to the correct answers.) Two demand schedules are given in the table below. One is the British demand for American dollars and the other is the American demand for British pounds. Change *either* of the two demand schedules to a supply schedule for the other money. (*Hint:* The work you did in problem 2 will help you.)

Demand for dollars		Demand for pounds	
Price, £	Quantity demanded	Price, $	Quantity demanded
½	400	$5.00	100
⅖	600	4.50	200
⅓	800	4.00	300
2/7	1,000	3.50	400
¼	1,200	3.00	500
2/9	1,620	2.50	620
⅕	2,000	2.00	788

a. What will be the rate of exchange for the pound? $_____ $4.00_____

b. What will be the rate of exchange for the dollar? £____ ¼ ____

c. How many pounds will be purchased in the market? ____ 360 ____

d. How many dollars will be purchased in the market? ____ 1,200 ____

e. Suppose the British government regulates the exchange rate of the pound and declares that the pound can only be sold at a price of $4.50:

(1) People in Great Britain will be able to buy one dollar at a price of £___ 2/9 ___
(2) The quantity of pounds supplied will exceed the quantity of pounds demanded at this price by ____ 160 ____
(3) The quantity of dollars demanded will exceed the quantity of dollars supplied at this price by ____ 720 ____

■ SELF-TEST

Circle the T if the statement is true, the F if it is false.

1. The importation by Americans of goods from abroad creates a supply of dollars in the foreign exchange market. **T F**

2. If a nation's exports of goods and services are less than its imports of goods and services, the nation has a balance of trade surplus. **T F**

3. A nation is in international equilibrium when its exports equal its imports. **T F**

4. The financial or balancing transactions are remittances and capital movements. **T F**

5. A nation is in international disequilibrium when the accommodating transactions exceed the autonomous transactions. **T F**

6. If a nation has a balance of payments deficit and exchange rates are freely flexible, the price of that nation's money in the foreign exchange market will tend to fall, and this will reduce its imports and increase its exports. **T F**

7. If country A defines its money as worth 100 grains of gold and country B defines its money as worth 20 grains of gold, then, ignoring packing, insuring, and shipping charges, 5 units of country A's money will be worth 1 unit of country B's money. **T F**

8. When nations are on the gold standard, foreign exchange rates fluctuate only within limits determined by the cost of moving gold from one nation to another. **T F**

9. If exchange rates are stable and a nation has a payments surplus, prices and money incomes in that nation will tend to rise. **T F**

10. A nation using exchange controls to eliminate a payments surplus might devalue its currency.   **T   F**

Underscore the letter that corresponds to the best answer.

1. If an American can buy £25,000 for $100,000, the rate of exchange for the pound is: (*a*) $40; (*b*) $25; ⓒ $4; (*d*) $.25.

2. Which one of the following is a financial or balancing transaction? (*a*) gifts of Americans to foreign persons and countries; ⓑ the export of gold from the United States; (*c*) a loan by an American bank to a foreign firm; (*d*) the income from United States investments abroad.

3. If a nation's international balance of payments shows that it is losing gold and foreign monies and that foreigners are increasing the amount of dollars they own, that nation has: (*a*) a trade surplus; (*b*) a trade deficit; (*c*) a payments surplus; ⓓ a payments deficit.

4. When its balance of trade exceeds its net remittances to other nations, its governmental loans and grants, and its capital outflow to other nations, a nation has a: (*a*) trade surplus; (*b*) trade deficit; ⓒ payments surplus; (*d*) payments deficit.

5. Which of these is an accommodating transaction? (*a*) a gift from an American to his uncle in Scotland; ⓑ an increase in the size of American bank accounts in England; (*c*) a loan by the United States government to Turkey; (*d*) the purchase by an American of stock on the French stock exchange.

6. Which of the following would be one of the results associated with the use of freely fluctuating foreign exchange rates to correct a nation's balance of payments surplus? (*a*) the nation's terms of trade with other nations would be worsened; (*b*) importers in the nation who had made contracts for the future delivery of goods would find that they had to pay a higher price than expected for the goods; (*c*) if the nation were at full employment, the decrease in exports and the increase in imports would be inflationary; ⓓ exporters in the nation would find their sales abroad had decreased.

7. If the nations of the world are on the gold standard and one nation has a balance of payments surplus: (*a*) foreign exchange rates in that nation will rise toward the gold import point; ⓑ gold will tend to be imported into that country; (*c*) the level of prices in that country will tend to fall; (*d*) employment and output in that country will tend to fall.

8. When exchange rates are stable and a nation at full employment has a payments surplus, the result in that nation will be: (*a*) a declining price level; (*b*) falling money income; ⓒ inflation; (*d*) rising real income.

9. The use of exchange controls to eliminate a nation's balance of payments deficit results in: ⓐ decreasing the nation's imports; (*b*) decreasing the nation's exports; (*c*) decreasing the nation's price level; (*d*) decreasing the nation's income.

10. A nation with a balance of payments surplus might attempt to eliminate this surplus by employing: (*a*) import quotas; (*b*) higher tariffs; (*c*) subsidies on items which the nation exports; ⓓ none of the above.

■ **DISCUSSION QUESTIONS**

1. What is foreign exchange and the foreign exchange rate? Who are the demanders and suppliers of a particular foreign exchange, say, the French franc? Why is a buyer (demander) in the foreign exchange markets always a seller (supplier) also?

2. What is meant when it is said that "a nation's exports pay for its imports"? Do nations pay for all their imports with exports?

3. What is an international balance of payments? What are the principal sections of a nation's international balance of payments? What are the three kinds of exports and imports listed in it?

4. What are the two kinds of financial or balancing transactions in an international balance of payments? Why are they called balancing transactions?

5. What is meant by international equilibrium and disequilibrium? How does a balance of payments surplus (or deficit) differ from a balance of trade surplus (or deficit)?

6. How can a nation have both a trade surplus and a payments deficit?

7. What is the difference between autonomous and accommodating transactions in a nation's international balance of payments? Which transactions are autonomous and which are accommodating?

8. How can freely fluctuating foreign exchange rates restore international equilibrium? What are the problems associated with this method of correcting international disequilibrium?

9. When is a nation on the gold standard? How does the international gold standard correct international disequilibrium? What are the disadvantages of this method of restoring international equilibrium?

10. Why does the operation of the international gold standard ensure relatively stable foreign exchange rates, that is, rates which fluctuate only within very narrow limits? What are the limits and what are the advantages of stable exchange rates?

11. How can foreign exchange controls be used to restore international equilibrium? Why do such exchange controls necessarily involve the rationing of foreign exchange? What effect do these controls have upon prices, output, and employment in nations that use them and in other nations?

12. What kinds of trade controls may nations with payments deficits employ to eliminate their deficits? Why do these controls often fail to achieve the desired result?

13. Why do nations devalue their currency during depressions or when faced with persistent balance of payments deficits? Why is devaluation seldom successful in solving these two problems?

INTERNATIONAL TRADE
AND FINANCE:
PROBLEMS AND POLICIES

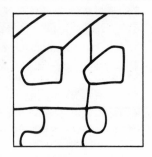

The title of this chapter is a brief but clear summary of its contents. Chapter 44 looks at the problems of the United States and of the world that arise because of international trade. It also examines actual and proposed solutions for these problems. The author concentrates his attention on three basic issues: (1) how to expand trade among nations and reap the benefits of international specialization; (2) how to eliminate the balance of payments deficits incurred by the United States over the past two decades and stop the outflow of gold; and (3) how to reform the international monetary system and thereby stabilize exchange rates, provide a sufficient quantity of international money, and create a system that brings about international equilibrium.

After briefly outlining the history of international trade from the 1920s through the cold war, Professor McConnell uses the same general method to attack each of the three problems. First he describes the problem. Next he notes its history and sources (or causes). Then he explains the actions already taken or the policies already employed in attempting to find solutions, and he appraises the success of these actions. Finally he ex-

amines suggested solutions to the still unsolved problems and comments on the merits and shortcomings of each solution.

While the student must examine each of these problems separately, he should not fail to realize that they are interrelated—and that their solutions will also be interrelated. A solution to the first problem, for example, is not possible without a solution to the third, and solving the third seems improbable if there is no solution to the second. These problems are, in fact, just one problem. Their solution requires an overall solution.

Again there are a number of new terms in the chapter. But there is really no new theory. The principles and basic notions necessary to understand these problems were developed in Chapters 42 and 43; the same principles and notions should enable the student to see how policies have been developed to solve the problems. In fact, the men and governments who designed the policies first had to understand principles, just as the student first has to understand principles, in order to understand the problems and develop solutions for them. One last point: In examining these policies and solutions note the wide variety of methods and devices which have been used to achieve the one basic objective of expanding the volume of international trade.

■ CHAPTER OUTLINE

1. Prior to 1930 the volume of international trade was large and was based on the principle of comparative advantage, a philosophy of laissez faire, and the automatic operation of the gold standard.

a. The Depression of the 1930s drastically reduced the volume of international trade and lending, and most nations erected trade barriers in a futile attempt to solve their domestic unemployment problems.

b. World War II increased the warring nations' demands for imports, reduced their willingness to export, and resulted in inflation and the destruction of productive capacity.

c. The cold war period has been marked by restrictions upon trade between the communist and free worlds, the pursuit of stable prices and full employment at home, and the economic independence of the underdeveloped nations.

d. The world (and especially Europe) at the close of World War II faced the problem of rebuilding its economy. To solve this problem the productive capacity of Europe had to be restored, an international monetary system had to be provided to facilitate trade, and trade barriers had to be reduced.

e. Postwar aid to rebuild Europe took many forms, including the Marshall Plan, and as time passed developed into a mutual security program.

2. In the postwar period nations have attempted to increase world trade by reciprocally reducing or eliminating tariffs and by integrating economically.

a. Until 1934 the United States steadily increased tariff rates to protect private-interest groups.

b. Since the passage of the Reciprocal Trade Agreements Act, tariff rates have been substantially reduced.

c. Many nations, including the United States, have signed the General Agreement on Tariffs and Trade in an attempt to eliminate trade barriers.

d. The European Common Market has sought the economic integration of Western Europe by the abolishment of internal tariffs and quotas, the establishment of common external tariffs, and the eventual free movement of labor and capital within the Common Market area. The Common Market nations have achieved considerable integration, have increased their growth rates, and have expanded trade; but their success has created problems for nonmember nations.

e. The Trade Expansion Act of 1962 permits closer economic ties between the United States and the Common Market.

f. The "Kennedy Round" of tariff negotiations, despite some disappointments, did produce substantial tariff rate reductions.

g. During the past few years the pressure to restrict American imports has increased.

3. The United States today is faced with a balance of payments problem.

a. Since 1949 the United States has had annual balance of payments deficits in all but two years and its gold reserves have decreased.

b. Because of productivity increases in many foreign nations and inflation in the United States, the American balance of trade surplus has been less than its foreign aid expenditures and investments abroad, and the result has been a payments deficit.

c. To control its payments deficit, the United States has already undertaken various measures which constitute a form of control and which limit and distort world trade.

d. Policies to reduce or eliminate the payments deficits would include having Western Europe assume a larger share of the costs of mutual defense and foreign aid; increasing productivity and limiting inflation in the United States; and devaluation of the dollar.

4. To rebuild the international monetary system and stabilize exchange rates, the International Monetary Fund was formed at the end of World War II.

a. The IMF, using the adjustable-peg technique, stabilizes exchange rates and provides for orderly changes in exchange rates to correct international disequilibria.

b. A well-functioning international monetary system requires a sufficient amount of international monetary reserves. Gold and key currencies (the United States dollar and the British pound) today provide these reserves.

c. But currently the world faces the problem of insufficient reserves, and it is doubtful whether international equilibrium can be achieved by using these reserves alone.

d. International trade in recent years has grown more rapidly than reserves. And without an expansion in reserves, further trade expansion may be limited.

e. The achievement of international equilibrium has been made difficult because exchange rate pegs are in fact rarely adjusted.

5. Three possible reforms have been suggested as a way of increasing international reserves and bringing about payments equilibrium.

a. If the United States raised the price of gold, reserves would increase; but two serious problems would be created.

b. It has been suggested that like nations' domestic monetary reserves, which are managed, international monetary reserves should also be managed.

(1) Professor Triffin has proposed to strengthen the IMF by allowing it to act as an international bank to create reserves.

(2) The Rio de Janeiro conference of 1967 resulted in the creation of new reserves called Special Drawing Rights (SDRs) which the IMF creates and lends to member nations.

c. It has also been suggested that the world return to freely fluctuating exchange rates. While this would solve the problem of insufficient reserves and would correct disequilibria, it would also result in several new problems.

6. With the suspension of the convertability of dollars into gold, demand and supply caused the international value of the dollar to float downward. The dollar was in effect devalued; and American goods became less expensive for foreigners and foreign goods became more expensive for Americans to buy. Designed to correct the American balance of payments deficit, floating the dollar upset the international monetary system; and made it necessary to develop a new system in which dollars and gold are less important and exchange rates are more flexible.

■ IMPORTANT TERMS

United Nations Relief and Rehabilitation Administration

European Recovery Program (Marshall Plan)

Mutual Security program

International monetary reserves

International Monetary Fund

Triffin Plan

Reciprocal Trade Agreements Act of 1934

Most favored nation clause

International Trade Organization

General Agreement on Tariffs and Trade

Economic integration

European Common Market (European Economic Community)

Trade Expansion Act of 1962

Kennedy Round

Adjustable pegs

Key currencies

Special Drawing Rights (SDRs)

"Floating" the dollar

Crawling-peg system

■ FILL-IN QUESTIONS

1. In the last half of the nineteenth century the volume of international trade in the world was _____; and this trade was primarily an exchange of the _____ of the _____ nations for the _____ of the _____ nations. Trade was based on the principle of _____, the ideology of _____, and the automatic operation of the _____ _____.

2. In the years following 1929 the amount of international trade was substantially reduced by _____, _____, and _____. The former event gave rise to reduced _____ _____, reduced long-term _____, and _____.

3. Nations at war usually want to increase

their _____

and decrease their _____

and this creates a _____
problem for these nations. War also tends to

result in _____

and the destruction of _____

4. The cold war environment has not been conducive to the reconstruction of international trade for at least three reasons:

    a. _____

    b. _____

    c. _____

5. The postwar programs and institutions to rebuild world trade had three related objec-

tives: to _____,

to _____,

and to _____

6. The most pressing economic problem facing the world at the end of World War II was

to _____.
The United States helped to solve this prob-

lem by contributing heavily to _____

_____,

by making _____

and _____

abroad, and by instituting the _____

and _____
programs.

7. Between 1790 and 1930 the trend of

tariff rates in the United States was _____,

but since the passage of the _____

Act in 1934 the trend has been _____.

This act empowered the President to _____

_____

and incorporated _____
in American trade agreements.

8. The three main principles set down in the General Agreement on Tariffs and Trade are:

    a. _____

    b. _____

    c. _____

9. The specific aims of the European Common Market were the abolishment of _____

_____,

the establishment of _____,

the free movement of _____,

and common policies with respect to _____

_____.

Its success, reflected in increased _____

_____

and _____
in the Common Market nations, can be attrib-

uted to a better _____

and to the _____
which have resulted from the creation of a
mass market.

10. The Trade Expansion Act of 1962 al-

lowed the President to _____

_____

and _____

11. The increasing pressures to restrict the imports of the United States are the result of greater _____ competition, discrimination against American _____ in foreign markets, and the _____ problem in the United States.

12. The current balance of payments position of the United States reflects:
    a. A smaller balance of trade surplus caused

by increases in the _____ of

foreign producers and by _____
in the United States.
    b. A payments deficit due to this smaller trade surplus, substantial American capital

_____, and _____

_____ from the United States government
to foreign nations.

13. The ad hoc measures which the United States has taken to reduce its payments deficit

are designed to increase its _____.

and decrease its _____ and

_____

14. Without restricting imports; the United States might alter its payments position by:

a. _____

b. _____

c. _____

d. _____

15. The IMF was established to bring about

_____ exchange rates. To accomplish this, it employs an _____ system of exchange rates.

16. The world is currently short of _____

_____ reserves because the demand for them has increased _____ rapidly than their supply. These reserves include both _____

and the "_____"
(which are basically the monies of two nations: _____ and _____).

17. A shortage of international monetary reserves makes it difficult to expand _____

_____

18. Reaching international equilibrium is also difficult in the world today because exchange

rate pegs are _____.
To increase reserves and foster balance of payments equilibrium, the following three reforms have been suggested.

a. _____

b. _____

c. _____

19. Following the suggestions in the _____

_____ Plan, the Rio de Janeiro conference adopted a proposal to have the IMF create and lend a new international

money called _____

20. Floating the dollar means that the dollar

can no longer be converted into _____;

and that _____ now determine the international value of the dollar.

■ **PROBLEMS AND PROJECTS**

1. Below is a list of acts, programs, institutions, etc., followed by a series of identifying phrases. Match the phrase with the act, program, institution, etc., by placing the appropriate letter in the space following each phrase. (*Note:* Not all the items in the list will have an identifying phrase.)

A. United Nations Relief and Rehabilitation Administration
B. European Recovery Program (Marshall Plan)
C. Mutual Security Program
D. European Common Market
E. Tiffin Plan
F. International Monetary Fund
G. Hawley-Smoot Act
H. Reciprocal Trade Agreements Act
I. International Trade Organization
J. General Agreement on Tariffs and Trade
K. Trade Expansion Act
L. Crawling-peg system
M. Rio de Janeiro conference

1. Makes short-term loans to member nations to stabilize foreign exchange rates and maintain exchange convertibility. _____

2. Agreement of 106 nations that authorized the IMF to create Special Drawing Rights. _____

3. Provides assistance to industries and workers adversely affected by the reduction or elimination of American tariffs on foreign goods. _____

4. Provided food, clothing, and medical aid to European nations in the immediate postwar period. _____

5. An organization (which the United States did not join) to foster international economic cooperation and freer trade. _____

6. Treaty signed by twenty-three nations in 1947 whose purpose was to reduce tariffs, eliminate import quotas, and secure equal treatment among all nations engaged in international trade. _____

7. Agreement of six nations to abolish tariffs and import quotas among the member nations and to establish common tariffs applicable to nonmember nations.

8. Program that would allow nations with chronic balance of payments deficits to increase the par value of their currencies by a small percentage each month. _____

9. Program that would require all member nations to deposit their international monetary reserves with the International Monetary Fund and allow the IMF to create new reserves by making loans in excess of the amount of the deposits with it. _____

10. American program to aid European nations in rebuilding their productive capacities destroyed during World War II. _____

11. Resulted in the gradual reduction of American tariff rates by allowing the President to reduce tariff rates up to 50 percent in return for lower foreign tariff rates on American goods. _____

12. Imposed the highest tariff rates in history on foreign goods imported into the United States. _____

2. Suppose France and the United States are the only two nations in the world. Assume that France defines the franc as worth $\frac{1}{120}$ of an ounce of gold and the United States defines the dollar as worth $\frac{1}{30}$ of an ounce of gold. The United States will buy from and sell gold to France at this price.

a. One ounce of gold is worth _____ francs and $_____.

b. In terms of gold, therefore, one dollar is worth _____ francs and one franc is worth $_____.

c. Imagine now that the United States has a payments deficit and France has a surplus, and the United States decides to devalue the dollar from $\frac{1}{30}$ to $\frac{1}{40}$ of an ounce of gold. This raises the price of the franc to $_____ and lowers the price of the dollar to _____ francs.

d. Suppose France has $120 million in United States banks and owns 1 million ounces of gold. The devaluation of the dollar de-

creases the value of these dollars from _____ to _____ ounces of gold and increases the value of this gold from $_____ to $_____.

e. If people in France had known this devaluation was coming, they would have converted their _____ to either _____ or _____

f. Anyone with one ounce of gold will realize a profit of $_____ and anyone with 100 francs will realize a profit of $_____; but a person with $240 will suffer a loss of _____ ounces of gold.

■ SELF-TEST

Circle the T if the statement is true, the F if it is false.

1. During the Depression of the 1930s most of the nations of the world lowered barriers to international trade in an attempt to increase domestic employment and output. **T F**

2. While the cold war has left the nations of the world ideologically divided, the volume of world trade has increased and the barriers to trade have been reduced to the levels of the 1920s. **T F**

3. Most experts agree that the European Recovery Program was highly successful in restoring the industrial and agricultural capacity of Western Europe. **T F**

4. The immediate postwar needs of Europe for food, clothing, and medical services were met by the United States through the establishment of the European Recovery Program (Marshall Plan). **T F**

5. Because the General Agreement on Tariffs and Trade committed its signers to eliminate their tariffs on imports, the U.S. Senate refused to ratify the agreement. **T F**

6. Since the establishment of the European Common Market its members' share of world trade has increased. **T F**

7. Before a firm can enjoy economies of scale it must enjoy a mass market. **T F**

8. In order to offset the loss of export markets that will result from the growing strength of the European Common Market, the United States will find it necessary in the future to increase its tariff rates.   **T   F**

9. The Trade Expansion Act of 1962 reversed earlier American economic policy and attempted to expand GNP by restricting imports.   **T   F**

10. The Kennedy Round resulted in fairly substantial reciprocal tariff rate reductions. **T   F**

11. The smaller American balance of trade in the 1950s and 1960s can be attributed to two main causes: the recovery of the economies of Japan and Western Europe and unemployment in the United States.   **T   F**

12. One suggested solution for the current United States balance of payments problem is an increase in American foreign aid to underdeveloped nations.   **T   F**

13. The rules of the International Monetary Fund prevent any member nation from devaluing its currency by more than 10 percent.   **T   F**

14. The "key currencies" are the American dollar and the British pound.   **T   F**

15. One of the basic shortcomings of the IMF management of the international monetary system has been its inability to bring about the changes in exchange rates needed to correct persistent balance of payments deficits and surpluses.   **T   F**

16. The world currently finds itself short of international reserves because the demand for them has not increased as rapidly as the supply.   **T   F**

17. The basic shortcoming of the adjustable-peg system is the failure to change exchange rates when permanent payments deficits exist.   **T   F**

18. The advocates of the Triffin Plan propose that the International Monetary Fund be allowed to create international monetary reserves by lending monies in excess of the amounts deposited with it.   **T   F**

19. The Rio de Janeiro conference of 1967 proposed that the world return to freely fluctuating foreign exchange rates.   **T   F**

20. Under the postwar international monetary system, foreign exchange rates remained relatively stable, but the American dollar became overvalued.   **T   F**

Underscore the letter that corresponds to the best answer.

1. Which one of the following was characteristic of international trade throughout most of the nineteenth century? (a) extensive barriers to trade; (b) the almost automatic operation of the gold standard; (c) a small volume of international trade; (d) government regulation of most foreign exchange rates.

2. Which one of the following was *not* characteristic of world trade during World War II? (a) trade was based on military objectives rather than on comparative advantages; (b) shortages of foreign exchange existed in most countries at war; (c) inflation in the warring nations made the exports of these nations more attractive to foreign buyers; (d) inflation in the warring nations made foreign goods more attractive to buyers in the warring nations.

3. The *most urgent* of the world's economic problems immediately following World War II was: (a) the elimination of trade barriers; (b) the development of an international monetary system; (c) the economic development of the underdeveloped nations; (d) the reconstruction of the European economies.

4. Which of the following has had as its basic objective the restoration of the productive capacity of European industry and agriculture? (a) the Triffin Plan; (b) GATT; (c) the Marshall Plan; (d) the Bretton Woods Conference.

5. Which one of the following specifically empowered the President of the United States to reduce their tariff rates up to 50 percent if other nations would reduce their tariffs on American goods? (a) the Underwood Act of 1913; (b) the Hawley-Smoot Act of 1930; (c) the Trade Agreements Act of 1934; (d) the General Agreement on Tariffs and Trade of 1947.

6. Which of the following is *not* characteristic of the General Agreement on Tariffs and Trade? Nations signing the agreement were committed to: (a) the elimination of import quotas; (b) the reciprocal reduction of tariffs by negotiation; (c) the nondiscriminatory treatment of all trading nations; (d) the establishment of a world customs union.

7. Which of the following was designed to produce some degree of economic integration in Europe? (a) UNRRA; (b) the Marshall Plan; (c) the Triffin Plan; (d) the European Common Market.

8. The European Common Market: (a) is designed to eliminate import quotas among its members during the next 12 to 15 years; (b) includes Great Britain, Denmark, France, and Germany among others; (c) aims to abolish tariffs imposed on all goods which member nations import over the next 12 to 15 years; (d) includes both East and West Germany.

9. During the late 1950s and 1960s the United States position in world trade has been characterized by: (a) a balance of trade deficit in the United States; (b) the importation of gold into the United States; (c) a balance of payments surplus in the United States; (d) American loans, grants, and investments abroad in excess of the rest of the world's balance of trade deficit with the United States.

10. Which of the following would be *least* effective in reducing or eliminating the American balance of payments deficit? (a) devaluation of the dollar; (b) reduction of America's loans and grants for economic and military aid; (c) restraint of inflation in the United States; (d) relaxation of foreign restrictions on American goods.

11. Which one of the following would *not* be a domestic readjustment which would tend to eliminate a nation's balance of payments deficit? (a) an increase in the productivity of a nation's resources; (b) an increase in the nation's price level; (c) an increase in the nation's growth rate; (d) an increase in the nation's exports.

12. Which one of the following is *not* one of the temporary ad hoc measures taken by the United States to ease its balance of payments deficit? (a) the interest equalization tax; (b) the rejection of SDRs by Congress; (c) the executive order by the President limiting for-

eign investment; (d) the "tying" of foreign aid to American goods.

13. In an attempt to reduce the American balance of payments deficit President Nixon (a) imposed a temporary freeze on wages and prices; (b) placed a temporary 10 percent tariff surcharge on imported goods subject to tariffs; (c) suspended the convertibility of dollars into gold; (d) did all of the above.

14. Which one of the following is *not* characteristic of the International Monetary Fund? (a) makes short-term loans to member nations with balance of payments deficits; (b) tries to maintain relatively stable foreign exchange rates; (c) attempts to maintain foreign exchange convertibility; (d) extends long-term loans to underdeveloped nations for the purpose of increasing the productive capacity of these nations.

15. All but one of the following are elements in the adjustable-peg system for foreign exchange rates. Which one? (a) each nation defines its monetary unit in terms of gold or dollars; (b) nations maintain foreign exchange stabilization funds; (c) nations are allowed to devalue their currencies when faced with persistent payments deficits; (d) the deposit by all nations of their international reserves with the IMF.

16. Which of the following is the best definition of international monetary reserves? (a) gold; (b) gold and dollars; (c) gold, dollars, and British pounds; (d) gold, dollars, British pounds, and Russian rubles.

17. "Floating" the dollar means (a) the value of the dollar will be determined by demand and supply; (b) the price of gold was raised from $35 to $40 an ounce; (c) the price of the dollar was allowed to crawl upward at a rate of one-fourth of 1 percent a month; (d) the IMF decreased the value of the dollar by 10 percent.

18. Which of the following is *not* true of SDRs? (a) they serve as international reserves; (b) they have no gold backing; (c) they are issued by the United Nations; (d) they are acceptable in payment of international debts by the members of the IMF.

■ DISCUSSION QUESTIONS

1. What were the extent and character of international trade in the nineteenth century?

2. Explain the effect of each of the following upon the volume and character of world trade and upon the international trade policies of the nations of the world: (a) the Depression of the 1930s; (b) World War II; (c) the cold war.

3. What was the condition of world trade at the end of World War II? What were the three objectives of the postwar programs and institutions used to correct this condition?

4. Which of the economic problems faced by the world at the end of World War II was the most urgent? How did the United States and the nations of Europe try to solve this problem?

5. What was the tariff policy of the United States: (a) between 1790 and 1930; (b) since 1934? Explain the basic provisions of the Reciprocal Trade Agreements Act. How has the United States cooperated with other nations since 1945 to reduce trade barriers? What are the reasons for the increased pressure within the United States in recent years to erect trade barriers?

6. What is meant by economic integration? What are the four main features of the European Common Market? How successful has it been in achieving its immediate goals and in increasing the economic well-being of its members? Why has it been successful?

7. What problems does the success of the Common Market create for the United States? How might the United States solve these problems?

8. What were the major provisions of the Trade Expansion Act of 1962? What were the accomplishments of the Kennedy Round?

9. In what way is the international trade position of the United States different from its position at the close of World War II? What has been the cause of this change?

10. What policies might the United States adopt to reduce or eliminate its balance of payments deficit? Why are increased tariff rates, the imposition of import quotas, and the devaluation of the dollar not "responsible programs"?

11. What temporary steps has the United States taken to ease its balance of payments problem? Why are these steps not beneficial to the long-run interests of the United States and of the world?

12. Explain why pressures to restrict the importation of goods into the United States have revived in recent years.

13. What are the chief goals of the International Monetary Fund? What means does it employ in the attempt to achieve these goals? How successful has it been in achieving these goals and why?

14. What are international monetary reserves? Why is there a shortage of these reserves, and why is this shortage a problem?

15. What is meant by the "adjustment problem"?

16. What three reforms have been suggested as solutions for the problems of inadequate reserves and international adjustment? What are the merits and shortcomings of each of these suggestions?

17. Explain (a) the Triffin Plan and (b) Special Drawing Rights (SDRs). How are SDRs created, what "backs" them, and how and for what purpose are they used?

18. Why did the President impose a temporary surcharge? Why did he in effect devalue the dollar by suspending the convertibility of dollars into gold? What do the nonconvertibility and the "floating" of the dollar do to the international monetary system and what changes will probably have to be made in this system in the future?

THE UNDERDEVELOPED
NATIONS:
A SPECIAL PROBLEM
IN ECONOMIC GROWTH

The economic study of underdeveloped countries found in Chapter 45 and the study of the economic system of Soviet Russia in Chapter 46 might well be placed in a separate section entitled "Current International Economic Problems." But because these two chapters concern the economies of foreign nations rather than American capitalism, they are grouped with the chapters dealing with international trade and finance. It should be noted that these final two chapters of the text bring together many of the principles of both macro- and microeconomics and the analysis of both American capitalism and international economics and apply them to two specific problems.

Probably no two problems today—with the possible exceptions of the problem of poverty —are so vitally important to the United States and its citizens and their future. Because these problems are so important, there is a considerable amount of debate in the United States over how much and what types of aid ought to be extended to foreign nations and how the economic challenge of the U.S.S.R. can best be met. These two chapters do not offer programs or policies or answers for these problems; rather they attempt to point out the nature of the problems and the more important facts surrounding them.

Chapter 45 is concerned with the problem of raising the standard of living faced by the underdeveloped nations. Both economic growth

in these nations and economic growth in the United States (discussed in detail in Chapters 20 to 22, to which the student might now find it useful to refer) require that the nation's resources and technological knowledge be expanded. Application of this very simple principle in the underdeveloped nations, however, faces a set of special obstacles quite different from those which limit economic growth in the United States. You may recall that in Chapter 1 it was pointed out that the principles and policies applicable to an economy in one set of circumstances might be quite inappropriate for another economy under another set of circumstances; and this is the case when dealing with the underdeveloped nations: The principles applicable to the economies of these nations and the policies appropriate to economic growth there are very different from the principles applicable to American capitalism and the policies conducive to growth here.

In this chapter emphasis is placed upon the obstacles to economic growth which exist in the underdeveloped nations of the world. While each of these nations faces its own particular obstacles, all of them face common obstacles, and it is these common obstacles which give rise to the special problems associated with the raising of their standards of living. The student should concentrate his attention on these obstacles; then he will be in a position to reach some conclusions for himself as to how growth in these countries can be fostered and how the United States can help this growth.

■ CHAPTER OUTLINE

1. The underdeveloped nations of the world comprise two-thirds of the world's population.

a. Most of the countries of Asia, Africa, South America, and Southeastern Europe are underdeveloped, and all of them have one common characteristic—poverty (that is, a low per capita income and standard of living).

b. Because of an increasing disparity between the standards of living in the developed and the underdeveloped nations, and because many of the underdeveloped nations have recently become politically independent, these nations are discontented and determined to raise their standards of living.

c. The more advanced nations have an economic, political, and military interest in furthering the development of the underdeveloped nations.

d. The economic and social environment of the underdeveloped nations is vastly different from that in which the United States found itself when it began its development; consequently, the underdeveloped nations cannot develop merely by following the examples of the United States and other advanced nations.

2. Economic development requires that the quantity and quality of natural resources, human resources, and capital equipment be increased and that technological knowledge be expanded in the underdeveloped nations.

a. There are many special obstacles to hinder the advancement of such a program; understanding these obstacles leads to an understanding of why these nations have not developed and of what must be done to foster development.

b. In addition, a nation must have a strong desire to develop and be willing to alter its own social and institutional environment to accomplish this.

c. It is probable the governments of these nations will have to sponsor and direct many of the early development plans if they are to succeed.

3. The more economically advanced nations can assist the underdeveloped ones by granting economic aid (directly in the form of loans and grants and indirectly through the World Bank), by increasing their trade with them, and by ensuring that their own economies maintain high levels of output and employment and stable prices.

a. The United Nations suggest that the advanced nations use 1 percent of their GNPs (about $20 billion) each year to aid the developing nations. This amount exceeds the aid granted in recent years and would require the United States to increase its aid.

b. Because of the relatively minor success of American aid, it has been suggested that American aid, which has been spread thinly among a number of nations, could be more effectively used if it were distributed among a few key countries.

c. In the 1960s real GNP increased at about the same rate in developed and underdeveloped nations; but the rate of growth in per capita output was much less in underdeveloped nations. The outlook for future growth in the latter nations is cautiously optimistic.

■ IMPORTANT TERMS

Underdeveloped nation	Capital-saving technological advance
Disguised unemployment	Capital-using technological advance
Basic social capital	World Bank
Internal capital formation	Key country
External capital formation	1 percent rule
Nonfinancial investment	Green revolution

■ FILL-IN QUESTIONS

1. The common characteristic of underdeveloped nations is _____

2. The underdeveloped nations are found chiefly in the following areas of the world:

_____,

_____,

_____,

and _____;

and they account for approximately _____

_____

of the world's population.

3. To grow, every economy must increase
its _____

_____ ,

and _____

and improve its _____

4. To use resources more efficiently involves
both the _____

and _____

5. Three characteristics of the human resources in underdeveloped nations are:

a. _____

b. _____

c. _____

6. The per capita standard of living = _____

_____

and social unrest = _____

minus _____

7. Disguised unemployment means that the

marginal product of workers is _____

_____

8. If the process of capital accumulation is

"cumulative," this means that _____

_____

9. Domestic capital accumulation requires

that a nation _____

and _____ .
The former is difficult in underdeveloped na-

tions because of a _____
and the latter is difficult because of a lack of

_____

and _____

10. An increase in the saving potential of the
mass of people in underdeveloped nations will
probably not increase their saving because

_____

and _____

11. Nonfinancial investment involves the

transfer of surplus labor from _____

to _____

or _____

12. If technological advances makes it possible to replace a worn-out plow, costing $10
when new, with a new $5 plow, the techno-

logical advance is _____

13. List five reasons why the role of government in fostering economic development will
need to be large in the underdeveloped nations, especially during the early stages of
development:

a. _____

b. _____

c. _____

d. _____

e. _____

14. The "will to develop" in underdeveloped
nations involves a willingness to change the

_____

of the nation.

15. The three major ways in which the United
States can assist economic development in

the underdeveloped nations are _____

_____ ,

_____ ,

and _____

16. The "1 percent rule" of the UN recommends that public and private flows of capital
from the developed to the underdeveloped na-

tions equal 1 percent of the _____
of the developed nations.

17. The "key country" approach to foreign

aid involves a reduction in _____

and an increase in _____ ;

key countries would be nations that ____ ____

_____ ,

_____ ,

and _____

18. During the 1960s real GNP in the under-developed nations grew at an average annual rate of _____ percent and per capita real GNP increased annually about _____ percent.

■ PROBLEMS AND PROJECTS

1. While economic conditions are not identical in all underdeveloped nations, there are certain conditions common to or typical of all. In the spaces after each of the following characteristics, indicate briefly the nature of this characteristic in the typical underdeveloped nation.

a. Standard of living (per capita income).

_____

b. Average life expectancy. _____

_____

c. Extent of unemployment. _____

d. Endowment of natural resources. _____

_____

e. Agricultural techniques employed. _____

_____

f. Percentage of the population engaged in agriculture. _____

g. Size of the population relative to the land and capital available. _____

h. The birth and death rates. _____

i. Quality of the labor force. _____

j. Amount of capital equipment relative to the labor force. _____

k. Level of saving. _____

l. Incentive to invest. _____

m. Amount of basic social capital. _____

_____

n. Extent of industrialization. _____

_____

o. Size and quality of the entrepreneurial class and the supervisory class. _____

_____

2. Suppose that it takes a minimum of 5 units of food to keep a person alive for a year, that the population can double itself every 10 years, and that the food supply can increase every 10 years by an amount equal to what it was in the beginning.

Year	Food supply	Population
0	200	20
10	_____	_____
20	_____	_____
30	_____	_____
40	_____	_____
50	_____	_____
60	_____	_____

a. Assume that both the population and the food supply grow at these rates. Complete the table by computing the size of the population and the food supply in years 10 through 60.

b. What happens to the relationship between the food supply and the population in the 30th year? _____

c. What would actually prevent the population from growing at this rate following the 30th year? _____

d. Assuming that the actual population growth in the years following the 30th does not outrun the food supply, what would be the size of the population in:

(1) Year 40: _____

(2) Year 50: _____

(3) Year 60: _____

e. Explain why the standard of living failed to increase in the years following the 30th even though the food supply increased by 75 percent between years 30 and 60. _____

_____

■ SELF-TEST

Circle the T if the statement is true, the F if it is false.

1. The United States has the highest per capita income in the world.   **T   F**

2. The difference between the per capita incomes in the underdeveloped nations and the per capita incomes in the developed nations has been decreasing over the past 20 years. **T F**

3. It is impossible to achieve a high standard of living with a small supply of natural resources. **T F**

4. Nations with large populations are overpopulated. **T F**

5. The chief factor preventing the elimination of disguised unemployment in the agricultural sector of underdeveloped nations is the small number of job openings available in industry. **T F**

6. The marginal propensity to consume of the mass of the people in underdeveloped nations is less than 1.0. **T F**

7. Before private investment can be increased in underdeveloped nations it is necessary to reduce the amount of investment in basic social capital. **T F**

8. The policies of the governments of underdeveloped nations have often tended to reduce the incentives of foreigners to invest in the underdeveloped nations. **T F**

9. Underdeveloped nations will not need foreign aid if the developed nations will reduce tariffs and import quotas on the goods which the underdeveloped nations export. **T F**

10. An increase in the output and employment of the United States works to the advantage of the underdeveloped nations because it provides the underdeveloped nations with larger markets for their exports. **T F**

11. Capital flows from the United States to the underdeveloped nations have consistently exceeded the amounts suggested by the "one percent rule." **T F**

12. The "key country" approach involves the distribution of American foreign aid to only those underdeveloped nations who are military allies of the United States. **T F**

Underscore the letter that corresponds to the best answer.

1. Which of the following is the most underdeveloped nation? (a) U.S.S.R.; (b) Israel; (c) Canada; (d) India.

2. Which of the following is the most serious obstacle to economic growth in underdeveloped nations? (a) the supply of natural resources; (b) the size and quality of the labor force; (c) the supply of capital equipment; (d) technological knowledge.

3. An increase in the total output of consumer goods in an underdeveloped nation may not increase the average standard of living because: (a) of diminishing returns; (b) it may provoke an increase in the population; (c) of disguised unemployment; (d) the quality of the labor force is so poor.

4. Which of the following best describes disguised unemployment? (a) an agricultural worker in an underdeveloped nation; (b) a worker whose marginal product is zero or less than zero; (c) an agricultural worker who cannot find employment in industry; (d) a worker whose productivity is subject to diminishing returns.

5. Which of the following is not a reason for placing special emphasis on capital accumulation in underdeveloped nations? (a) the inflexible supply of arable land; (b) the low productivity of workers; (c) the low marginal productivity of capital equipment; (d) the possibility that capital accumulation will be "cumulative."

6. Which of the following is not a factor limiting saving in underdeveloped nations? (a) the incomes of the mass of people are too low to allow saving; (b) those who are able to save are unwilling to save; (c) the highly unequal distribution of income; (d) the low marginal productivity of capital equipment.

7. Which of the following is an example of basic social capital? (a) a steel plant; (b) an electric power plant; (c) a farm; (d) a demand deposit in a commercial bank.

8. Which of the following seem to be the most needed and widespread institutional change required of underdeveloped nations? (a) adoption of birth control; (b) development of strong labor unions; (c) increase in the nation's basic social capital; (d) land reform.

9. The role of government in the early stages of economic development will probably be a major one for several reasons. Which one of the following is not one of these reasons? (a) only government can provide a large amount

of the needed basic social capital; (b) the absence of private entrepreneurs to accumulate capital and take risks; (c) the necessity of creating *new* money to finance capital accumulation; (d) the slowness and uncertainty of the price system in fostering development.

10. Which of the following was *not* true during the 1960s? (a) Real GNP increased at about the same average rate in developed and underdeveloped nations; (b) real GNP increased more rapidly than population in the underdeveloped nations; (c) the rate of growth of real GNP per capita was more rapid in the developed than in the underdeveloped nations; (d) real GNP per capita was approximately constant in the underdeveloped nations.

■ DISCUSSION QUESTIONS

1. What nations of the world can be called "developed"? Which can be classified as "semideveloped"? Where are the "underdeveloped" nations of the world found?

2. What recent events have increased the desire of the underdeveloped nations to improve their standard of living? Why should social unrest increase in the underdeveloped nations even though their standards of living have been increasing?

3. Why is it to the interest of the United States to assist development in the underdeveloped nations?

4. Why is advice to the underdeveloped nations to follow the example of the United States inappropriate and unrealistic?

5. What must any nation, developed or underdeveloped, do if it is to increase its standard of living? Answer in terms of the production possibilities curve concept.

6. What obstacles do the human resources of underdeveloped nations place in the path of economic development? Why is it difficult to eliminate disguised unemployment in underdeveloped nations?

7. What reasons exist for placing special emphasis on capital accumulation as a means of promoting economic growth in underdeveloped nations?

8. Why is domestic capital accumulation diffi-cult in underdeveloped nations? Answer in terms of both the saving side and the investment side of capital accumulation. How does a lack of basic social capital inhibit investment in underdeveloped nations?

9. In addition to the obstacles which limit domestic investment, what other obstacles tend to limit the flow of foreign capital into underdeveloped nations?

10. Why is it possible for underdeveloped nations to improve their technology without engaging in slow and expensive research?

11. What is meant by the "will to develop"? How is it related to social and institutional change in underdeveloped nations?

12. Why is the role of government expected to be a major one in the early phases of development in underdeveloped nations?

13. How can the United States help underdeveloped nations? What types of aid can be offered?

14. Discuss the World Bank in terms of its purposes, characteristics, sources of funds, promotion of private capital flows, and success. What are its affiliates and their purposes?

15. How is it possible for the United States to assist underdeveloped nations without spending a penny on "foreign aid"? Is this type of aid sufficient to ensure rapid and substantial development in the underdeveloped nation?

16. How much does the United States contribute in relative and absolute amounts to underdeveloped nations? How much do you think it should contribute?

17. What reasons are there—aside from its total cost—for dissatisfaction with the present United States program of aid to the underdeveloped nations? How would the key country approach involve a change in American foreign aid policy? Which nations would be key countries? What are the merits and the weaknesses of this approach?

18. What was the growth record of the underdeveloped nations during the 1960s and what are their prospects for growth during the 1970s?

THE ECONOMIC CHALLENGE OF SOVIET RUSSIA

For many years people in the United States were convinced that the economic system of the Soviet Union was totally unworkable and that it would sooner or later break down— proof that Marx, Lenin, and Stalin were unrealistic dreamers—and that the reconversion of their economy to a free enterprise, price-market system would follow. Slowly it has dawned upon the American people that the breakdown would not soon occur and that, on the contrary, the Soviet economy was becoming more workable, more productive, and, therefore, a greater challenge to the United States. In part the early American belief that Soviet Russia would collapse was based on prejudice—they wanted it to collapse in order to prove to themselves that the system employed by American capitalism was both the only feasible system of economic organization and the most perfectly operated system—and in part it was based on ignorance of the institutions and methods employed by Russian communism.

The aim of Chapter 46 is to dispel some of the ignorance surrounding Soviet institutions and methods and by doing so eliminate the basis for much of the unwarranted prejudice against the Soviet *economic system*. (Chapter 46, of course, does not try to convince the reader that the United States should adopt the Soviet system, nor does it try to persuade the reader that the Russian way of life *as a whole* is morally, politically, or socially preferable.) To accomplish its aim the chapter first examines the two institutions of the Soviet economy which are remarkably different from anything found in American capitalism and which are the framework of the Russian economy. Within this framework the Fundamental Economic Problems are solved through central economic planning. Central economic planning has no counterpart in the United States, and it is to further central economic planning that the Soviet institutional framework is maintained. The better part of the chapter is devoted to explaining what central planning is and how it is employed in the U.S.S.R. to obtain answers to the Fundamental Economic Problems.

If the student learns anything from this chapter he ought to learn that it is the Soviet *economy* which is the greatest threat to the Western way of life, not only because economic strength is the basis for political and military strength, but also because the performance and growth of the Soviet and American economic systems (and the social and political institutions that accompany them) are being compared by people throughout the world who will be inclined to adopt the economic *and* political *and* social system which promises them the best prospect of improving their own material well-being. In addition, the student should be aware that it is not a question of "Will the Soviet system work?" but of how well it does work *compared* with the American system.

There is great strength in the Soviet Union

because the government is able to compel the economy to do as it wishes. The large and almost continuous increases in Soviet output are mostly the result of central economic planning and the direction of the economy toward the achievement of these plans by central authority. It is both the strength and weakness of the American economy that it lacks central direction. It was once assumed that central planning was too complex to be practical and that only the impersonal price-market system could coordinate the various parts of the economy, just as it was once imagined that only monetary self-interest and private property could provoke increased efficiency, effort, and output. The Soviet experiment suggests the contrary.

Of course, economic and political freedom is lacking in the Soviet Union, but for the underfed, the illiterate, the sick, and those without hope, this would be a small price to pay for even a slightly improved standard of living. Whether the challenge of the Soviet system can be met successfully depends not only upon how successful the Soviet system is in the future, but also upon how well the American system functions in improving its own and others' standards of living, and upon the moral, political, and social costs of this improvement.

Although nondiscussion questions and problems are provided in this study guide, studying these questions is not sufficient to develop and test fully the student's understanding of the Soviet Union. The nature of the material is such that the student should spend considerable time and effort on the discussion questions.

■ CHAPTER OUTLINE

1. The major economic characteristics of the U.S.S.R. are:
   a. The public ownership of most property resources (as opposed to private ownership).
   b. Central economic planning or government direction (as opposed to the price-market system).
   c. The limited freedom of choice of consumers and workers (as opposed to consumer sovereignty and freedom of occupation).

2. Central planning is used in the Soviet Union to answer the Five Fundamental Economic Questions.

   a. Government in the U.S.S.R. sets forth the goals of the economy in its Five- and Seven-Year Plans.
   b. The basic problem encountered in planning for an entire economy is the difficulty of coordinating the many interdependent segments of the economy and the avoidance of the chain reaction that would result from a bottleneck in any one of these segments.
   c. To coordinate the different sectors of the economy, *Gosplan* plans by negotiation, employs the priority principle, and uses inventories to offset bottlenecks.
   d. To achieve the objectives of central planning the Soviet government relies upon control agencies such as *Gosplan* and other planning groups and especially upon *Gosbank*.
   e. To motivate economic units to fulfill the plan the U.S.S.R. employs monetary and non-monetary incentives and coercion.
   f. Prices in the Soviet economy are established by the state and are used to promote the achievement of the plan.

3. Microeconomic problems troubled the Soviet economy in the late 1960s, and a number of reforms were instituted.
   a. The three principal problems were the production of unsalable goods, distorted production and poor-quality goods, and resistance to innovation by producing enterprises.
   b. At the suggestion of Liberman and others, the government introduced a modified profit motive, less central planning and more planning from below, and greater autonomy for the managers of individual enterprises.

4. The U.S.S.R. has sought the macroeconomic goal of rapid economic growth.
   a. The GNP of the U.S.S.R. is about one-half that of the United States; but its growth rate has been greater than that of the United States.
   b. The sources of this rapid growth in the Soviet Union were its large endowment of natural resources, its totalitarian government, its surplus farm labor, its adoption of the superior technologies developed in Western nations, and its virtual elimination of cyclical unemployment.
   c. There are at least six factors which slowed Soviet growth in recent years.
   d. But there are four reasons to believe that the U.S.S.R. may be able to continue to grow at the same rate.

e. On balance it is not possible to predict the Soviet growth rate in the future.

5. Any evaluation of the Soviet system requires an examination of its principal accomplishments and shortcomings.

a. Its major accomplishments are the great improvements in education and its complete system of social insurance.

b. The shortcomings are the small increases in the consumers' standard of living and the general absence of personal freedom.

c. The successes of the Soviet economy mean that if the United States is to retain its independence and freedom, it must strive to improve the performance of the American economy and the efficiency of its own resource allocation.

■ IMPORTANT TERMS

Public ownership

Central economic planning

Gosplan

Libermanism

Priority principle

Gosbank

Turnover tax

Forced economic growth

■ FILL-IN QUESTIONS

1. The two institutions of the U.S.S.R. which are in sharp contrast with private property and the price-market system of the United States are _____ and _____

2. In the U.S.S.R. the _____ determines the goals or objectives of the economy while in the United States it is the _____ _____ which sets goals or objectives.

3. The basic planning problem in the Soviet Union is the _____ of the various sectors of the economy. The failure of any one of these sectors to produce its planned output results in a _____ which causes a _____ throughout the remainder of the economy.

4. To coordinate the various segments of the economy the Soviet government plans by _____; and when bottlenecks appear it applies the _____ principle and draws upon _____

5. _____ is the agency primarily responsible for the construction of the economic plan in the Soviet Union, and _____ is the agency primarily responsible for ensuring that the provisions of the plan are enforced.

6. Production in the Soviet Union is motivated by _____,

_____,

and _____

7. In the U.S.S.R. prices perform two essential functions, namely, _____ and _____

8. Profits in the Soviet Union are essentially a means of determining _____ while in the United States profits serve to _____

9. The Soviet economy in recent years has had serious microeconomic problems and has had to undertake reform to reduce these problems.

a. Three problems which plagued planners were:

(1) The production of _____ goods and the accumulation of _____ inventories.

(2) A distorted _____ of goods which were of poor _____

(3) The reluctance of enterprise managers to _____

b. The reforms undertaken include:

(1) The introduction of a modified _____ _____

(2) More _____ in the economy and more _____ for enterprise managers.

(3) More planning from _____

c. These reforms were suggested by _____
_____ and others.

10. The gross national product of the U.S.S.R. is about _____ of the GNP of the United States and grew during the 1960s at a rate of about _____% per year.

11. List five specific reasons why there has been economic growth in the U.S.S.R.

a. _____

b. _____

c. _____

d. _____

e. _____

12..What six factors may retard future economic growth in the Soviet Union?

a. _____

b. _____

c. _____

d. _____

e. _____

f. _____

13. What considerations suggest that the Soviet economy may be able to sustain its rate of economic growth?

a. _____

b. _____

c. _____

d. _____

14. What have been the two most significant accomplishments of the U.S.S.R. since central planning began?

a. _____

b. _____

15. The two chief shortcomings of the Soviet economy over the past years have been

_____

and _____

■ PROBLEMS AND PROJECTS

1. On the left side of the table below are several of the major institutions or characteristics of American capitalism. In the spaces to the right, name the institution or characteris-

American institution or characteristic	Russian institution or characteristic
Private ownership of economic resources	_____
Consumer freedom to spend income as he sees fit	_____
Consumer sovereignty	_____
Worker freedom to select occupation and place of work	_____
Profit motive	_____
Entrepreneurial freedom to select product, output, price, etc.	_____
System of prices and markets	_____
Self-interest	_____
Privately owned farms	_____
Privately owned industrial firms and retail stores	_____

tic of the Soviet economy which compares with the American institution or characteristic.

2. Below is a market demand schedule for product X.

Price, rubles	Quantity demanded (million)
90	25
80	30
70	35
60	40
50	45
40	50
30	55

a. If Soviet planners decide to produce 50 million units of product X, the price of the product *plus* the turnover tax will be set at

_____ rubles.

b. If the accounting cost of producing product X is 25 rubles, the turnover tax *rate* will

be set at _____ percent.

■ SELF-TEST

Circle the T if the statement is true, the F if it is false.

1. The Soviet government sets the economic objectives of the economy, directs the resources of the economy toward the achievement of these objectives, and uses the price system as one of the means of achieving these objectives.   **T   F**

2. Consumers in the U.S.S.R. are free to spend their incomes on any of the consumer goods provided by the economy's central plan.   **T   F**

3. *Gosplan* is the agency in the Soviet Union primarily responsible for preparing the economic plan.   **T   F**

4. In the U.S.S.R. individual plants and industries play no part in the formulation of the final economic plan.   **T   F**

5. The basic planning problem in the Soviet Union is the determination of the overall goals of the economy.   **T   F**

6. Application of the priority principle means that when production bottlenecks develop in

the economy, inventories are used to prevent a chain reaction.   **T   F**

7. Most workers in the Soviet Union are paid on a piece-rate basis.   **T   F**

8. The turnover tax does not affect the price of consumer goods, but it does affect the consumer income available for the purchase of consumer goods.   **T   F**

9. The GNP of the U.S.S.R. is about one-half the size of GNP in the United States, and the rate of growth of the GNP in the Soviet Union has been greater than the rate of growth of GNP in the United States.   **T   F**

10. GNP in the U.S.S.R. will undoubtedly expand at a more rapid rate in the future than it has in the past.   **T   F**

Underscore the letter that corresponds to the best answer.

1. Which of the following is *not* true of the Soviet economic challenge to the American economy? (*a*) the economy which achieves the most efficient allocation of resources and the highest standard of living will probably obtain the friendship or political domination of the underdeveloped and uncommitted nations of the world; (*b*) the output of the Russian economy exceeds the output of the American economy; (*c*) the output of the Russian economy is growing at a more rapid rate than the output of the American economy; (*d*) the Soviet economy devotes a larger percentage of its output to capital accumulation than does the American economy.

2. In the U.S.S.R.: (*a*) all property is owned by the state or by collective farms and cooperatives; (*b*) all property except urban housing and farms is owned either by the state or by cooperatives; (*c*) all property except retail and wholesale enterprises is owned either by the state or by collective farms and cooperatives; (*d*) all property except small tools, clothing, household furnishings, and rural homes is owned either by the state or by collective farms and cooperatives.

3. Which of the following is the most important agency in enforcing and carrying out the central economic plan in the Soviet Union? (*a*) *Gosplan;* (*b*) *Gosbank;* (*c*) the Communist party; (*d*) the secret police.

4. Prices in the Soviet Union: (a) are used as a device for rationing consumer goods; (b) are determined by the demands for and the supplies of products and resources; (c) are used to allocate resources among different firms and industries; (d) perform a guiding function, but not a rationing function.

5. Profits and losses in the U.S.S.R. are used to determine whether: (a) the production of various consumer goods should be expanded or contracted; (b) various goods are being produced efficiently or inefficiently; (c) more or fewer resources should be devoted to the production of various goods; (d) a product should be taxed or subsidized.

6. Suppose the Soviet government determined that the annual output of a certain quality of wristwatch would be 100,000 and that the accounting cost of producing a watch is 300 rubles. If the demand schedule for these watches were as given in the table below, what turnover tax rate would be placed on watches? (a) 33⅓%; (b) 66⅔%; (c) 100%; (d) 133⅓%.

Price, rubles	Quantity demanded
700	85,000
600	90,000
500	100,000
400	120,000
300	150,000
200	190,000
100	240,000

7. In the late 1960s the Soviet government undertook a number of economic reforms. These include: (a) the abolition of central planning; (b) the introduction of a modified profit motive; (c) the return of public property to private ownership; (d) the reduction of the autonomy of the managers of individual enterprises.

8. In comparing the composition of GNP in the U.S.S.R. and the United States it can be said that: (a) over 25 percent of the GNP in the United States is devoted to capital goods while less than 20 percent is so devoted in the U.S.S.R.; (b) government in the U.S.S.R. absorbs over 20 percent and in the United States absorbs less than 10 percent of the GNP; (c) over 75 percent of the GNP in both

nations is represented by consumer goods; (d) investment in the U.S.S.R. is over one-half again as large as it is in the United States.

9. Which of the following is *not* a significant factor in explaining the rapid rate of economic growth in the Soviet Union? (a) extensive investment by foreigners in the Soviet economy; (b) high levels of domestic investment in basic industries; (c) adoption of the advanced technological methods employed in Western nations; (d) the reallocation of labor from the agricultural to the industrial sector of the economy.

10. Which of the following is apt to make it possible for the Soviet Union to sustain or increase its rate of economic growth? (a) conditions in the agricultural sector of the economy; (b) the past efforts to improve education and technology; (c) the overall manpower situation; (d) increases in the level of replacement investment.

■ **DISCUSSION QUESTIONS**

1. What is meant by "the Soviet economic challenge"? How is it related to Russian military strength and to Russian political domination of underdeveloped nations?

2. What are the two principal economic institutions of the U.S.S.R.? How do these institutions compare with the economic institutions of the United States?

3. What is the basic planning problem in the U.S.S.R.? What techniques are used to overcome this problem and make central planning workable?

4. How is an economic plan drawn up in the Soviet Union? How is such a plan made "realistic and workable"? Why is the process of obtaining the final plan referred to as a "down-and-up evolution"?

5. What means and agencies are used in the Soviet Union to facilitate the achievement of the objectives of the economic plan? What types of incentives and inducements are offered to encourage the achievement of these objectives?

6. What is meant by the priority principle of resource allocation? What sectors of the Soviet economy have received high priorities in the past?

7. Explain the role *Gosbank* plays in the enforcement of the central economic plan in the U.S.S.R.

8. What functions do prices perform in the U.S.S.R.? How does the Russian government use the turnover tax to set the prices of consumer goods?

9. Plants and firms in the U.S.S.R. can earn profits or suffer losses just as plants and firms can in the United States. What role do profits and losses play in the U.S.S.R. and what role do they play in the United States?

10. How is the turnover tax used in the Soviet Union to match the quantities demanded of various consumer goods with the quantities

of these goods which *Gosplan* has already decided to produce?

11. What microeconomic problems did the Soviet government encounter in the late 1960s, and what reforms did they introduce in an attempt to resolve these problems? What role did Professor Liberman play in these reforms?

12. Compare the GNP of the Soviet Union and the United States with respect to size, composition, and rate of growth.

13. Why has it been possible for the U.S.S.R. to achieve economic growth? Why is economic growth in the Soviet Union called "forced economic growth"?

14. What have been the major accomplishments of central planning in the U.S.S.R.? What are its chief shortcomings?

ANSWERS

CHAPTER 1

Fill-in questions

1. production, exchange, consumption

2. generalizations, abstraction

3. economics is not a laboratory science and economics deals with the behavior of human beings

4. control economic events

5. economic growth, full employment, price stability, economic freedom, equitable distribution of income, economic security

6. *a.* a clear statement of the objectives and goals of the policy; *b.* a statement and analysis of all possible alternative solutions to the problem; *c.* an evaluation of the results of the policy selected after it has been put into operation

7. *a.* failure to distinguish between relevant and irrelevant facts; *b.* failure to recognize economic models for what they are—useful first approximations; *c.* tendency to impute ethical or moral qualities to economic models

8. the economy may be in a different phase of the business cycle

9. employ two different terms to mean the same thing

10. total, general, individual industry, particular product

Problems and projects

1. An increase in the demand for an economic good will cause the price of that good to rise.

2. All the factors are relevant to *some degree.* However, the degree of relevance of the factors varies; and, depending upon the degree of abstraction and generally desired in the analysis of the production and the price of automobiles, the factors may be included or excluded from consideration. The noneconomic factors are c (political), i (sociological), k (ecological), l (psychological), and m (political).

5. *a.* The validity of the statement depends upon the phase of the business cycle; *b.* the fallacy of composition; *c.* dual terminology; *d.* the *post hoc, ergo propter hoc* fallacy.

6. *c.* (1) direct, (2) inverse

Self-test

1. F; **2.** T; **3.** T; **4.** T; **5.** T; **6.** F; **7.** F; **8.** F; **9.** F; **10.** F

1. *b;* **2.** *c;* **3.** *a;* **4.** *a;* **5.** *d;* **6.** *b;* **7.** *a;* **8.** *d;* **9.** *a;* **10.** *b*

CHAPTER 2

Fill-in questions

1. *a.* society's material wants are unlimited; *b.* economic resources, which are the ultimate means of satisfying these wants, are scarce in relation to these wants

2. *a.* property resources; (1) land or raw materials, (2) capital; *b.* human resources; (1) labor, (2) entrepreneurial ability

3. rental income, interest income, wages, profits

4. the social science concerned with the problem of using or administering scarce resources to attain maximum fulfillment of our unlimited wants

5. *a.* the economy is operating at full employment and full production; *b.* the available supplies of the factors of production are fixed; *c.* the state of technology does not change during the course of the analysis

6. directly, indirectly

7. *a.* fewer, more; *b.* unemployed, underemployed; *c.* more, more; *d.* increase resource supplies, improve its technology

8. less

9. economic resources are not completely adaptable between alternate uses

10. *a.* takes initiative of combining the other resources—land, labor, and capital; *b.* makes basic business policy decisions; *c.* takes position of innovator; *d.* takes position of risk bearer

11. *a.* determination of what is to be produced; *b.* determination of how the total output should be produced; *c.* determination of distribution of total output; *d.* determination of the extent of resource use; *e.* determination of provisions for flexibility and adaptability to change

12. opportunity cost

13. apparent, disguised

14. full employment, full production

15. willing, able

16. consumer tastes, supplies of resources, technology

17. values (or goals or priorities), nonscientific (or moral or subjective)

18. goals, institutions, organizations, pure (or laissez faire) capitalism, communism

Problems and projects

1. *a.* land; *b.* C; *c.* land; *d.* C; *e.* EA; *f.* land; *g.* C; *h.* C; *i.* labor; *j.* EA

CHAPTER 3

Fill-in questions

1. private property

2. enterprise, choice

3. attempts to do what is best for itself, competition

4. *a.* large numbers of independently acting buyers and sellers operating in the markets; *b.* freedom of those buyers and sellers to enter or leave these markets

5. control price

6. price, market

7. innovators, profit

8. the extensive use of capital, specialization, the use of money

9. interdependent, exchange

10. medium of exchange

11. coincidence of wants

12. product, resource

2. *b.* 1, 2, 3, 4, 5, 6, 7; *c.* ⅐, ⅙, ⅕, ¼, ⅓, ½, 1

4. *a.* DEP; *b.* CAP; *c.* CAP; *d.* CAP; *e.* CAP; *f.* CAP; *g.* DEP; *h.* DEP; *i.* DEP; *j.* DEP; *k.* CAP; *l.* DEP

Self-test

1. T; **2.** T; **3.** F; **4.** F; **5.** T; **6.** T; **7.** F; **8.** T; **9.** T; **10.** F

1. *d;* **2.** *b;* **3.** *c;* **4.** *b;* **5.** *b;* **6.** *d;* **7.** *a;* **8.** *c;* **9.** *d;* **10.** *d*

13. generally acceptable by buyers and sellers in exchange

14. the prices received for resources, the amount of resources sold, the prices received for products, the amounts sold

Problems and projects

1. *a.* (1) 4, (2) ½; *b.* (1) 5, (2) ⅓; *c.* (1) 8, (2) 2; *d.* (1) 15, (2) 3; *e.* Brobdingnag, Lilliput; *f.* bananas, apples; *g.* 2, 3, ⅓, ½; *h.* 69, 18, (1) 75, 20, (2) 6, 2

2. *a.* (1) ⅔, (2) 1½; *b.* (1) ½, (2) 2; *c.* (1) Schaffner, ½, ⅔; (2) Hart, 1½, 2; *d.* 60, 50, 10 pairs of trousers; *e.* ½, ⅔, 1½, 2

3. *a.* goods and services; *b.* expenditures for goods and services; *c.* money income payments (wages, rent, interest, and profit) *d.* services of resources (land, labor, capital, and entrepreneurial ability)

Self-test

1. F; **2.** T; **3.** T; **4.** F; **5.** T; **6.** T; **7.** F; **8.** T; **9.** F; **10.** F
1. *c;* **2.** *c;* **3.** *c;* **4.** *a;* **5.** *a;* **6.** *d;* **7.** *c*

CHAPTER 4

Fill-in questions

1. business firms, households; demand decisions of households, supply decisions of business firms

2. vertical, horizontal

3. indirect, direct

4. *a.* the tastes or preferences of consumers; *b.* the number of consumers in the market; *c.* the money income of consumers; *d.* the prices of related goods; *e.* consumer expectations with respect to future prices and incomes

5. smaller, less

6. inferior, normal (superior)

7. complementary, substitute

8. demand for, a change in the quantity demanded of the product

9. *a.* the technique of production; *b.* resource prices; *c.* prices of other goods; *d.* price expectations; *e.* the number of sellers in the market

10. increase, decrease

11. less

12. *a.* +, +; *b.* −, +; *c.* −, −; *d.* +, −; *e.* ?, +; *f.* +, ?; *g.* ?, −; *h.* −, ?

13. rationing

14. quantity demanded and quantity supplied are equal

Problems and projects

2. Total: 5, 9, 17, 27, 39

3. Each quantity in column 3 is greater than in column 2, and each quantity in column 4 is less than in column 2.

4. *a.* 30, 4. *b.* (1) 20, 7; (2) inferior; (3) normal (superior)

5. *a.* complementary; *b.* substitute

6. *a.* 0.60; *b.* 25

7. 45,000; 33,000; 22,500; 13,500; 6,000; 0

8. 0.60, 0.55; 33,000, 31,000

9. *a.* decrease demand, decrease price; *b.* decrease supply, increase price; *c.* decrease supply, increase price; *d.* increase demand, increase price; *e.* decrease supply, increase price; *f.* increase demand, increase price; *g.* increase supply, decrease price; *h.* decrease demand, decrease price; *i.* increase demand, increase price; *j.* decrease demand, decrease price

10. Each price in column 3 is less than in column 1 and each price in column 4 is greater than in column 1.

Self-test

1. F; 2. F; 3. F; 4. F; 5. T; 6. F; 7. F; 8. F
1. a; 2. b; 3. b; 4. a; 5. c; 6. d; 7. a; 8. c

CHAPTER 5

Fill-in questions

1. communicating, coordinating

2. maximizes the satisfaction received from its income

3. resources are scarce, substitutes

4. it is payment which must be made to a businessman or entrepreneur to retain his services

5. enter, fall, larger, larger; fall, zero

6. *a.* determination of money incomes; *b.* determination of product prices

7. *a.* is the price system adaptable to change; *b.* is the price system conducive to change

8. artificial barriers

9. profits, borrowed funds

10. private, public (or social), invisible hand

11. it leads to an efficient allocation of resources; it emphasizes personal freedom

12. *a.* competition tends to break down; *b.* it allocates resources poorly; *c.* it fails to adjust rapidly to drastic changes in society's production objectives; *d.* it does not ensure the continuous full employment of the economy's resources.

13. it is irksome to individual producers, technological advance contributes to its decline.

Problems and projects

1. $6, −$5; $10.00; *a.* C; *b.* produce A and have an economic profit of $14; *c.* it would increase

2. *a.* method 2; *b.* −$5, $5; *c.* (1) 13, 8; 3, 4; capital: 2, 4; entrepreneurship; no change; (2) −$5, $4

3. *a.* product B; *b.* (1) 40, (2) 9, (3) 10, (4) 1; *c.* $14; *d.* (1) product C; (2) increase to 90, increase to 12, increase to 12, remain constant at 1; (3) increase to $90

Self-test

1. T; 2. T; 3. T; 4. T; 5. T; 6. T; 7. T; 8. F; 9. T; 10. T
1. b; 2. b; 3. c; 4. d; 5. d; 6. c; 7. a; 8. a; 9. c; 10. b

CHAPTER 6

Fill-in questions

1. market, planned

2. *a.* provide legal foundation and social environment; *b.* maintain competition; *c.* redistribute income and wealth; *d.* reallocate resources; *e.* stabilize the economy

3. the situation wherein the number of sellers becomes small enough so that each can influence total supply and the price of the commodity being sold

4. *a.* regulate, natural; *b.* ownership of; *c.* antitrust (antimonopoly)

5. inequality; *a.* public assistance; *b.* direct market; *c.* income

6. *a.* demand; *b.* supply; *c.* benefit, cost

7. spillover costs, spillover benefits

8. people other than the buyers and sellers

9. *a.* over, cost, benefit; *b.* under, benefit, cost

10. *a.* (1) enact legislation, (2) pass special taxes; *b.* (1) subsidize production, (2) take over the production of the product

11. divisible, individuals, indivisible, spillover

12. exclusion, private, social

13. taxing, spends the revenue to buy

14. *a.* increases, increasing, decreasing; *b.* decreases, decreasing, increasing

15. stabilizing the economy

16. public goods, private goods

17. *a.* estimate; *b.* output and price level, distribution

18. private sector

19. limited decisions

20. the high levels of expenditures for military purposes, the relative growth of government in the economy, ⅕

Problems and projects

1. *a.* reallocates resources; *b.* redistributes income; *c.* provides a legal foundation and social environment *and* stabilizes the economy; *d.* reallocates resources; *e.* maintains competition; *f.* provides a legal foundation and social environment *and* maintains competition; *g.* reallocates income; *h.* reallocates resources; *i.* provides a legal foundation and social environment; *j.* reallocates income

2. *a.* p_2, p_1; *b.* p_2, p_1; *c.* optimum, p_e

3. *a.* a supply curve to the left of the one shown should be drawn in, (1) decreases, increases, (2) greater; *b.* a demand curve to the right of the one shown should be drawn in, (1) increases, increases, (2) less

4. *a.* marginal cost: $500, $180, $80, $100; marginal benefit: $650, $100, $50, $25; *b.* yes; *c.* (1) 2, (2) $500, (3) $650, (4) $150

Self-test

1. F; 2. F; 3. F; 4. F; 5. T; 6. T; 7. F; 8. T; 9. T; 10. T; 11. F; 12. T; 13. F; 14. F; 15. F

1. *a*; 2. *a*; 3. *b*; 4. *a*; 5. *d*; 6. *c*; 7. *b*; 8. *c*; 9. *a*; 10. *d*; 11. *b*; 12. *b*

CHAPTER 7

Fill-in questions

1. furnish resources, buy the bulk of the total output of the economy

2. 70

3. composition of national output, level

4. contribution of resources

5. personal consumption, personal saving, personal taxes

6. 15, Federal, income

7. services, nondurable goods, durable goods

8. stock or accumulation, flow

9. security, speculation

10. increase

Problems and projects

1. 73.3%, 8.7%, 11.2%, 4.0%, 2.9%

2. *a.* −20, −10, 0, 10, 20, 30, 40, 50; *c.* Percent of income spent: 120, 106.67, 100, 96, 93.33, 91.4, 90, 88.9; Percent of income saved: −20, −6.67, 0, 4, 6.67, 8.6, 10, 11.1; *d.* (1) increases, (2) increases; *e.* (1) decreases, (2) increases

Self-test

1. F; 2. F; 3. T; 4. T; 5. T; 6. T; 7. F; 8. T; 9. T; 10. T

1. *c*; 2. *d*; 3. *d*; 4. *b*; 5. *b*; 6. *a*; 7. *a*; 8. *a*

CHAPTER 8

Fill-in questions

1. 11.6 million

2. unlimited, limited

3. *a.* CORP; *b.* PRO and PART; *c.* PRO; *d.* CORP; *e.* CORP; *f.* CORP; *g.* PART; *h.* PART; *i.* CORP

4. *a.* desire to achieve greater productive efficiency; *b.* seeking of power and prestige; *c.* security and insurance of long-run survival; *d.* seeking of greater financial rewards

5. internal growth, combination, combination

6. Any of the following: foundations, mutual insurance companies, Blue Cross and Blue Shield, savings and loan associations, professional societies, trade associations, consumer cooperatives, farmer cooperatives, private colleges and universities, research institutions, and museums and libraries

7. employ economic resources, produce goods and services; those who receive the goods and services they produce pay none or only part of the cost of producing them

8. producing goods and services, hiring the bulk of the economic resources

9. the sources of a firm's receipts, how these receipts were dispersed

10. the amount of capital equipment worn out in the process of producing goods during a year

11. consumers, businesses, government

12. the product sold is the final good or service; the output of the business sector, the value of the intermediate transactions are included in the value of the final product

Problems and projects

3.

Allocations			Receipts	
(1) Wages and salaries		$ 42,000	(8) Sales of output	$128,000
(2) Materials		37,000		
(3) Interest		2,000		
(4) Rents		5,000		
(5) Depreciation		6,000		
(6) Taxes		21,000		
(a) Payroll	$ 4,000			
(b) Indirect Business	1,000			
(c) Corporate profits	16,000			
(7) Corporate profits (after taxes)		15,000		
(a) Dividends	7,000			
(b) Undistributed profits	8,000			
Total allocations		$128,000	Total receipts	$128,000

4.

Allocations			Receipts	
(1) Wages and salaries		$186	(8) Sales of output	$375
(2) Interest		6	(a) To consumers	$270
(3) Rents		11	(b) To other businesses	58
(4) Depreciation		37	(c) To government	47
(5) Taxes		64		
(a) Payroll	$ 5			
(b) Indirect business	35			
(c) Corporate income	24			
(6) Corporate profits after taxes		19		
(a) Dividends	11			
(b) Undistributed profits	8			
(7) Proprietors' income		52		
Total allocations		$375	Total receipts	$375

Self-test

1. F; 2. T; 3. T; 4. T; 5. F; 6. T; 7. F; 8. T; 9. F; 10. T; 11. F

1. c; 2. b; 3. d; 4. a; 5. a; 6. b; 7. b; 8. d; 9. c; 10. a; 11. b

CHAPTER 9

Fill-in questions

1. taxation, expenditures

2. voluntary, compulsory

3. money expenditures for which government currently receives no products or services in return

4. personal income, payroll, war and defense

5. corporate profits are taxed and then the dividents paid out of these profits are taxed as personal income

6. sales, property, education, highways, public welfare

7. Heller Plan, 2, 3, personal income

8. benefits-received, ability-to-pay

9. constant, increasing, decreasing

10. a. P; b. R; c. R; d. R; e. P; f. P

11. regressive, progressive, roughly proportional

Problems and projects

1. tax: $520, $770, $1,060, $1,400, $1,800,

$2,270; average tax rate: 20.8%, 22%, 23.6%, 25.5%, 27.7%, 30.3%

2. Tax A: average tax rate: 3, 3, 3, 3, 3, 3, 3; type of tax: proportional. Tax B: average tax rate: 1, 2, 3, 3, 2.5, 2, 2; type of tax: combination. Tax C: average tax rate: 10, 9, 8, 7, 6, 5, 4; type of tax: regressive

3. *a.* $200, $232, $264, $296, $328, $360; *b.* 4%, 3.87%, 3.77%, 3.70%, 3.66%, 3.6%; *c.* regressive

Self-test

1. T; **2.** F; **3.** F; **4.** T; **5.** T; **6.** F; **7.** F; **8.** T

1. c; **2.** a; **3.** d; **4.** b; **5.** c; **6.** a; **7.** b; **8.** a

CHAPTER 10

Fill-in questions

1. level of production in the economy at some point in time and to plot the long-run course the economy has been following, public policies to improve the performance of the economy

2. market prices

3. the value of money (i.e., the price level) changes

4. double counting

5. value added

6. the market value of the final product

7. purely financial

8. nonincome

9. all final purchases of machinery, tools, and equipment by business firms; all construction; changes in inventories; depreciation

10. expanding, declining, stationary

11. supplements; social insurance programs; private pension, health and welfare funds

12. corporation income taxes, dividends, undistributed corporate profits

13. make allowance for that part of this year's output which is necessary to replace the capital goods consumed in the year's production

14. depreciation

15. indirect business taxes; earned

16. *a.* old age and survivors' insurance and unemployment compensation insurance payments; *b.* relief payments; *c.* veterans' payments; *d.* private pension and welfare payments; *e.* interest payments made by government and consumers

17. transfer payments, social security contributions, undistributed corporate profits, corporation income taxes; personal consumption expenditures, interest paid by consumers, personal saving, personal taxes

18. personal taxes; personal consumption expenditures, interest paid by consumers, personal saving

19. personal consumption expenditures, interest paid by consumers

20. depreciation

Problems and projects

1. *a.* (1) price index (1927 = 100): 100, 122, 67, 78, 89; (2) price index (1935 = 100): 113, 138, 75, 88, 100. *b.* (1) adjusted GNP in 1927 dollars (billions): 90, 98.4, 89.6, 83.3, 78.7; (2) adjusted GNP in 1935 dollars (billions): 79.6, 87, 80, 73.9, 70

2. *a.* 445 billion; *b.* 426 billion; *c.* 361 billion; *d.* 324 billion; *e.* 6 billion

3. All figures are in billions of dollars.

Income (allocations) method		Output (expenditures) method	
Gross National Product			
(1) Compensation to employees	$238	(1) Personal consumption expenditures	$217
(2) Rents	9	(2) Government expenditures for goods and services	71
(3) Interest	6	(3) Gross private domestic investment	56
(4) Proprietors' income	21	(4) Net exports	5
(5) Dividends	13		$349
(6) Corporate income taxes	15		
(7) Undistributed corporate profits	14		
(8) Indirect business taxes	11		
(9) Depreciation	22		
	$349		

Income (allocations) method		Output (expenditures) method	
Net National Product			
(1) Compensation to employees	$238	(1) Personal consumption expenditures	$217
(2) Rents	9	(2) Government expenditures for goods and services	71
(3) Interest	6	(3) Net private domestic investment	34
(4) Proprietors' income	21	(4) Net exports	5
(5) Dividends	13		$327
(6) Corporate income taxes	15		
(7) Undistributed corporate profits	14		
(8) Indirect business taxes	11		
	$327		
National Income			
(1) Compensation to employees	$238	(1) Net national product	$327
(2) Rents	9	(2) Less: indirect business taxes	11
(3) Interest	6		$316
(4) Proprietors' income	21		
(5) Dividends	13		
(6) Corporate income taxes	15		
(7) Undistributed corporate profits	14		
	$316		
Personal Income			
(1) National income	$316	(1) Personal consumption expenditures	$217
(2) Plus: transfer payments	26	(2) Personal saving	29
(3) Less: social security contributions	7	(3) Personal taxes	55
(4) Less: Corporate income taxes	15	(4) Interest paid by consumers	5
(5) Less: Undistributed corporate profits	14		$306
	$306		
Disposable Income			
(1) Personal income	$306	(1) Personal consumption expenditures	$217
(2) Less: personal taxes	55	(2) Personal saving	29
	$251	(3) Interest paid by consumers	5
			$251

4. *a.* personal income and disposable income, a public transfer payment; *b.* none; a second-hand sale; *c.* all, represents investment (additions to inventories); *d.* all; *e.* none, a purely financial transaction; *f.* all; *g.* none, a nonmarket transaction; *h.* all; *i.* none, a private transfer payment; *j.* all; *k.* none, a nonmarket transaction; *l.* all; *m.* all, represents additions to the inventory of the retailer; *n.* personal income and disposable income, a public transfer payment; *o.* all; estimate of rental value of owner-occupied homes is included in rents

Self-test

1. F; 2. F; 3. T; 4. T; 5. F; 6. T; 7. F; 8. F; 9. T; 10. T

1. *b*; 2. *d*; 3. *d*; 4. *b*; 5. *a*; 6. *c*; 7. *c*; 8. *a*; 9. *a*; 10. *d*

CHAPTER 11

Fill-in questions

1. total spending
2. larger, more, increases, increase
3. premature, pure
4. 96 to 97, frictional (or normal)
5. potential, actual

6. rising general level of prices, falling general level of prices

7. money income, the prices which he must pay for the goods and services he purchases

8. The following is a partial answer. Inflation: hurt—savers, creditors, fixed-income groups; benefit—debtors, some profit receivers; Deflation: hurt—debtors, some profit receivers; benefit—savers, creditors, fixed-income groups

9. 1, 3

10. prosperity, recession, depression, recovery; expansion, contraction, upswing, downswing

11. seasonal variations, secular trends

12. capital and durable, nondurable, low

13. expand, low, stable; high and prolonged, capital equipment, construction

14. *a.* strong demand for capital goods; *b.* development of new products and industries; *c.* declining labor costs and general business optimism

15. excess industrial capacity, decline in residential construction

16. increased, decreased

17. a backlog of demand, the means to finance expenditures, rising

18. *a.* a backlog of demand for capital goods; *b.* confidence that the Federal government would prevent unemployment; *c.* a high level of foreign demand for American goods as a result of Marshall Plan aid; *d.* inflation created an expectation of rising prices

19. 1954, 1958, economic growth, rising

20. *a.* a change in economic policy; *b.* expansion of the Vietnam war; *c.* increased spending

by state and local governments; *d.* suburban growth and an increase in the number of people driving automobiles; *e.* rapid rate of technological progress

21. increased, declined, fairly stable, the worst inflation in two decades

22. employment, output, expectations

Problems and projects

1. The following figures complete the table. 1968: 78,737, 58.1, 2,817, 96.4, 3.6; 1969: 80,733, 58.6, 2,831, 96.5, 3.5; 1970: 82,715, 59.0, 4,088, 95.1, 4.9, *a.* the labor force increased more than employment increased; *b.* because unemployment and employment in relative terms are percentages of the labor force and *always* add to 100 percent; if one increases the other must decrease; *c.* yes, because unemployment was between the 3 to 4 percent considered normal; 1970 was a year of less than full employment because unemployment was greater than 4 percent; *d.* because the number of people looking for jobs expands

2. *a.* B, B, B, A; *b.* B. B. B. B.; *c.* C, A, A, C

3. Prices: % decline—34, 7; output; % decline—22, 38. *a.* A; *b.* B; *c.* B; *d.* B

4. *a.* D, B; *b.* I, I; *c.* B, D; *d.* D, B; *e.* D, B; *f.* D, B; *g.* I, I; *h.* D. B

5. *a.* $1,260, $1,323; *b.* $24, $37

Self-test

1. T; **2.** T; **3.** F; **4.** F; **5.** T; **6.** F; **7.** T; **8.** F; **9.** F; **10.** F; **11.** F; **12.** T

1. *d*; **2.** *c*; **3.** *b*; **4.** *b*; **5.** *c*; **6.** *a*; **7.** *d*; **8.** *b*; **9.** *a*; **10.** *a*; **11.** *c*; **12.** *a*

CHAPTER 12

Fill-in questions

1. closed economy, personal, neither taxes nor spends; net national product, national income, personal income, disposable income

2. demand for these goods and services

3. the rate of interest

4. decrease, increase; stabilize

5. Say's Law, price-wage flexibility

6. decrease; unemployment; down, increase; all who are willing to work at the going wage rate are employed, and total output equals total spending

7. it does not exist in the degree necessary for ensuring the restoration of full employment in the face of a decline in total spending, lower money incomes, reductions in total spending, lower prices

8. the fallacy of composition

9. different groups, different reasons

10. income, increase

11. consumption

12. increase, decrease

13. *a.* stocks of liquid assets which households have on hand; *b.* the stocks of durable goods consumers have on hand; *c.* expectations with respect to incomes, prices, and the availability of goods; *d.* the current volume of consumer credit outstanding; *e.* attitudes toward thrift; *f.* taxation of consumer income

14. the amount consumers will consume (save) will be different at every level of income, the level of income has changed and that consumers will change their consumption (saving) as a result

15. expectations of net profit, capital goods

16. *a.* technological advance and innovation; *b.* costs of acquiring, maintaining, and operating the proposed capital equipment; *c.* the interest rate; *d.* government policies; *e.* the stock of capital on hand; *f.* expectations

17. stable, unstable

18. durability, irregularity, variability

Problems and projects

1. *a.* 6, 50, 50. *b.* (1) decrease, increase, increase; (2) increase, decrease, decrease. *c.* (1) increase, increase, increase; (2) decrease, decrease, decrease. *d.* (1) increase, income; (2) decrease, income. *e.* (1) a rate of interest less than zero; (2) because savers are not willing to pay other people for the privilege of allowing them to use or borrow their money; (3) depression; (4) decrease, increase

CHAPTER 13

Fill-in questions

1. aggregate demand–aggregate supply, saving-investment

2. aggregate demand

3. consumption, investment, saving, investment

4. *a.* less than, increase; *b.* greater than, decrease; *c.* equal to, remain unchanged

5. actual, actual, increase, equal to 1/MPS times; decrease, an amount equal to 1/MPS times $5

6. greater than, increase, remain constant, increase, remain constant, inflation

7. 1/MPS, 1/(1-MPC); the economy is characterized by repetitive, continuous flows of expenditures and income; any change in income will cause changes in both consumption and saving to vary in the same direction as, and by a fraction of, the change in income

8. decrease, decrease, remain constant, paradox of thrift

9. less, increase, the multiplier

10. inflationary, aggregate demand, the amount

CHAPTER 14

Fill-in questions

1. Employment, 1946; Council of Economic Advisors, Joint Economic Committee

2. consumption, investment, government expenditures for goods and services; saving, taxes, investment, government expenditures for goods and services

3. marginal propensity to consume, marginal propensity to save

4. decrease, the decrease in taxes or in government spending

5. decreased, increased, increased, decreased

2. saving: −1, 0, 1, 3, 5, 8, 11, 15; APC: 100.3%, 100%, 99.7%, 99.2%, 98.7%, 98%, 97.3%, 96.4%; APS: −0.3%, 0, 0.3%, 0.8%, 1.3%, 2%, 2.7%, 3.6%; MPC: 90%, 90%, 80%, 80%, 70%, 70%, 60%; MPS: 10%, 10%, 20%, 20%, 30%, 30%, 40%

3. *a.* −; *b.* −; *c.* +; *d.* +; *e.* +; *f.* none; *g.* −; *h.* −

4. *a.* +; *b.* +; *c.* −; *d.* +; *e.* +; *f.* −; *g.* −; *h.* −; *i.* +; *j.* −

Self-test

1. F; **2.** F; **3.** T; **4.** T; **5.** F; **6.** F; **7.** T; **8.** F

1. *c;* **2.** *a;* **3.** *a;* **4.** *b;* **5.** *b;* **6.** *c;* **7.** *d;* **8.** *d*

by which equilibrium NNP exceeds the full-employment noninflationary NNP

Problems and projects

1. *a.* S: 10, 12, 14, 16, 18, 20, 22, 24, 26, 28, 30; I: 22, 22, 22, 22, 22, 22, 22, 22, 22, 22; 22; C + I: 312, 320, 328, 336, 344, 352, 360, 368, 376, 384, 392. *b.* 360. *c.* 0.80, 0.20. *d.* 5. *e.* 15. *f.* 20

2. change in income: $8.00, $6.40, $5.12, $4.10, $16.38, $50.00; change in consumption: $8.00, $6.40, $5.12, $4.10, $3.28, $13.10, $40.00; change in saving: $2.00, $1.60, $1.28, $1.02, $0.82, $3.28, $10.00

3. *a.* 350, 15; *b.* 0.20, 5; *c.* 10, 20; *d.* 10; *e.* (1) decrease, 340, 15; (2) decrease, 330, 13; (3) decrease, decrease, leave unchanged the amount of, paradox of thrift; (4) multiplier

4. *a.* 2½; *b.* 620, 30, inflationary, 12; *c.* 570, 20, deflationary, 8

Self-test

1. T; **2.** T; **3.** T; **4.** F; **5.** F; **6.** F; **7.** T; **8.** T

1. *c;* **2.** *d;* **3.** *a;* **4.** *b;* **5.** *b;* **6.** *c;* **7.** *c;* **8.** *a*

6. deficit, surplus

7. 5, 4

8. tax receipts, government expenditures

9. increase, decrease; decrease, increase

10. borrowing from the public, creating new money; latter, financing in this manner will avoid the depressing effects upon consumption and investment which borrowing from the public may have

11. *a.* public works spending stimulates the construction and capital goods industries which are typically hardest hit by depression; *b.* public works expenditures, as opposed to relief payments, and subsidies, guarantee that government funds will be spent at least once

12. progressive

13. *a.* difficulty in predicting accurately the future course of economic activity; *b.* the expenditure aspect of fiscal policy is lacking in flexibility; *c.* Congress may be slow to enact the required changes in taxes and expenditures

14. progressive, regressive

15. down, decreased

Problems and projects

1. *a.* C′: 316, 325, 334, 343, 352, 361, 370, 379, 388, 397, 406, 415, 424; S′: 24, 25, 26, 27, 28, 29, 30, 31, 32, 33, 34, 35, 36; S′ + T: 34, 35, 36, 37, 38, 39, 40, 41, 42, 43, 44, 45, 46. *b.* I + G: 35, 35, 35, 35, 35, 35, 35, 35, 35, 35, 35, 35, 35; C′ + I + G: 351, 360, 369, 378, 387, 396, 405, 414, 423, 432, 441, 450, 459. *d.* 360. *e.* 100. *f.* 90. *g.* increase, $10

2. *a.* 60; *b.* 70; *c.* second; *d.* 30; *e.* 45; *f.* second

3. *a.* (1) −, −, −; (2) +, +, +; (3) +, +, +; (4) −, −, −; (5) +, +, +. *b.* (1) +, 0, 0; (2) +, 0, 0; (3) +, 0, 0; (4) −, −, −; (5) −, −, −

4. *b.* built-in stability; *c.* (1) decreased, (2) decreased, (3) increased; *d.* more; *e.* 6, 36, 3.6

5. *a.* 0.8, 5; *b.* (1) Number 2, (2) Number 1, (3) Number 3; *c.* (1) 40, 10, 0, (2) 0.8, 5; *d.* (1) 36, 9, 5, (2) 0.72, 3.6; *e.* (1) (*a*) 27.2, 6.8, 16, (*b*) 54.4, 2.2, (2) (*a*) 25.6, 6.4, 18, (*b*) 51.2, 2.1, (3) (*a*) 28.8, 7.2, 14, (*b*) 57.6, 2.4; *f.* (1) does not, (2) decreases, (3) decreases, (4) decrease, increase

Self-test

1. T; **2.** T; **3.** T; **4.** F; **5.** T; **6.** T; **7.** F; **8.** F; **9.** F; **10.** T; **11.** T; **12.** T

1. c; **2.** b; **3.** b; **4.** a; **5.** b; **6.** c; **7.** a; **8.** b; **9.** d; **10.** d; **11.** d; **12.** b

CHAPTER 15

Fill-in questions

1. *a.* annually balanced budget; *b.* cyclically balanced budget; *c.* functional finance

2. it intensifies both inflation and contraction (tax receipts tend to decrease and expenditures to increase during inflation while taxes tend to increase and expenditures to decrease during depression)

3. depression, inflation, the upswing and downswing of the cycle may not be of equal magnitude and duration

4. full employment without inflation, deficits, public debt

5. 40, 1.9

6. *a.* private debt is one between distinct economic units, while public debts is one held within a single economic unit; *b.* retirement of public debt which is internally held need not entail a loss of purchasing power from the economy as a whole, whereas retirement of private debt entails a redistribution of wealth which can lead to a loss of purchasing power; *c.* public debt, because nations are immortal, need never

be retired, but private debt, because persons are mortal, must be retired at some time.

7. internally

8. the goods and services that could not be produced because of the production of war goods; receive the interest paid

9. investment, income inequality, monetary policy

10. highly liquid and virtually riskless securities for small and conservative investors, cyclical downswings, monetary

11. increases, borrowed, spent

12. government; *a.* decrease; *b.* increase

Problems and projects

1. *a.* (1) Debt as % of GNP: 22, 80, 100, 120, 120, 118.75; (2) interest as % of GNP: 13.33, 4.00, 4.00, 4.92, 6.00, 9.50. *b.* (1) 1, 4; (2) 4, 5; (3) 5, 6; *c.* (1) 3, 6; (2) 2, 3; (3) 1, 2

Self-test

1. T; **2.** T; **3.** T; **4.** F; **5.** T; **6.** F; **7.** T; **8.** T

1. a; **2.** b; **3.** d; **4.** a; **5.** b; **6.** c; **7.** d; **8.** b

CHAPTER 16

Fill-in questions

1. *a.* medium of exchange; *b.* standard of value; *c.* store of value

2. coins, paper money, bank money (or demand deposits), banks, government

3. banks, the Federal government

4. savings accounts (or time deposits), government bonds

5. it can be exchanged for goods and services which people desire; inversely, price level

6. demand deposits, currency

7. control of the money supply; Federal Open Market Committee, Federal Advisory Council

8. *a.* set the discount rate; *b.* set the reserve ratio; *c.* open-market operations

9. *a.* they are central banks; *b.* they are quasi-public banks; *c.* they are bankers' banks

10. it accepts deposits of banks, makes loans to banks

11. *a.* holding the deposits of member banks; *b.* providing for the collection of checks; *c.* supplying the economy with paper currency; *d.* acting as fiscal agent for the government; *e.* supervising member banks; *f.* regulating the supply of money

12. accept deposits, make loans, create money

13. create money, destroy money

14. hold most of the treasury's checking accounts, aid the government in collecting taxes, administer sale and redemption of government bonds

15. regulating the supply of money

Problems and projects

1. *a.* $220.0 = (53.7 + 6.5 + 0.6 + 171.9) - (10.4 + 0.2 + 0.1)$; *b.* $396.9 = 230.2 + 166.7$

2. remained unchanged, changed to include $500 less in currency and $500 more in bank money (demanded deposits)

3. *a.* rise, 25; *b.* fall, 9.1

Self-test

1. F; **2.** F; **3.** T; **4.** T; **5.** F; **6.** T; **7.** T; **8.** T

1. *d*; **2.** *c*; **3.** *b*; **4.** *d*; **5.** *a*; **6.** *b*; **7.** *d*; **8.** *b*

CHAPTER 17

Fill-in questions

1. assets, liabilities

2. vault cash, till money

3. demand deposit; time deposit

4. Federal Reserve Bank in its district, deposit liabilities, reserve ratio

5. actual reserves, required reserves

6. fractional

7. not changed

8. decreased, increased; decreased, increased

9. excess reserves

10. increases, 10,000

11. decreases, 2,000

12. profits, liquidity

13. reciprocal of the reserve ratio (deposit multiplier)

14. smaller

15. decrease, 36 million

Problems and projects

1.

	(1)	(2)	(3)	(4)
Assets:				
Cash	$100	$100	$100	$100
Reserves	150	150	260	300
Loans	500	500	500	500
Securities	200	200	200	100
Liabilities:				
Demand deposits	850	850	960	900
Capital stock	100	100	100	100

2. column 2: 8, 6, 5, 4, 3⅓, 3; column 3: 1, 1, 1, 1, 1, 1; column 4: 8, 6, 5, 4, 3⅓, 3

3.

	(1a)	(2a)	(3a)	(4a)	(5a)
A. Required reserve	$35	$40	$30	$36	$44
B. Excess reserve	5	0	−5	4	1
C. New loans— single bank	5	0	*	4	1
D. New loans— monopoly bank	25	0	*	20	5

* If an individual bank or a monopoly bank is $5 short of reserves it must either obtain additional reserves of $5 by selling loans, securities, or its own IOUs to the reserve bank or contract its loans by $25.

	(1b)	(1c)	(2b)	(2c)	(3b)	(3c)	(4b)	(4c)	(5b)	(5c)
Assets:										
Cash	$ 10	$ 10	$ 20	$ 20	$20	$20	$ 20	$ 20	$ 15	$ 15
Reserves	40	40	40	40	25	25	40	40	45	45
Loans	105	125	100	100	*	*	104	120	151	155
Securities	50	50	60	60	30	30	70	70	60	60
Liabilities:										
Demand deposits	180	200	200	200	*	*	184	200	221	225
Capital stock	25	25	20	20	25	25	50	50	50	50

* If an individual bank or a monopoly bank is $5 short of reserves it must either obtain additional reserves of $5 by selling loans, securities, or its own IOUs to the reserve bank or contract its loans by $25.

4.

	(1)	(2)	(3)	(4)	(5)	(6)
Assets:						
Cash	$ 50	$ 50	$ 50	$ 50	$ 50	$ 50
Reserves	105	105	108	108	110	110
Loans	200	220	200	240	200	250
Securities	200	200	192	192	200	200
Liabilities:						
Demand deposits	505	525	500	540	500	550
Capital stock	50	50	50	50	50	50
Loans from Federal Reserve	0	0	0	0	10	10
Excess reserves	4	0	8	0	10	0
Maximum possible expansion of the money supply	20	0	40	0	50	0

Self-test

1. F; **2.** T; **3.** F; **4.** F; **5.** T; **6.** T; **7.** F; **8.** F; **9.** F; **10.** F; **11.** T; **12.** T; **13.** T; **14.** T; **15.** F

1. c; **2.** d; **3.** b; **4.** a; **5.** b; **6.** b; **7.** d; **8.** b; **9.** a; **10.** b

CHAPTER 18

Fill-in questions

1. a full-employment noninflationary level of total output; Board of Governors of the Federal Reserve, the Federal Reserve Banks

2. decrease, contract, rise, decline

3. securities, gold certificates, Federal Reserve Notes, reserves of member banks

4. influence the ability of commercial banks to create money by lending, influence the rate of interest

5. securities held by the Federal Reserve Banks, loans to commercial banks by the Federal Reserve Banks

6. the reserve ratio, the discount rate, open market operations

7. excess reserves, the multiple by which the banking system can lend

8. decrease, decrease, buy; increase, increase, sell

9. 10 million, 10 million, 7.5 million; none, 10 million, 10 million

10. a. −; b. +; c. +

11. a. margin requirements; b. consumer credit regulations; c. the maximum interest rate commercial banks may pay on time deposits

12. M: the supply of money; V: the income (circuit) velocity of money; P: the price level; Q: the physical volume of output

13. a. +, 0; b. 0, +; c. +, +; d. 0, +; e. +, 0

14. a. one month; b. 6

15. a. decreased; b. good, bad; c. deflation, inflation

16. $34.39

17. refuse to make loans, refuses to borrow from commercial banks

18. speed and flexibility

Problems and Projects

1. Assets: securities, gold certificates, loans to member banks, cash; liabilities: Federal Reserve Notes, member bank reserves, Treasury deposits

2. *a.* (1) reduce, 20; (2) buy, 25; (3) decrease, 1; *b.* (1) increase, 28⅖; (2) sell, 12½; (3) increase, 2½

3.

	(2)	(3)	(4)	(5)	(6)
Federal Reserve Banks					
Assets:					
Gold certificates	$ 25	$ 25	$ 25	$ 25	$ 25
Securities	27	34	30	30	30
Loans to commercial banks	10	10	10	10	4
Liabilities:					
Reserve of commercial banks	47	54	50	55	44
Treasury deposits	5	5	5	0	5
Federal Reserve Notes	10	10	10	10	10
Commercial Banks					
Assets:					
Reserves	$ 47	$ 54	$ 50	$ 55	$ 44
Securities	70	66	70	70	70
Loans	90	90	90	90	90
Liabilities:					
Demand deposits	197	200	200	205	200
Loans from Federal Reserve	10	10	10	10	4
A. Required reserves	49.25	50	40	51.25	50
B. Excess reserves	−2.25	4	10	3.75	−6
C. Initial change in the money supply	−3	0	0	+5	0
D. Total potential change in money supply	−12	+16	+50	+20	−24

4. *a.* year 1: 450; year 2: $2; year 3: 4; year 4: $450; year 5: $4; year 6: 750. *b.* (1) *Q*, 33⅓; (2) *P*, 14½, *Q*, 16⅔; (3) 31¼, 7½; (4) *P*, 33⅓; (5) *P*, 20

Self-test

1. F; **2.** T; **3.** T; **4.** F; **5.** F; **6.** T; **7.** F; **8.** F; **9.** F; **10.** F

1. *b*; **2.** *a*; **3.** *c*; **4.** *b*; **5.** *d*; **6.** *c*; **7.** *d*; **8.** *d*; **9.** *d*; **10.** *c*

CHAPTER 19

Fill-in questions

1. aggregate demand, consumption, investment, government expenditures for goods and services

2. *a.* net national product (or disposable income), consumption schedule; *b.* profit expectations; *c.* public policy

3. fiscal, monetary

4. *a.* government, aggregate demand; *b.* tax, consumption, investment

5. money, rate of interest, investment

6. complex, quantify, noneconomic

7. fiscal

8. *a.* demand, velocity, supply; *b.* real GNP, 3, 5

9. net, employment, inflation

10. *a.* prices, wages, rents; *b.* (1) an investment tax credit, (2) reducing the excise tax on automobiles, (3) setting ahead the date on which personal income tax exemptions increase by one year; *c.* imports subject to tariff, foreign currencies

Problems and projects

1. *a.* *C'*: $150, 190, 230, 270, 310, 350, 390, 430, 470; *S'*: $0, 10, 20, 30, 40, 50, 60, 70, 80; *b.* $200; *c.* $250, 300, 350, 400, 450, 500, 550, 600; *e.* (1) −, +; (2) +, −; (3) +, −; (4) +, −; *f.* (1) −, +; (2) +, −; (3) +, −; (4) +, −; *g.* increase in net taxes, decrease in government expenditures, decrease in investment demand, decrease in consumption schedule; decrease in net taxes, increase in government expenditures, increase in investment demand, increase in consumption schedule

2. *a.* greater; *b.* smaller; *c.* (1) $20; (2) $80, 1.0%; *d.* 1.5, 2.0, 2.5, 3.0, 3.5, 4.0, 4.5, 5.0; *f.* (1) decrease, 0.5%; (2) increase, 0.5%; *g.* (1) a curve to the right of LM_2; (2) a curve to the left of LM_2

3. *a.* (1) 400; (2) 3.0; *b.* (1) 400; (2) 3.0; *c.* (1) +, +, +, −; (2) −, −, −, +; (3) +, −, +,

+; (4) −, −, −, ?; (5) +, +, +, −; *d.* increase the supply of money, increase government expenditures for goods and services, decrease net taxes; *e.* decrease the supply of money, decrease government expenditures, increase net taxes

Self-test

1. T; 2. F; 3. T; 4. T; 5. T; 6. T; 7. F; 8. T; 9. F; 10. T

1. *c*; 2. *b*; 3. *c*; 4. *c*; 5. *b*; 6. *a*; 7. *d*; 8. *c*; 9. *a*; 10. *a*

CHAPTER 20

Fill-in questions

1. fixed, changes (increases)

2. total real output, per capita real output

3. increases, decreases, existing wants, new needs

4. quantity and quality of natural resources, quantity and quality of human resources, the supply or stock of capital goods, technology, demand, allocative

5. $30, $18, $12

6. 8

7. increase, decreasing

8. 10

9. average, decrease

10. optimum population

11. population, decrease

12. productivity

13. increase, increasing

14. aggregate demand, productive capacity, capital-output ratio

15. reallocate, speed, completeness

Problems and Projects

1. *a.* 80, 120, 130, 70, 50, 30, 10, −10; *b.* third, fourth; *c.* positive, negative; *d.* 80, 100, 110, 100, 90, 80, 70, 60; *e.* increasing, decreasing; *f.* 3, average product, a maximum

2. *a.* 100; *b.* 100, 110, 120, 125, 120, 110, 100, 90; *c.* 25; *d.* capital, technology, labor; *e.* increased, 4; *f.* (1) increased, 120; (2) remained constant; (3) decreased to 90

3. *a.* full-employment consumption: 192, 224, 256, 288, 320; full-employment saving: 48, 56, 64, 72, 80; investment required: 48, 56, 64, 72, 80; *b.* 20, 20; *c.* 11.1, 11.1; *d.* the rate at which full-employment output increases; *e.* the marginal propensity to save

4. *a.* (1) 330, 363, 399.3; (2) full-employment consumption: 231, 254.1, 279.51; full-employment saving: 99, 108.9, 119.79; (3) 99, 108.9, 119.79; *b.* 10, 10; *c.* increasing, increasing; *d.* 0.3, ⅓, 10, the rate at which investment must increase to ensure full employment

Self-test

1. T; 2. F; 3. T; 4. F; 5. T; 6. T; 7. F; 8. F; 9. T; 10. F; 11. F; 12. T

1. *a*; 2. *d*; 3. *b*; 4. *a*; 5. *b*; 6. *c*; 7. *b*; 8. *c*; 9. *b*; 10. *b*

CHAPTER 21

Fill-in questions

1. *a.* 6; *b.* 2½

2. 3.6%, 1.9%

3. Japan, France, Italy, Canada

4. improvements in product quality, sizable increases in leisure

5. increase, employ substitutes, increase production, foreign countries

6. achieving greater economy in the use of available supplies of resources, developing means for the economical recovery of known sources of raw material, discovering new substitute materials

7. the size of the population; health, education, training, versatility

8. new products, new productive techniques

9. the size, vigor, and ability of the entrepreneurial class

10. $30,000, 11%

11. 42%; improved education and training, improved technology, the economies of large-scale production

12. a GNP gap and a slower rate of growth, inflation

13. it must encourage those changes in products, productive techniques, and capital facili-

ties vital to economic growth; it must provide a mechanism which will efficiently reallocate resources in a way appropriate to these changes; price system

14. virtually no social or moral taboos upon production and material progress, healthy attitudes toward work and risk-taking, a stable political system.

15. artificial impediments, inherent resource immobilities

Problems and projects

1. *a.* $300, 400, 500, 550, 600, 550, 500; *b.* 150 million; *c.* (1) $15 billion; (2) $100; *d.* (1) 46⅔%; (2) 9.1%

CHAPTER 22

Fill-in questions

1. standard of living, domestic problems, image (reputation)

2. spillovers, domestic problems, anxiety, insecurity, good life

3. continuous full employment, increased investment, more basic scientific research, more education

4. aggregate demand

5. expansionary ("tight"), contractionary; *a.* interest rates, investment; *b.* corporate income, personal income, reducing

6. increase, research and development

7. social benefits, social goods

8. technological unemployment, gradual, so many production processes cannot be automated, it is not economically feasible (profitable) to automate

9. aggregate demand, productivity of labor

10. the demand for labor, displaced workers, new industries

11. *a.* education and training for displaced workers; *b.* improving the flow of information in labor markets and the mobility of workers; *c.* rehabilitating distressed areas; *d.* reducing social obstacles to employment

12. demand increases, demand decreases, price level in the economy, output, price level, unemployment

CHAPTER 23

Fill-in questions

1. *a.* a large number of independent sellers in a highly organized market; *b.* the firms produce a standardized or virtually standardized product; *c.* individual firms exert no significant

2. *a.* $200.0, 210.0, 242.0, 266.2; *b.* 5%, less, aggregate demand did not increase by enough to induce the economy to produce at capacity; *c.* (1) $10; (2) 4.5%; *d.* (1) $22; (2) $55; (3) more; (4) 15.2%; (5) rise, aggregate demand in constant dollars was greater than the constant dollar productive capacity; (6) by having idle productive capacity in year 2; *e.* (1) greater, equal to; (2) fall; (3) would

Self-test

1. T; **2.** T; **3.** T; **4.** F; **5.** T; **6.** F; **7.** T; **8.** T; **9.** F; **10.** F

1. *d*; **2.** *c*; **3.** *b*; **4.** *c*; **5.** *b*; **6.** *d*; **7.** *c*; **8.** *b*; **9.** *a*; **10.** *c*

13. market power, market power, less than full employment, something extra, higher prices

14. upward, downward, increase, remain constant, increase the price level

15. of pattern bargaining and escalator clauses, they use materials produced by industries which have experienced a structural increase in demand

16. inflation, unemployment

17. wage increases, productivity, labor costs per unit of output or product prices

18. voluntary restraint, reduction of market power, increased government participation and control, an excess wage settlement tax

Problems and projects

1. *a.* 3; *b.* 6

2. *a.* unemployment; *b.* inflationary pressures; *c.* full employment

3. *a.* S; *b.* D; *c.* S; *d.* S and C; *e.* S and C; *f.* S; *g.* D and S

4. *a* 4; *b.* (1) increase, increase; (2) decrease, decrease; (3) remain constant, remain constant; *c.* (1) remain constant; (2) increase, decrease; remain constant; (3) equally

Self-test

1. F; **2.** F; **3.** F; **4.** F; **5.** F; **6.** T; **7.** T; **8.** T; **9.** T; **10.** F; **11.** T; **12.** F

1. *b*; **2.** *b*; **3.** *b*; **4.** *b*; **5.** *c*; **6.** *b*; **7.** *a*; **8.** *d*; **9.** *c*; **10.** *d*; **11.** *d*; **12.** *a*

control over product price; *d.* new firms are free to enter and existing firms are free to leave the industry; *e.* there is virtually no room for nonprice competition

2. sellers', buyers'

3. fully employed, allocated among alternative uses in the most efficient way; latter

4. standardized, differentiated; close substitutes

5. there are barriers to entry into the industry

6. public relations, good-will

7. there are large numbers of sellers, entry into the industry is fairly easy, the firm has some control over the price of its product

8. *a.* there is only one firm in the industry; *b.* the firm produces a product for which there are no close substitutes; *c.* the firm exercises considerable control over the price of its product; *d.* there are barriers to entry into the industry; *e.* advertising is limited and of a good-will or public relations nature

9. each firm produces a fairly small share of the total industry output

10. *a.* a large number of independent sellers; *b.* the product is differentiated; *c.* the firm has a limited amount of control over the price of its product; *d.* entry into the industry is relatively easy; *e.* there is extensive and vigorous non-price competition

11. the product is standardized in pure competition and differentiated in monopolistic competition

12. standardized, differentiated

13. raw materials, semifinished goods

14. few, a significant percentage

15. the number of rivals the firm has, the extent to which the products of rival firms are substitutes for the product of the oligopolistic firm.

16. (1) pure competition, monopsony, monopsonistic competition, oligopsony; (2) large number of buyers, one buyer, fairly large number of buyers, a few buyers

17. the geographic size of the market, the extent of interindustry competition, the extent of nonprice competition, the rate of technological advance

18. *a.* the legislation and policies of government; *b.* business policies and practices; *c.* technological development and the role of research in industry; *d.* the permissive characteristic of American capitalism

CHAPTER 24

Fill-in questions

1. inelastic, elastic

2. sensitive, insensitive

3. negatively (inversely), positively (directly)

4. elastic: greater than 1, decrease, increase; inelastic: less than 1, increase, decrease; of

Problems and projects

1. number of firms: d, a, c, b; type of product: e, e, f, e or f; control over price: m, h, g, g; entry: i, j, k, l; nonprice competition: m, g, h, g or h

2. pure competition–pure competition, agricultural markets; pure competition–pure monopsony, many labor markets; pure competition–monopsonistic competition, agricultural products used as raw materials in manufacturing; pure competition–oligopsony, raw tobacco; pure monopoly–pure competition, public utilities; pure monopoly–pure monopsony, many labor markets; pure monopoly–monopsonistic competition, public utilities servicing industry; pure monopoly–oligopsony, many labor markets; monopolistic competition–pure competition, many consumer goods markets; monopolistic competition–pure monopsony, many labor markets; monopolistic competition–monopsonistic competition, many consumer goods markets; monopolistic competition–oligopsony, original-equipment automobile parts; oligopoly–pure competition, aluminum; oligopoly–pure monopsony, missiles and rockets; oligopoly–monopsonistic competition, many local markets for consumer goods; oligopoly–oligopsony, original-equipment tires

3. *a.* oligopoly or monopolistic competition; standardized product, number of firms is fairly large, easy entry; *b.* oligopoly or monopolistic competition; differentiated product, number of firms is fairly large, entry is moderately difficult; *c.* pure competition; large number of firms, standardized product, easy entry; *d.* oligopoly; small number of firms, difficult entry; *e.* oligopoly or monopolistic competition; differentiated product, number of firms is fairly large, easy entry; *f.* oligopoly; small number of firms, entry is fairly difficult

4. *a.* yes; railroads, buses, automobiles; *b.* yes; synthetic fibers (nylon, rayon); *c.* yes; aluminum, steel, wood, copper, glass; *d.* yes; radios, movies, books, records, all forms of entertainment; *e.* yes; aluminum, steel, wood, glass, plastics

Self-test

1. F; 2. F; 3. T; 4. T; 5. T; 6. F; 7. T; 8. F; 9. T; 10. F; 11. T; 12. T; 13. F; 14. F; 15. F

1. *d;* 2. *c;* 3. *b;* 4. *b;* 5. *a;* 6. *a;* 7. *b;* 8. *b;* 9. *d;* 10. *a;* 11. *b;* 12. *b*

unitary elasticity: equal to 1, remain constant, remain constant

5. perfectly inelastic, perfectly elastic, parallel to the vertical axis, parallel to the horizontal axis

6. *a.* greater than; *b.* less than; *c.* equal to

7. *a.* the number of good substitutes for the

product which are available; *b.* the relative importance of the product in the total budget of the buyer; *c.* whether the good is a necessity or a luxury; *d.* the period of time in which demand is being considered; *e.* the durability of the good

8. the amount of time which a producer has to respond to a price change

9. *a.* 7.00, 15,000; *b.* shortage, 4,000; *c.* surplus, 2,000

10. war, shortages, rationing

11. rationing

12. minimum wages, agricultural price supports

13. surplus, attempt to reduce supply or increase demand, purchase the surplus and store or dispose of it

14. remains constant, decreases, equal to, less than

15. elastic, inelastic

16. the amount the price of the commodity rises as a result of the tax; *a.* less, more; *b.* more, less

Problems and projects

1. *a.* 0.70, 0.80, 0.75; *b.* 500, 600, 550; *c.* total revenue: $300, 360, 400, 420, 420, 400, 360; elasticity coefficient: $2\frac{5}{7}$ (2.72), $1\frac{8}{9}$ (1.89), $1\frac{4}{11}$ (1.36), 1, $\frac{11}{15}$ (0.73), $\frac{9}{17}$ (0.53); character of demand: elastic, elastic, elastic, unitary elasticity, inelastic, inelastic; *d.* elasticity coefficient: $1\frac{4}{15}$ (1.27), $1\frac{4}{13}$ (1.31), $1\frac{4}{11}$ (1.36), $1\frac{4}{9}$ (1.44), $1\frac{4}{7}$ (1.57), $1\frac{4}{5}$ (1.8); character of supply: elastic, elastic, elastic, elastic, elastic, elastic; *e.* (1) shortage, 300; (2) surplus, 500

2. *a.* (1) S_3; (2) S_2; (3) S_1; *b.* p_1, q_1; *c.* (1) p_4,

remain at q_1; (2) p_3, q_2; (3) p_2, q_3; *d.* more; *e.* less, greater

3. *a.* $3.60; *b.* (reading down) 600, 500, 400, 300, 200, 100; *c.* $4.00; *d.* (1) $.40, $66\frac{2}{3}$; (2) $.20, $33\frac{1}{3}$

4. *a.* (2) has not changed; (3) none, all; (4) smaller, larger; (5) larger, smaller; *b.* (2) increased by the amount of the tax; (3) all, none; (4) larger, smaller; (5) smaller, larger

5. *a.* average revenue: $11.00, 10.00, 9.00, 8.00, 7.00, 6.00, 5.00, 4.00, 3.00, 2.00; total revenue: $0, 10.00, 18.00, 24.00, 28.00, 30.00, 30.00, 28.00, 24.00, 18.00; marginal revenue: $10.00, 8.00, 6.00, 4.00, 2.00, 0, −2.00, −4.00, −6.00; elasticity coefficient: 21.0, 6.33, 3.4, 2.14, 1.44, 1.0, 0.7, 0.47, 0.29; *b.* imperfectly competitive; price (average revenue) decreases as the output of the firm increases and is greater than marginal revenue; *d.* (1) elastic, positive; (2) inelastic, negative; (3) of unitary elasticity, equal to 0; *e.* in order to sell a larger quantity, it is necessary for the firm to lower its price not only on the additional units but also on the units which it could have sold at the higher price

6. *a.* average revenue: all are $10.00; total revenue: $0, 10.00, 20.00, 30.00, 40.00, 50.00, 60.00; marginal revenue: all are $10.00; *b.* purely competitive, because price (average revenue) is constant and equal to marginal revenue; *d.* infinity; *e.* they are equal

Self-test

1. F; **2.** T; **3.** F; **4.** T; **5.** T; **6.** F; **7.** F; **8.** T; **9.** F; **10.** T; **11.** T; **12.** T

1. c; **2.** b; **3.** a; **4.** a; **5.** c; **6.** b; **7.** c; **8.** c; **9.** a; **10.** b; **11.** a; **12.** b

CHAPTER 25

Fill-in questions

1. increase, decrease, income

2. more, lower, less, more, substitution

3. rational, tastes

4. limited, prices, budget restraint

5. ratio of the marginal utility of the last unit purchased of a product to its price

6. *a.* the income of the consumer; *b.* the prices of other products

7. increase, decrease

8. marginal utility, decrease

Problems and projects

1. *a.* (1) increase, $1\frac{1}{2}$; (2) inelastic; *b.* (1) decrease, 1; (2) elastic

2. marginal utility of good A: 21, 20, 18, 15, 11, 6, 0; marginal utility of good B: 7, 6, 5, 4,

3, 2, 1.2; marginal utility of good C: 23, 17, 12, 8, 5, 3, 2

3. *a.* marginal utility per dollar of good A: $4\frac{1}{5}$, 4, $3\frac{3}{5}$, 3, $2\frac{1}{5}$, $1\frac{1}{5}$, 0; marginal utility per dollar of good B: 7, 6, 5, 4, 3, 2, $1\frac{1}{5}$; marginal utility per dollar of good C: $5\frac{3}{4}$, $4\frac{1}{4}$, 3, 2, $1\frac{1}{4}$, $\frac{3}{4}$, $\frac{1}{2}$; *b.* the marginal utility per dollar spent on good B (7) is greater than the marginal utility per dollar spent on good A (3), and the latter is greater than the marginal utility per dollar spent on good C (2); he would not be maximizing his utility; *c.* he would be spending more than his $37 income; *d.* (1) 4; (2) 5; (3) 3; 151; 3. *e.* A, he would obtain the greatest marginal utility for his dollar ($2\frac{1}{5}$)

4. *a.* MU/$ of good A: 15, 10, $6\frac{2}{3}$, 5, 4, $3\frac{1}{3}$, 3, $2\frac{1}{2}$; MU/$ of good B: 6, $5\frac{1}{2}$, 5, $4\frac{1}{2}$, 4, $3\frac{1}{2}$, 3, $2\frac{1}{2}$; MU/$ of good C: 10, 9, 8, 7, 6, 5, 4, 3; MU/$ of good D: 8, $6\frac{4}{5}$, 6, $5\frac{2}{5}$, 5, $4\frac{3}{5}$, 4, 3; MU/$ of saving: 6, 5, 4, 3, 2, 1, $\frac{1}{2}$, $\frac{1}{4}$; *b.* (1) 4; (2) 3; (3) 6; (4) 5, 2, 490; *c.* (1) 2;

(2) 3; (3) 6; (4) 8; d. price of A: 6.00, 4.00, 3.00, 2.00, 1.50; quantity of A demanded: 2, 3, 4, 6, 8. The relationship between price and quantity is the demand schedule

CHAPTER 26

Fill-in questions

1. other products, opportunity, alternative

2. attract the resources, explicit, implicit

3. implicit, the services of entrepreneurs, total, explicit, implicit

4. amounts of variable resources (labor, raw materials, etc.), the fixed resources (the size of the plant) it employs

5. enter, leave, fixed (constant)

6. variable resource, fixed resource, extra or marginal product, variable resource, decline

7. fixed, variable, variable

8. increase, decreasing, increase, increasing

10. average variable, average total, marginal

11. total variable, total cost

12. decreasing, increasing

13. had time to make all appropriate adjustments in its plant size

14. a. increased specialization in the use of labor; b. better utilization of and increased specialization in management; c. more efficient productive equipment; d. greater utilization of by-products

15. managerial inefficiency

Problems and projects

1. a. 15 units of good Y; b. 1½ units of good Y; c. 7 units of good Y

Self-test

1. F; 2. T; 3. T; 4. F; 5. F; 6. T

1. c; 2. b; 3. a; 4. b; 5. c; 6. c

2. a. 5, 6, 7, 6, 5, 4, 3, 2, 1, ½; b. $0, 10, 20, 30, 40, 50, 60, 70, 80, 90, 100; c. $2.00, 1.67, 1.43, 1.67, 2.00, 2.50, 3.33, 5.00, 10.00, 20.00; d. (1) decreases; (2) increases

3. a.

Total cost	Average fixed cost	Average variable cost	Average total cost	Marginal cost
$ 200	—	—	—	—
250	$200.00	$50.00	$250.00	$ 50
290	100.00	45.00	145.00	40
320	66.67	40.00	106.67	30
360	50.00	40.00	90.00	40
420	40.00	44.00	84.00	60
500	33.33	50.00	83.33	80
600	28.57	57.14	85.71	100
720	25.00	65.00	90.00	120
870	22.22	74.44	96.67	150
1,100	20.00	90.00	110.00	230

4. a. $7.00, 6.00, 5.00, 4.00, 4.00, 3.00, 4.00, 5.00, 6.00, 5.00, 7.00, 10.00; b. (1) 10, 40; (2) 50, 80; (3) 90, 120

Self-test

1. F; 2. T; 3. T; 4. F; 5. F; 6. T; 7. T; 8. T; 9. F; 10. F

1. a; 2. b; 3. d; 4. a; 5. d; 6. c; 7. d; 8. b; 9. b; 10. a

CHAPTER 27

Fill-in questions

1. a. a large number of independent sellers; b. a standardized product; c. no single firm supplies enough to influence market price; d. no obstacles to the entry of new firms or the exodus of old firms

2. total revenue minus total cost

3. total-receipts—total-cost, marginal-revenue—marginal-cost

4. it can realize a profit or a loss which is less than its fixed costs; its profit is the greatest or its loss the least, marginal revenue equals marginal cost

5. the minimum average variable cost

6. that portion of the firm's marginal-cost curve which lies above the average-variable-cost curve, the sum of the short-run supply curves of all firms in the industry

7. total quantity demanded, total quantity supplied, the quantity demanded and supplied at the equilibrium price

8. fixed (constant), variable

9. price (average revenue), marginal revenue, long-run marginal cost, a minimum

10. the firms in the industry are realizing profits in the short run, the firms in the industry are realizing losses in the short run

11. increasing cost

12. the industry's demand for resources is small relative to the total demand for these resources, the industry is using unspecialized resources which are used by other industries

13. total satisfaction of consumers; consumers most want, the most efficient way

14. a. the best available (least-cost); b. price, cost; c. are essential to produce the product; d. minimum

15. marginal cost, price

16. a. The competitive price system does not accurately reflect the needs of consumers; b. the competitive price system does not accurately measure costs and benefits where spillover costs and benefits are significant; c. the competitive price system does not entail the use of the most efficient productive techniques; d. the competitive price system may not provide for a sufficient range of consumer choice or for the development of new products

Problems and projects

1. a. (see table below); b. (1) 0, $-300; (2) 5, $-100; (3) 7, $380;

c.

Price	Quantity supplied	Profit
$360	10	$1,700
290	9	1,070
230	8	590
180	7	240
140	6	0
110	5	−150
80	4	−270
60	0	−300

d. (1) quantity supplied: 1,000, 900, 800, 700, 600, 500, 400; (2) (a) 180; (b) 7; (c) 240; (d) enter, profits in the industry will attract them into the industry

2. a. 140; b. 6; c. 133 = 800 (the total quantity demanded at $140) ÷ 6 (the output of each firm); d. 150 = 900 ÷ 6

Self-test

1. F; 2. T; 3. T; 4. T; 5. F; 6. F; 7. T; 8. T; 9. F; 10. T; 11. T

1. c; 2. a; 3. d; 4. b; 5. b; 6. b; 7. c; 8. c; 9. b; 10. a; 11. b

Market price = $55		Market price = $120		Market price = $200	
Revenue	Profit	Revenue	Profit	Revenue	Profit
$ 0	$ −300	$ 0	$ −300	$ 0	$ −300
55	−345	120	−280	200	−200
110	−340	240	−210	400	−50
165	−345	360	−150	600	90
220	−370	480	−110	800	210
275	−425	600	−100	1,000	300
330	−510	720	−120	1,200	360
385	−635	840	−180	1,400	380
440	−810	960	−290	1,600	350
495	−1,045	1,080	−460	1,800	260
550	−1,350	1,200	−700	2,000	100

CHAPTER 28

Fill-in questions

1. reasonable approximations, monopolistic competition, oligopoly

2. a. nonexistent; b. strongest; c. weak; d. strong

3. a. the economies of scale; b. natural monopolies; c. ownership of essential raw materials; d. patents and research; e. unfair competition; f. the economies of being established

4. their costs of production will be greater than those of the large-scale firms, they will find it difficult to obtain the money capital necessary to acquire a large-scale plant

5. natural, regulated

6. tying agreement

7. product disparagement, pressure on resource suppliers and banks to withhold materials and credit, hiring away of strategic personnel, aggressive price cutting designed to bankrupt competitors

8. advantages over potential new firms, easier access to the capital market; an efficient administrative framework staffed by competent and experienced personnel; past profits from which to finance expansion; a product which is highly advertised, which is sold through well-established

marketing channels, and for which customers have a preference

9. less than, less than, will decrease

10. marginal revenue, marginal cost, greater than

11. *a.* highest possible; *b.* a maximum; *c.* profit

12. public criticism, the entry of new firms into the industry

13. entry of new firms

14. a minimum, price (or average revenue), marginal cost

15. costs (or cost schedule), economies of scale

16. the amount by which price exceeds average cost becomes the income of stockholders who are largely in the upper income groups

17. past profits, the profits, automatic impetus

18. less evident than in a static economy

19. marginal cost, average (total) cost

20. average (total) cost, the misallocation of resources caused by monopoly

Problems and Projects

1. *a.* total revenue: $0, 650, 1,200, 1,650, 2,000, 2,250, 2,400, 2,450, 2,400, 2,250, 2,000; marginal revenue: $650 550, 450, 350, 250, 150, 50, −50, −150, −250; *b.* (1) 6; (2) 400; (3) 1,560; (4) 260; *c.* $250, 750, 1,140, 1,410, 1,550, 1,560, 1,430, 1,150, 710, 100

2. output of the firm: 3, 0; price it will charge: $150, −; total profit: $−60, $−300; average profit: $−20, −

3. *a.* 4, 11.50, 4.00; *b.* 6, 8.50, −7.50, bankrupt, subsidize; *c.* 5, 10.00, zero; *d.* b, a, c

Self-test

1. F; **2.** T; **3.** T; **4.** F; **5.** T; **6.** F; **7.** F; **8.** T; **9.** T; **10.** T

1. *b;* **2.** *c;* **3.** *a;* **4.** *d;* **5.** *a;* **6.** *c;* **7.** *b;* **8.** *c;* **9.** *a;* **10.** *d*

CHAPTER 29

Fill-in questions

1. relatively large, differentiated, collude, price, nonprice, fairly easy

2. limited, rivalry

3. *a.* more, less; *b.* number of rivals the firm has, the degree of product differentiation; *c.* marginal cost, marginal revenue

4. reduce, increase

5. equal average cost, equal zero, greater

6. average cost is greater than minimum average cost, price is greater than marginal cost

7. product differentiation, product promotion

8. a wider variety of goods, an improved quality of goods.

9. informative, competitive

10. (a) information; (b) newspapers, magazines, radio, and television; (c) new products; (d) costs; (e) spending in the economy

11. (a) informative; (b) wastes; (c) social costs; (d) costs; (e) spending; (f) barrier to entry

12. product, promotion

Problems and projects

2. *a.* marginal cost: $30, 10, 20, 30, 40, 50, 60, 70, 80, 90; marginal revenue: $110, 90, 70, 50, 30, 10, −10, −30, −50, −70; *b.* (1) 4; (2) $80; (3) $180; *c.* (1) decrease; (2) average cost; (3) equal to zero

Self-test

1. F; **2.** F; **3.** T; **4.** F; **5.** T; **6.** T; **7.** F; **8.** F

1. *c;* **2.** *b;* **3.** *c;* **4.** *d;* **5.** *b;* **6.** *c;* **7.** *a;* **8.** *b*

CHAPTER 30

Fill-in questions

1. few, standardized, differentiated, difficult

2. mutually interdependent, the reactions of rivals, no, so many

3. the economies of scale, the advantages of merger

4. oligopoly encompasses many specific market situations, the element of mutual interdependence which fewness adds complicates analysis

5. inflexible, simultaneously

6. price, nonprice

7. elastic, elastic, inelastic

8. not raise their prices, lower their prices

9. gap, price the oligopolist will charge in order to maximize his profits

10. would be set by a pure monopolist

11. *a.* legal obstacles (the antitrust laws); *b.* a large number of firms in the industry; *c.* differentiated products; *d.* price breaks

12. set price or output, divide the market

13. informal, prices, the ingenuity of each seller (i.e., nonprice competition), price leader

14. prices one firm might charge, prices the other firm might charge, profits of the two firms

15. *a.* the price charged by the other firm; *b.* decrease, not raise its price, also lower its price; *c.* collusion, merger

16. price cuts can be quickly and easily met by a firm's rivals, oligopolists are typically blessed with substantial financial resources which allow them to support such measures as advertising and product development

17. substantial profits; *a.* technological advance provides an alternative means for enlarging total profits; *b.* technological superiority is a basic means by which survival is ensured; *c.* the presence of strong rivals places the oligopolist under severe pressure to seek maximum productive efficiency; *d.* existence of barriers to entry give the progressive oligopolist some assurance that he will realize some of the profit rewards of research

18. have not, modest, financed from public funds.

19. resource suppliers, customers, abuses of original power, share in the profits of original power

20. costs, better, countervailing power, smaller, higher

CHAPTER 31

Fill-in questions

1. resources, incomes, costs

2. derived, productivity of the resource, value of the product produced from the resource

3. marginal revenue product, marginal resource cost; price, marginal resource cost

4. marginal revenue product, quantities, prices

5. lower, less

6. 15.00, 27, 5.00, 20, 6.00

7. adding up the demand curves for the resource of all the firms hiring the resource

8. product, productivity, prices

9. *a.* +; *b.* −; *c.* +; *d.* +; *e.* +

10. more, less, substitution, more, output

11. marginal physical product, substituted, elasticity of demand, portion of total production costs accounted for by the resource

12. marginal revenue product, price

13. marginal physical product, price

14. one

CHAPTER 32

Fill-in questions

1. unit of time, the wage rate multiplied by the amount of time worked; the goods and services money wages will purchase

Problems and projects

1. *a.* total revenue: 290, 560, 810, 1,040, 1,250, 1,260, 1,265, 1,265, 1,260; *b.* marginal revenue: 2.70, 2.50, 2.30, 2.10, 0.40, 0.20, 0, −0.20; elasticity of demand: 19, 11, 7.57, 5.67, 1.2, 1.1, 1.0, 0.9; *c.* 2.50, 500; *e.* (1) 2.50, 500; (2) 2.50, 500, they have decreased; (3) 2.50, 500, they have increased

2. *a.* marginal cost: $30, 20, 30, 40, 50, 60, 70, 80; marginal revenue: $130, 110, 90, 70, 50, 30, 10, −10; *b.* $90; *c.* (1) 5; (2) $280; *d.* (1) 15; (2) $840; *e.* no; *f.* $90

3. *a.* $3, $2, $2; *b.* (1) would not, its profits would decrease; (2) would not, its profits would decrease; (3) would, this would prevent an even larger decrease in its profits; (4) would not, its profits would decrease; *c.* (1) $4, $49; (2) $4, $50; (3) $99

Self-test

1. T; **2.** F. **3.** F; **4.** T; **5.** F; **6.** F; **7.** T; **8.** T; **9.** F; **10.** T

1. *c*; **2.** *d*; **3.** *c*; **4.** *c*; **5.** *d*; **6.** *a*; **7.** *b*; **8.** *c*; **9.** *d*; **10.** *d*

15. *a.* marginal revenue product, marginal resource cost, marginal revenue product, marginal resource cost, one; *b.* marginal physical product, marginal resource cost

Problems and projects

1. *a.* marginal physical product of A: 12, 10, 8, 6, 4, 2, 1; *b.* total revenue: 0, 18.00, 33.00, 45.00, 54.00, 60.00, 63.00, 64.50; marginal revenue product of A: 18.00, 15.00, 12.00, 9.00, 6.00, 3.00, 1.50; *c.* 0, 1, 2, 3, 4, 5, 6, 7

2. *a.* total product: 0, 22, 43, 62, 78, 90, 97, 98; *b.* (1) total revenue: 0, 22.00, 38.70, 49.60, 54.60, 54.00, 48.50, 39.20; (2) marginal revenue product of B: 22.00, 16.70, 10.90, 5.00, −0.60, −5.50, −9.30; *c.* 0, 1, 2, 3, 4, 4

3. *a.* (1) 1, 3; (2) 3, 5; *b.* 5, 6; *c.* the marginal physical product of C divided by its price, the marginal physical product of D divided by its price; *d.* purely, $.50; *e.* (1) 114; (2) $57; (3) $28; (4) $29

Self-test

1. T; **2.** F; **3.** T; **4.** T; **5.** T; **6.** F; **7.** F; **8.** T

1. *c*; **2.** *c*; **3.** *a*; **4.** *c*; **5.** *c*; **6.** *c*; **7.** *d*; **8.** *a*

2. capital equipment, natural resources, technological, work

3. it is necessary for employers to pay higher wages to attract workers from alternative employment; total quantity of labor demanded, total quantity of labor supplied; marginal-revenue-product schedules for labor

4. perfectly, an individual employer is unable to affect the market wage rate

5. marginal revenue product, wage rate, marginal labor cost

6. marginal revenue product, marginal labor cost; marginal labor cost, the wage rate, the marginal revenue product of labor, marginal labor cost

7. lower, less

8. increase wages, increasing the demand for labor, restricting the supply of labor, imposing above-equilibrium wage rates on employers

9. restricting the supply of labor, imposing above-equilibrium wage rates, decreased

10. marginal revenue product of labor, competitive and monopsonistic equilibrium wage, the relative bargaining strength of the union and monopsonist

11. *a.* increase, decrease; *b.* increase, increase; *c.* increase, decrease

12. increase, decrease, leave uneffected

13. homogeneous, attractiveness, imperfect

14. noncompeting, equalizing differences, they must be paid to compensate workers for the nonmonetary differences or unattractive aspects of various jobs

15. immobilities, geographical, sociological, artificial-institutional

16. *a.* education, health, mobility; *b.* productivity, wage rates (income); *c.* real wages; *d.* groups

Problems and projects

1. *a.* quantity of labor demanded: 100, 200, 300, 400, 500, 600, 700, 800; *b.* (1) 10.00; (2) 600; *c.* (1) 10.00; (2) 6; (3) 10.00; *f.* 400

2. *a.* total labor cost: 0, 4.00, 12.00, 24.00, 40.00, 60.00, 84.00, 112.00, 144.00; marginal labor cost: 4.00, 8.00, 12.00, 16.00, 20.00, 24.00, 28.00, 32.00; *b.* (1) 5; (2) 12.00; (3) 20.00; *d.* 6, 14.00

3. *a.* wage rate: 16.00, 16.00, 16.00, 16.00, 16.00, 16.00, 16.00, 18.00; *b.* total labor cost: 16.00, 32.00, 48.00, 64.00, 80.00, 96.00, 112.00, 144.00; marginal labor cost: 16.00, 16.00, 16.00, 16.00, 16.00, 16.00, 16.00, 32.00; *c.* (1) 6; (2) 16.00; (3) 96.00; *d.* increased, increased, increased

Self-test

1. F; **2.** T; **3.** T; **4.** F; **5.** T; **6.** F; **7.** T; **8.** T; **9.** T; **10.** T

1. *a*; **2.** *c*; **3.** *d*; **4.** *d*; **5.** *d*; **6.** *a*; **7.** *a*; **8.** *a*; **9.** *b*; **10** *d*

CHAPTER 33

Fill-in questions

1. land, natural resources, fixed (perfectly inelastic)

2. demand, supply, incentive, surplus

3. unearned, confiscated, the single tax

4. land differs in productivity (quality), individual, alternative uses

5. money, loanable funds, they can use them to purchase capital equipment

6. risk, the length of loan, the amount of the loan, market imperfections

7. business firms, the expected net return from the purchase of capital

8. negative, inelastic

9. current, past, households, business firms, newly created, commercial banks, government

10. transactions, precautionary, speculative

11. administered, investment, rations

12. entrepreneurial ability, resources, non-routine decisions, innovating, uncertain

13. uncertain, insurable, uninsurable, economy as a whole, innovation

14. investment, employment, output

15. allocation, monopoly

Problems and projects

1. *a.* 250.00; *b.* 300,000; *d.* 0, 300,000

2. *a.* —; *b.* ?; *c.* ?; *d.* —; *e.* +; *f.* +; *g.* +; *h.* +

Self-test

1. F; **2.** T; **3.** T; **4.** T; **5.** T; **6.** F; **7.** T

1. *a*; **2.** *d*; **3.** *b*; **4.** *c*; **5.** *d*; **6.** *b*; **7.** *c*

CHAPTER 34

Fill-in questions

1. particular, interrelationships

2. *a.* the resources used to produce Z; *b.* other products which use these same resources; *c.* products which are substitutes for or complements to product Z; *d.* resources which are substitutes for the resources used to produce Z and other products

3. equilibrium, product, resource

4. tastes, availability of resources, technology

5. downward, upward; *a.* (1) diminishing marginal utility, (2) diminishing marginal productivity; *b.* (1) increasing marginal cost, (2) work-leisure preferences and increasing marginal cost

6. *a.* increase, decrease; *b.* P, Q; *c.* increase, decrease; *d.* C, D

7. *a.* P, Q; *b.* increase, decrease; *c.* increase, decrease; *d.* C, D; *e.* increase, decrease

8. *a.* substitutes, complements; *b.* increase, decrease; *c.* Q, P

9. maximizes the satisfaction of the wants; *a.* price, marginal cost; *b.* minimum; *c.* the same

10. imperfectly, less than ideal, incomplete, slow

11. technological progress, product variety

12. *a.* spillover costs, spillover benefits, social goods; *b.* distribution, income

CHAPTER 35

Fill-in questions

1. small number of, all or a large portion, major, relative, absolute

2. workable, economies of mass production, high rate, investment, pricing, social responsibility

3. *a.* pervasive competition; *b.* interproduct competition; *c.* innovative competition; *d.* countervailing power; *e.* potential competition

4. *a.* technological imperatives, capital, technology, planning; *b.* security, stability, vertically, internally, advertising, salesmanship, government

5. restrict, charge higher, misallocate, greater inequality, slow rate, instability, political

6. competition, monopoly

7. natural, agencies, commissions

8. monopoly, restraint of trade

9. price discrimination, tying contracts, acquisition of stock of competing corporations to lessen competition, interlocking directorates

10. investigate unfair competitive practices, public hearing on such complaints, "cease and desist" orders, the courts, interpret the meaning of antitrust laws

13. producing, consuming (using), output, input

14. 7.5

15. performance of the economy, economic problems, economic policies

Problems and projects

2. *a.* From left to right: 75, 0, 75, 10, 400; *b.* 25; *c.* (1) 37½; (2) 15; (3) 8¾; (4) 35; *d.* (1) 8.8; (2) 13.6; (3) 2.9; (4) 8.97; *e.* each sector will have to increase its inputs in order to increase its output, and this will require still further increases in the outputs of the various sectors

Self-test

1. F; 2. T; 3. T; 4. F; 5. T; 6. T; 7. T; 8. F; 9. F; 10. T

1. *c;* 2. *b;* 3. *c;* 4. *a;* 5. *d;* 6. *d;* 7. *c;* 8. *a;* 9. *c;* 10. *c;* 11. *d;* 12. *a*

11. Celler Antimerger, Clayton

12. Wheeler-Lea, Robinson-Patman, price discounts

13. conglomerate, other industries

14. exempts, patients, protective tariffs

15. Webb-Pomerene, Miller-Tydings; labor unions, agricultural cooperatives

16. patent laws, protective tariffs

17. *a.* maintenance of the status quo; *b.* move toward public regulation and ownership; *c.* restore vigorous competition

18. no individual firm possess considerable market power, collusion, entry into markets is relatively unrestricted

Problems and projects

1. G; 2. C; 3. I; 4. A; 5. E; 6. F; 7. D; 8. B; 9. H

Self-test

1. F; 2. F; 3. T; 4. F; 5. F; 6. T; 7. F; 8. F; 9. T; 10. F

1. *d;* 2. *b;* 3. *c;* 4. *a;* 5. *a;* 6. *b;* 7. *b;* 8. *d;* 9. *c;* 10. *b*

CHAPTER 36

Fill-in questions

1. *a.* prosperity; *b.* prosperity; *c.* depression; *d.* prosperity; *e.* depression

2. less, highly unequal

3. falling farm prices and incomes over the years, extreme year-to-year fluctuations in farm prices and incomes

4. inelastic demand for agricultural products, the fact that the supply of agricultural products

has tended to increase more rapidly than the demand for these products, the relative immobility of agricultural resources

5. farm products have few good substitutes

6. technological advances in the production of agricultural products

7. the increase in the size of the American population has not been rapid enough; as the income of Americans has increased, their expenditures for farm products have not increased proportionately

8. immobile

9. inelastic, small, large, small, large

10. resources, agriculture, the nonagricultural sectors of the economy

11. *a.* cost, economic growth; *b.* purely competitive, price

12. *a.* prices, incomes, output; *b.* soil conservation; *c.* agricultural research; *d.* farm credit; *e.* crop insurance; raise farm incomes by raising the prices of farm products

13. given, a fixed amount of goods and services

14. surpluses, purchase

15. increase, decrease

16. acreage-allotment, soil bank; new uses, domestic consumption, export

17. reallocated, already have high incomes, increase agricultural production

18. *a.* the free-market solution; *b.* the production controls solution; *c.* the optimum R & D solution

19. *a.* free markets should be restored in agriculture by the eventual elimination of price and income supports; *b.* the return to free agricultural markets should be implemented by an adaptative approach; action by government working with and not against the free market; *c.* the exodus of human resources from agriculture should be hastened by improvements in the labor market; *d.* present support prices should be replaced by adjustment prices; *e.* two temporary land retirement programs

20. rural education, nonfarm occupations, nonfarm employment, the retraining and moving costs of farm workers who seek nonfarm employment

21. government subsidy, the nonfarm economy, support, government farm programs were ended immediately

Problems and projects

1. 0.42; 0.6125; 0.735; 0.70; 0.805

2. *a.* inelastic; *b.* decrease, 1,200.00, 700.00, 16⅔, decrease, 41⅔; *c.* fall, 1.00, 0.80, fall, 700.00, 560.00; *d.* 100, 180.00; *e.* (1) 0.80, 1.00; (2) 720.00; (3) greater, disposing of a surplus; (4) inelastic

3. *a.* increase, 153,750.00, 200,000.00; *b.* increase, 153,750.00, 205,000.00

Self-test

1. T; 2. T; 3. F; 4. T; 5. F; 6. T; 7. F; 8. F; 9. T; 10. T

1. *c*; 2. *d*; 3. *a*; 4. *c*; 5. *d*; 6. *c*; 7. *b*; 8. *c*; 9. *a*; 10. *b*

CHAPTER 37

Fill-in questions

1. 150, 75, increase

2. where, transport, resources, buyers

3. surplus, labor

4. near each other and their markets; *a.* internal economies of scale; *b.* locational (transport) economics; *c.* urban economies

5. higher, internal, external, society, spillover

6. the advantages and opportunities of a metropolitan area, the disadvantages, fragmentation, imbalance

7. *a.* property, base, rates; *b.* large, welfare, densely, high

8. *a.* jobs; *b.* transportation; *c.* highways, congestion, pollution; *d.* highways, suburbs, automobiles, highways; *e.* public mass transit

9. *a.* user charge, peak pricing; *b.* public masstransmit systems

10. weight, wastes, nature (the ecological system), absorb (reabsorb or recycle), population, per capita income, technology, incentives

11. *a.* prosperous, trained and educated, suburbs, buildings; *b.* educated, low, South; *c.* central city, suburbs, mass transit, discrimination

12. jobs, education, training, maintenance

13. public mass-transit system, Black capitalism

14. consolidation, revenues

15. decision, needs, means

16. sharing, the Federal government, property, land, buildings

Problems and projects

1. *a.* 1,800, 900; *b.* $.50; *c.* $.50; *d.* (1) 810, (2) Total revenue: 225, 67.50, 90, 45, 270, 90, 22.50; 810, (3) 7am–9am, 4pm–6pm; *e.* (1) 55, (2) 64

2. *a.* 4,000, 2,500; *b.* 5,000; *c.* 7,500,000; *d.* 1,000, 1,500,000

3. *a.* grossly inadequate; *b.* high; *c.* low; *d.* inadequate; *e.* old, deteriorated, crowded; *f.* high; *g.* deplorable; *h.* high

CHAPTER 38

Fill-in questions

1. considerable

2. native abilities; education, training, and opportunity; property resources; misfortune

3. decreased, significant

4. has not changed significantly

5. consumer satisfaction, occupational opportunities, productivity, social and political

6. a high volume of saving; incentives to work, produce, and innovate; the incomes necessary to bring forth improved products and cultural advances

7. *a.* $3,700; $1,800; *b.* 10, 24

8. *a.* the aged; *b.* farmers; *c.* children; *d.* families headed by women; *e.* the unhealthy; *f.* the unemployed; *g.* the poorly educated and trained

9. nonwhites, higher, discrimination

10. *a.* much of it is isolated and unseen in the hearts of large cities; *b.* the sick and old seldom venture onto the streets; *c.* rural poverty is away from the main highways; *d.* the poor can be well dressed because clothes are inexpensive; *e.* the poor have no political voice

11. old age, survivors, disability and health; unemployment; public assistance

12. least, most

13. the fault of the individual, social forces

14. prosperous, rapidly expanding

15. negative income, workfare

Problems and projects

1. *a.* (1) column 4: 18, 30, 44, 61, 80, 91, 100; (2) column 5: 4, 10, 22, 36, 51, 71, 100; *b.* (1) 30, 10; (2) 20, 49

2. *a.* 5,000, 4,000, 3,000, 2,000, 1,000, 0; *b.* Income subsidy: 3,000, 2,400, 1,800, 1,200, 600, 0; Total income: 3,000, 3,400, 3,800, 4,200, 4,600, 5,000; *c.* 600, 400; *d.* 5,000; *e.* Income subsidy: 5,000, 4,000, 3,000, 2,000, 1,000, 0; 1,000, 0; *f.* (1) 8,333⅓, 7,333⅓, 6,333⅓, 5,333⅓, 4,333⅓, 3,333⅓; (2) Income subsidy: 5,000, 4,400, 3,800, 3,200, 2,600, 2,000; Total income: 5,000, 5,400, 5,800, 6,200, 6,600, 7,000; (3) 600, 400; (4) 5,000, 0

Self-test

1. T; **2.** T; **3.** T; **4.** F; **5.** T; **6.** T; **7.** T; **8.** F; **9.** T; **10.** F

1. *d*; **2.** *b*; **3.** *c*; **4.** *d*; **5.** *c*; **6.** *a*; **7.** *b*; **8.** *d*; **9.** *c*; **10.** *d*

1. T; **2.** T; **3.** T; **4.** F; **5.** F; **6.** F; **7.** F; **8.** T; **9.** T; **10.** F

1. *b*; **2.** *c*; **3.** *a*; **4.** *a*; **5.** *d*; **6.** *d*; **7.** *a*; **8.** *c*; **9.** *b*; **10.** *c*

CHAPTER 39

Fill-in questions

1. 20, 28

2. of the attitude of the courts, the resistance of employers to recognizing and bargaining with unions

3. criminal conspiracy, injunctions

4. discriminatory discharge, blacklisting, lockout, strikebreakers, yellow-dog contracts, paternalism, company unions

5. business unionism, political neutrality, craft unionism

6. Norris-La Guardia, Wagner; CIO, industrial, unskilled mass-production

7. organize, bargain collectively; National Labor Relations Board, unfair labor practices of management

8. Taft-Hartley, Landrum-Griffin, merger of the AFL and the CIO, static (constant), stagnation

9. *a.* provisions which designate and outlaw certain "unfair union practices"; *b.* provisions which regulate the internal administration of unions; *c.* provisions which specify collective bargaining procedures and regulate the actual contents of bargaining agreements; *d.* provisions for the handling of strikes which threaten to imperil the health and safety of the nation

10. elections, finances, union members, union officers

11. *a.* the degree of recognition and status accorded the union and the prerogatives of management; *b.* wages and hours; *c.* seniority and job opportunities; *d.* a procedure for settling grievances

12. what are others getting, productivity, ability to pay, cost of living

13. status, security, administering, interpreting

14. monopolies, above-equilibrium, misallocate; unemployment, inflation, abolished, regulated, price-wage controls, three-party bargaining

15. employment, prices, socially responsible; resisting wage demands, labor unions did not exist, monopoly power, aggregate demand

CHAPTER 40

Fill-in questions

1. 80, 8, 41

2. civilian goods and services

3. *a.* the Federal government budget, the sale of products in the market; *b.* nonprofit, profit; *c.* rival military establishments in other nations; *d.* conscripting, competing

4. *a.* defense budget; *b.* central-management, subsidiaries, expand its size; *c.* cost, progress payments, patent

5. distribute, less, occupational choice

6. monetary cost, professional mercenaries, racial, too small

7. *a.* taxes, demand-pull, borrowing, money; *b.* instability

8. civilian goods and services, military goods and services

CHAPTER 41

Fill-in questions

1. private goods, public (social) goods, ethical

2. recreation, advertising, tobacco, automobiles

3. increased, sixteen

4. a misallocation of resources, instability, a low rate of growth

5. demand, supply, Wagner's Law

6. *a.* the mechanisms and mores of capitalism; *b.* the political realities in the United States; *c.* the character of social goods; *d.* the tax obstacles; *e.* advertising and emulation; *f.* inflation

7. median family income, GNP, the public attitude that government spending is costless to them, the fact that those who expect to benefit most from increased public spending are a majority of the population and are in the lower-income tax brackets, the vocal and active minorities who request and obtain increased public spending

Problems and projects

1. 1. K; 2. D; 3. Q; 4. E; 5. O; 6. G; 7. A; 8. C; 9. F; 10. J

2. *a.* C; *b.* B; *c.* B; *d.* A; *e.* D; *f.* C; *g.* C; *h.* B

Self-test

1. F; **2.** F; **3.** F; **4.** T; **5.** F; **6.** F; **7.** T; **8.** T; **9.** T; **10.** T

1. *b;* **2.** *b;* **3.** *d;* **4.** *a;* **5.** *a;* **6.** *d;* **7.** *b;* **8.** *b;* **9.** *c;* **10.** *d*

9. decrease, increase, easy

10. *a.* military, civilian; *b.* spillover; *c.* private, inevitable; *d.* fiscal, monetary; *e.* conflict, development

11. national priorities, civilian, military

12. *a.* benefit, hurt; *b.* longsightedness, third party

Problems and projects

1. *a.* 8, 0; *b.* 7, 100; *c.* 300; *d.* 200

2. *a.* 3, 6; *b.* −6, −3; *c.* −3, −6; *d.* −3, 3; *e.* (1) 3, (2) 3

Self-test

1. F; **2.** F; **3.** F; **4.** T; **5.** F; **6.** T; **7.** T; **8.** F; **9.** T; **10.** F

1. *b;* **2.** *a;* **3.** *a;* **4.** *c;* **5.** *a;* **6.** *d;* **7.** *d;* **8.** *b;* **9.** *a;* **10.** *c*

8. *a.* (1) it will not necessarily be spent for high-priority items at the expense of low-priority private items, (2) many of the "new needs" of society are for private rather than public goods; *b.* (1) the overproduction of social goods because of their "free" and nonmarket character, (2) the overproduction of social goods because public spending tends to increase across the board when it increases, (3) the loss of individual freedom

9. an end to the Vietnam war and an effective disarmament agreement, increased output that results from economic growth

10. sales

Self-test

1. F; **2.** F; **3.** T; **4.** F; **5.** T; **6.** T; **7.** T; **8.** T; **9.** T; **10.** F

1. *d;* **2.** *d;* **3.** *b;* **4.** *a;* **5.** *a;* **6.** *c;* **7.** *b;* **8.** *b;* **9.** *a*

CHAPTER 42

Fill-in questions

1. less mobile, money, restrictions

2. 4, 59, 63

3. machinery, automobiles and tractors, chemicals; autos and parts; petroleum and products, electrical machinery

4. comparative advantage, comparative disadvantage

5. more output, inputs (resources); resources, uneven, different combination of resources

6. *a.* inexpensive, expensive; *b.* expensive, inexpensive; *c.* hats, bananas; *d.* 3, 4, world demand and supply for hats and bananas; *e.* (1) ⅓, 2/7, (2) 4, 3½

7. cost, increases

8. *a.* efficient; *b.* prices; *c.* resource

9. tariffs, import quotas, protect special interest groups, attempt to increase net exports, protect domestic producers of essential war goods, industrialize and diversify their economies

10. a better allocation of resources, a higher standard of living; *a.* military self-sufficiency; *b.* infant industry; *c.* increase domestic employment; *d.* diversification for stability; *e.* protect high wages and the high standard of living

Problems and projects

1. *a.* constant; *b.* (1) 8, 2, (2) 4, 2; *c.* (1) it has a comparative advantage in producing wheat (its cost of producing wheat is less than Chile's), (2) it has a comparative advantage in producing copper (its cost of producing copper is less than the United States); *d.* one of the two nations would be unwilling to trade if the terms of trade are outside this range; *f.* (1) 1, 0, (2) 1, 0

2. *a.* (1) increase, decrease, (2) decrease, increase; *b.* (1) rise, fall, equal, (2) fall, rise, equal; *c.* (1) increase, decrease, (2) decrease, increase; *d.* (1) rise, fall, they are the same as the prices for these resources in the United States, (2) fall, rise, they are the same as the prices for these resources in France; *e.* (1) chicken, wine, (2) wine, chicken

Self-test

1. T; **2.** F; **3.** T; **4.** F; **5.** F; **6.** T; **7.** T; **8.** T

1. *a*; **2.** *b*; **3.** *d*; **4.** *a*; **5.** *a*; **6.** *a*; **7.** *c*; **8.** *a*

CHAPTER 43

Fill-in questions

1. dollars, one French franc

2. 4

3. imports, exports, exports, imports

4. increase, decrease, increase, decreases

5. *a.* exports of goods and services; *b.* imports of goods and services; *c.* net balance due on exports and imports; *d.* net remittances; *e.* net government transactions; *f.* net capital movements; *g.* balance due to or from rest of world; *h.* financing (balancing) transactions

6. goods, services, and the services of money capital; surplus

7. loans, investments, gold, foreign money

8. inpayments (outpayments), outpayments (inpayments), gold, foreign money, decreases (increases)

9. surplus, deficit

10. gives, loans, invests

11. foreign, exports, unemployment

12. gold, foreign money, its own money owned by foreigners, autonomous

13. risks, reduce, terms of trade, prices, output

14. freely fluctuating foreign exchange rates, changing price and income levels, public controls

15. defines its monetary unit in terms of gold and will buy and sell gold at the rate set down in its definition of the monetary unit, allows gold to be exported and imported freely

16. the gold equivalent of monetary units, the cost of transporting gold; gold export point, gold import point

17. *a.* decrease; *b.* less, more; *c.* decrease, increase; *d.* decreases, increases

18. stable exchange rates, price levels, outputs, levels of employment

19. legally establishes, imports, exports, ration, prices, national output (or employment)

20. gold, demand and supply

Problems and projects

1. *a.* (1) +47.9, (2) −39.1, (3) −7.2, (4) +4.6; *b.* (reading down) +47.9, +32.5, +8.1, +7.3, −39.1, −31.1, −6.2, −1.8, +8.8, −1.5, −4.7, −7.2, −10.2, +3.0, −4.6, +0.7, +3.9; *c.* deficit, 4.6; *d.* +4.6, −4.6

2. ½, ⅖, ⅓, 2/7, ¼, 2/9, ⅕, lower

3. *a.* 5.00, ⅕; *b.* 5.03, 4.97; *c.* 0.201, 0.199

4. The two supply schedules will be as follows:

Supply of dollars		Supply of pounds	
Price, £	Quantity supplied	Price	Quantity supplied
½	1576	$5.00	400
⅖	1550	4.50	360
⅓	1500	4.00	300
2/7	1400	3.50	286
¼	1200	3.00	267
2/9	900	2.50	240
⅕	500	2.00	200

The quantity of dollars supplied at any price (in pounds) is found by multiplying the equivalent dollar price by the quantity of pounds demanded at that price. The quantity of pounds supplied at any price (in dollars) is found by multiplying the equivalent pound price by the quantity of dollars supplied at that price. *a.* 4.00; *b.* ¼; *c.* 300; *d.* 1,200; *e.* (1) 2/9, (2) 160, (3) 720

Self-test

1. T; 2. F; 3. F; 4. F; 5. F; 6. T; 7. F; 8. T; 9. T; 10. F

1. *c*; 2. *b*; 3. *d*; 4. *c*; 5. *b*; 6. *d*; 7. *b*; 8. *c*; 9. *a*; 10. *d*

CHAPTER 44

Fill-in questions

1. large, raw materials, underdeveloped, manufactured goods, manufacturing nations; comparative advantage, laissez faire, gold standard

2. depression, war, cold war; exports, capital flows, trade barriers

3. imports, exports, balance of payments; inflation, productive capacities

4. *a.* political objectives have been placed above economic objectives; *b.* nationalistic tendencies and the pursuit of domestic stability often conflict with the rebuilding of international trade; *c.* the underdeveloped countries have restricted trade in order to industrialize and diversify their economies

5. assist European recovery, create an international monetary system, reduce trade barriers

6. rebuild the European economies; the United Nations Relief and Rehabilitation Administration, grants, loans, European Recovery, Mutual Security

7. upward, Reciprocal Trade Agreements, downward; lower tariff rates up to 50 percent in return for a reduction of foreign restrictions on American goods, most-favored-nation clauses

8. *a.* equal, nondiscriminatory treatment of all trading nations; *b.* reduction of tariffs by negotiation; *c.* elimination of import quotas

9. tariffs and import quotas among members, common tariffs on goods imported from nonmembers, capital and labor among member nations, other matters, growth, trade, allocation of resources, economies of scale

10. lower or eliminate tariffs on products where the United States and the Common Market have 80 percent or more of the world's trade, lower tariffs on other goods up to 50 percent over five years

11. *a.* productivity, inflation; *b.* outflows, military and economic aid

12. *a.* getting Western Europe to assume a larger share of the costs of mutual defense and economic aid to underdeveloped nations; *b.* increasing the productivity of American firms; *c.* using monetary and fiscal policies to restrain domestic inflation; *d.* negotiating the reduction or elimination of the foreign restrictions on the import of American goods

13. higher, increase, out, increasing

14. exports, imports, capital outflow

15. stable, adjustable peg

16. international monetary, more, gold, key currencies, the United States, Great Britain

17. world trade

18. seldom changed; *a.* increase the dollar price of gold (devalue the dollar); *b.* have nations manage international reserves, return to freely fluctuating foreign exchange rates

19. Triffin, Special Drawing Rights (SDRs)

20. gold pool, two-price, the private gold market, themselves and to central banks of other nations who agree not to resell it in the private gold market

Problems and projects

1. 1. F; 2. M; 3. K; 4. A; 5. I; 6. J; 7. D; 8. L; 9. E; 10. B; 11. H; 12. G

2. *a.* 120, 30; *b.* 4, 0.25; *c.* 33⅓, 3; *d.* 40 million, 30 million, 30 million, 40 million; *e.* dollars, gold, francs; *f.* 10, 8⅓, 2

Self-test

1. F; 2. F; 3. T; 4. F; 5. F; 6. T; 7. T; 8. F; 9. F; 10. T; 11. F; 12. F; 13. F; 14. T; 15. T; 16. F; 17. T; 18. T; 19. F; 20. T

1. *b*; 2. *c*; 3. *d*; 4. *c*; 5. *c*; 6. *d*; 7. *d*; 8. *a*; 9. *d*; 10. *a*; 11. *b*; 12. *b*; 13. *d*; 14. *d*; 15. *d*; 16. *c*; 17. *a*; 18. *c*

CHAPTER 45

Fill-in questions

1. poverty (i.e., a low standard of living)

2. Asia, South America, Africa, southeastern Europe, $\frac{2}{3}$

3. supplies of raw materials, capital equipment, effective manpower, technology

4. elimination of unemployment, greater efficiency in the allocation of resources

5. a. overpopulation; b. widespread disguised unemployment; c. the poor quality of the labor force

6. consumer goods (food) production ÷ population, aspirations, standard of living

7. zero or less than zero

8. capital accumulation increases output and increased output allows a greater volume of saving and more capital accumulation

9. save, invest; low saving potential, investors, incentives to invest

10. their level of income is low, their standard of living is far below the standard of living of the advanced nations

11. agriculture, the improvement of agricultural facilities, the construction of basic social capital

12. capital saving

13. a. the absence of a sizable and vigorous entrepreneurial class; b. the great need for social goods and services; c. government action may be the only means of promoting saving and investment; d. government can more effectively deal with the social-institutional obstacles to growth; e. government may be the only mechanism for speeding up the rate of growth

14. institutions and social arrangements

15. loans and grants, expanding the volume of international trade, maintaining America's economic stability

16. GNP

17. the number of countries receiving aid, the aid received by the key countries, have the greatest growth potential, have the will to develop, are strategic

18. 5.2, 2.7

Problems and projects

1. a. low; b. short; c. widespread; d. poor; e. primitive; f. large; g. large; h. high; i. poor; j. small; k. low; l. absent; m. small; n. small; o. small and poor

2. a. food supply: 400, 600, 800, 1,000, 1,200, 1,400; population: 40, 80, 160, 320, 640, 1,280. b. the food supply is just able to support the population. c. the inability of the food supply to support a population growing at this rate. d. (1) 200, (2) 240, (3) 280. e. the population increased as rapidly as the food supply.

Self-test

1. T; 2. F; 3. F; 4. F; 5. T; 6. F; 7. F; 8. T; 9. F; 10. T; 11. F; 12. F

1. d; 2. a; 3. b; 4. b; 5. c; 6. d; 7. b; 8. d; 9. c; 10. d

CHAPTER 46

Fill-in questions

1. public ownership of property resources, central economic planning

2. central planning commission, many small economic units

3. coordination, bottleneck, chain reaction

4. negotiation, priority, reserve stocks

5. Gosplan, Gosbank

6. monetary incentives, nonmonetary incentives, coercive techniques

7. as an accounting device for checking productive efficiency, as a means of rationing products among consumers

8. the efficiency of production, affect the allocation of resources

9. a. (1) unsalable, unwanted, (2) production, quality, (3) innovate; b. (1) profit motive, (2) decentralized planning, autonomy, (3) below; c. Professor E. Liberman

10. one-half, 5

11. a. the large natural resource base; b. the totalitarian government has allocated resources to promote growth; c. the surplus of farm labor; d. the employment of the superior technologies developed in Western nations; e. the absence of cyclical unemployment

12. a. the diversion of resources to consumer goods, foreign aid, and military goods; b. increasing replacement investment; c. the closing of the technological gap between Soviet and Western methods of production; d. a manpower shortage; e. the backwardness of Soviet agriculture; f. the increasing complexity of economic planning as the economy grows

13. a. the large annual increases in GNP available for consumer goods, foreign aid, and military goods; b. improvements in education and technology promise to make the economy more productive; c. possible improvements in planning techniques; d. the ability of the Soviet Union to force economic growth

14. *a.* the increased quantity and quality of education; *b.* the development of a complete system of social insurance

15. the failure of the consumer's standard of living to increase by as much as is possible; the limited freedom of Soviet citizens

Problems and projects

1. public ownership of property resources; relative consumer freedom to spend income as he sees fit; central economic planning; workers are generally free to choose occupation and place of work; central economic planning and various forms of incentives; central economic planning; central economic planning with prices playing an implemental role; central economic planning and various forms of incentives which appeal to self-interest; state and collective farms; state-owned and cooperative firms and retail stores

2. *a.* 40; *b.* 60

Self-test

1. T; **2.** T; **3.** T; **4.** F; **5.** F; **6.** F; **7.** T; **8.** F; **9.** T; **10.** F

1. *b*; **2.** *d*; **3.** *b*; **4.** *a*; **5.** *b*; **6.** *b*; **7.** *b*; **8.** *d*; **9.** *a*; **10.** *b*

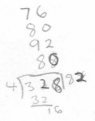